THE OXFORDSHIRE HUSSARS IN THE GREAT WAR

Swaine.

COLONEL ARTHUR DUGDALE, C.M.G., D.S.O.
Commanded Queen's Own Oxfordshire Hussars, 1914–1919.

THE
OXFORDSHIRE HUSSARS
IN THE GREAT WAR
(1914–1918)

BY ADRIAN KEITH-FALCONER

WITH PORTRAITS, ILLUSTRATIONS AND MAPS

LONDON
JOHN MURRAY, ALBEMARLE STREET, W.

TO

THE OFFICERS, NON-COMMISSIONED OFFICERS,
AND MEN

OF THE QUEEN'S OWN OXFORDSHIRE HUSSARS,

IN MEMORY OF THEIR

FALLEN COMRADES

" And you, good yeomen,
Whose limbs were made in England, show us here
The mettle of your pasture."

SHAKESPEARE, *King Henry V.*

BATTLE HONOURS OF THE REGIMENT

SOUTH AFRICA, 1900–1901

MESSINES, 1914
ARMENTIÈRES, 1914
YPRES, 1915
ST. JULIEN
BELLEWAARDE
ARRAS, 1917
SCARPE, 1917
CAMBRAI, 1917, 1918
SOMME, 1918
ST. QUENTIN
LYS
HAZEBROUCK
AMIENS
BAPAUME, 1918
HINDENBURG LINE
CANAL DU NORD
SELLE
SAMBRE
FRANCE AND FLANDERS, 1914–1918

BATTLE HONOURS SELECTED TO BE BORNE ON THE APPOINTMENTS

SOUTH AFRICA, 1900-1901

MESSINES, 1914
ARMENTIÈRES, 1914
YPRES, 1915
ARRAS, 1917
CAMBRAI, 1917, 1918
SOMME, 1918
LYS
AMIENS
HINDENBURG LINE
FRANCE AND FLANDERS, 1914-1918

PREFACE

THIS book has been written for the officers and men of the Queen's Own Oxfordshire Hussars as a record of the Regiment in the Great War. It is essentially a war book, and the very brief introductory chapter must not be regarded as a substitute for a full history of the Regiment—a task which, if ever attempted, would require a separate volume.

It is based primarily on the regimental war diary, supplemented by such private letters and diaries as have come into my hands. To all those who have kindly lent me letters, diaries, or photographs, I desire to express my warmest thanks.

I am greatly indebted to the Director and staff of the Historical Section (Military Branch) of the Committee of Imperial Defence for free use of the divisional and brigade war diaries, and especially to Mr. E. A. Dixon for unfailing readiness to help at all times. I have also to thank the staff of the War Office library for the use of their old army lists in the preparation of Chapter I ; the War Office (Records Section) for some additions to Appendices A and C ; the Controller of H.M. Stationery Office for kind permission to reproduce Major A. F. Becke's map of the Antwerp operations from the *Official History of the War, Military Operations, France and Belgium*, Vol. II ; and the Director of the Imperial War Museum for a similar permission to reproduce the panorama photograph of Messines.

I am particularly indebted to Engineer-Commander Benson Freeman, R.N., whose exceptional knowledge of early yeomanry history, freely placed at my disposal, has been of the greatest help in compiling Chapter I ; to Major-General T. T. Pitman, C.B., C.M.G., for kindly reading the typescript, and making many helpful suggestions, and also lending me the MS. of articles by him on the Battles of

ix

Cambrai (1917), and Amiens (1918) ; to Lieutenant-Colonel W. T. Willcox, C.M.G., for generous permission to reproduce ten of the maps from his *3rd (King's Own) Hussars 1914–1919*, thereby greatly lightening my task ; and to Lieutenant-Colonel John Murray, D.S.O., for much kindly help in seeing me safely through the intricacies of publication.

I have further to thank the Viscount Churchill, G.C.V.O., for kindly allowing me to reproduce his picture of the 1st Lord Churchill, and the Viscount Valentia, C.V.O., for similar kind permission to reproduce his picture of the late Viscount.

I am grateful to those officers of the Regiment who have been good enough to read through the typescript, in whole or in part, and have helped me with criticism, encouragement, or suggestions. My thanks are specially due to Major J. S. S. Churchill, D.S.O., for an interesting account of the Regiment between 1899 and 1914, most of which I have incorporated in the concluding pages of Chapter I, and to Captain G. T. Hutchinson, M.C., for valuable additions to my sketch of the Regiment as it was in 1914 (Chapter II), and of the Cassel operations in Chapter III, and particularly for the description of the Regiment and its transition from irregular to regular standards given at the beginning of Chapter VII. Finally, to Major the Honourable A. G. C. Villiers, D.S.O., and to Major Philip Fleming I owe a very special debt of gratitude. Major Villiers has made numerous suggestions and saved me from sundry errors ; Major Fleming has also been helpful in many ways ; while both, having originally inspired me to undertake the work, have encouraged me throughout with their constant and unfailing interest.

A. K.-F.

CONTENTS

CHAPTER I

CHAPTER II

CHAPTER III

CHAPTER IV

CHAPTER V

CHAPTER VI

CHAPTER VII

CHAPTER VIII

CHAPTER IX

CHAPTER X

CHAPTER XI

LIST OF ILLUSTRATIONS

LIST OF MAPS

* From Willcox's *3rd (King's Own) Hussars, 1914–1919.*

THE OXFORDSHIRE HUSSARS
IN THE GREAT WAR

CHAPTER I

INTRODUCTORY

MANY centuries before the yeomanry were embodied as a volunteer mounted force for home defence, they formed an important part of the nation in peace and the pick of its fighting forces in war. The point is of interest, for, long afterwards, in the hundred years before the Great War, the county yeomanry regiments were more than mere military units ; they had a political and social value, and represented the ancient traditions of the stock from which they sprang.

The term " yeoman " had two chief meanings :

(1) " a servant or attendant in a royal or noble household, usually of a superior grade," (2) " a man holding a small landed estate ; a freeholder under the rank of a gentleman ; hence vaguely, a commoner or countryman of respectable standing, especially one who cultivates his own land." (Oxford English Dictionary.)

The word occurs frequently in both senses in books and documents six hundred years ago, but it is the second meaning which concerns us here. The exact limits of the class which it covered are uncertain, and probably varied from time to time, but it seems to have included (1) the small freeholders and landed proprietors, (2) the tenant farmers, (3) retainers, men-at-arms, and archers drawn from the families of (1) and (2). The following extracts (taken from the O.E.D.) illustrate their social standing and their value in war.

1

" 1375. Barbour : Bruce, iv, 386. Schir Iohne the Hastyngis, With knychtis of full mekill pryde, With squyaris and gude yhemanry.

" 1477. Earl Rivers : Dictes, F iii. The nombre of his knyghtes were comonli of his retenew . . . were ccc.xiii. thousand wythout yomanrye and other men necessary to his warres.

" 1538. Starkey : England, 79. Yf the yeomanry of Englond were not, in tyme of warre we schold be in schrode case.

" 1549. Latimer : 1st Sermon before Edward VI, 40. My father was a Yoman and had no landes of his owne, onlye he had a farme of iii. or iiii. pound by yere at the uttermost. . . . He had walke for a hundred shepe, and my mother mylked xxx. kyne." [1]

Long before the regular standing army came into existence in the seventeenth century, England had fought her wars with troops raised on a county basis and mainly composed of ordinary civilians serving only for the duration of the war. A few semi-regular mercenaries, feudal retainers, and ex-criminals formed such standing army as there was, but the men that fought at Crécy and Agincourt were for the most part drawn from the yeoman class.

It must, however, be admitted that the yeomen commonly fought on foot. The cavalry of those days was mainly provided by the knights and barons, and manned by their own retainers. But besides these, who were the regular cavalry, used for shock action, there was an auxiliary force of light cavalry called " hobelers," raised in the country districts, primarily intended for home defence, and used chiefly for scouting, thus faintly foreshadowing the yeomanry of later days.

Two or three centuries later we find a more direct ancestor of our present-day yeomanry in the troops of " volunteer horse " raised during the civil war, in the mounted troops of

---

[1] Hugh Latimer, born 1490, became Bishop of Worcester in 1535, and was burnt at the stake opposite Balliol College, Oxford, in 1555. The value of his father's farm would be equivalent to between £40 and £50 a year in present-day money.

yeomen formed in Northamptonshire in 1744, and in the
Royal Regiment of Hunters raised by the gentlemen of
Yorkshire in 1745, at the time of the Jacobite rebellion.
But these units had no permanent existence, and were
disbanded after the crisis had passed.

The French Revolution led to war with France in 1793
and the formation of all kinds of auxiliary forces. Among
these were the yeomanry cavalry, first embodied in 1794.
The war encouraged recruiting, and many troops were
quickly enrolled all over the country, the first three coming
from the little county of Rutland. But many counties,
including Oxfordshire, hung back at first, and though meetings of the " Nobility, Clergy, Gentry, Freeholders, and
Yeomanry of the County " were held at Oxford to discuss
the matter in April 1794, no mounted troops were raised,
except a regiment of Fencible Cavalry under Colonel the
Hon. Thomas Parker. (Fencible regiments were regular
troops enlisted for home service and for the duration of the
war only.)

Two years passed. The response to the call for mounted
troops had been insufficient ; the war was still going on ;
and the regular cavalry was fighting overseas. It was calcu-
lated that 200,000 riding horses were being kept in England
for " purposes of pleasure alone." The Government accordingly passed a " Provisional Cavalry Act," by which all
who kept a certain number of horses were obliged to find
and equip a proportionate number of men and horses, while
those who owned less than four were grouped together with
other small horseowners for the purpose of finding their
quota.

This new force was highly unpopular, partly because the
farmers and smaller gentry found themselves riding in the
ranks with their own labourers, partly because, being raised
on a militia basis, it was thought liable for long periods of
service outside the county. But as it was to be raised only
in counties which did not supply the required quota of
yeomanry, it soon led to a great increase in the latter force.

The gentlemen and yeomen of Oxfordshire, as of other

2

counties, were now forced to rouse themselves, if they wished to escape the hated Provisional Cavalry Act.

The first yeomanry unit raised in Oxfordshire was the Watlington Troop, embodied in May 1798, under the following officers : Captain George, Earl of Macclesfield, Lieutenant William Lowndes Stone, Cornet Richard Clerk (gazetted 20th June 1798).

It was quickly followed by others, the next being the Bullington, Dorchester, and Thame Troop, under Captain Sir Christopher Willoughby, Bart., Lieutenant John Weyland, Cornet William Henry Ashurst ; the third the Oxford (or Wootton) Troop,[1] Captain Oldfield Bowles, Lieutenant William Samuel Churchill, Cornet John Duffell ; the fourth, the Bloxham and Banbury Troop, Captain Thomas Cobb, Lieutenant John Davies, Cornet George Councer, Surgeon John Shorter.

These four troops all date from 1798. They were each about 50 strong, and entirely independent units. They were armed with swords and pistols, and met for drill at least once a week throughout the year, except during harvesting, haymaking, and sheep-shearing. All ranks provided their own horses. They were only liable to be called out of the county " for the suppression of riots or tumults within their own or adjacent counties ; or by Royal warrant in case of invasion, in either case to receive pay as cavalry and to be subject to military law." The uniform was blue, with white facings and white breeches and large white scarves, black leather light cavalry helmet with bearskin crest and side hackle feather plumes.

Peace was signed in 1802, but the Oxfordshire troops continued to serve, and when war broke out again in 1803, the strength of these troops was raised from 50 to 80, and the Bloxham and Banbury Troop was doubled and made into a squadron, under Major-Commandant George Frederick Stratton. Further units raised were the so-called " Oxfordshire Cavalry," really a Woodstock Troop, under

---

[1] This appears as the Oxford Troop in the Yeomanry List of 1798, but seems to have become definitely known as the Wootton Troop by about 1803.

Captain Lord Francis Spencer [1]; the Oxford Troop, under Captain Henry Whorwood; and the Ploughley (or Bicester) Troop, under Captain John Harrison. The uniform of some of these later troops varied in some respects, e.g. Lord F. Spencer's troop wore scarlet, with yellow facings. The yeomanry force of the county had thus been more than doubled, and now consisted of eight strong troops, all, however, still strictly independent of one another, except the two Bloxham and Banbury troops which formed a squadron. The total strength of the eight troops was 586. (An independent unit was often known as a corps. Thus either the Watlington Troop or the Bloxham and Banbury Squadron of two troops would often be spoken of as the Watlington Corps or the Bloxham and Banbury Corps.) Twelve men per troop were now allowed carbines and acted as flank men.

Weekly drills and monthly inspections were strictly enforced, so great was the fear of a French invasion, until Nelson's victory at Trafalgar in 1805 relaxed the strain, and the drills henceforth became less frequent.

In 1803, and again in 1813, the Government ordered all yeomanry troops to be amalgamated into regiments of not less than six troops each, but the order was not carried out in Oxfordshire.

For fifteen years after the battle of Waterloo the yeomanry were chiefly employed in the preservation of order at home. Then, as now, peace after a long war was full of troubles, and there was much rioting, owing to bad trade, high taxes, high prices, and other causes. There was no police force until 1829, and the country relied on the yeomanry to keep order. Sir John Fortescue says :

" Little though the fact is recognised, England owes much to the yeomanry during the first trying years of the peace. . . . The temper of the nation was certainly menacing, not without reason, and it found vent in repeated acts of violence. Troops were in request in all quarters of Great Britain, and the Commander-in-Chief had not a single battalion to

[1] Afterwards Lord Churchill, and first Colonel of the united regiment.

spare. . . . It seems in fact to be no more than the truth that, but for the yeomanry, the trouble would have been very serious indeed ; but the yeomanry did its duty when ordered . . . it was they mainly who stood between the country and insurrection." (*History of the British Army*, xi, 43, 57, 85.)

The yeomanry of Oxfordshire did their share in this duty, some incidents of which will be noted later. Meanwhile, important changes of organization were taking place. In 1817 Lord Francis Spencer's (now Francis Lord Churchill's) troop was increased to a corps or squadron of three troops under a Major, and in 1818 the old Wootton Troop was amalgamated with the new corps, which was now formed into a regiment, known as the North-western Oxfordshire Regiment of Yeomanry Cavalry, under Lieutenant-Colonel Lord Churchill.[1] But the Bloxham and Banbury Squadron and the Watlington, Bullington, and Oxford Troops still remained independent. The Ploughley Troop had been disbanded in 1807. Among the officers of the new regiment we find Captain Charles Cottrell-Dormer, and two Churchills besides the C.O. The uniform was blue, with scarlet facings.

In 1823 the title of the Regiment was changed from North-western Oxfordshire Regiment of Yeomanry Cavalry to First Oxfordshire Regiment, and in 1824 the Watlington, Bullington, and Oxford Troops were disbanded, but the Bloxham and Banbury Squadron continued to exist as an independent unit till 1831.

In 1827 the Government ordered the disbandment of all but eighteen of the fifty odd yeomanry corps in existence, with the usual conventional thanks for past services. This was done in the name of economy, but there is reason to suppose that the hostility of radical elements in Parliament and outside to any force composed of country gentlemen and farmers and used to maintain order had much to do with the Government's decision.

The disbandment was to take effect from the 1st April 1828,

---

[1] Lord Francis Spencer had been created Lord Churchill in 1815. He died in 1845 and was succeeded by his son, Colonel of the regiment from 1857 to 1874.

FRANCIS, 1st LORD CHURCHILL.
Commanded Oxfordshire Yeomanry, 1818-1845.

but several corps, including the 1st Oxfordshire and the Bloxham and Banbury, offered a renewal of their services without
pay or allowances, and were accepted by the King in March
1828. Among the troops thus accepted was the Wootton
Troop, first raised in July 1798, united with Lord Churchill's
regiment in 1818, and never afterwards disbanded. And on
the date of this troop the seniority of the Regiment should
have been based. But unpaid patriotism did not prevent the
loss of its place in the table of precedence, on which, and on
which alone, was based the selection of the yeomanry regiments to be disbanded a second time, ninety-four years later.

It was not long before the civil power was glad to have the
services of the yeomanry it had thought to dispense with. Six
miles from Bicester there is a large tract of marshland called
Otmoor. In 1820 an Act was passed to drain the moor, and
for this purpose the course of the river Ray was diverted by
a mound. This was all very well for Otmoor but in time
of heavy rains led to the flooding of other people's lands.
In the spring of 1830 the floods were unusually bad, and the
owners of the flooded land, losing patience, forcibly removed
the mound and turned the Ray into its old channel. For
this they were brought to trial, but acquitted. This enraged
the inhabitants of the Otmoor villages, who had recently
lost their ancient right of common on the moor under the
Enclosure Acts, but who seem to have found some sort of
compensation in the diversion of the river Ray ; at any rate,
they were infuriated by the acquittal of those who had
turned it back into its old channel, and accordingly broke
into open riot, destroying gates, posts, fences, and sheds on
the enclosed lands. On the 5th September Lord Churchill's
regiment was called out to keep order, and on the 6th they
were reinforced by five troops of the Mid-Buckinghamshire
Yeomanry and two guns of the latter's artillery. The Riot
Act was read, but the mob refused to disperse, and fifty-
seven were taken into custody and conveyed to Oxford
under a troop of twenty-one yeomen. It happened to be
the time of St. Giles's Fair in Oxford, and in passing through
the town the escort was set upon by a mob over a thousand

strong, armed with stones, sticks, and brickbats, which
they hurled at the yeomanry. In the midst of the confusion
the prisoners, who were unbound, quietly escaped, while
the officer in charge of the escort, wishing to avoid bloodshed,
ordered his men to retire. The yeomen are said to have
shown great steadiness in repelling the assaults and insults
of the mob without using their firearms. The prisoners
were subsequently recaptured, and Lord Churchill was
publicly thanked for the services of his regiment.

Owing to the Enclosure Acts, the increasing use of agricultural machinery, the starvation wages of farm labourers,
and other causes, rioting still continued in many parts of
the kingdom and Lord Churchill's regiment was again
required for service at Otmoor in November 1830 and May
1831. A correspondent at Islip, writing to the *Oxford
Journal* of the 24th May 1831, says :

" Our quiet village has become a garrison town. Monday
last two troops of yeomanry commanded by Major Bowles,
Captain Lord Norreys, Captain Lord Villiers, Captains
Hamilton and Peyton, arrived summoned by a despatch of
the magistrates. Yesterday they paraded in front of the
headquarters (Lion and Cross Keys) at 10 a.m. and marched
towards Otmoor. Just on coming within sight of the moor
they were saluted with a peal of ' Heaven's own artillery '
in the shape of a terrible thunderstorm which sent them
quickly back to quarters."

Otmoor continued to be a centre of disturbance for some
time, and the yeomanry were on duty at Islip in July and
September 1831 and again in April and May 1832, remaining
there for eighteen days on one occasion.

The 1st Oxfordshire Regiment, under Lord Churchill,
was restored to the pay list in December 1830, and in the
following year the Watlington Troop was revived under
Captain John Fane. In October 1835 Queen Adelaide
visited Oxford, and guards of honour were furnished by
the county yeomanry, which was now given the title of
" Queen s Own Royal Oxfordshire Yeomanry Cavalry."
(The word "Royal" dropped out of the title before 1855.

The present style, " Queen's Own Oxfordshire Hussars," was first used in 1881.) They now adopted the well-known mantua purple facings instead of the scarlet hitherto worn, mantua purple being a favourite colour of the Queen.

An incident which occurred in 1847 illustrates the strong spirit of independence still surviving from the old days when each troop was an independent command, and which was not quite dead in 1914, or even in 1918, if less openly displayed. Lord Villiers—

" who raised his own troop and provided and trained his own private band, which always accompanied him during permanent duty, considered himself so much outside the authority of the commanding officer of the Regiment that on one occasion, when ordered to take up a position with his troop which he had not been accustomed to occupy during drill, said . . . that ' as right troop of the 3rd Squadron he and his men had always been accustomed to work, and he would be —— before either he or his men worked anywhere else.' " (*Army and Navy Gazette*, 5th November 1898.)

Lord Villiers actually wrote to the Home Secretary in June, 1847, requesting that his troop might be separated from the rest of the Regiment, so the story is not merely a regimental legend. [1]

The Duke of Marlborough became commanding officer in 1845 and was succeeded by Lord Churchill in 1857.

From 1831 the Regiment consisted of six troops. The establishment varied from time to time, but was usually from 20 to 25 officers, and about 350 other ranks. Until 1874 the commanding officer had the rank of Lieutenant Colonel-Commandant, and the second-in-command was a Lieutenant-Colonel. There was a regular Adjutant, but no commissioned Quartermaster in those days ; each troop had its own Quartermaster, who was a warrant officer. The ancient rank of Cornet was abolished in 1871, but lingered on in the yeomanry till 1873, when it was replaced

[1] Lord Villiers joined the Regiment in 1831, became Lieutenant-Colonel and second-in-command in 1857, and died in 1859. He was the grandfather of Major the Hon. A. G. C. Villiers.

by that of Sub-Lieutenant, and some years later by that of Second-Lieutenant.

In 1848 the whole Regiment, instead of only 12 men per troop, was armed with carbines.

The uniform varied so often during the nineteenth century that it is impossible to give a full account of it here. From about 1835 it consisted of a dark blue light dragoon coatee with mantua purple facings and stripes and light dragoon shako, and dark blue breeches with mantua purple stripes ; some time between 1856 and 1863 the Regiment adopted the Hussar tunic and busby.

The Regiment assembled annually for eight days' training, which was mostly confined to drill and parade movements. Such subjects as musketry, reconnaissance, outpost duty, and map reading, were little thought of, but it must be remembered that as late as 1870 these subjects were still hopelessly neglected in the Regular Army, the scientific soldier unknown, and professional zeal wholly at a discount.

On the 6th May 1869 Viscount Valentia was gazetted Lieutenant, from the 10th Hussars. He died on the 20th January 1927, after nearly sixty years unbroken connection with the Regiment, including ten years in command and over twenty years as Honorary Colonel. When the Regiment was converted into artillery in 1922, he continued to serve as Honorary Colonel of the new brigade. No one ever took a more active interest in the Regiment, or was so universally beloved and admired by all ranks for so many years.

Lord Churchill was succeeded as commanding officer by Lieutenant-Colonel Henry Barnett in 1874, and the latter was followed by Lieutenant-Colonels Edmund Ruck-Keene (1878), John Baskerville (1885), Albert Brassey (1892), Viscount Valentia (1894), H. C. Norris (1904), Sir Robert Hermon-Hodge (1905), Duke of Marlborough (1910), Arthur Dugdale (1914), Charles Nicholl (1919).

In 1893 the yeomanry regiments were brigaded, the Q.O.O.H. with the Royal Bucks Hussars. The squadron system was also introduced in this year, the Regiment forming two squadrons, " A " Banbury and " B " Bicester.

ARTHUR, 11TH VISCOUNT VALENTIA, K.C.V.O., C.B. (1843–1927)
Commanded Queen's Own Oxfordshire Hussars, 1894–1904, Honorary Colonel, 1904–1927.

Thirty years ago the Oxfordshire Yeomanry could only muster between 150 and 200 men on parade. The annual training lasted eight days and took place in Oxford. The men were of the old-fashioned yeoman class. Many were past forty years of age, some wore beards, and the tight stable jackets and forage caps did not add to their dignity. But there were many younger men and the territorial spirit was very strong. In many cases the troop leader was himself the landlord of all his troopers, or at any rate belonged to the family which for generations had lived in the district from which the men were recruited. The training consisted in practising the parade movements on Port Meadow. One day was given up to dismounted work and carbines were laboriously drawn from their buckets. This was considered very tiresome and not of great importance. The lessons of mounted infantry had not been learnt, and the yeomanry did not consider they could ever be needed without their swords and their horses.

But under the command of Lord Valentia, an old 10th Hussar, the Regiment acquired a considerable reputation for smartness, horsemanship, and horses. The discipline was good and the *esprit de corps* was tremendous. King Edward, then Prince of Wales, honoured the Regiment by becoming Colonel-in-Chief in 1896. A gorgeous full-dress uniform was designed. Mantua purple breeches, the Churchill family colours, and Hessian boots with pink heels were admired at the levee, when the whole of the officers paraded annually to bow before their Colonel.

It is unfortunately impossible here to follow the history of the Regiment during the South African War (1899–1902). It soon became evident that mounted men were greatly wanted, and on 18th December 1899 the War Office issued an appeal for yeomanry and volunteers. Fifty men of the Regiment enrolled next day, and a new corps, the "Imperial Yeomanry," was formed, recruited from the Yeomanry, volunteers, and civilians, armed and organized purely as mounted infantry. To this force the Oxfordshire Hussars contributed two companies, the 40th Company of the 10th

Battalion, and the 59th Company of the 15th Battalion. Among the officers of the Regiment who went out were Lord Valentia, the Duke of Marlborough, Captain Leonard Noble, Captain Cecil Boyle, Lieutenant the Hon. Eustace Fiennes, Lieutenant Jack Churchill; also Lieutenants Ferdinand St. John and Brian Molloy, both of whom joined the Regiment later; and Lieutenant H. C. Jagger as Veterinary Officer.

Lord Valentia served as Assistant Adjutant-General for the Imperial Yeomanry, and the Duke of Marlborough as Staff Captain. Lieutenant Churchill served with the South African Light Horse.

The Regiment took part in the successful attack on the Boer position at Dreifontein, in which Cecil Boyle, Captain of the Banbury Troop, was killed. He was the first yeomanry officer ever killed in action. Those who wish to follow the experiences of the Regiment in the rest of the campaign cannot do better than read Colonel Sidney Peel's interesting book, *Trooper 8008 I.Y.*, in which he says :

" Since the beginning of the war they cannot have been less than sixty or seventy times in action, and the miles that they have marched are beyond counting."

Viscount Valentia, the Duke of Marlborough, Major Fiennes, Staff Sergeant-Major Goldie, and Sergeant A. Barnsby were mentioned in despatches ; Lord Valentia also received the C.B.

In 1901 the yeomanry was reorganized on a four-squadron basis.

After the war a great advance was made and the lessons of South Africa began to be taught in earnest. The annual training was increased to fourteen days and took place under canvas in many of the beautiful private parks of the county, which were generously lent by their owners. Recruiting improved in every way and the farmers sent their sons to join. These young men were splendid material. They could shoot and ride and many of them brought their own horses. Working dress also improved and the blue serge superseded the stable jacket and was in its turn superseded by khaki. The War Office began to take a more intelligent interest in the yeomanry. Under the command of Sir Robert Hermon-Hodge, now Lord Wyfold, the efficiency of the Regiment grew rapidly. The strength of the Regiment increased and several young officers joined. The friendly rivalry with the neighbouring county developed, and a fierce battle took place every year against the Royal Bucks Hussars. This necessitated night marches and bivouacs. Among the officers who joined at this time were Mr. Winston Churchill, who had seen service in five campaigns, and Mr. F. E. Smith, now Lord Birkenhead. The connection of these officers with the Regiment was of considerable service in influencing the fate of the Regiment in 1914.

Many distinguished Generals visited the Regiment. Sir John French and Sir Ian Hamilton were always ready to give their help. Regular staff officers fresh from the Staff College came down and made suggestions to the C.O. and the squadron leaders.

In 1908 the War Office instituted a new organization of the Territorial Forces. It is not necessary here to discuss the scheme by which the county associations managed the affairs of their own Territorial regiments. With Lord Valentia, whose popularity and influence in Oxfordshire were so great, as Chairman of the Association, the Oxfordshire Yeomanry was sure to fare well.

In 1909 a small book was issued to the members of the Regiment, marked secret. In it was given, down to the smallest detail, the secret orders to be carried out in the event of a mobilization order being issued. The story of the mobilization will be given later, but it is interesting to place on record that when the telegram " mobilize " was sent out, the instructions in the little book, issued years before, were carried out almost to the letter with ease and punctuality.

The Territorial scheme was the outcome of much labour at the War Office, in which Sir Henry Wilson played a prominent part, and it was launched under the aegis of Lord Haldane, the Secretary of State for War. An officer of the

Regiment met Lord Haldane at the time at a country house. He asked about the yeomanry and then said that if ever the country needed a large army the Territorial scheme was there, by means of which a great expansion could rapidly be made with ease and economy.

This, then, was the machine ready at hand in 1914 for the War Minister to use. But Lord Kitchener ignored it. To him Territorials were useless. At vast expense and with great difficulty the wonderful new armies were formed and the Territorial scheme was not used.

The Duke of Marlborough next became Colonel, and through his hospitality the squadrons continued to train under the shadow of the Great Duke's monument in Blenheim Park. One year the whole Brigade of Bucks, Berks, and Oxfordshires camped in the park. Half the county came to see a brigade field-day, and in the evening a ball was given at Blenheim Palace. On another occasion Major Winston Churchill—then First Lord of the Admiralty—took the Henley and Woodstock Squadrons to Portsmouth, where they were shown the latest Dreadnoughts and the dockyard.

During these years the Regiment was nearly always up to strength and it was the ambition of many to be allowed to join. These were pleasant years for members of the Regiment to look back to. With a Cabinet Minister to intercede at times with the Secretary of State for War, and Second-Lieutenant F. E. Smith to answer conundrums of inspecting generals, the Regiment throve.

The rest of this book is devoted to a record of the Regiment's activities in the Great War, memories of which—still so fresh in our minds—have perhaps tended to obliterate in some measure the long years of its previous history. But in estimating the character and efficiency of the Q.O.O.H in this last great struggle, the work of three generations of former officers and N.C.O.s must never be forgotten. It was they who year by year recruited and trained the men who made the Regiment what it eventually became, and by their efforts built up a standard and tradition of which we their successors may well be proud to-day.

CHAPTER II

MOBILIZATION AND TRAINING IN ENGLAND

(5th August—18th September 1914)

ON the morning of Tuesday, 4th August 1914, the officers
and men of the Oxfordshire Yeomanry were scattered about
the country, engaged for the most part in their ordinary
peacetime occupations. Some few were at work in city
offices in London ; others, more numerous, were attending
to their shops and businesses in the county ; but the great
majority would probably have been found at work on the
farm. Only ten days earlier the officers had assembled for
the regimental dinner at the Ritz Hotel in London, and
though the cloud of war had already appeared on the horizon
it was not then sufficiently threatening to suggest the thought
of our mobilization. But in those ten days many startling
and momentous things had happened. Diplomatic notes
culminating in ultimatums had been exchanged among the
Great Powers with alarming rapidity, and already on the
4th August the forerunners of great armies were on the march.
It is not within my power, nor is it within the scope of this
book, to describe the events of those first few days of August,
or the thoughts and feelings of the nation as the hours of
crisis drew slowly on to their appointed end. By Monday
the 3rd (Bank Holiday) most of us felt pretty sure we should
have to come into the war ; by Tuesday the 4th, after Sir
Edward Grey's speech, probability had become a practical
certainty. And, of course, no one doubted that if we went
to war, the whole Territorial Force would be immediately
called up. Still, even with this certainty, there was little
that the average yeoman could do by way of preparation.

The order to mobilize reached Headquarters at 6 p.m.
on the 4th August, and was immediately repeated to every

15

officer and man on the strength. The receipt of that laconic
telegram containing the one word " mobilize " was the signal
for all that the hour of action had come. Less dramatic
than the fiery cross or beacon of old, its message was the
same. Henceforth until the end we were to have but one
duty, the service of our country, but one goal for our ambition,
the final achievement of victory over our enemies. Few
perhaps thought much about this ; most of us were fully
occupied getting together such kit as we had, and making
other preparations of a practical nature ; but even the most
unemotional and unimaginative member of the Regiment
must have been stirred in some degree by the greatness of
the hour, and of the destiny calling him to fill a place, however humble and obscure, in the history of his country.

A few enthusiasts joined up that night, but the great
majority received the order too late, or lived too far from
their mobilization centre, to report for duty till the next
day. Wednesday, the 5th August, was a pouring wet
morning, when the earliest comers began to arrive about
7 a.m. By 8.30 a.m. some forty men had arrived at " D "
Squadron Headquarters at Banbury, and were being rapidly
sworn in and put through their medical examination.
During the next six days mobilization proceeded apace at
Oxford, Banbury, and Henley, strength being made up,
horses delivered, and stores obtained. On Monday, the
10th August, " D " Squadron was able to have its first
mounted parade, marching from Banbury to Wroxton and
drilling there.

A word must be said here about an important reorgani-
zation in the Regiment caused by the change from peace
to war establishments. Under the old peace establishment
there had been four squadrons, with their Headquarters
respectively at Oxford, Woodstock, Henley, and Banbury,
and a machine-gun section attached to Regimental Headquarters. But the war establishment of a yeomanry
regiment was Headquarters (including a machine-gun
section) and three squadrons, and it therefore became
necessary to break up one of the four existing squadrons

and distribute its officers and men among the three other
squadrons. The Woodstock Squadron was the one selected
for sacrifice, and the distribution of the officers and men who
had been trained together in peace time, and had developed
a strong feeling of *esprit de corps* and a legitimate pride in
their squadron, naturally caused much disappointment
and-heartburning, besides disturbing the organization of
the troops in the three other squadrons. The newcomers
took some little time to settle down in their new surroundings, and in at least one squadron, if not in all, the troop
formed from the old Woodstock Squadron never wholly
lost its individuality of character.

The Regiment was commanded by Lieutenant-Colonel
Arthur Dugdale, who had succeeded to the command in
March 1914, after twenty-two years' previous service.
Second-in-Command was Major the Hon. E. E. Twisleton-
Wykeham-Fiennes, who had seen service in Canada, Egypt,
Mashonaland, and the South African War, and who had
commanded the Banbury Squadron until mobilization.
Captain Guy Bonham-Carter, of the 19th Hussars, had been
our Adjutant since February 1913, and on him, and on the
Regimental Sergeant-Major, Mr. J. L. Goldie, formerly of
the 3rd Hussars, fell the bulk of the strain and responsibility
of mobilization.[1] The three squadron leaders were Major
J. S. S. Churchill (" D," or Banbury), Major C. R. I. Nicholl
(" C," or Henley), and Captain J. W. Scott (" A," or Oxford).
Of these both Major Churchill and Captain Scott had served
in the South African War, the former in the South African
Light Horse, and the latter in the Royal Artillery.

The Regiment formed part of the 2nd South Midland
Mounted Brigade, under the command of Brigadier-General
the Earl of Longford, formerly Lieutenant-Colonel commanding the 2nd Life Guards, Major H. G. Watkin, of the
4th Hussars, being Brigade Major. The other units com-

[1] It may be added that no small share of the credit for the general
efficiency and preparedness of the Regiment at the outbreak of war was
due to Mr. Goldie's keenness and energy. He had joined the Regiment in
1896 as private instructor to the Duke of Marlborough's Troop, and was
appointed R.S.M. in 1905.

posing the Brigade were the Bucks Yeomanry, the Berkshire Yeomanry, the Berkshire R.H.A. (Battery and Ammunition Column), the 2nd South Midland Mounted Brigade, Transport and Supply Column, A.S.C., and the 2nd South Midland Mounted Brigade Field Ambulance, R.A.M.C.

On mobilization the Brigade, which in peace time had been an independent formation under the direct orders of the Southern Command, was incorporated in the South Midland Mounted Division, commanded by Major-General E. A. H. Alderson. The latter had as his Chief Staff officer during the time the Oxfordshire Yeomanry were in the division, first, Colonel W. E. Peyton, afterwards to command the division on Gallipoli, and later to become Military Secretary to Sir Douglas Haig ; and secondly, Lieutenant-Colonel Hon. H. A. Lawrence, the future Chief of the General Staff of the British Armies in France.

The Brigade was ordered to concentrate at Reading on the night of Tuesday, 11th August. The Regiment was by now fully up to strength in officers, men, and horses ; indeed, eager recruits were already being turned away on the second day of mobilization, so great had been the rush to join. The move to Reading was carried out by squadrons independently, Headquarters, " A " and " C " Squadrons marching by road from Oxford and Henley, while " D " Squadron came by train. The last-named squadron had paraded at Banbury Cross at 9.30 p.m. and marched to the G.W.R. station amid the cheers of the townspeople. Although there was no conceivable likelihood of our meeting the enemy for many long months—many credulous people said " never "—it was a memorable and stirring moment for those who left Banbury that night, none knowing when or in what circumstances they might return again. But any feelings of sentiment or romance were quickly dispelled on reaching the station, where a scene of much bustle and activity took place. The process of entraining some 150 horses, all quite unused to such adventures, in the dark, and in the rather inadequate sidings not constructed to

deal with such large numbers, occupied nearly two hours
and entailed a good deal of shouting by officers and sergeants
and much perspiration by the men. However, at last the
most unwilling horse was safely in his box, and we steamed
out of Banbury at 11.20 p.m. On reaching Reading at 12.55
a.m. we were met by the Brigadier, the Brigade Major, the
Colonel, the Second-in-Command, and the Adjutant. No
billets had been arranged for the men, who mostly had to
sleep on the floor in a big schoolroom. A good deal of
" hot air " ensued, not because either officers or men expected
to spend the war in luxury, or even in comfort, but because
it was felt that no trouble whatever had been taken over a
matter to which it was most certainly the duty of someone
in authority to attend. Dissatisfaction with billets was to
be a most fruitful source of " grousing " and grievance
against the " Staff " throughout the war, and often it was
justified. On the other hand, it is only fair to say that the
fault did not usually lie so much with the unfortunate Staff
Captain (who got all the complaints) as with the Staffs of
higher formations.

We were now concentrated as a brigade, and began to
devote our time seriously to troop and squadron training.
On the evening of Thursday, 13th August, Mr. Winston
Churchill (then First Lord of the Admiralty) and Sir Ian
Hamilton (then Commander-in-Chief of the Home Forces)
dined with the officers of " C " and " D " Squadrons
at the Caversham Bridge Hotel, where the latter were
billeted. Mr. Churchill rather astonished some of the
more optimistic of the officers by informing them that
they were in for two years of war at least, adding the
comment that few people realized the immense military
strength of Prussia.

On the evening of Saturday the 15th, the Brigade entrained for Bury St. Edmunds, arriving there in the early
morning of the 16th. Here we continued troop and squadron training till Thursday the 20th, when the Brigade
marched to Thetford and went into billets there. Training,
including much useful work in riding school, continued till

3

Thursday the 27th, when the Brigade marched to East Dereham, where it billeted for the night.[1]

Next day we continued our march to Blickling, where it had been intended the Brigade should stay for some weeks' training. At 6 p.m., however, the Regiment received the startling orders to prepare to proceed to Southampton for service overseas. Needless to say that, as soon as this became known, there was the wildest excitement in all ranks, and all officers were summoned to a conference at Regimental Headquarters at Blickling Hall after dinner. As it happened, all the officers were billeted there, except those of " D " Squadron, who were close by at Blickling Lodge.

Next morning, however, the order to go to Southampton was cancelled, and the Brigade was ordered to march to Cromer that afternoon and entrain for Churn at dawn the following day. There was naturally a good deal of disappointment at this sudden change, but it turned out very well in the end. For we learnt not long afterwards that it had been intended to send us to Egypt, the last place most of us wanted to go to, whereas we had all jumped to the conclusion that the order for service overseas had meant France. Had we gone to Egypt then, as we very nearly did, we should almost certainly have spent the whole war in the Near East, and probably never landed in France at all.

We went on to Cromer that same afternoon, the 29th, and entrained the next morning, Sunday the 30th, for Churn. The whole Brigade filled about twelve trains, the first starting about 8 a.m. and the last about 12 noon. The journey, via Cambridge, Bletchley, and Oxford, took about eight hours. It was a hot August day, and the journey, though rather a comfortable day of rest for the officers, was hot and trying for the horses. During the journey the " D " Squadron train stopped at Norwich. Two young officers of the 7th Division, which was in the neighbourhood, came on the platform and said they had come to settle a

[1] " Going into Dereham the black mare driven by Toms in the ration cart bolted going down the hill, cart overturned, horse shoes, nails, and rations all mixed up ; was Corporal in charge at the time." (Sergeant Stroud's Diary.)

bet. All day trains had been seen passing full of troops in white uniforms (most of our men had taken off their coats and many still wore white shirts), and the officers had wagered that we were the Russians passing through the country.

On the arrival of Brigade Headquarters at Churn it was found that no provision had been made for the encampment of troops, and the men had to bivouac in the open until tents were issued a day or two later. Fortunately the weather was fine.

This was the first night on which the officers' horses had been picketed in the open, and Lieutenant Keith-Falconer's second servant distinguished himself by driving in the pegs so lightly that both his master's chargers walked off at daybreak, and, in spite of all attempts to coax them back to captivity, finally kicked their heels in the air and disappeared over the skyline, never to be seen again.

During the next three weeks troop and squadron training was continued, and the whole Regiment was inoculated twice against enteric. On the 1st September orders came to form a reserve regiment of all those who would not volunteer for service abroad, and to fill their places by recruiting, and on the 5th 106 N.C.O.s and men were sent to Oxford to form the nucleus of a second regiment under Lieutenant-Colonel A. N. Hall, an old member of the Q.O.O.H. The rest of this period was tedious and uneventful, and we began to resign ourselves to the unattractive prospect of a winter on the Berkshire downs, all hope of active service having now been abandoned.

On the afternoon of the 18th General Peyton visited Churn and sent for commanding officers. Colonel Dugdale being away at Oxford seeing about stores, Major Churchill attended in his place. General Peyton gave an outline of our immediate future and explained that we should remain at Churn for a considerable time, probably several months, during which we should have severe regimental training.

Thirteen years have now passed since the war began, and

as these pages may soon be read by the sons of those who
served with the Regiment then, it is worth while to recall
for their benefit what sort of fighting force their fathers
composed, on the eve of active service against the first
military Power of the day. The official conception of the
yeoman was based on the experience of the South African
War. He was not a cavalry man ; he was not an infantry
man ; he was a mounted rifleman. Counsels of perfection
would require of him mobility and marksmanship. Common
sense suggested that if, within the small proportion of the
year which he could devote to his military duties, he could
learn to move in a formed body, and to pass a not too exact-
ing standard on the range, it was about as much as could be
reasonably expected. A few preliminary drills enabled
him to present himself at the annual training of fourteen
days at the end of May, with his own or a hired horse, which
he was able to ride, but which had probably never been in
the ranks before. For the first few days he was drilled in a
troop, then in a squadron, finally in a regiment. Once or
twice during the training the image of war without its guilt
was provided by an issue of blank cartridges for a " scheme "
or field day. Once in three years the Regiment was
brigaded, when, in company with two other yeomanry
regiments and a Territorial battery, the yeoman seemed to
form part of a veritable army. His only weapon was the
rifle, and having once passed as a "marksman," his
subsequent musketry practice usually consisted of one
annual appearance on the range, to pass his standard test.

The ordinary routine at the annual training was by no
means irksome—a kind of " holiday " atmosphere was
encouraged in the interests of recruiting. Certain enthusiasts specialized on scouting, signalling, or in the machine-
gun section. But for the majority of officers, N.C.O.s, and
men, no ambitious standard of military training was aimed
at. They were there to provide good material, and the
permanent staff, consisting of the Adjutant, Regimental
Sergeant-Major, and Squadron Sergeant-Majors—all ex-
Regulars—were there to answer technical questions.

Members of the pre-war Regiment can recall more than one
humorous incident in the career of the so-called " agricultural cavalry." One subaltern, very distinguished in other
walks of life, asked by the Brigadier how much his horses
got to eat, said, " I'm sure I don't know ; but this man here "
(indicating the Squadron Sergeant-Major) " will tell us."
On another occasion a squadron leader, convicted by an
inspecting General of a deplorable ignorance of his military
duties, was asked with bitter sarcasm if he " thought that
he was a soldier." " Oh no, sir," was the bland reply ;
" I'm a stockbroker." A parallel case was provided by a
harassed subaltern, manœuvring his troop for examination
under the eye of the Brigade Major, and reduced by the
vagaries of his command and the comments of the expert
to a state of nervous prostration. " Now, Mr. ——," said
the Brigade Major, " can you tell me why on earth that man
is standing there ? " " Because he is a damned fool,"
answered the overwrought officer, not with any idea of
indiscipline, but forgetful of half-learnt military convention
under the strain of independent command.

At the last pre-war training the Regiment was assembled
for inspection, when an anxious troop leader was startled
to see one of his men leave the ranks with an abrupt excla-
mation, " Gawd ! I've forgot me gun," gallop past the
approaching squadron leader to his tent, and return
triumphantly with the missing weapon.

But on mobilization it was immediately recognized by all
ranks that they were entering on a new phase—they were
still amateurs, but they must become professionals as soon
as possible. From Brigade Headquarters came the order
that the necessarily compressed exercises of the annual
training must be replaced by regular cavalry training,
methodically undertaken, and starting from the beginning.
The first step was an officers' riding school, taken by the
Adjutant in the discreet privacy of the early morning, to
teach the officers how to give proper instruction to their
troops. Stirrups were crossed in front of the saddle, and
more than one officer seriously imperilled a reputation gained

on the hunting-field or " between the flags." But fortified
by this experience, the troop leaders were able to instruct
their troops daily, with beneficial results to men and horses,
so that the subsequent troop drill and squadron drill were
greatly simplified. Another difficulty of early days was the
matter of equipment. The peace-time yeoman travelled
light, and it took some time for him to accustom himself to
the numerous articles of equipment to be carried by the man
or the horse on active service—and to retain them on the
march. Indeed, to the civilian mind the start of every
day's march in August suggested all the horrors of packing
against time indispensable articles into inadequate luggage.
Nor must it be forgotten that the horses were even more
untrained than the men—good enough as raw material, but
collected hastily from the farms and villages, many of them
straight off grass, and inevitable victims to girth galls, and
all the other injuries to which animals picketed in horse
lines for the first time are liable.

At the same time the Regiment had to absorb an abnormal
number of recruits. On mobilization, the Mounted Band,
which was " on the strength," and all who could not be
passed fit for service, were replaced by recruits. No sooner
had these been absorbed than it became necessary to fill
the places of N.C.O.s and men who were unable to volunteer
for service abroad. Three of the troop leaders had not yet
done an annual training with the Regiment.

A large part of the seven weeks since mobilization had
been consumed in moving about from place to place in
England, and the always tiresome business of packing up to
leave, and then settling down into new quarters, had considerably disturbed the progress of training. But field
days, regimental and squadron " schemes," and still less
mere formal drill, though all necessary, are by no means the
only, or even the most important, parts of the soldier's
training. The hundred and one lessons in horsemastership,
discipline, and control of men, that can be learnt in constantly marching and moving billets, were a very useful
foundation of practical experience.

Still, even so, it cannot be said that the Regiment would have been regarded by any professional soldier in September 1914 as anything but raw, untrained material, at best only fit for garrison duty in some town far behind the lines, and a source of danger rather than strength if sent into battle with seasoned troops. But the regular officer too often overlooked the compensating advantages of civilian life, and especially the high standard of education among the men, their independence, resource, and self-reliance, combined with a real sense of duty and responsibility.

The officers of the yeomanry were drawn from the land-owners and country gentlemen of the district ; actually more than half of them were engaged in other pursuits. Some were members of Parliament, others were barristers, bankers, or merchants ; one was a solicitor, another a King's messenger, yet another an Oxford don.[1] All, however, had spent much of their life in the country, and had been accustomed to horses and hunting from their earliest days. Many had travelled in various parts of the world ; and even the least gifted were endowed with that common sense which, next to courage, is perhaps the most necessary quality in the regimental officer. Above all, five combatant officers [2] and the Medical Officer had served in the South African War, where they had acquired that practical experience in the field which makes the old soldier, and which is not to be gained in a lifetime spent on the barrack square. Finally, in the Adjutant all ranks had an expert adviser, trained in the latest school of military thought, who could supply that technical and professional knowledge which was necessarily lacking in themselves.

A similar combination of the countryman's shrewd

---

[1] Colonel Dugdale was a cloth manufacturer, Major Fiennes and Captain Fleming members of Parliament, Major Churchill a stockbroker, Major Nicholl a solicitor, Captain Scott a barrister, Captain Molloy a King's messenger, Lieutenant Fleming a banker, Lieutenant Hutchinson Bursar of Christ Church.

[2] Major Fiennes, Major Churchill, Captain Scott, Captain Molloy, and Lieutenant Hermon-Hodge. Captain Scott and Lieutenant Hermon-Hodge were both ex-Regular officers, as was also Second-Lieutenant Gill.

common sense, hardy physique, and knowledge of horse-flesh, with the townsman's business ability and quickness of perception, existed among the non-commissioned ranks. The majority were drawn from the tenant farmers of the county, a class not only remarkably well educated, but also accustomed to ride and shoot from boyhood, and to mix freely with other classes in the sport and business of the countryside. Hitherto they had lived in surroundings of solid comfort and abundance, and their general standard of living was probably not far below that of the country gentlemen their neighbours. The discomforts and hardships of active service were to be far greater for them than for their officers, and the way in which they endured them was beyond all praise.

The remainder came from the towns and larger villages and formed a valuable addition to the strength of the Regiment. They were especially strong in " A " Squadron, which was mainly recruited from the city of Oxford, and in which almost all trades were represented.

Here, also, as among the officers, there was a strong nucleus of veterans from the South African War, headed by the Regimental Sergeant-Major, Mr. J. L. Goldie, and the three Squadron Sergeant-Majors, all of whom were also Regular soldiers.

Finally, the relations between all ranks were the happiest and most cordial possible. Among the officers who sailed with " the original Regiment," as it came to be called afterwards, there existed the most complete and intimate friendship, while between officers and men there was a true feeling of comradeship and mutual confidence. If to the outward eye discipline was not up to the Prussian, or even to the British Regular Army standard, to those who knew the Regiment there was no anxiety on this score. With these men discipline was largely a matter of goodwill and confidence, and, as already said, both flourished in the Regiment at that time.

The average age of the officers was thirty-three ; none were over fifty or under twenty-three. Most of the senior officers were about thirty-four, while the junior officers varied widely in age, between twenty-three and forty-one, only one being below twenty-five, while no less than three junior subalterns were forty or upwards. These figures serve to illustrate still further the difference between the yeomanry and the average Regular regiment. Later experience seemed to show that the best age for active service is between twenty-five and thirty-five. The very young tended to crack more easily under the strain, especially showing the effects of lack of sleep more quickly than their elders, while soldiers once past forty were apt to develop ague, rheumatism, and other kindred ailments. Brilliant exceptions of course there were, the most notable being the Colonel himself, who was probably the hardiest man in the whole Regiment.

CHAPTER III

EARLY DAYS IN FRANCE

(19th September—29th October 1914)

ON the evening of Friday, the 18th September, the Regiment went to bed with the full expectation of another dull day of routine on the morrow. But away in Whitehall, in some busy room at the War Office, orders were already being drafted which were to change all this, and to fulfil our now almost forgotten hopes of active service. The civilians and regular officers who had scoffed at the idea of the untrained yeomanry being employed in France for at least six months, if then, were to be signally confuted.

Unknown to most people, the Admiralty had already begun the organization of the Royal Naval Division, afterwards to become famous at Antwerp, Gallipoli, and in France. It was now in process of formation in England, but one marine brigade was already in existence, and had been on an expedition to Ostend in August. On the 16th September Marshal Joffre had telegraphed to Lord Kitchener asking for marines to co-operate with French troops in the neighbourhood of Dunkirk, and Mr. Churchill had agreed to send them if he could have some yeomanry to act as divisional cavalry. The War Office refused to part with a whole brigade, but agreed to send a regiment, and orders were issued for the Oxfordshire Yeomanry to be detached from the 2nd South Midland Mounted Brigade and to entrain for Southampton, there to embark for service overseas. The order to hold the Regiment in readiness for this purpose was received at 1.30 a.m. on Saturday, the 19th September, and at 2 a.m. further orders arrived for the first squadron to entrain at 7.30 and start at 9 a.m., the other squadrons, Regimental Headquarters, and the machine-gun section to follow at intervals of an hour and a half.

All this, however, remained unknown to the bulk of the
Regiment for another two or three hours. But towards
4.30 some of the officers were surprised by the sound of men
afoot in the lines, and by 5 a.m. the whole Regiment had
been roused with the news that we were to entrain at 7.30 a.m.
for service abroad. There was a good deal to be done.
For some reason we were short of about 68 horses, and
these had to be made up from the Berks and Bucks, who
showed the utmost goodwill and generosity in giving us
the pick of their lines. Kits had to be got together, and a
number of recruits, who had only arrived the day before,
were deficient in various articles of equipment. Some even
had not yet got a uniform, and actually sailed the next day
in civilian suits and bowler hats ! At least two landed in
France wearing black-and-white check breeches.

The first train, containing " D " Squadron, left Churn
punctually at 9 a.m., Lord Longford being at the station
to see them off. Everybody was in the highest spirits,
and there was but one regret—the Brigadier was being left
behind. To many of the Regiment Lord Longford had
been known personally, in the hunting-field and elsewhere,
for many years, and he had commanded the Brigade since
1912. Everybody liked him and not a few were deeply
devoted to him. His quiet and unassuming manner concealed a strong character and a resolute will. But the
quality which most won our admiration, and by which
we most remember him, was his rare and exceptional
courage. Those who knew him well were convinced that
no danger would ever daunt his purpose, and that among
many brave men they knew none braver. When eleven
months later, on the 21st August 1915, he fell on Gallipoli,
personally leading his brigade in the frontal assault on the
hills behind the Suvla Plain,[1] the Regiment lost a valued
and a trusted friend.

The first train, containing " D " Squadron, arrived at
Southampton Docks at 11.15 a.m. During the journey

[1] Major Watkin, our former Brigade Major, and the majority of the
Brigade Staff, were also killed in this attack.

there had been much speculation as to where we were
going. It was known to be somewhere overseas and we
hoped it would be to France. Many thought that, in view
of the incomplete state of equipment of the Regiment, and
especially of the new recruits, we should probably spend a
week or so in camp at Southampton until all deficiencies
had been made up. When therefore we became aware
that our train was slowly passing through the dock gates at
Southampton, and finally drew up alongside the quay
itself, we realized with surprised excitement that we were
to be off in earnest this time. But where, and for what
duties, we did not yet know. Major Churchill, however,
had a wire from his brother to say we were in for a jolly
good show, and would be well looked after by the Admiralty,
which encouraged our already exuberant spirits.

In the course of the morning " C " Squadron arrived,
followed at intervals by " A " Squadron and Regimental
Headquarters, the last train arriving about 3.30 p.m. We
immediately began embarking the horses, which continued
all through the night. Meanwhile kits and stores of every
description were being got on board, while officers and men
settled down into their quarters. The ship was the
Bellerophon, 13,000 tons, speed 13 knots—a fine cargo
steamer of the Blue Funnel Line, ordinarily engaged in
trade to Vancouver and Japan, now converted into a
transport. The accommodation for both officers and men
of the Regiment was very rough and ready ; for the officers
a large, unfurnished, iron-walled cabin amidships, with
improvised bunks all round the sides, and a table and
benches in the centre. The men were all on one large lower
deck in the stern, while the horses were all packed together
in the fore part of the ship. In addition there were no less
than eight three-ton motor-lorries, attached to the Regiment
by Admiralty orders ; four or five private motor-cars
belonging to officers and taken on board in the absence
of any orders to the contrary ; and finally, an immense
quantity of personal baggage. So little warning of departure
had been given that there had been no time to go through

kits before leaving Churn, and consequently all ranks had
brought with them everything they possessed. Most
officers had valises weighing anything from 50 to 100 lb.,
instead of the regulation 35 lb., while every man carried on
board a fair-sized kit-bag. Probably no regiment ever went
to France accompanied by such a fleet of motor transport,
solely for its own personal use. This we owed to the
generous provision of the Admiralty, whose large ideas on
the subject we found sadly lacking in the War Office and
G.H.Q., France, when later on we came under their command.

During the day Major Churchill telephoned two or three
times to Mr. Winston Churchill and gave his secretary a
long list of stores and equipment which we needed. Mr.
Churchill promised that we should receive the stores before
we landed the other side.

The officers were allowed to go ashore in small parties by
turn for dinner, relieving one another in charge of the embarkation of the horses, which went on all through the night
and was still unfinished when morning came.[1]

Breakfast presented difficulties. Not only were our
sleeping-quarters unattractive as a dining-room, but it had
also been impossible as yet to make any proper messing
arrangements. Most of the officers did the best they could
at a dirty little pub near the docks, but two members of a
squadron which afterwards gained the reputation of looking
after itself with singular success had already made friends
overnight with the Captain and Chief Engineer, and now
had an excellent breakfast with the ship's officers, who did
everything in their power to make the Regiment comfortable.
After the ship sailed, arrangements were made for all our
officers to have their meals in the cabin, after the ship's
officers. As the cabin was only made to hold about ten or
a dozen, this necessitated three separate services for every
meal, which must have been a great nuisance to the rightful
occupants. But the arrangement made all the difference

---

[1] The real cause of our delay in starting was the non-arrival of the special
train containing all the transport, swords and equipment which were to be
sent down by the Admiralty.

to our comfort during the voyage, and the hospitality shown us by the officers of the *Bellerophon* should not be forgotten.

At last by 11 a.m. all was ready and the Regiment was paraded in the docks, the roll called, and the men marched on board. We sailed at 11.15. It was a perfect September day, not a cloud in the sky, and the sea as smooth as glass.

The strength of the Regiment at the time of its departure from England was 24 officers, 447 other ranks, and 455 horses.

By the time we sailed it had become fairly generally known that we were bound for Dunkirk. We had heard that a force of British naval aeroplanes and seaplanes had established a base there, which we were intended to guard, and that we should probably be employed in patrolling the surrounding country for a radius of about twenty-five miles.

Towards evening, after we had been at sea some five hours and were now well out in the Channel, the ship began to develop an increasing roll, and by 10 p.m. there was a heavy swell. During the night we were held up for nearly half an hour while a destroyer examined us with its searchlight. We arrived off Dunkirk at 1 a.m. in a rough sea and waited some hours for the pilot to come out. At last he arrived, and we started for the harbour. Owing to the wind, however, it was found impossible to get in, and after some delay we had to go out and lie at anchor till Tuesday morning. Meanwhile the Colonel and Major Fiennes went ashore to prospect and make billeting arrangements, returning to the ship at night.

The sea grew calmer on Monday evening, and was quite smooth again by Tuesday morning, the 22nd. A few of the officers and many of the men had been laid low by sea-sickness, but the horses had not suffered very much. About 10.30 a.m. we began to make a move, and eventually got alongside the quay by 11.15, just forty-eight hours since we left Southampton. The work of disembarkation started at once, and all the horses were ashore and picketed in a large shed alongside by 9.15 p.m. This was much quicker

than had been expected. At Southampton they had all
been hoisted on board in special boxes, whereas here they
were just slung ashore in ropes, none being injured.

As we entered Dunkirk harbour a fussy little tramp
steamer pushed in in front of us and berthed just ahead.
An officer came from her to us and informed the Colonel
that all stores, etc., we had asked for were on board the little
steamer, ready to be taken over as soon as possible. They
had been rushed to Dover by lorry and sent over to catch
us on arrival. The Admiralty had kept their word.

The officers and men were all comfortably billeted in
houses about the town, as near the docks as possible, and
an officers' mess was established at the Restaurant des
Arcades.

The Regiment was now at last safely landed in France,
and it is to be noted that it was the first Territorial unit to
leave for the theatre of war, though not actually the first to
land in France, the London Scottish having arrived on the
16th September, and the Honourable Artillery Company on
the 20th.   (See *Official History of the War, Military Operations, France and Belgium*, vol. ii, pp. 7, 486, 487.)   It was
also the first to come into action, as will be seen later.

Here we must pause a moment to review briefly the
general military situation in France at that time. The
battle of the Marne had ended on 10th September, and for
nearly ten days now the British Army had been fighting on
the heights of the Aisne, the passage of which it had secured
on the 13th. Since then little progress had been made, and
casualties were heavy and increasing. Lord French's own
account reveals some of the secret anxieties and difficulties
of the high command at that time. He writes [1] :

" It is from this particular evening of the 16th September
that I date the origin of a grave anxiety which then began
to possess me. . . . So long as the Germans were being
driven back, whether by frontal or flank attack, the Channel
ports might be considered comparatively safe ; but on the
particular night of which I am speaking (16th September) I

[1] " 1914," pp. 154-7.

had arrived at the conclusion that a frontal attack was
hopeless, whilst it began to appear that any threat against
the German flank would be effectually countered if not
turned against ourselves.

" This, then, was my great fear. What was there to
prevent the enemy launching a powerful movement for the
purpose of securing the Channel ports, whilst the main
forces were engaged in practically neutralizing one another ?

" From this time I sent constant and urgent warnings
to London by wire and by letter to look out for the safety
of these same ports.

" It was just about now that I began to conceive the idea
of disengaging from the Aisne, and moving to a position in
the north, for the main purpose of defending the Channel
ports and, as a secondary reason, to be in a better position
to concert combined action and co-operation with the Navy."

In the latter days of September Mr. Winston Churchill
paid a visit to the Commander-in-Chief. Lord French says :

" It was at this time that we first discussed together the
advisability of joint action by the Army and Navy. It was
then that we sketched out plans for an offensive towards
the sea. . . ."

About the day that the Oxfordshire Yeomanry sailed from
England, the so-called " race to the sea " was beginning in
France. It was to continue for three weeks, until the 7th
Division landed at Ostend and joined hands with the I Corps
arriving from the Aisne, but its true significance was not immediately realized and only gradually became apparent.
On the 23rd–24th September the French left had reached the
Somme, five miles west of Péronne ; by the 27th–28th it
was at Bapaume ; by the 1st October at Lens. A corresponding movement was taking place on the German side,
and it was impossible to say which army would outflank the
other. In these circumstances a diversion by allied troops
operating from the neighbourhood of Lille seems to have
been contemplated, but was subsequently abandoned.

The Regiment was now attached to the Royal Naval
Division, commanded by Brigadier-General Sir George

Aston. The division at present had only its marine brigade at Dunkirk, the two naval brigades being still in process of formation in England. There appeared to be nothing between a raiding force of Germans and the Channel ports, except some French territorial troops, headquarters, and one brigade of the Royal Naval Division, Commander Samson with an advanced aeroplane base and some armoured cars near Hazebrouck—and the Oxfordshire Yeomanry. These few troops were intended to act as a threat to the German communications, and General Aston had instructions to give the impression that they were the advanced guard of a large British force. It is significant that special prominence was given in the Press at this time to the exploits of Commander Samson's armoured cars, and that the arrival of the yeomanry was recorded locally in somewhat exaggerated terms as follows :

LA SITUATION À DUNKERQUE

" Il n'y a plus qu'un but de promenade à Dunkerque ; c'est l'immense camp anglais des Glacis de Rosendael. Par le Square dévasté, ou par les avenues dénudées on se rend aux abords de cette petite ville de toile, qui rappelle un peu de loin, les installations des grands cirques américains.

" Et les habitants, qui portent à la boutonnière ou au corsage les petites broches de cuivre, offertes par les soldats, retrouvent ces derniers près de leurs tentes où, avec des gestes et de rares mots, ils disent tous leurs regrets d'avoir perdu leurs lits et la table de famille.

" ' I will come back ! ' avaient dit les soldats à leurs hôtes et ils profitent des premiers instants de liberté pour rendre les visites qu'on leur a faites au camp et retrouver les charmes de la vie familiale, réservée maintenant aux seuls cavaliers de yoemanry."

On the 22nd September Major Fiennes joined Divisional Headquarters as Intelligence Officer, and was followed there three days later by Lieutenant Keith-Falconer as A.D.C. On the 29th Sir George Aston, whose health had temporarily broken down, left for home, and was succeeded in the command by Brigadier-General A. Paris, hitherto commanding the Marine Brigade.

The Regiment remained a week at Dunkirk, doing squadron training and musketry practice on the sands at Malo-les-Bains, a pleasant little seaside resort adjoining the town. All deficiencies of kit and equipment had been made good, and check breeches and tweed caps disappeared. Swords had been issued to the men as soon as they landed, and the brief period of training at Dunkirk gave them a welcome opportunity of acquiring some knowledge of their new weapon. It was a time of suppressed excitement, and though the days passed uneventfully enough, everybody was on tiptoe with expectation.

On the 29th September the Naval Division moved inland to Cassel, $19\frac{1}{4}$ miles away, and the Regiment went on to Hazebrouck, 5 miles farther south, a town of about 12,000 inhabitants, 28 miles W.N.W. of Lille, and a railway junction of great strategical importance.

On arrival at Hazebrouck the Regiment was met by a priest, who informed them that the advanced guard of " D " Squadron had been taken by the inhabitants for Germans. He was introduced to the officers, and on meeting Major Churchill said, " Are you the son of the man who made a great speech about ' Trust the people ' ? " On being answered in the affirmative, he began quoting Lord Randolph Churchill's speech at length. It was then discovered that the priest was the Abbé Lemire, a member of the Chamber of Deputies, and a considerable personality in the district.

On 1st October R.S.M. Goldie was promoted Quartermaster in place of Major Lidington, who had remained at Dunkirk with the Base Commandant. S.S.M. Pearce, of " D " Squadron, became R.S.M., and Sergeant Warren took Pearce's place as S.S.M.

The first few days here were spent in patrol work and outpost schemes. On the 2nd October the Regiment took part in a field day round Flêtre, in which they acted the part of rearguard to the marines, while the latter were withdrawn from an imaginary battle in motor-buses, fresh from London, with all their names, colours, and advertisements still on them. It was strange to see twenty or so following one another along the narrow, twisting French country roads. This turned out to be our last day with the Naval Division. During the night unexpected orders arrived from London, and early next morning the marines left for Antwerp. The Regiment was ordered to remain at Hazebrouck, but a few of its members accompanied Divisional Headquarters to Antwerp. A brief account of the expedition must suffice.

The Marine Brigade left Cassel at 10.30 a.m. on the 3rd October, and reached Antwerp twelve hours later. Next morning they took up an entrenched position about seven miles south-east of Antwerp. All was quiet on their immediate front, but towards evening a steady bombardment began and continued through the night and all next day.

During the night of the 5th–6th the Belgians on our right made an unsuccessful attack, whereupon the Germans counter-attacked and forced them to give way all along the line. In consequence, our troops had to be withdrawn to a partially entrenched position some two miles in rear of the original line. Here they remained all day, but late at night the Allied commanders jointly decided to withdraw all troops within the inner line of fortifications protecting Antwerp, the movement to begin at 3 a.m.

At 11 p.m. on the 7th the bombardment of the city began. Hitherto the Germans had not used their biggest guns, and the attack on the outer defences had been supported by an immense weight of high explosive and shrapnel from pieces of smaller calibre. But now the huge Austrian howitzers were brought into play, and for upwards of thirty hours continued to devastate Antwerp.

About 5 p.m. on the evening of Thursday the 8th it was decided to evacuate the city. This is not the place to discuss whether it could have been held or not, but more than one of the battalion commanders that night expressed surprise at the order to retreat, and declared that they

could have held on with ease for much longer. The real
danger lay in the threat to our line of retreat across the
Scheldt. On the evening of the 7th the Germans had forced
a passage twenty-five miles south-west of Antwerp, and
thrown more than a brigade across. This, combined with
the weakness of the Belgian fortress troops, made our
withdrawal inevitable.

The retreat of the Naval Division began about 7 p.m. and
continued through the night. The leading units reached
St. Gilles Waes about 6 a.m. on the 9th. Here a railway
runs westward along the Dutch frontier, and rolling-stock
had been provided. Four trains containing two brigades
eventually reached Ostend, but the fifth never got through,
being cut off by the Germans *en route*, and its occupants
either killed, captured, or interned in Holland.

The few members of the Regiment with the Division
mostly went by road, and all arrived safely at Ostend that
night or the next morning. Sergeant Hine, an Oxfordshire
yeoman serving as despatch rider, distinguished himself
by a performance which attracted some attention in the
newspapers. During the bombardment of Antwerp he
found a Belgian girl outside her blazing home. He was on
his way to the coast with despatches, and took her to
Calais on the carrier of his motor-bicycle. Arrived there,
he was ordered to London, so conducted her across the
Channel to England, where his people befriended her.

The following members of the Regiment took part in the
expedition to Antwerp : Major Fiennes (Intelligence Officer),
Lieutenant Keith-Falconer (A.D.C.), Sergeant Hine, Sergeant
Winterbottom, and Private Worsley (motor-cyclist despatch
riders), Private Broad and Private Rice (officer's servants).

We must now return to the Regiment, which we left at
Hazebrouck on the morning of Saturday, the 3rd October.[1]
With their nominal commander far away at Antwerp, and
gravely preoccupied with the task there confronting him ;
with the nearest British troops over 20 miles away at
Dunkirk, and those but a few details under a Base Com-

[1] See map in pocket at end of book.

mandant ; with that Commandant, the only possible
remaining authority to whom they could look for orders,
deeply involved in the far more urgent and vital duty of
forwarding reinforcements and supplies to the troops at
Antwerp ; with no sources of information as to the movements of the enemy except their own vigilance ; it was a
strange situation for yeomanry who had left England less
than a fortnight before.

A continuous stream of troop trains began to pass through
the station at Hazebrouck, containing French troops who
had entrained on the Aisne—mainly at Châlons—to be
carried *via* Calais to Armentières, and continue the outflanking movement northwards. As the trains stopped for
a time at Hazebrouck, the opportunity was taken to exchange
civilities with some of the French officers, and to gain some
first-hand information of their experiences, which might
prove valuable at no distant date. There was a general
feeling that the Regiment must depend very much on its
own resources, but it is noteworthy that this was accepted
as nothing unusual—various possibilities of action were
closely debated by the officers, and the absence of other
British troops, of guns, and of the Divisional Commander,
caused no apparent concern.

A system of telephoning was arranged, by which the
mayors of the towns and villages in the neighbourhood
reported regularly to Hazebrouck. On the 3rd there was
no answer from Armentières, and it was rightly concluded
that German cavalry were in possession.

On the 3rd October " D " Squadron was sent to Morbecque,
a small village 2 miles S.S.W. of Hazebrouck, to guard the
advanced base of Commander Samson's aeroplanes and
armoured motor-cars. These motor-cars with their improvised armour had had many adventures with patrols
of Uhlans. Their home-made shields riddled with bullets
told a tale of encounters with the Germans, who in some cases
wreaked their vengeance on harmless village folk because they
had not warned them of the ambushes prepared by the
gallant occupants of these cars. Undoubtedly the presence

of this force increased the difficulties of the Germans in their endeavour to obtain information as to developments on their right flank, and possibly the knowledge that British cavalry had been seen in the neighbourhood may have caused them to make false deductions as to our numbers.

The task allotted to " D " Squadron and the machine guns was to guard the approaches to Morbecque and to post patrols to give early information of the advance of the Germans whom rumour credited with being in the neighbourhood. It was the first experience of night outpost duty, and the possibility of an encounter with the Germans made everyone realize the acute difference between field days and the genuine article. The few yeomen who had served in South Africa were reminded most vividly of the days of war in that far-off land, realizing even at this early stage that those experiences, hard as they were, would be considered as a picnic compared with the war which they were about to take part in. The experience of these South African veterans was of great assistance, and they were able to give many " tips " as to campaigning which proved most useful.

Trenches were dug in suitable—or more likely unsuitable —positions, and, much to the annoyance of the inhabitants, the roads were barricaded with carts, ploughs, harrows, and other implements. On the whole the population was friendly and delighted to see for the first time " les Anglais," but they could not believe that war or any act of man should hamper their harvest activities on a fine autumn day. Lieutenant Gill and his troop had built a particularly imposing barricade which all the prayers and curses of the good folk of Morbecque failed to make him move, so that they had to unharness their horses and leave their carts for the night.

Major Churchill paid a visit to Lille, and Lieutenant Pepper motored Captain Molloy to Béthune, where they saw the General commanding the French forces, who told them of the " grand mouvement " which was taking place in that area. As the Q.O.O.H. had been left without orders after

the departure of the Royal Naval Division for Antwerp,
Captain Molloy told the French General that there was a
regiment of British cavalry at Hazebrouck which would be
proud to co-operate with him !

On Sunday, the 4th, the Colonel motored to Dunkirk
to get orders for the Regiment, the aeroplane base at
Morbecque having been evacuated. On his return he
found French cavalry detraining at Hazebrouck, and was
requested by the French commander to cover this operation
by throwing out a protective screen to the east towards
Bailleul. The Germans were reported to be a few miles
away and advancing rapidly.

Accordingly " C " Squadron, commanded by Major
Nicholl, was sent to Strazeele, a small village situated on
comparatively high ground 4¼ miles due east of Hazebrouck,
and halfway between that town and Bailleul. Here they
were to form a line of outposts in conjunction with the
French to cover the detrainment.

On arrival at Strazeele, No. 1 Troop, under Lieutenant
Fleming, was sent to Flêtre, a mile or two away to the north,
on the main Bailleul-Cassel road, while Nos. 2 and 4 Troops,
under Lieutenants Palmer and Chinnery respectively, formed
the outpost line immediately east of Strazeele. Meanwhile Captain Fleming took No. 3 Troop on a reconnoitring
patrol over the squadron front, but finding no sign of the
enemy, returned peacefully to Squadron Headquarters at
Strazeele.

The night passed very quietly, disturbed only by the
frequent passage of refugees through the outpost line.
Lieutenant Palmer's troop had made use of a large farm
wagon as a barricade, placing it across the road so as to
block it completely from side to side. Very late at night
an old peasant came slouching along, considerably the worse
for liquor. The spectacle of a wagon without horses sideways across the road at this time of night, surrounded by
armed men who halted and questioned him in a strange
tongue, was mysterious and disturbing—a portent not to
be explained to his befuddled mind. " Mais, qu'est-ce

qu'il y a ? Qu'est-ce qu'il y a ? " he asked in thick and
troubled accents. Unable to understand a word of what
was said to him, he could make nothing of this strange
obstacle and the strange figures round it. But at last a
dim perception of the mystery began to dawn upon him.
"Ah ! c'est un accident," he exclaimed with relief, and
waddled off on his zigzag course homewards.

At 10 p.m. that night the Germans blew up the main
Calais–Lille railway at Steenwerck, 6½ miles E.S.E. of
Strazeele, and this was seen and reported by our
outposts.

Meanwhile at Hazebrouck a miniature council of war
was held in the railway-station by the Colonel and Adjutant,
with the French Colonel Commandant, assisted by a variety
of interpreters and advisers. Outside, the correct course
for the Regiment to take was debated in the democratic
spirit characteristic of a Territorial regiment. It was felt
that little support was to be expected from the French in
the event of fighting, as their orders for concentration in
the opposite direction were specific, and that if the Regiment should get into trouble, it would have to find its own
way out. " D " Squadron was recalled from Morbecque,
and " A " Squadron relieved " C " Squadron in Strazeele
at dawn. Here they also encountered an outpost of French
dragoons, magnificent in cuirass and casque, under an
officer who introduced himself correctly enough as " a good
sport." He stated that the Uhlan patrols were always
" très peureux," but that incautious pursuit was usually
penalized by a concealed machine gun ; he also begged that
if our patrols were driven in they should be careful not to
mask his fire—a somewhat discouraging request on a dark
autumn morning, with the situation, to say the least of it,
obscure. Happily his apprehensions were groundless.
" A " Squadron patrols advanced beyond the outpost lines
and barricaded the roads south of Meteren, but were attacked
by nothing more formidable than a stream of so-called
refugees, civilians leaving the Lille district in cars, country
carts, and on foot. From these and other sources it was

soon apparent that there were no Germans south of the
Hazebrouck–Bailleul road, and the squadron was accordingly moved to Flêtre, where Regimental Headquarters
had been established. From this point " D " Squadron was
despatched to patrol the country north of the road towards
Bailleul, in which direction Germans were reported. " A "
Squadron held a barricade at Flêtre, and sent a patrol to
get touch with " C " Squadron, which had watered and fed
at Eecke, farther to the north, and was then to patrol
towards the Mont des Cats, the only dominating feature in
the landscape, and afterwards well known to the British
Armies in France. None of the " D " Squadron patrols
encountered Germans, though one of them, under Lieutenant
Pepper, entered Bailleul. Burning buildings could be seen
on the other side of the town, and it was reported that the
Germans were approaching rapidly from the east. On the
left, the main body of " C " Squadron speedily discovered
that Germans were in force on the Mont des Cats, and was
fired at from the high ground. Captain V. Fleming, with
one troop, acting as flank guard to the squadron and on
the extreme left of the Regiment, reached Godewaersvelde [1]
and " spied " the Mont des Cats with his stalking-glass
from the church tower. He was able to telephone to Headquarters at Flêtre, confirming the report received from
" C " Squadron, and then led on a reconnoitring patrol
until it rejoined the Regiment later in the evening.

Meanwhile the Higher Command, with better information before it, had become apprehensive for the safety of
the Regiment, which was 25 miles from the coast, and unsupported, in view of the reported German advance from
the north, and orders were received at Flêtre to withdraw
at once to Dunkirk. The patrols were called in, and the
Regiment moved back to Cassel for the night. The front
covered by the patrols had been not less than 9 miles, in
an enclosed undulating country, with abundance of hedge-
row timber—not unlike parts of Oxfordshire—and when
every man was safe back in Cassel the Regiment could

[1] Which the men called " Gertie-wears-velvet."

congratulate itself that, if it had achieved nothing glorious in its first engagement, it had at any rate done nothing foolish.

At Cassel it was hoped to make up arrears of food and sleep, and it was disconcerting to be met there by an anxious staff officer who exclaimed, " It's all right, Colonel ; I've started all your transport back to Dunkirk." The men were tired and hungry, and the horses—not yet in hard condition—could not by any stretch of imagination do a night march to the coast. This may account for the startling reply from the Colonel, " Well, I wish you hadn't, because now I shall have to get it all back again." Whatever may be the historical accuracy of this anecdote, the Regiment remained for the night at Cassel, " A " Squadron and " C " Squadron finding pickets for the various approaches to the town, and in touch with French cavalry, now detraining at St. Sylvestre and Cassel.

The next day, Tuesday, the 6th October, the Regiment marched to Bergues (14 miles), " C " Squadron providing a rearguard and " D " Squadron a flankguard. At Bergues they stayed two nights, and marched into camp at Malo-les-Bains on Thursday, the 8th October.

So ended a very interesting episode in the Regiment's war experience. They had been engaged in operations petty indeed in comparison with the vast events then taking place at Antwerp and in northern France, but none the less significant of the enemy's purpose. The race for the sea was in full swing. On the 6th October the French official communiqué reported the presence of large masses of German cavalry in the country round Lille and Armentières, and infantry and artillery were believed to be following up the cavalry. Everything pointed to the opening of a new German offensive, directed especially against England and the Channel ports. The moment Antwerp fell, a fresh army would be liberated to act against us. The presence of British cavalry in the gap between Lille and Dunkirk may well have caused a momentary surprise in the German Intelligence Staff, just as we know the landing of British

marines at Ostend in August had mystified, and even
alarmed, them.

But however that may be, these little adventures round
Cassel must always have a singular interest and importance
in the history of the Regiment itself. Not only was it the
first time that British troops had met the enemy so far
north—except, of course, at Antwerp—not only was it
the first occasion in this war that the yeomanry—or for
that matter any British Territorials—had come under fire,[1]
but, above all, it was the Regiment's first encounter with the
enemy, its first taste of real war since 1902. And the
excitement and interest of the operations had been height-
ened by the fact that they were working alone, practically
isolated from any British troops, under the orders of a
French General, with whose force alone they were in contact.

They were now to enter on a period of inaction. For
a week they remained at Malo-les-Bains, where the men
were under canvas, while the officers were mostly billeted
in a hotel, except one or two sterner spirits [2] who preferred
to live in tents, with the idea of hardening off for the
campaign! The Regiment continued training on the
beach, doing some very useful work, and improving the
shooting of recruits. Antwerp fell on the 9th October, and
the Naval Division withdrew to Ostend, where the Colonel
visited them on the 10th or 11th to get orders or information. However, on the 12th the whole division was withdrawn to England to refit, and the Regiment was once more
left high and dry at Dunkirk. The future was obscure,
and our best chance of further useful service seemed to lie
in the possibility of getting attached to the British Expeditionary Force, under Sir John French.

After a week at Dunkirk, orders were received from the
Base Commandant there to move to Boulogne, and on
Thursday, the 15th October, the Regiment marched out
of the town, with drawn swords—reminiscent of its cere-
monious progress through the smaller towns of Oxfordshire.

---

[1] See *Official History of the War*, vol. ii, p. 46.
[2] Captain Val Fleming and Lieutenant Villiers.

A German aeroplane afforded a mark for some random rifle fire by French Territorials or details from the Belgian Army. All added to the prevailing confusion and panic, and the railway-station was besieged by civilians trying to escape. The Germans were said to be at Ostend, and Dunkirk might fall at any moment. The road to Calais was crowded with refugees—the saddest and most depressing spectacle of war—and Belgian soldiers, not in formed bodies, but moving steadily west. Neither the surroundings nor the prospect was exhilarating. Whatever the British Army might be doing, it was very evident that the Regiment was in retreat ; Boulogne was not regarded favourably as a field for its activities after Hazebrouck, and there was an unpleasant rumour that from Boulogne it was to be sent back to England.

In these circumstances a halt was called for lunch, and after a brief debate the Regiment took what may perhaps be described as the most yeomanlike step of its career. It was decided to billet for the night at Oye, a small village 19 miles west of Dunkirk, while the Adjutant was despatched —in an unauthorised motor-car—to G.H.Q., which it was now known had just moved to St. Omer. There he was to " put it "—presumably to Sir John French—that the Regiment merited a better fate than Boulogne, and in case his instincts as a regular soldier might prevent him from doing justice to this irregular appeal, he was accompanied by Lieutenant Fane, who was generally regarded as one of the most adventurous spirits in the Regiment. The appeal achieved the success which it perhaps deserved, and orders were received to march on the following day to St. Omer.

On the 15th October Lieutenant Keith-Falconer rejoined the Regiment from Antwerp.

We left Oye at 7.30 a.m. next morning and marched 25 miles via Guines to Nordausques, a pleasant little village where we billeted for the night.

Next day, Saturday the 17th, we marched the remaining 9½ miles to St. Omer, arriving there about 12 noon. The officers were billeted in houses along the Rue de Dunkerque, and an officers' mess was established at the Café Hersent. The men were all billeted in the French infantry barracks, which were in a most filthy condition, alive with vermin. It took two or three days' hard work and much fumigation to make them habitable. The horses were picketed out in a sort of drill ground close by.

The next fortnight was devoted to training, little schemes of reconnaissance and outpost work, field firing and bayonet exercise, etc. At the outbreak of war the Regiment was armed only with the Lee-Enfield Mark VI, the old rifle with the long barrel, carried slung on the back of the man. We continued to use these till we got to St. Omer, when the new Regular Army rifle, the Lee-Enfield Mark VII, was issued to us ; we did not get rifle buckets for some time, and rifles were carried slung on the back as before. Finally, at St. Omer our equipment was completed by the issue of bayonets, and a part of the time available for training was devoted to this purely infantry weapon.[1] As time went on the Regiment became very proficient with the rifle, but the bayonet was seldom used, and the sword never.

Two lessons at St. Omer marked a definite step forward in training. (1) The Regiment learnt to dig deep narrow trenches, 18 inches wide at the top, as the best protection against shell fire. (2) Field firing. The Regiment advanced mounted, in squadron column, behind a ridge, dismounted for action, advanced in line, and fired a specified number of rounds without misadventure.

We had to provide a daily guard for the town, consisting of 2 officers, 3 sergeants, 6 corporals, and 99 men, relieved every twenty-four hours. Sentries had to be found for the Commander-in-Chief's house, the G.H.Q. offices, and sundry other buildings, and the officers of the guard had to go round them twice between midnight and 6 a.m. and also at other times during the day. By way of recreation the men got a good deal of football, while the

---

[1] Bayonets were first issued to the Regular cavalry about the time of the battle of the Aisne.

officers went for rides and walks in the country round. A favourite walk was up to the aerodrome near by, where we made friends with the R.F.C. officers and heard from them much interesting news of the battle. We still had our private motor-cars, and a few officers went for what they called "joy-rides" up to the front. One at least of these joy-rides nearly ended in disaster. The party was driving gaily down the Menin road, in search of some particular unit of the front line, when they came on a few British infantry-men busily digging themselves in. Stopping to ask how far it was to the front line, they received the startling answer that this *was* the front line. A moment later came the order for the infantry to retire. Another few hundred yards and three of our best officers[1] would have spent the rest of the war looking through barbed wire.

During the last few days of October it became increasingly evident that a terrific battle was in progress not very far away in the east. Reliable information was scarce, but many stray fragments of news were picked up from our friends in the R.F.C., from small parties of battered troops returning through St. Omer to rest and refit, and from the joy-riding excursionists mentioned above. All these reports pointed the same way. The battle was growing fiercer day by day, and our troops, though apparently holding their own, were clearly hard-pressed. On the 28th and 29th the roar of a great artillery duel was plainly heard while we were out at exercise.

On the morning of the 30th we received some news of our future movements. Major Churchill had dined with the C.-in-C. on the previous evening. Sir John French told him that the Regiment must not be impatient, and that it would be kept at St. Omer for some time. Regular officers would be lent to help with the training.

This chapter may fittingly close with an extract from a letter written by the Adjutant on the 30th October :

"The Regiment, officers, men, and horses, are all pretty fit and as far as possible ready to go and fight the G.s any

[1] Major Scott, Captain Hermon-Hodge, and Lieutenant Gill.

day, and I think only want the experience of war that even the best regular regiments must have and for which especially in this war of heavy losses every regiment has unfortunately got to pay pretty heavily. The C.O. and self had a short interview with Sir John French yesterday, and he asked whether the Regiment was fit to go and take its place in the firing line, and we told him it was, and from what he said our job will probably be divisional cavalry to one of the infantry divisions. The Regiment has had a lot of practice in shooting since we've been here, which I believe has improved all ranks, and we only now wait to see what its effect will be when we get into the trenches. The cavalry are taking their turn in the trenches now just as much as the infantry, and often don't see their horses for days at a time, as they have to leave them billeted in farms well behind the firing line, and this has been the case since the beginning of the war, when they had to cover our retirement first and then pursue the G.s when they retired in their turn from the Marne to the Aisne ; but since then there have been no moving fights at all, and we appear to have arrived at another stage of stalemate all along the line, though our Army have had some desperate fighting lately, as the G.s have done their uttermost to break through, at Nieuport, Ypres, and La Bassée, especially. The Indians have joined the firing line now and are, I believe, doing very well ; some of their officers told me they were rather nervous as to how they would stand shell fire at first, but I've since heard that the difficulty is to make them sufficiently careful in taking cover from it. I've had two days up in the front line as a spectator, which was very interesting.

" As I write we have just received orders to go and join the Cavalry Division to-night."

CHAPTER IV

WULVERGHEM AND MESSINES

(30th October–22nd November 1914)

THE battle of Ypres had now been in progress for about ten days. The essential feature of the struggle was the threat to the Channel ports, the capture of which was the real objective of the enemy at this time. Had they fallen into German hands, the consequences would have been more disastrous to the Allied arms than any other conceivable event, always excepting the complete destruction and dispersal of our Army in the field.

Lord French fixes the close of the first phase of the battle " as the night of 26th October," and summarizes it [1]—

" as the conclusion of the successive attempts, begun a month previously, to effect a great turning movement round the German right flank. The operations up to the night of the 26th certainly failed in their original intention of clearing the coast line and driving the enemy from Bruges and Ghent, but they succeeded in establishing a line to the sea which, if it could be held, brought the Germans face to face with the challenge : ' Thus far shalt thou go, and no farther.' "

During the next two days there was a lull while the enemy reinforcements were coming up. But on the morning of the 29th the attack was renewed and the real crisis began. Our troops more than held their own that day, and even gained some ground, but next day fresh assaults were made, this time against the left centre of our line, held by the 3rd Cavalry Division, under General Byng. General Gough's 2nd Cavalry Division was also hard-pressed on the right, while the 1st Cavalry Division, under General de Lisle, was heavily engaged at Messines, where the Germans fought their way into the village, but were driven out again.

[1] " 1914," pp. 235–6.

This then was the position on the evening of Friday, 30th October. The II Corps, under Sir Horace Smith-Dorrien, was on the right of the British line, south of Armentières, and its fortunes do not concern us here. In the centre from Armentières to the river Douve was the III Corps, under Sir

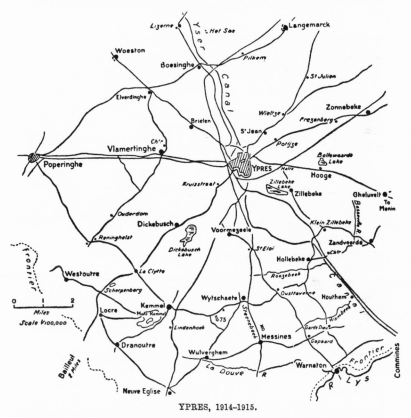

YPRES, 1914–1915.

William Pulteney, with the Cavalry Corps, under General Allenby, on its left from the Douve to the Comines Canal.[1] Then came Bulfin's Force (six battalions) from the canal to opposite Zandvoorde, with a French cavalry brigade and three French battalions at Zillebeke ; while the I Corps

[1] The 1st Cavalry Division held the right from the Douve to Messines (inclusive) ; the 2nd the left from Messines to the Canal ; the 3rd was in reserve at and south of Zillebeke.

(three divisions), under Sir Douglas Haig, held the extreme left from opposite Zandvoorde to the Zonnebeke–Roulers road, where they joined the French.

At 3.45 p.m. on Friday, 30th October, the Oxfordshire Yeomanry received orders to proceed to Neuve Eglise and there report to Headquarters, 1st Cavalry Division. For the next two hours everybody was feverishly engaged in packing kits, drawing rations, and other necessary preparations for a move. At 5 p.m. the officers met for a hasty meal at the Café Hersent. As it turned out, this was to be the last occasion on which the officers of the Regiment were to dine together until Christmas 1916. There had been some slight changes in organization since we sailed from England, and the following list of officers serving with the Regiment when we left St. Omer may be of interest here.

Headquarters : Lieutenant-Colonel A. Dugdale (commanding) ; Major J. S. S. Churchill (second-in-command) ; Captain G. Bonham-Carter, 19th Hussars (Adjutant) ; Lieutenant J. J. Pearce (Machine-gun Officer), Lieutenant J. L. Goldie (Quartermaster), Surgeon-Captain A. H. Hogarth (Medical Officer) ; Captain W. S. Carless, A.V.C. (Veterinary Officer).

"A" Squadron : Major J. W. Scott (commanding), Captain R. E. U. Hermon-Hodge (1st Troop), Lieutenant G. T. Hutchinson (2nd Troop), Lieutenant H. A. Fane (3rd Troop), Second-Lieutenant R. H. E. Hall (4th Troop).

"C" Squadron : Major C. R. I. Nicholl (commanding), Captain V. Fleming (second-in-command), Lieutenant P. Fleming (1st Troop), Lieutenant G. H. Palmer (2nd Troop), Second-Lieutenant A. J. Muirhead (3rd Troop), Second-Lieutenant E. H. Chinnery (4th Troop).

"D" Squadron : Captain B. C. B. Molloy (commanding), Lieutenant the Hon. A. G. C. Villiers (4th Troop), Lieutenant W. Pepper (3rd Troop), Second-Lieutenant A. W. Keith-Falconer (2nd Troop), Second-Lieutenant F. A. Gill (1st Troop).

The warrant officers and sergeants were :

Headquarters : R.S.M., A. Pearce ; R.Q.M.S., S. A.

Wright ;   F.Q.M.S.,   Stow ;   Sergeant-Cook W. Butter-
field,   Transport-Sergeant   H.   Shrimpton,   Sergeant
A. D. Goldie (Orderly-room Clerk), Sergeant-Trumpeter
Thomas, Signalling-Sergeant Basson, Saddler-Sergeant A·
E. Bryant.
" A " Squadron :   S.S.M.,   W.   Eltringham ;   S.Q.M.S.
Pinder ; Sergeants F. F. Jones, W. Shrimpton, R . T. King-
ston, W. Perrin, J. S. McFie, Farrier-Sergeant Cleverly.
" C " Squadron : S.S.M., A. Collier ; S.S.M., R. Buswell ;
S.Q.M.S., E. Wright ; Sergeants W. Batty, J. Grant, E. M.
Potter, W. Roberts, W. Maisey, Prince, Farrier-Sergeant T.
Kerr, Lance-Sergeant Stanwell.
" D " Squadron :   S.S.M.,   J. C.   Warren ;   S.Q.M.S., F.
Webb ; Sergeants H. Tompkins, G. H. Elliott, G. F. Sansom,
J. J. List, W. Miles, G. Raynham, M. Rice, Riley, Farrier-
Sergeant H. Clifton, Lance-Sergeant Hyde.

Parade was ordered for 6 p.m., but it was nearly 7 before
we got off.   Headquarters led the way, followed by " C,"
" D," and " A " Squadrons in the order named.   Last of
all came the transport, somewhat reduced since our first
landing at Dunkirk, but still considerably in excess of regulations and still including two lorries and four or five private
cars.   The lorries were to be taken from us in a day or two,
but the officers' motor-cars still had a long and useful career
in front of them, until in April 1915 a ruthless Quartermaster-
General finally banished them from the area of the British
Army.

The afternoon had been drab and rainy, and it was pitch
dark and raining steadily when we moved off.   Our progress
was exceedingly slow, and we seemed to be perpetually
halting for long periods, and then leading our horses on
foot.   Fortunately the rain stopped after we had been
going for about an hour.   We reached Hazebrouck about
10 p.m. and halted in the square to feed the horses, starting
off again at 11 p.m. and reaching Bailleul between 2 and
3 a.m. in the morning.   Here we halted to water the horses.
We seemed to stay an interminable time at Bailleul, and
it was nearly 4 a.m. before we started again.   By now

everybody was pretty tired and it was difficult to keep
some of the men awake on their horses. Still, no one
actually fell off, though one or two dropped asleep from
time to time. At Bailleul many slept for a time on the
pavements or on the doorsteps of houses. Here we first
distinctly heard the sound of rifle and machine-gun fire,
and it sounded uncomfortably close. On moving off, the
head of the column took what appeared on the map as the
more direct of two alternative routes, but it very soon
degenerated into a deep and muddy lane, along which we
floundered and scrambled for some way. We now first
saw the flash of a battery in action somewhere on our right
front. It gradually grew light and we eventually reached
Neuve Eglise at 7 a.m., after a good long march of nearly
30 miles. The Colonel reported to General de Lisle and
received orders to feed the horses and have breakfast and
then report to him at Wulverghem at 9 a.m.

Neuve Eglise is a small village standing on comparatively
high ground halfway between Bailleul and Messines, and
about 3½ miles from either place. Eastwards from Neuve
Eglise the ground falls in a gradual slope to the little river
Douve, on which is situated Wulverghem, a tiny village of
560 inhabitants, halfway between Neuve Eglise and
Messines. A mile or two to the north-east is Hill 75, from
which a broad and gently sloping spur descends southwards
to the river Douve, which here flows due east and almost
exactly parallel to the road. Just beyond the spur the
road dips again to the level of the little stream called the
Steenbeek, which flows southwards from Wytschaete to
join the Douve a mile S.S.W. of Messines. The whole
country round is very highly cultivated arable land, inter-
spersed here and there with pretty little pastures enclosed
by thick hedges or " bullfinches " and generally surrounded
by rows of tall Lombardy poplars.

Before proceeding to an account of the Regiment's share
in the day's work, we must pause for a moment to take
another look at the situation on our immediate front.

We have already seen how the battle was renewed on the morning of the 29th, and was fast approaching its crisis on the evening of the 30th.   Lord French says : [1]

" Shortly after dawn on this fateful 31st October we had news that a serious infantry attack was developing on the left of the 4th Division in the valley of the river Douve. The 4th Division was able to extend its line some little way to the north of the river and thus release troops of the 1st Cavalry Division, which subsequently fought fiercely all day at Messines. . . .

" Early in the morning Allenby reported that Messines was being heavily attacked, and that the 9th Lancers had been withdrawn after suffering severely ; that the eastern exit of the town was held by the 4th and 5th Dragoon Guards, and that the situation was ' decidedly critical.'

" A heavy attack had been delivered against the right of the 1st Cavalry Division shortly after 7 a.m., and an Indian battalion of rifles (the 57th, attached to the 1st Cavalry Division) were driven from their trenches. The reserves, however, held on, and the Inniskilling Fusiliers retook the trenches which the 57th had lost. . . .

" The most critical fighting of the day in this part of the line was at Messines, on Allenby's right.

" By 9 a.m. the cavalry were driven out of Messines, holding only one or two houses on the eastern side. Owing to heavy pressure elsewhere, no support was available until Shaw's (9th) Infantry Brigade could arrive. It reached Kemmel at 10 a.m. . . .

" General de Lisle, commanding the 1st Cavalry Division, was commanding at Messines. The Oxfordshire Yeomanry and an Indian battalion were the last reserves sent up to him."

(*Note.*—The 1st Cavalry Division at that time contained only two brigades ; the 1st, under Brigadier-General Briggs, consisting of the 2nd and 5th Dragoon Guards and the 11th Hussars, commanded by Lieutenant-Colonel T. T. Pitman, our future Brigadier and Divisional Commander ; and the 2nd, under Brigadier-General Mullens, consisting of the 4th Dragoon Guards, the 9th Lancers,

[1] " 1914," pp. 245–7.

and the 18th Hussars. The 2nd Cavalry Division contained three brigades.)

Shortly before 9 a.m. we rode out of the square at Neuve Eglise. Order of march : " A," " D," " C." There was a good deal of rather indiscriminate shelling of the country on either side of the road, but nothing came at all near us. A certain number of people were still working in the fields, and here and there cows were still peacefully grazing. Ahead of us, getting nearer and nearer as we rode on, was the sound of continuous and heavy bombardment. All night we had heard it, at first faintly, like the distant rumble of a thunderstorm, and then ever more and more distinctly. Now it was close upon us. We passed through Wulverghem and on along the Messines road.

At Wulverghem the Colonel received orders for half the Regiment to report to the G.O.C. 1st Cavalry Brigade, at Messines. He therefore detailed Major Churchill to take " A " Squadron and two troops of " D " Squadron on, while he remained with the other half of the Regiment digging trenches on the right of the road, nearly halfway between Wulverghem and Messines. Let us follow the fortunes of the leading half of the Regiment, under Major Churchill.

After continuing some way down the road they presently halted, and the order was given to dismount for action. The order, which should have been passed down the line from man to man, failed to reach the rear troop, which was consequently left behind for some minutes. Soon realizing, however, that the others had gone on down the road, they handed the horses over to the number three's, and followed up the main body. As they went they met streams of wounded, mostly limping back, some few being carried. Shells were falling freely all round. After marching perhaps a quarter of a mile they came to a small cottage standing by the road on the right-hand side and just west of the Steenbeek. In front of the cottage were standing a General and his Staff Officer.

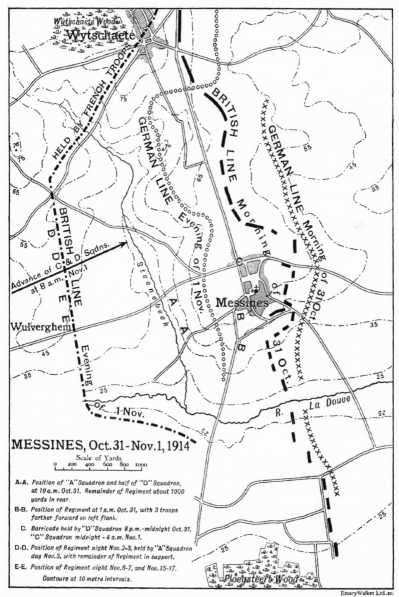

Wytschaete Wood
Wytschaete

75

76
76

65

55

HELD BY FRENCH TROOPS

BRITISH LINE

BRITISH LINE
D—D Sqdns.
D D

Advance of C & D Sqdns.
at 8 a.m. Nov.1

E E

Evening

of 1 Nov.

Wulverghem

45

35

25

GERMAN LINE

GERMAN LINE Evening of 1 Nov.

Steenbeek

65

A

A

C

B

B

Messines

GERMAN LINE Morning of 31 Oct.

55

45

35

35

25

31 Oct

R. La Douve

25

25

25

25

MESSINES, Oct. 31-Nov. 1, 1914

Scale of Yards
0   200   400   600   800   1000

A-A. *Position of "A" Squadron and half of "D" Squadron,*
at 10 a.m. Oct.31. Remainder of Regiment about 1000
yards in rear.

B-B. *Position of Regiment at 1 p.m. Oct.31, with 3 troops*
farther forward on left flank.

C. *Barricade held by "D" Squadron 8 p.m.-midnight Oct.31,*
"C" Squadron midnight - 4 a.m. Nov.1.

D-D. *Position of Regiment night Nov.2-3, held by "A" Squadron*
day Nov.3, with remainder of Regiment in support.

E-E. *Position of Regiment night Nov.6-7, and Nov.15-17.*

Contours at 10 metre intervals.

Ploegsteert Wood

EmeryWalker Ltd.sc

No detailed orders were given to Major Churchill, nor was the general situation explained. He was simply told to get on to the Messines Ridge, choose a place out of shell fire, and act as support to the cavalry in the village of Messines. He crossed the Steenbeek and took up a position south of the road under cover of a low ridge. "A" Squadron, which had been leading, now formed the left of the line, with the two troops of "D" Squadron, under Lieutenants Gill and Keith-Falconer, on the right. The latter were in a grass field with a small dry ditch running down the middle of it, in which most of the men sat or lay down. In front the ground sloped upwards for about 100 yards, and a hedge on or about the crest of the slope still further blocked the view. Away to the right the ground fell gradually away into the plain, but here again observation to our front and flank was limited by hedges and rows of trees. There seemed no particular reason why the enemy should not at any moment appear either over the crest in front of us or round the enclosures to our right front and flank. As our right was entirely in the air, instructions were given to keep a sharp look-out in this direction. In reality we must have been well behind the front line, but the front line at that time was extremely vague and fluctuating, and no one knew exactly where it was. We knew nothing of the situation of our own or the enemy's forces, nor had we any maps of any kind. The fog of war was at its thickest.

Meanwhile the battle continued to rage. Shells were falling on all sides, and far away in the plain to our right châteaux and farm houses could be seen burning and smoking. Although apparently under cover of the slope, we were bothered by frequent sudden storms of bullets whizzing past our heads. Suddenly heavy machine-gun and rifle fire broke out on our right flank. A patrol sent to investigate reported that they could see nothing and had been heavily fired on. This could not have been direct fire, but must have been the " overs " from the fighting going on over the next ridge.

About eleven o'clock the whole line began to move forward in a half-right direction. We crossed two or three fields, and scrambled over ditches and through barbed-wire fences, and eventually came to the Messines–Ploeg-steert road. Captain Hermon-Hodge and Lieutenant Fane, with the 1st and 3rd Troops of " A " Squadron, and Lieutenant Gill, with the 1st Troop, " D " Squadron, went on over the road, in single file along a track, and took what cover they could a little farther on, where they remained for the rest of the day.

Lieutenant Keith-Falconer, with No. 2 Troop, " D " Squadron, was left to line the road the others had crossed. On the eastern side it was unfenced, but a low bank gave some cover from rifle and machine-gun fire. Beyond the bank stretched a large open ploughed field, with some cottages and hedges in the distance, and a good field of fire in this direction. A mile or so away to the right the road disappeared in a wood. On the western side of the road there was a high thick hedge, behind which were Lieutenants Hutchinson and Hall, with Nos. 2 and 4 Troops, " A " Squadron.

We must now return to the second half of the Regiment, which we left digging trenches on the right of the Messines–Wulverghem road. About 11 a.m. the Colonel was ordered to send one squadron to support the other squadron and a half on the Messines–Ploegsteert road, and later to take up the rest of the Regiment.

" C " Squadron was sent up first. A German observation balloon was overhead and probably saw the squadron going across the fields, for some enormous shells came hurtling over and landed close by. Eventually the squadron halted in a ditch by a road facing the German positions, and a little to the right of No. 2 Troop, " D " Squadron.

The remaining half of " D " Squadron came up shortly afterwards and was in close support for the rest of the day.

All day the bombardment continued, and shells frequently came pretty close, but we were not much troubled by rifle fire. The afternoon dragged on slowly. From time to time

MESSINES FROM THE SOUTH-WEST, JULY, 1915. *Imperial War Museum Photo : Crown Copyright.*

Showing ground crossed by Regiment on morning of 31st October, 1914.

a few Germans could be seen running from a little spinney towards a farm building, and Captain Fleming and one or two of the men tried to pick them off with a rifle as they crossed the open. But they were a good distance away. Some time in the afternoon we were rather puzzled by a line of men crossing the road in single file about half a mile away on our right, coming from the direction of the enemy. We could hardly believe they were Germans, but it was difficult to distinguish their uniforms. However, we eventually concluded they were our own men, though we could not be sure whether they were retreating or merely being relieved. For most of the Regiment this was the first experience of being shelled. What chiefly struck them was the stupendous noise the shells made on bursting, and it was wonderful how soon the men got accustomed to it, and did not seem to mind very much. Luckily there were very few casualties.

Somewhere about 4 p.m. there was a sudden very notable increase in the machine-gun fire, and the road became extremely unhealthy, though one was safe enough under the bank. The machine-gun fire continued pretty fiercely, and an attack seeming possible, those troops which had not fixed bayonets were now ordered to do so. Nowadays of course it seems incredible that this had not been done long before, but we knew little enough of war in those early days.

About 5 p.m. the Adjutant appeared on the scene and said we were going to retire to a position about 500 yards farther back. This we presently did, and the whole Regiment withdrew to practically the same line that " A " Squadron and half " D " had occupied in the morning before advancing to the Messines-Ploegsteert road.

The Regiment was still practically intact. " A " Squadron had 2 men wounded, Sergeant Kingston and Private B. Smith ; " C " Squadron 1, Private M. Batting ; and " D " Squadron 2, Corporal J. Beesley and Private Sheasby. All recovered in course of time except Sheasby, who was badly wounded in the stomach and died in hospital.

It was now growing dark. " D " Squadron took up a position under cover of a bank, on the left of the Regiment, and approximately holding the line of the Steenbeek. It was a cold, starry night. S.S.M. Warren made all the men take off their cap badges, as they were glinting in the moonlight. Everybody was pretty cold and hungry. Rations had been issued in the morning, and only the improvident had been at least without biscuit and bully beef during the day, but that was all. Greatcoats had been left with the horses.

Heavy fighting had been in progress throughout the day in and about Messines, but at nightfall the line held there was the same as in the morning.

"Not many hours of darkness had elapsed, however, before new anxieties arose in connection with the line held by the cavalry on the Wytschaete–Messines Ridge.

"Events hardly less momentous than those of 31st October were before us." [1]

The Colonel reported to the G.O.C. 2nd Cavalry Brigade (General Mullens), to which we were attached, and received orders that one squadron was to hold the barricade in Messines for the night. He detailed " D " Squadron to do so till midnight, when they were to be relieved by " C " Squadron, while " A " Squadron was ordered to occupy the trenches dug in the morning.

It was about 8 o'clock when " D " Squadron moved off along the road towards Messines. On the way they met a party of 26 German prisoners being escorted back from the direction of Messines, walking right into them in the darkness before they realized who they were. As they got nearer Messines they came more and more under the fire of a light field gun firing down the road from behind the barricade they were to take over. Almost every minute there were loud bursts of shrapnel overhead, but fortunately no one was hit. They kept close into the side of the road, marching strung out in single file. At last they halted. On the left of the road were the ruins of a farmhouse or estaminet, some parts of which were still burning. The squadron was kept under cover of these buildings, while

[1] French, " 1914," p. 256.

Captain Molloy and Lieutenant Villiers went forward to reconnoitre. During their absence Lieutenant Pearce appeared on the other side of the road, having come up to inquire whether he could be of any use with his machine gun, but from what he was told of the situation he did not seem to think he could do any good, and presently went away. After waiting perhaps half an hour behind the buildings, the squadron was brought up to the barricade, a short distance farther up the road. It is impossible to give an adequate idea of the scene. The darkness was lit up on all sides by the flames of burning houses, and the air resounded with the incessant roar of shells and rattle of machine-gun and rifle fire. We were now in the streets of Messines, and in front of us stood what appeared to be a solid barricade, through a peep-hole in which one could see the enemy running about. They had a machine gun a short distance away shooting directly at us, and a light field gun firing down the road. We had to be on our guard against a sudden attempt to rush the barricade, which was bound to come sooner or later. Our flanks were very insecure, for we did not appear to be in touch with anybody. However, sentries were posted to watch the approaches to the houses or buildings on our flanks, while we kept firing on the Germans, whom we could see moving about on the other side and working their gun, less than 100 yards away.

At 1.30 a.m. "D" Squadron was relieved by "C" Squadron, who continued to hold the barricade until relieved by the 18th Hussars about 5 a.m. The shelling of the barricade continued as before, but no attempt was made to rush it. Captain V. Fleming reconnoitred the left flank and reported that he could find no one there.

"C" Squadron now marched back to Wulverghem, where they found the regimental transport. Rations were issued and the men set about getting breakfast.

"D" Squadron meanwhile had been given no rest. After being relieved at the barricade they had started back towards Wulverghem, but were kept just outside Messines for a long time in case the Germans should break through.

Everybody was very cold, hungry, and tired. At last, after long delays, they reached Wulverghem about 4 o'clock, and had just time to snatch a few moments' sleep and get some tea and biscuits before being sent off again at 5.30 to dig trenches. Even this was welcomed as affording some prospect of a comparatively quiet day, but the squadron had hardly arrived, carrying picks, spades and greatcoats, besides, of course, rifles and ammunition, when it was ordered back to Wulverghem.

" A " Squadron was moved back from the trench line and remained in reserve for the next twenty-four hours. During the night there had been desperate fighting not only in Messines, but also in Wytschaete and all along the intervening ridge. By 6.30 a.m. on Sunday, the 1st November, Wytschaete and the northern half of the ridge were in German hands, thus exposing the left flank of our troops in Messines, which now became untenable. At 7.30 a.m. they were ordered to retire slowly to an entrenched line half a mile east of Wulverghem.

Meanwhile " C " and " D " Squadrons were busy preparing for breakfast. Suddenly a motor-cyclist despatch rider arrived and said that about 200 Germans had broken through somewhere and were now behind our lines. He said we should probably be able to round them up. I don't think the news particularly excited us, but it made us suspect that we should probably be turned out again before long. It did not strike us as particularly dangerous that " 200 Germans " were wandering about behind our lines nor did we in the least want to leave our sleep and join in the sport of " rounding them up." We had no idea of what had been going on elsewhere during the night, nor did we much care ; what mainly interested us was the thought of food and sleep. At 7 a.m. we were ordered to fall in at once dismounted, leaving number three's in charge of horses.[1] We

[1] So little was the " rounding up " of the 200 Germans regarded as a serious undertaking that Private Wilkins, Capt. Fleming's servant, who was at that moment busy frying bacon for the mess, fell in with the rest " just to see the sport," as he put it, and took part in the whole advance, without rifle or bayonet.

fell in, two squadrons in line, " D " on the right and " C "
on the left, in a field just outside the village, while the
Colonel briefly explained the plan of operations on the map
to the Adjutant and squadron leaders. They were standing
some 30 or 40 yards in front of the line. Suddenly a man
accidentally let off his rifle in their direction. " Take that
man's name," roared the Colonel, which was done, but
nothing more was ever heard of the incident, and the offender
doubtless owed his escape to the more exciting events that
followed.

We moved off in line, but owing to obstacles, such as
fences and brooks, it was difficult to keep straight. The
Divisional Commander's orders were for the Regiment to
occupy and hold the ridge east of Wulverghem, covering
the retirement of our troops from Messines, and also to drive
back or capture the 200 Germans who were reported to have
broken through. But no one below the rank of squadron
leader had any very precise idea of the scheme, beyond the
fact that we were going to carry out an advance of some sort.
We marched roughly due east, with the Wulverghem–
Messines road about a mile away on our right and parallel
to our line of advance. Lieutenant Gill's troop acted as
advanced guard. As we ascended the slopes of the first
ridge we passed a good many men of the London Scottish
coming back in twos and threes. They had been in the
line all night, and had suffered severely in attacks and
counter-attacks. About the top of the ridge, or just on
the Messines side of it, there was a farmhouse. We passed
this, and presently found ourselves lying down in line in a
grass field behind a thick hedge. It was then about 7.45
a.m. and the sun was coming out and a fine morning promising. After perhaps half an hour behind the hedge we moved
on into some root fields sloping down to the Steenbeek
stream, beyond which the ground rises steeply up to Messines. The Colonel received word that there were some
Germans in the wood just over the stream—perhaps they
were the 200 we were looking for—and that the 3rd Hussars
and Indians were on our left. We were not in touch with

anyone on our right flank, which was entirely in the air, and the troops on our left were not advancing with us. Some discussion took place, one party urging that we should continue the advance independently, while others were of opinion that we should keep in touch with the 3rd Hussars. The Colonel finally decided to find out whether the latter and the Indians would co-operate with us in an attack on the ridge.

However, other events were now to decide our course of action. While still awaiting an answer from the 3rd Hussars, we suddenly noticed infantry coming out of the houses in Messines and streaming down the hill towards us. They were British troops retiring. They came down the hill in ones and twos, under an officer, who blew his whistle from time to time to give some order. They came right down to the Steenbeek and crossed it, after which they bore away to the right and disappeared from view. The enemy had evidently seen them, for now a great noise of cheering and blowing of bugles arose in the village of Messines. At the same time Germans in large numbers were observed coming over the ridge from behind Wytschaete towards Messines. Fire was opened on them at about 900 yards' range and a few were seen to fall.

But it was now obvious that we could not stay where we were, and the order was given to retire. We were totally unsupported on the right flank, the troops on our left were unwilling to advance further without orders from higher authority, and we were entirely ignorant of the opposition likely to meet us on the next ridge. Moreover, our orders were to hold the ridge farther back, over which we had already passed, and only to go on if the Messines Ridge were held.

The Regiment now began to retire to the ridge about half a mile west of the Steenbeek. Squadrons were ordered to retire independently, keeping in touch with one another as far as possible. " C " Squadron retired on the left, while " D " Squadron took up a position along a lane enclosed with hedges, about 500 yards east of the ridge over

which we had advanced earlier in the day. Captain Molloy
was very indignant at the order to retire and declared that
he must at any rate remain here for a time and cover the
withdrawal of " C " Squadron. He had got hold of a
German sword, which he had picked up somewhere during
the morning, and earlier in the day, during our advance,
had been waving it about with great enthusiasm. The
squadron took up the position he indicated, with Lieutenant
Keith-Falconer's troop on the right and Lieutenant Villiers'
on the left. Lieutenant Gill was now on the left of the line
with " C " Squadron, and Lieutenant Pepper was ordered
to take his troop back a short distance and remain in
immediate support to " D " Squadron. The following
account is taken from the author's notes written some time
afterwards, when the events were still fresh in his memory :

" Our position was not a good one. We were behind
a hedge, which, while affording no cover, made it impossible
either to observe the enemy or to direct our own fire. On
our right was a very enclosed country, through which the
enemy could easily approach unseen. Moreover, the ground
we occupied offered no natural protection of any kind.
We were completely in the dark as to the movements and
position of the enemy. I fully expected to see them appear
suddenly either in front of us or on our flanks. I was
particularly anxious about our right flank. But we never
saw any of them, and I do not know whether they had come
down from Messines and crossed the Steenbeek. But,
wherever they were, they evidently had seen us, and knew
approximately where we were, for bullets soon began to
whistle through the hedge in great numbers, and most of
us made ourselves as flat on the ground as we could. Two
sleepless nights had made most of us pretty tired, and one
man fell sound asleep in spite of the enemy's fire, his snoring
plainly audible amid the din of the battle.
" After some time, perhaps half an hour, I noticed that
the men on the left of the line were beginning to retire one
by one, towards the farm near the crest of the first ridge.
A message was passed down to say we were to retire one by
one, leaving a distance of 3 yards between each man. To
keep ourselves concealed as much as possible, I told the men

to follow the line of the hedge till they came to the corner
of the field, and then turn left-handed at right angles and
make straight for the farm, by way of a line of trees which
might afford some protection from the enemy's fire. I
remained till all the men had gone, and then followed along
the hedge till I came to where Brian Molloy and S.S.M.
Warren were standing near the corner of the field. There
were still two or three men with them, and Molloy told us
to keep on firing to divert the enemy's attention. I stepped
across the lane to get behind a big tree, but they must have
seen me, for a shower of bullets hit the tree and flew all
round me. I fired a shot or two into the blue, hoping it
might hit someone of the enemy. After a minute or
two Warren, who was with Molloy close by, said, ' For
God's sake go now, sir. We shall have to get out of this.'
I looked round and saw all the others had gone, and so
made a bolt for the nearest tree in the direction of the farm.

" How I, or any of us, ever reached that farm, I don't
know. A veritable hail of bullets was storming on to the
ground in all directions. The trees were big Lombardy
poplars, large and thick, and about 10 yards apart, one
from another. One's only chance was to make a dash from
tree to tree. The whole distance to the farm was perhaps
200 yards. As soon as I reached it I took cover behind one
of the buildings, and waited a minute or two, expecting to
see Molloy and Warren any moment. There were a few of
our men also waiting in the farmyard. Several minutes
passed and I began to wonder why neither Molloy nor
Warren came. At last, after what seemed an age, but was
probably about five minutes, Warren appeared round the
corner of the building, breathless and excited, and said,
' Captain Molloy's dead, sir.' He told me how, almost
immediately after I had left them, Molloy had been hit by
a bullet in the forehead and had died almost instantaneously.
Warren had stopped to make sure he was dead, and to take
a few papers and belongings from his body. It was of
course impossible to bury or carry away his body then,[1]
and it was important that we should rejoin the squadron
as soon as possible. We therefore continued our retreat
over the crest of the ridge."

The death of Brian Molloy so early in the campaign was

[1] He was buried that night by a party from the 5th Dragoon Guards.

a great loss to the Regiment. He was one of the few officers with previous war experience, and his impetuous bravery, unchecked by any thought of danger, was a valuable asset to untried troops in so desperate a conflict. He was a typical Irishman, and though at times he may have been carried away by enthusiasm for the battle, he was a very gallant leader. He had left the Regiment several years before and become a King's Messenger, and had only rejoined on the outbreak of war. Among the older members of the Regiment he was very popular and had many friends by whom his loss was keenly felt.

The Colonel now received orders to withdraw his two squadrons to the Wulverghem–Wytschaete road, close to the cross-roads near Hill 75. Here the Regiment, less " A " Squadron, which was still in reserve near Wulverghem, was reassembled about 11 a.m. " C " Squadron had had one man wounded, Private B. Bury. We were extraordinarily lucky not to have had more casualties, for both squadrons had been exposed to really heavy rifle and machine-gun fire, besides a certain amount of rather desultory shelling, while retiring across the open.

The rest of the day was spent on the road under fairly heavy shell fire. Lieutenants Pepper and Keith-Falconer were sent with their troops to support the 18th Hussars on the ridge west of the Steenbeek, which we had already crossed and recrossed twice during the day. On their right were the 18th Hussars ; on their left no one. They were told to dig themselves in, but as they had only one shovel and one pick between the two troops, they could do little more than scrape out a meagre head-cover with bayonets, knives, and forks. About 2 o'clock heavy shells began to fall all round and within a few yards of their position, but though, being on the crest of the ridge and having no trenches, they were an easy mark for the German observers, their luck still held and no one was hit. After dark a party of sappers came up and dug some deep, narrow trenches.

Apart from shell fire, the chief discomforts of the day
6

were hunger and thirst, cold and weariness. A little bully beef and biscuit and a mug of tea were all the great majority, including officers, had had since leaving St. Omer two days before. Lieutenant Fleming ate a swede and thought it very good ; others drank water from a pond in which they would have hesitated even to dip their hands in normal times ; while another officer was reduced to quenching a raging thirst with neat brandy in the middle of the day and quantities of water from a farmyard pump in the evening. As to the weather, it was warm and sunny in the middle of the day, but grew rapidly colder after 3 p.m., and all great-coats were still back with the horses. By the time we got into billets that night everybody had been over sixty hours without sleep.

At night " C " Squadron moved into some trenches which the 4th Dragoon Guards had been holding, but were relieved soon afterwards by the 9th Lancers.

About 10 p.m. both " C " and " D " Squadrons were withdrawn to billets in a deserted farmhouse on the Messines road just outside Wulverghem, the two troops of " D " with the 18th Hussars being relieved by the 5th Dragoon Guards. Here they had a scratch meal and a cup of tea, while someone on the transport told them how Sir Douglas Haig had carried out a great turning movement in the north, and that the battle was as good as won.[1] Supper finished all were quickly asleep. As we were within a mile of the front line we were warned to be careful about showing lights. A few preferred to sleep out of doors, but the majority, officers and men, lay down as they were, fully dressed and armed, on the stone floor inside. There was a large sort of attic which accommodated most of the men. One junior officer undressed completely and slept in pyjamas, but, on being suddenly roused at 4 in the morning, found himself totally unable to get into the polo boots which he

---

[1] This was the first time we had heard this sort of statement since reaching the front line, but even so I don't think we put much faith in it. In the next few weeks we were to hear many more remarkable stories of a similar nature.

habitually wore. When, after a terrific struggle, he at last succeeded, the Regiment had already gone, but fortunately his private car was there for him to overtake them.

This car was a godsend to the squadron in the first winter of the war. It always turned up when most required ; it carried an immense quantity of unauthorized kit, food, and wine ; and when in billets it took people on leave, fetched provisions from the neighbouring towns, and did many other useful jobs.

On being turned out, the two squadrons marched back through Wulverghem, where they were rejoined by " A " Squadron and the horses.

It was now about 6 a.m. on the morning of the 2nd November. The whole Regiment was marched back about 2 miles to the neighbourhood of Lindenhoek, where after a good deal of marching and counter-marching, mounting and dismounting, searching for a spot where the horses would be screened from observation by aeroplanes—" those grim harbingers of destruction," as Captain Fleming once called them—it was finally set to work digging trenches on a commanding ridge running south from Lindenhoek on the east side of the Kemmel–Neuve Eglise road. We saw a lot of led horses belonging to General Conneau's Cavalry Corps, like us, temporarily transformed into infantry, and sent up to relieve or support our own cavalry. Both men and horses looked thoroughly war-stained and unkempt. We also saw a lot of French infantry, and their artillery was firing busily near by. The sight of our allies, and especially the sound of their guns, was encouraging. With a feeling of relief everyone removed his equipment and felt his shoulders free from bandoliers, haversacks, waterbottles, etc. It was a lovely autumn day, and we got a good panorama of the terrific struggle for the Wytschaete–Messines Ridge. One could not, at any rate without glasses, see much or anything of the infantry on either side, but all along the line of the ridge there was a continual succession of great clouds of black and white smoke caused by the bursting of our own and the enemy's shells. The roar of guns was incessant, but we were not the target. For us the day seemed a holiday and our work a not unpleasant way of passing a fine autumn day. Here were no shells, no angrily whizzing machine-gun bullets, no need for constant scanning of the foreground with our field-glasses, no anticipation of sudden rushes of the enemy against our position. In spite of the terrific roar of the battle, and the fact that we might at any moment become the target of some observant Hun artilleryman, we were chiefly conscious of the bliss of being for the moment out of the battle, able to remove our equipment and relax the strain of nervous tension in which we had passed the two previous days. Altogether it was a very pleasant day.

But how were we going to spend the night ? Were we to be sent up to the front again to relieve some tired unit, or were we to occupy the trenches we were then digging ? Or was it possible we might be relieved and sent back to billets for a night or two ? Of these alternatives the second seemed the most probable, the third almost too good to hope for, while the first we rather discounted in view of the fairly trying time we had experienced since the evening of the 30th October.

But any hopes of a night's rest were soon shattered. Towards 4 p.m. the Colonel suddenly appeared with the news that we were " for the trenches " almost at once. We soon had our kit and equipment buckled on again and were marching down to Wulverghem. It was dark when we reached the entrance to the village, where we halted for some time, while the Adjutant was explaining to the squadron leaders the situation on the map and the exact position of our sector of the line, with other necessary information. After a while we moved on again towards the trenches. The line we were to occupy ran from near the cross-roads halfway between Wulverghem and Wytschaete, southwards along the ridge we had crossed the day before, towards the Wulverghem–Messines road. The position was almost identical with that occupied by half " D " Squadron the day before. They had been relieved by the 5th Dragoon Guards, from

whom we now took over. " C " Squadron was on the right,
" D " on the left, with " A " in the centre. No. 4 Troop,
" A " Squadron, under Lieutenant Hall, was with the 9th
Lancers, on our right ; on our left were the 4th Dragoon
Guards, who held the line up to Hill 75.

On the left part of the " D " Squadron sector the trenches
were only a few feet deep, and the squadron had to work hard
for an hour or two to make them habitable. This was our
first night in the trenches, and by good fortune a quiet and
peaceful one. The trenches were simply a narrow slit in
the ground about 5 feet 6 inches deep. There were no
dugouts or communication trenches, and very few traverses.
One man in every two was posted as sentry and relieved
hourly. Few, if any, of the officers or sergeants slept that
night. The complete absence of any place where one could
lie down, the novelty of the situation, and the obvious need
for perpetual vigilance, drove away all desire or indeed possibility of sleep. The Germans must have been some distance
off, for one could get out of the trenches and walk about
behind without being shot at, although it was not a very
dark night. By far the most striking object in our immediate
surroundings was the farm on the crest of the ridge in front
of us, through which we had passed in our advance on the
1st November. It had been set on fire by the 5th Dragoon
Guards in order to prevent the enemy using it either as a
strong-post or as cover for their troops when we evacuated
it, and it was now burning fiercely, throwing great tongues
of flame up into the air. From time to time the dancing
flames gave the appearance of moving figures to what were
probably beams and posts silhouetted against the firelight.
The fire lasted through the night and finally burnt itself
out towards morning. As the war went on the Regiment
grew accustomed to many strange sights, but this homestead
burning to its destruction in the darkness and the loneliness
of the battle-scarred countryside left a weird and unforget-
table impression.

" A " Squadron had been ordered to hold this farm at
all costs. Major Scott immediately placed a picket from

No. 1 Troop close to the farm, in order to obtain timely
warning of the approach of any attacking force in the dead
ground behind the ridge. While reconnoitring the neighbourhood of the farm, Captain Hermon-Hodge found
Captain Molloy's grave close to the ruins, and brought the
Colonel to see it. Before daybreak the picket was relieved
by a sergeant and three men from No. 2 Troop. The squadron spent the night improving and extending the trenches
which it was to occupy during the day.

Just before dawn on Tuesday, 3rd November, both " C "
and " D " Squadrons were withdrawn to the Wulverghem–
Wytschaete road. The reasons for reducing the strength of
the garrison were that during the hours of daylight there
was (a) far less danger of a surprise attack, (b) far greater
danger from shells. On the west side of the road there was
a farm, with the usual enclosure, and on the east side was
a bank affording some protection from shells. Just off the
road, on that side, there were two ricks. As soon as the two
squadrons had got to their positions they were told to dig
in under the bank as quickly as possible. The men were
naturally very tired, and were under the impression that,
having just been relieved from the front line, they were
entitled to a little rest and sleep. When therefore they
heard the order to dig in at once there was some little mur-
muring and a distinct disinclination to start work. Suddenly
and without warning a couple of shrapnel shells burst quite
close. I have seldom seen such a sudden transformation.
From a crowd standing about and " grousing," the whole two
squadrons were as if by magic changed into a body of men
working with furious energy and activity. Where only a
minute before picks and shovels had been lying idle on the
ground, and the question was who was going to pick them
up and use them, there was now not a tool of any sort to be
seen that was not in use, and a number of men were forced
to remain idle through lack of anything to dig with. In
about half an hour every man in the squadron had dug
himself, not indeed a shell-proof dugout, but at least a
" cubby-hole " undercut from the side of the bank and

sufficiently large to enable him to get his head and shoulders under cover, if not always the whole of his body. So tightly packed in these miniature shelters that they could not move a limb and consequently got cramp, they were obliged to stay for nearly two hours without moving, as there was heavy and continuous shelling between 8 and 10 o'clock. Then came a temporary lull.

The morning gradually wore away. Of the progress of the battle little was heard except occasional stray scraps of information. Once a badly wounded man came limping hastily down the road, shouting to us to clear out at once as the enemy had broken through and were coming along the road after him. No attention was paid to this beyond sending a man a short way up the road to see if anything unusual was happening, but it is just those sort of baseless and incoherent statements that sow the first seeds of a panic and are often the real cause of many an otherwise inexplicable withdrawal.

It was a day of tremendous shell fire, incessant and violent, due, it was said, to the presence of the Kaiser, and the two squadrons in the road were plastered with high explosive and shrapnel.

Meanwhile " A " Squadron was being even more severely tested. Daybreak had disclosed a level field of fire of about 300 yards in front of the unwired trenches. This ended in a slight ridge, on which the ruins of the farm still smouldered, and beyond was a long expanse of dead ground, in which a considerable force might be massed unseen for an attack on the trenches. The only warning of such an attack must come from the small advanced post at the farm, and the gaps left by " C " and " D " Squadrons to the right and left increased the sense of isolation felt by the four troops and machine-gun section.

However, the wisdom of holding the line lightly by day soon became apparent. It was a day of bright sunshine, and the line of freshly dug trenches provided an excellent mark for the German artillery. At any rate it was subjected to practically continuous shelling from dawn to dusk, and, as the day advanced, there were increasing indications of an infantry attack. Early in the bombardment Private Napper returned from the advanced post to report that though no Germans had approached, two of the men had been wounded by shrapnel and were now in an improvised rifle pit behind a haystack with Sergeant Shrimpton. Major Scott ordered the men to lie down in the bottom of the deep trench, leaving one look-out man for every troop front. But, as the shrapnel swept the trench, Private Archer was killed on this duty, and for the rest of the day observation was carried on by hasty glimpses over the parapet whenever no shell was heard approaching. The squadron escaped heavy casualties partly through these precautions, but mainly by sheer good fortune. The trench was deep and narrow—so narrow that progress along it was only possible for the troop leaders by walking over their recumbent men. The latter were practically safe from shrapnel, and the most serious danger was that of a 5.9-inch shell actually dropping in the trench. The fire was extremely accurate, and when —as happened in about six different places—a 5.9 inch dropped near enough to the trench, the sides collapsed, and the men were buried until they were dug out by their comrades.

In the middle of the morning Captain V. Fleming with great gallantry came up from behind to ascertain how the squadron was getting on, and if more ammunition was required ; but so far not a German had been seen. About 3 p.m. a few Germans appeared at the farm, and were fired at by the squadron. About the same time Captain G. Hermon-Hodge, F.O.O. for " H " Battery, R.H.A., reported Germans massing in the dead ground beyond for an attack on the trench line, part of which was held by his brother's troop. The battery responded with rapid and effective gun fire, and apparently broke up the attack, for no infantry advanced beyond the farm. The squadron had good reason to be thankful for this timely assistance, as the trenches were shattered by shell fire, many rifles had jammed from the effect of dust and grit, several men had

been buried, and all ranks had felt the effect of the
continuous shelling.   At dusk the shelling ceased.
Lieutenant Fane took out No. 3 Troop as a reconnoitring
patrol, and brought in the two wounded men from
the farm.

As usual during all this period, there was a great scarcity
of entrenching tools.

Meanwhile the 4th Dragoon Guards on our left were
suffering heavy losses under the bombardment. Towards
4 p.m., after consultation with Major Solly-Flood, their
commanding officer, the Colonel sent the 1st and 3rd
Troops of " D " Squadron, under Lieutenants Gill and
Pepper, to advance across the open towards the cross-roads
near Hill 75 and support the Dragoon Guards. To do
this they had to cross a very dangerous piece of open
ground in full view of the enemy, and they got very badly
shelled. By great good fortune they only had one casualty
—Sergeant Rice, wounded. They were accompanied by
S.S.M. Warren, who for his share in this exploit received the
D.C.M. long afterwards in April 1915, while Lieutenant
Gill, Private Checkley, and Private Dallow were mentioned in Despatches, but not till February 1915. It was
a really fine performance, considering the *very* heavy fire
which was going on all the time.

Later on, " C " Squadron also was sent up to support the
4th Dragoon Guards. They went up the road in single
file, to avoid casualties, but they were in luck, for very soon
after they started the shelling entirely ceased. After dusk
the two remaining troops of " D " Squadron went up to
the front line again, but were assured that it would only
be for a very short time, and that the whole division was
to be relieved in an hour or two by the 2nd Cavalry Division.
After about two hours the long and anxiously expected
relief appeared, the 16th Lancers taking over from
the 4th Dragoon Guards and the 4th Hussars from
ourselves.

Rations and rum had somehow found their way up, and
the Regiment halted by the roadside while they were issued.

The rum, of course, was the chief attraction, and, as usual,
the distribution was accompanied by much heated argument. There were two jars for each squadron, about
4 pints for each troop, or rather less than a quarter of a pint
per man—a fairly liberal allowance compared with the
amount generally issued in later years of the war. However,
each jar had to be divided between two troops, and this
delicate operation was carried out by one of the sergeants,
closely watched by his colleagues from the other troop.
The aggrieved party might—and did—protest to its troop
leader, but it was generally found that possession was nine
points of the law, and that the only way of adjusting the
balance was to hold the jar oneself next time.

As soon as all the rations had been issued we set off along
the Wulverghem road to meet the horses. After marching
a mile or two we met them, mounted, and rode on towards
Dranoutre, where we were to billet.

It was a foggy night, calm and still. Everyone felt
supremely happy. Behind us lay four days of extreme
strain and exertion, not to mention a certain amount of
danger. Ahead of us was the hope of a square meal, a
sound sleep, and a good wash the next day, in fact all that
we soon came to associate with the magic word " billets."
Dranoutre is probably one of the most unattractive of the
many unattractive villages of Flanders, but not Paris in
her fairest moments ever had half the charm that this
dirty little village had for us that night. We soon got the
horses off-saddled and tied up for the night in a field. Major
Churchill and Lieutenant Goldie had made excellent
arrangements, and all ranks had a good meal. And with
it letters, newspapers, parcels, etc.—the first since leaving
St. Omer. The men were housed in barns, the officers in
a little deserted house. The ground-floor was full of refugees,
but we didn't much mind what was there as long as we
could sleep somewhere. A very few of the officers found
beds of a sort, but the majority slept on their valises spread
on the floor upstairs, above the refugees. And so ended
four ever-memorable days.

Before continuing the narrative, we may make one last quotation from Lord French.   He says : [1]

"In the great onslaught made by the enemy on 31st October and 1st November, sufficient recognition has never yet been given to the glorious stand made by the cavalry corps under Allenby, and when I speak of the gallantry of the cavalry, I hasten to add that the splendour of their work was equally shared by Shaw's 9th Brigade of the 3rd Division (1st Battalion Northumberland Fusiliers, 4th Battalion Royal Fusiliers, 1st Battalion Lincoln Regiment, and 1st Battalion R. Scots Fusiliers), Egerton's Brigade of the Indian Corps (1st Connaught Rangers, 129th Duke of Connaught's Own Beluchis, 57th Wilde's Rifles, 9th Bhopal Infantry), the London Scottish, and the Oxfordshire Yeomanry.

"For close upon forty-eight hours these troops held the Wytschaete–Messines Ridge against the utmost efforts of no less than two and a half German Army Corps to dislodge them.   Here was the centre of our line of battle, and, had it given way, disaster would have resulted to the entire left wing of the Allied line. . . .

"Reviewing the situation as it presented itself on 31st October and 1st November 1914, I believe that the vital interests of the British Empire were in great danger on both these days.   That is to say, the whole coast-line from Havre to Ostend was within an ace of falling into the hands of the enemy.

"In recalling the fateful hours of those two wonderful days and nights, I think we were perhaps in the greatest danger between 2 a.m. and 11 a.m. on Sunday, 1st November. Had the French XVI Corps arrived only an hour later than it did, the German advance from the line Wytschaete–Messines would have gained such volume, strength, and impetus, that nothing could have saved Mont Kemmel from falling into their hands.   A vital wedge would have been driven into the very centre of our line. . . .

"The greatest threat of disaster with which we were faced in 1914 was staved off by the devoted bravery and endurance displayed by the cavalry corps. . . ."

Lord French goes on to explain the great disadvantages

[1] " 1914," pp. 238, 260–1.

under which cavalry fights on foot. First there are the horses, which have to be looked after, and which take many men from the fighting line. A cavalry division gets little more than half its strength into the firing line, when employed in the trenches.

" But the mobility of the cavalry arm will always be found to compensate in large degree for these manifest disadvantages. Taking into account the losses they had suffered, they can hardly have opposed 2,000 rifles to the onslaught of what has been computed as more than two German Army Corps. . . .

" I must add a few words as to the fine part played in the fighting of 1st November by the Oxfordshire Hussars and the London Scottish. They were the first Territorial troops who fought in the war.

" After disembarking at Dunkirk the Oxfordshire Hussars took part in the important operations connected with the Belgian retreat from Antwerp, and rendered most valuable aid in the defence of the Wytschaete–Messines Ridge when that piece of ground was held with such marvellous tenacity by the cavalry division against overwhelming odds." [1]

And finally :

" I say without the slightest hesitation that without the assistance which the Territorials afforded between October 1914 and June 1915, it would have been impossible to have held the line in France and Belgium, or to have prevented the enemy from reaching his goal, the Channel seaboard." [2]

The Regiment spent Wednesday, 4th November, spreading itself into billets around Dranoutre. The billets were nothing to boast about, squalid little farms surrounded by mud and manure, but still they were billets, and the worst billet is a great deal better than the best bivouac. Each squadron had its own farm, the officers living and sleeping in one room, the sergeants in another—probably the kitchen —while the men slept in a barn. The horses were picketed in lines in the adjoining pasture, close under the hedge to avoid observation by enemy aircraft.

Lieutenant F. A. Gill was now appointed to command

[1] " 1914," p. 262.   [2] " 1914," p. 294.

" D " Squadron in place of Captain Molloy. Captain Fleming and Captain Hermon-Hodge did not wish to leave their respective squadrons, and Lieutenant Villiers, on whom the command would thus normally have devolved, and who had actually been in charge of the squadron from midday on the 1st to the evening of the 3rd November, specially requested that it should be given to Lieutenant Gill. The latter was some years older than the other officers in " D " Squadron and, as already mentioned, was an ex-Regular officer of the 3rd Dragoon Guards. His promotion was welcome to all, but most especially to the officers of his own squadron.

Thursday, 5th November, was spent resting quietly in billets. No work was done beyond what was absolutely essential, that is to say, watering, feeding, and grooming the horses, and thoroughly cleaning rifles and bayonets. General de Lisle visited the Colonel and expressed his great satisfaction with the way in which the Regiment had carried out everything which it had been called upon to do, and said that he could not pay it a greater compliment than by treating it in the future on the same level, and relying on it to perform exactly the same duties, as a Regular regiment.

At 4.30 a.m. on Friday, 6th November, the Regiment was turned out and marched to Lindenhoek, where it was held in reserve against an expected attack, However, the attack never materialized, or if it did, was repulsed ; anyhow, we were not required, and eventually, after being kept standing to till noon, we returned to another group of farms, about 2 miles from Dranoutre. Here we just had time to have tea and begin to settle down comfortably before being suddenly turned out again at 4 p.m. to go and relieve a regiment of the 1st Cavalry Brigade in the trenches east of Wulverghem. The turn-out was so sudden and hasty that at least one squadron, if not more, had to move at a fast canter in order to be on time at the regimental rendezvous, with the inevitable result that it arrived in a fragmentary condition, the rear half galloping desperately to catch up the head of the column.

After riding some way we dismounted near Wulverghem and marched up to the trenches in a dense fog, arriving about 6 p.m. " D " Squadron was on the right, " C " on the left, and " A " in support. The right flank of the Regiment rested on the Wulverghem–Messines road, and we were in touch with other troops on both flanks, for the trench line was now continuous. The trenches were good as far as they went, deep and narrow, affording good protection from rifle and shell fire. But there were practically no dugouts or communication trenches, and no drainage system. Fortunately there had not been enough rain yet to make them really wet. And though trenches should be narrow rather than wide, these were almost too much so, for it was impossible to walk along them without getting above ground. Consequently all orders and messages during the daytime had to be passed along from man to man.

An officer of " A " Squadron, marching up to the line at the head of his troop, received word through the fog that the troop in front of him had lost touch. " Who the hell's Touch ? " was his reply.

Soon after midnight the Germans suddenly opened heavy rifle and machine-gun fire, to which we replied vigorously. Owing to the fog we could not see what we were firing at, but they cannot have been much more than 200 yards away, as their shooting was pretty accurate. We were well entrenched, and no one was hit, but one man had a bullet through his waterbottle and another through his bayonet. Later in the night Corporal L. Gale and Private Franklin, belonging to Lieutenant Muirhead's Troop (No. 3, " C " Squadron) captured our first prisoner, an officers' mess cook, who had lost his way in the fog and was wandering about between the lines. He had two little mess-tins of a disgusting-looking white mixture, food for German officers.

The rest of the night and the following day passed off quietly. The weather was fine, and though there was a certain amount of shelling, it was never very serious. During the afternoon the Germans made a small attack on some French infantry away on our left front. The line curved forward in this direction, forming a small salient, and from our position we had an admirable view of the attack. So few orders and messages of this period have been preserved that it may be of interest to quote the two following :

To Lieutenant Gill, " D " Squadron, Q.O.O.H.
No. 1. Date 7.11.14.

Captain Fleming, on left of my trenches, reports that the Germans are coming out of trenches at Point 75 and are advancing in small bodies down the road leading to Wulverghem which we all lined when " A " Squadron were in forward trenches. Have reported this to Headquarters and sent verbal message to " A " Squadron. In the event of their enfilading my trenches, or coming round left rear of French outposts, shall have to withdraw " C " Squadron to the line of trenches running at right angles to you and parallel with the road, where " A " Squadron now is. This will leave your left unprotected, so will notify you if I have to do this.

From C. R. I. Nicholl.
Time 1.23 p.m.

The second message is from the left troop of " D " Squadron :

1.30 p.m.
About 50.

Germans are advancing on our left flank, beyond the French trenches. If we are enfiladed I will put my troop in the other trench, out at an angle to this.

Second-Lieutenant Wilfred Pepper.

To C.O., " D " Squadron.

The Germans crept very slowly and cautiously forward on their hands and knees through what looked like a root field. They must have been in dead ground, for the French infantry, in their dark blue uniforms, could be seen sitting placidly in their trenches, apparently quite unconcerned. Suddenly, when quite near the French position, the Germans leapt to their feet and began to move hurriedly forward. Instantly the French opened fire, and the Germans began to fall like ninepins. Not one reached the French trenches and the whole attack fell to pieces.

About this time the Regiment was slowly becoming aware of the importance of everybody keeping out of sight in the trenches and not attracting the enemy's fire. At first we had been blissfully ignorant of the extent to which every movement of our troops above ground was watched by the German observers, but we all learnt by experience sooner or later.

About 8 p.m. on Saturday, the 7th November, the Regiment was relieved by the composite regiment of Household Cavalry, and marched back to new billets near Bailleul, being met by the horses outside Wulverghem. The new billets were farther back from the line than we had been since the 31st October, and were also rather cleaner and generally better than those we had last occupied.

All next day we rested in billets.

The following extract from an officer's diary gives a striking account of his first impressions under fire, and of what many of us thought and felt in those days.

" We have now been fighting for nine days and I will try and describe truthfully my present feelings and what I have felt in the past nine days. On first coming under fire, I was not in any way scared, although I rushed to take advantage of any cover ; a shrapnel shell burst right over me but nothing hit me. Shortly afterwards a sniper had a shot at me and I jumped into a ditch full of water which came up over my knees. One very soon realizes that it is no good trying to dodge bullets or shells except by taking cover, and that as regards ' black marias ' and shrapnel it is a question of going several miles before you can be really safe. Everything depends on being warm and having plenty to eat. Once in Messines I was very cold and felt wretched, but apart from that I have merely a feeling of loathing for the whole thing ; the burning houses, churches, farms, dead and wounded men and horses, all tell the same story—misery and grief to themselves or someone else, and who will be better for it all ? In a district like that round Messines it must be a generation before there can be any real restoration of happi-

ness to the people.   I intensely dislike exposing myself (or
my men) to fire unless it is absolutely imperative, and I am
afraid that each time the Regiment goes under fire the
dislike of everybody will increase rather than diminish.
The men have been very good and cool so far, and this is
most creditable, as the whole thing has been a great bewil-
derment to them.   The shell fire was something which they
had never contemplated at all.   I am sure that as long as
people's nerves stand they will do their duty to the best of
their ability. . . . The prospect of a long war is what
depresses people.   It is the hopeless feeling that we shall
have to go on day after day, night after night, always ready
to move and fight, never knowing what is happening and no
end in sight.   It is not wounds or death people mind ; it is
the uncertainty, discomfort, loss of friends and home life,
and the sole goal is victory for one's country—a fine goal
it is true, but the part each man plays is so minute that it is
hard to realize that what I or any other single man does can
effect the result in the slightest degree."

The Regiment was turned out again at 2 p.m. on Monday,
9th November, and went into bivouac close to the 16th
kilometre stone on the Dranoutre–Neuve Eglise road, where
it remained in reserve till next day, expecting to be sent up
to the trenches any moment.

During the day a rumour was going about that we were
likely to be sent to Egypt, and there was some discussion as
to whether the prospect was agreeable or the reverse.   A
few thought that the voyage alone would be such a blessed
relief from the trenches as to outweigh any considerations
of what might happen the other end, while the idea of un-
limited sunshine seemed particularly attractive to anyone
in the cold and wet and squelching mud of Flanders.   But
I think the majority took the view that it was better on the
whole to remain where we were.

This was the first appearance of a rumour which in later
stages of the war sprang up again in many different shapes.
Sometimes we would be bound for Serbia ; another time
for Palestine ; more often for Italy.   But we never
went.

7

That night we slept in a field round a camp fire, but it was so cold that we didn't get much sleep. Someone had a copy of *The Times*, from which he read extracts to the officers and sergeants by the light of the fire. A generous issue of rum helped to keep us going through the night, though from time to time the cold would drive one to get up and stamp about in a vain endeavour to get warm. All Tuesday, 10th November, we remained in reserve ; but Tuesday night half the Regiment was sent to the trenches, while the rest were kept in reserve in a house a mile behind the trenches, where they managed to get a bit of sleep. This house was full of dried bundles of tobacco-leaf, which no doubt represented a substantial portion of the proprietor's annual income. These we found tolerable, if not very comfortable, substitutes for beds.

The half-regiment in the trenches consisted of " A " Squadron, under Major Scott, and the 1st and 4th Troops of " D " Squadron, under Lieutenant Villiers. They were east of Wulverghem, close to the Wulverghem–Messines road. There was a semblance of a night attack, but nothing serious. Lieutenant Villiers was in support to the 9th Lancers, with one of whose squadron leaders he had the following conversation on reaching the line :

9TH LANCER : " What regiment is that ? "
VILLIERS : " The Oxfordshire Yeomanry."
9TH LANCER (in a tone of the deepest disgust) : " Good God ! Who's on your left ? "
VILLIERS : " The 4th Dragoon Guards."
9TH LANCER : " Thank God ! "

The Regiment was relieved at daybreak on Wednesday, 11th November, and returned to billets near Bailleul. That day we were transferred to the 4th Cavalry Brigade (Brigadier-General the Hon. C. E. Bingham), forming part of the 2nd Cavalry Division, under Major-General H. de la P. Gough. Here we took the place of the composite regiment of Household Cavalry, which was transferred to the 3rd Cavalry Division. The other two regiments in the Brigade were the 6th Dragoon Guards (Carabiniers) and the 3rd (K.O.) Hussars, with whom we were destined to serve for the next four years, and among whom we made many friends.

At first we were rather sorry to leave the 2nd Cavalry Brigade. There had not been enough time to get to know them, but—in spite of the little conversation with the 9th Lancers recorded above—we already felt ourselves part of the Brigade with which we had made our first serious entry into action, and we should have been glad to remain in their company. However, we soon settled down in our new surroundings, which indeed made very little difference for a long time to come.

As a result of the change into the 2nd Cavalry Division we now went into new billets about 2 miles south of Bailleul. Regimental Headquarters was at an estaminet called "La Blanche Maison," and the three squadrons were in farms at La Becque, close by. The billets were fairly good for those times—we should not have liked them a year later—and the inhabitants fairly friendly. The officers of "C" Squadron christened their farm "the Duck Billet," in memory of the remarkably fine birds which they killed and ate there, much to the fury of the old harridan their owner— till she was paid.

On Friday, 13th November, we stood to from 5 a.m. to 8.30 a.m., when we moved to a new area somewhere between Bailleul and Dranoutre. Our new billets were, I think, the worst we ever had. The farms were small and filthy beyond words, and the inhabitants equally disagreeable.[1] To add to our discomforts, the weather, which hitherto, though cold at night, had been generally fine and sunny, now took a turn for the worse, and soon settled down to rain almost incessantly for weeks. The horses, picketed out in the field, were over their fetlocks in mud ; the men, once

---

[1] We were now just inside the Belgian frontier, and it was our almost universal experience that whereas the French peasants, even in the Flemish-speaking area, welcomed us with every hospitality—at any rate in the early stages of the war—the Belgians, on the contrary, generally received us with scowls and blank refusals to do anything for us.

wet—and they had to go out in the rain at least three times a day to water and feed—never got properly dry, and even the officers were none too comfortable. For example, in " D " Squadron the officers ate and washed and slept in one small dirty brick-floored room, with a fireplace, but no possibility of lighting a fire because the chimney had been bricked in. Next door, in the kitchen, ten sergeants, four officers' servants, the sergeants' cook, and a number of exceedingly dirty and unpleasant inhabitants were herded together, while the servants struggled with the inhabitants for a place on the fire to cook. And of course everybody was smoking, and the windows all shut to keep out the wind and rain. The atmosphere may be imagined, but anyway it was warm. Conditions in the other squadrons were no doubt much the same.

We were about 5 miles behind the trenches, in support of another brigade now in the line, whom we were due to relieve on the 15th. About this time we were much cheered by the news of the Russians having got into Germany and captured the Kaiser's hunting-box, also by the sinking of the *Emden*, and there was a rumour that the German ships off the coast of Chile had been sunk by the Japanese.

At 2.30 p.m. on Sunday, 15th November, we marched off to the trenches, the same that we had occupied on the night of the 6th–7th. The weather was perfectly foul, pouring rain and cold. We had to ride about $3\frac{1}{2}$ miles at a walk ; we then dismounted and marched another 3 miles to the trenches in an absolute downpour of rain. The men hated marching on foot, not being accustomed to it. The worst part about it was the weight one had to carry ; full haversack and waterbottle, rifle and ammunition, waterproof sheet and blanket. Many of the officers also carried a rifle and ammunition, besides field-glasses and revolver. On top of all this everybody wore a heavy greatcoat or British warm, and very often a light Burberry or mackintosh over it. Later in the war British warms were issued to the men, but at this period, and for long afterwards, they wore long heavy greatcoats, the lower part of which became caked with mud in the trenches, and the whole soaked through and through with rain, adding greatly to the weight. Although the head of the column generally moved at a foot's pace, the rear troops usually had to march at four or five miles an hour, and often to double, in order to keep up, owing to the congested state of the roads and the difficulty of keeping close touch in the darkness. The result was that, whatever the weather, hot or cold, dry or wet, one almost invariably arrived at the trenches in what is coarsely, but exactly, described as a " muck sweat."

We got into our trenches at 5.55 p.m., relieving the 4th Hussars. " D " Squadron was on the right of the line, " C " on the left, and " A " in support. The 3rd Hussars were on the right of the Regiment, with the Wulverghem–Messines road between us, and the 6th Dragoon Guards on our left.

We had a most unpleasant night. The trenches were inches deep in water and the sides a mass of thick, clammy slime, so that everything one touched—rifles, ammunition, food—was immediately covered with it. The trenches were so narrow that it was impossible to get along them ; there was only one miserably inadequate communication trench, full of water, which led nowhere ; there were no sanitary arrangements and no drainage. The men were not supposed to get out of their trench even at night, and as a matter of fact it was no easy matter to get out, climbing up the steep, slippery side in one's full equipment. Above ground the muddy surface was equally slippery, and even in well-nailed boots it was almost impossible to keep one's feet, so that troops relieving or being relieved slithered and fell in all directions, often into some ditch or shell hole full of water.

It rained at intervals throughout the night, and at 3 a.m. began a steady downpour which lasted several hours. It was a quiet night and there was no attack, but the wet and cold and cramp made everyone very glad to be relieved at 6 a.m. by " A " Squadron. " C " and " D " spent the day in comparative comfort in a farmhouse half a mile behind, where they got warm, had plenty of food and some sleep. About midday " C " Squadron was sent to dig trenches behind " A," but the Germans soon saw them, and " A " Squadron got badly shelled, losing one man—Private A. E. Horne—killed, and one—Sergeant W. Perrin—wounded. " C " Squadron was then withdrawn to the farm.

We expected to spend the whole of the coming night in the trenches, but about tea-time heard the joyful news that we were to be relieved by an infantry brigade at 8 p.m. " C " and " D " Squadrons relieved " A " at 5 p.m., hoping to be relieved themselves in a few hours, but to their disgust the hours went by and no relief came. It was very cold, but luckily not raining. They had carried up bundles of faggot sticks to sit on, which slightly reduced the discomfort. At last, when they had almost given up hope, the relief arrived at 1.30 a.m., and the Regiment marched off to the horses 3 miles away, and then rode on to the billets near La Becque, which it had left on the 13th, getting in at 4 a.m., the 17th November.[1]

The next two days we rested in billets. On the 18th we were roused at 6.15 a.m. by a sudden order to " stand to," ready to move at a moment's notice. However, nothing came of the alarm (said to have been caused by a General being woken up by the noise of shelling on Kemmel Ridge), and we were left in peace for the rest of the day. The wet weather was now temporarily interrupted by a few days of sharp frost, and, though very cold, it was a welcome change after the incessant rain.

A story is told of these days that on one occasion an enterprising sergeant's batman, on getting into billets late one night, found a convenient cowshed, not, as usually happened, snaffled by the officers. Being zealous for the

[1] In those days the only method of relieving cavalry in the trenches was by bringing up the led horses. Here is an example of how it worked : Major Churchill went back to La Becque on the morning of the 16th to fetch them. They started at about 4 p.m., each man with four horses, and blocked the Dranoutre road from about 7 p.m. until 1 a.m. During that time no one could dismount and the men had at least nine hours in the saddle, most of which were spent halted.

well-being of his nags, and perhaps thinking to avoid inspection by officers, he tied up his two horses in the shed, instead of putting them out on the lines. It was a bitterly cold night with a hard frost. Next morning, before dawn, there was a sudden alarm and orders to turn out and saddle up at once. Our man hurried off to his shed, and began groping about in the inky darkness to find his horses. At last, after much stumbling about, he found what he took to be one of them, and hoisted the heavy saddle on to its back. He then set about bridling it. After some difficulty, he got the bit in its mouth and was drawing on the headstall when his numbed hands suddenly hit against something hard on the top of its head. " Gorblimey, you are the sort of beggar that would go and get its ears frozen on a night like this, cuss you," he said. It was an old cow.

At 1 p.m. on Thursday, 19th November, the Regiment suddenly received orders to march at 2 p.m. to Locre to take over a line of trenches held by French infantry. This unwelcome news reached the squadrons just as they were settling down to lunch. By now we were getting fairly well accustomed to these sudden turn-outs, but they were none the less disagreeable. Lunch was abandoned, while we hastily saddled up, got into fighting kit, slung waterbottles, haversacks, revolvers, and the rest of the " Christmas-tree " paraphernalia over our shoulders, and stuffed pockets and haversacks with as much bully beef, biscuits, and chocolate as we could carry. " D " Squadron had to turn out with only two officers—Lieutenants Villiers and Keith-Falconer—the other two having gone off on leave for the day to Dunkirk.

Just before we started Major Churchill received orders to report to G.H.Q. to take up an appointment as Camp Commandant of a training centre near St. Omer. Lieutenant Hutchinson was also ordered to G.H.Q. for duty under the Director of Supply.

The three squadrons left their billets at 1.30 p.m.—not a bad turn-out at such short notice—and marched to the rendezvous, where the whole Regiment assembled and moved off at 2 p.m.

A blinding snowstorm now set in and lasted continuously for eight hours. We marched through Bailleul to Locre, where we formed mass in a ploughed field, halted, and dismounted. Squadron leaders were summoned to a conference at Brigade Headquarters, while the rest waited with the horses. It was now growing dark and snowing harder than ever. Mr. Pearce, the Regimental Sergeant-Major, informed us that we were probably going to make a charge, because we had been drawn up in mass formation, which, he said, was the usual preliminary to such an operation. In view of the snow and the darkness, it seemed rather unlikely, but we felt that anything was possible.

After waiting some time we got orders to mount, and moved off at a steady trot up the road to Kemmel. The roads were getting very slippery with the snow, which froze as it fell, but we had to keep trotting, even down a steepish hill, to avoid being left behind and cut off by other traffic. Halfway to Kemmel we turned into a field, where we dismounted and handed over the horses, while ammunition, rum, and rations were issued. Then we set off down the road again, leaving the horses behind. We halted for some time in Kemmel, where there was a block in the traffic, while a squadron of the Royal Scots Greys, which had got cut off, went by at the double, with strange oaths in a strange tongue. On we went again across the snow-clad fields towards Wytschaete.

The snow had stopped and it was a bright starry night. We pursued a very uneven course in order to avoid crossing exposed ground as far as possible. Every now and then we advanced short distances at a great pace, the head of the column passing down messages to keep closed up, while the tail replied with urgent entreaties not to go so fast in front. Then we would halt for long periods, while presumably the leaders took their bearings, and their sweating followers cooled in the frosty air. No one behind Headquarters knew where we were going, and anyone who lost touch would have cut off all those following him and had no small difficulty in joining up again. However, no one was cut off, and eventually, at 9.30, we reached our position, where we were met by the squadron leaders.

The French troops from whom we were to take over did not stand on ceremony, but simply streaked off as hard as they could go directly they saw the head of the relieving column. Not a very formal relief, but no doubt they had had a hard time, and anyway no harm came of it, as things turned out. Still, it made it rather difficult for our men to distribute themselves in their proper places in the line, especially as one could not speak above a whisper, for fear of arousing the Germans. As it was, they were sniping busily, and the men were obliged to move to their positions over the top of the ground, as the trenches were not continuous, but merely a series of disconnected holes and a few dugouts.

The Regiment was on the left of the Brigade with the Royal Scots Greys on its left, on the other side of a small unfenced road. The line here bent rather sharply back to the left, enabling the enemy to enfilade our trenches. and their snipers gave us a lot of trouble. " A " and " C " Squadrons held the front line, with " D " in close support in a tiny spinney 100 yards behind. The front trenches were in some places within 30 yards of the Germans, and nowhere more than 200 yards from them.

We remained in these trenches seventy-two hours, unable to move a limb by day or by night without being shot at by snipers at close range, and desperately cold, with the temperature some 15 degrees below freezing-point all the time. Many of the men got frost-bitten, and in some cases lost one or more toes, while a few eventually died from gangrene setting in and poisoning the whole system. During all this time we had nothing but cold bully and biscuit to eat and ice-cold water to drink, except for a mouthful of rum.[1] We found several dead Frenchmen, whom it was impossible to bury, owing to the hardness of the ground.

---

[1] Someone had carried off from billets a bottle half full of what he took to be the officers' rum ration, but which turned out to contain lamp-oil when drunk in the cheerless dawn next morning. A bitter moment !

Some time in the middle of the night the two other " D " Squadron officers arrived back from Dunkirk and found their way up to the trenches.

About the middle of the morning of Friday, 20th November, Private N. Harcourt, " C " Squadron, was hit rather badly through the shoulder. Captain V. Fleming at once went along to him, had him bandaged up, and though it was of course daylight and they were in full view of the enemy, Captain Fleming, helped by Sergeant Hoddinott, carried the man back to the dressing-station. It was freezing cold, and if the man had been left in the trench till dark, he might have died of exposure.

Lance-Corporal R. Holmes, " C " Squadron, was also wounded on this day.

After dark on the 20th, " D " Squadron relieved " C " in the front line, where they remained for the next forty-eight hours.

The 21st passed off quietly, and in the evening " C " Squadron relieved " A " in the front line.

About 9 a.m. on the morning of Sunday, 22nd November, Private F. B. Dallow, " D " Squadron, stood up to throw a biscuit to the man in the next bit of trench, and was immediately shot in the mouth by a sniper hidden in a tree, and died in half an hour. Dallow was a first-rate young soldier, who had greatly distinguished himself with the party supporting the 4th Dragoon Guards on the 3rd November, for which, as already recorded, he was mentioned in Despatches three months after his death. He was buried in Kemmel churchyard.

There were no other casualties this day, except Saddler S. Harris, " C " Squadron, wounded. About midday there was an intensive bombardment for about an hour, which, however, did no damage beyond covering us with dirt.

After dark the cooks and servants managed to make some tea in a farm half a mile behind and bring it up to the front line. Though nearly cold by the time it reached us, it was none the less welcome.

We were relieved at 8.30 p.m. by the 4th Dragoon Guards

and marched back to billets at Noote Boom, 10 miles away, getting in just after midnight. The horses met us between Kemmel and Locre. On our way we heard the first rumours of " leave," an idea incredible but exciting.

For sheer hardship the three days and nights in the Kemmel trenches were the most trying the Regiment ever experienced. Often, before and afterwards, they were in greater peril, were more heavily shelled, carried out and withstood attacks and counter-attacks and raids, suffered more casualties. But never, not even at Arras in April 1917, were they so continuously exposed to the fiercest wintry weather with absolutely no alleviating conditions. They started by getting thoroughly wetted in the eight hours' snowstorm on the way up, and then sat or stood practically motionless in holes in the ground for seventy-two hours, the only break being when a squadron moved the short distance from the front line to the support trenches. All the rest of the time there could be no movement, even within the trenches, because, as already explained, they were nowhere continuous, while it was death to walk about above ground. Added to the intense cold was the total lack of hot food or drink for three days, the partial lack of sleep, and the continuous strain of sitting within 100 yards of the Germans.

A word may be said here about casualties. It will have been remarked that the Regiment had singularly few during these three weeks' fighting—4 killed, 1 died of wounds, 13 wounded, and an indefinite number more or less permanently invalided by frost-bite. What is the explanation ? Partly, no doubt, that we spent several quiet days and nights in the trenches, even when most uncomfortable ; but partly also that we undoubtedly had the most amazing luck. Once at least during the four days' fighting round Messines each squadron in turn might easily have been wiped out ; both " C " and " D " Squadrons at the Messines barricade on the night 31st October–1st November ; " D " Squadron in the retirement from the Steenbeek on the 1st November when Captain Molloy was killed ; and " A " Squadron in the fierce shelling of the 3rd November. On each of these occasions we had scarcely any casualties, and this can only be attributed to rifle and shell fire constantly missing its mark by a hairsbreadth, and to failure of the enemy to press their attack at those particular moments.

This, though we did not realize it at the time, was the close of an epoch in the war. The Oxfordshire Yeomanry had only come in for the last phase, but that phase included the two most critical days of the First Battle of Ypres, in which the British cavalry were outnumbered by more than 20 to 1 for more than forty-eight hours and stood their ground.

After this the war was never the same again. The dark side of war is never likely to be forgotten by this generation, and is especially prominent in trench warfare, which ceases to be an adventure and becomes a business. But till now there had been movement, variety, and novelty in all we did. The sudden turn-out, the disgust at leaving comfortable billets, the saddling up in haste, the long ride through the darkness with the sounds of battle coming ever nearer, the excitement and uncertainty of every next half-hour, the long weary waits, the anxious whispering and the sharp " ping " of the sniper's bullet as one got near the line, the process of relieving, settling down, and taking stock of one's position, the long hours of cold and wet and sleeplessness, the perpetual strain, always expecting an attack, the inferno of shells, and then at last, after goodness knows how many days, the relief, the light-hearted ride back to billets, the intense comfort of warmth and hot food, of warm blankets with one's boots off and one's head on some sort of pillow, and then—blessed sleep ; all these—so soon to become items in the routine of war—were in 1914 still part of a great adventure. Above all, the Regiment—officers and men—was still almost the same happy company which had sailed from England two months before, but with friendships now tested by the most searching ordeal in the world, made strong by the common memory of great experiences.

CHAPTER V

THE FIRST WINTER

(23rd November 1914—22nd April 1915)

THE war was now becoming a form of siege in which for cavalry mounted action would be impossible, and infantry, artillery, and engineers would bear the brunt of the fighting. But this was hardly realized yet, at any rate by the majority of regimental officers and men, who settled down in their billets with the full expectation of being turned out again before long, either for attack, defence, or pursuit.[1] The possibility that we should be left undisturbed—except for a move to a more comfortable billeting area—for ten weeks, and that it would be nearly twelve weeks before we saw the front line again, never entered our heads. Yet so it was to be.

The fact was, the German bid for Ypres and the Channel ports having definitely failed, both sides settled down to watch one another in miserable water-logged trenches until the spring. The cavalry was greatly reduced in strength by the heavy fighting of the last five weeks, and the horses were naturally not in the best of trim after standing out in all weathers, never under cover at night, and looked after for most of the time by only one man to four horses.

---

[1] An officer, writing home on the 26th November, less than four days since leaving the trenches, says : " We have been allowed quite a long rest this time, and have been in our billets since we came out of the trenches last Sunday night. I expect we shall be turned out again now at any moment. We heard a rumour from a young staff officer this afternoon that the Germans had begun to retreat from their present position ; of course, if that is the case, the cavalry would be required to be up and at them without delay, and we should be kept pretty busy chasing them. We also heard that Allenby was very anxious to keep the cavalry out of the trenches as much as possible, so as to prevent the possibility of his being left with very few or very tired men in the event of their being called on to perform proper cavalry work."

Moreover, it would of course have been folly to waste a specially trained arm of the service, which it was hoped would be required for its own proper duties later on, on the ordinary routine of trench warfare. So the cavalry was now left quietly in billets and given a chance to restore its horses and to brighten up the cavalry spirit in general.

Our first business was to settle down and make ourselves comfortable in billets—or at least as comfortable as the conditions allowed. Our area comprised the scattered hamlet of Noote Boom and a few houses in Steentje,[1] which village we shared with " E " Battery R.H.A. and other units. Headquarters and the machine-gun section established themselves here, while each squadron had a farm to itself in the Noote Boom area, about a mile from Steentje and 2½ miles south-west of Bailleul.

These farms were rather squalid affairs. Nearly all built on the same model for miles round, though varying in size and lack of cleanliness, they generally consisted of a square enclosure, one side of which formed the living-rooms, the second stables, cow-byres, and pigsties, and the third and fourth huge barns and granaries, often very dilapidated, and built mainly of mud and straw supported by a few stout beams. The middle space was invariably taken up by a large manure heap on which pigs and poultry browsed and slumbered. Adjoining the buildings was a small enclosed pasture, surrounded by Lombardy poplars, and sometimes an orchard as well.

The problem of housing 6 officers and 150 men and horses in one of these farms, in addition to the inhabitants and their livestock, was a difficult one, and, as a matter of fact, was incapable of solution with any comfort to the men and horses. The officers themselves were far from comfortable. They generally found a tiny cottage outside the squadron farm, and with luck secured one fair-sized room, or two small ones, in which to live and sleep, while the servants slept on the kitchen floor, and the owner and his family squeezed into a spare room or attic. Beds were rare. The four officers

---

[1] Pronounced, not inappropriately, " Stench."

of " D " Squadron were lucky in finding three beds in two very small rooms, one of which served as the mess, but in the other squadrons most of the officers slept on the floor. In the squadron farms the sergeants had one room, or part of a room shared with the inhabitants, as a mess, and slept where they could ; while the men ate, lived, and slept in the hay and straw in the barns. The horses were picketed in lines in the adjoining pasture or round the sides of the farmyard. When it rained, which it did two days out of three, the men got wet and remained so till next morning. They had no change of clothes, beyond a shirt and socks, which, being carried in their haversacks, were usually wet by the time they were wanted. And even on the rare fine days the men's feet were practically always wet from going about the muddy horse lines in the one and only pair of boots which they possessed, and which in most cases they had worn continually every day for three months.

As time went on we built rough wattle shelters for the horses with the scanty materials available.

The brightest feature of these days was leave. This began on the second day after our arrival at Noote Boom, the first party of five officers going on the 24th November and arriving in England next day. Batches of four or five officers and eight men per squadron went every five days after this, for ninety-six hours each. As far as is known there is only one authentic case of anyone voluntarily refusing to take his leave : Sergeant Hepworth, of " D " Squadron, who was eventually taken prisoner in June 1917.

Just as the first three weeks of fighting was an experience unique and sharply differentiated from all the rest of the war, so also the first leave was a pleasure never to be quite so intensely enjoyed again. Later leaves, though always delightful, long awaited, and quickly passed, gradually grew longer and came at rarer intervals, but never again gave quite the thrill of the first. Moreover, in those days we went on leave in comfort, travelling to Boulogne in our own motor-cars, unharassed by officious R.T.O.s.

On the 28th November the first draft arrived from

England, consisting of 3 officers—Second-Lieutenants J. A.
Moncreiffe, J. Kingscote, and L. Winterbottom, and 40 men.
Of these officers Moncreiffe and Kingscote were both posted
to " D " Squadron, and Winterbottom to " A," but Moncreiffe was very soon afterwards put in charge of the
machine-gun section in place of Lieutenant Pearce.

On the 1st December a number of officers were promoted,
Captains V. Fleming and Hermon-Hodge to be Majors, and
Lieutenants Villiers, P. Fleming, Hutchinson, Fane, and
Gill to be Captains. Major Nicholl went to Headquarters
as second-in-command, in place of Major Churchill, and
Major Fleming succeeded to the command of " C " Squadron.

During the three weeks' fighting in November we had
grown accustomed to the use of the terms " Echelon A " and
" Echelon B " to describe the first- and second-line transport respectively. At first no one had the slightest idea
what they meant or what the difference was between the
two. But they did not take long to find out. Whereas
Echelon A, consisting solely of limbers, was liable to follow
the Regiment into action, and was used to bring rations and
ammunition up to the trenches at night, frequently a very
disagreeable business, as the Germans, knowing what was
going on, habitually shelled the roads at night, Echelon B,
consisting of the heavy G.S. wagons loaded with officers'
kits, squadron stores, and other heavy baggage, always
remained in billets miles behind the line. In the event of
an advance, Echelon B follows at a safe distance behind
the fighting troops, while in the event of a retreat it is the
first to be sent back out of the way. In a word, Echelon
A goes to the trenches, and Echelon B doesn't. An officer
wrote at the time :

" There is considerable competition among all [1] parties,
particularly ——, to be in Echelon B, in fact I have rele-
gated —— to Echelon Z. He holds the record from Wulverghem church to ' out of shell fire.' "

Several of the Guards battalions were billeted not far
—————
[1] This is rather too comprehensive.

from our area, and some of their officers used to come to lunch with ours occasionally, and we picked up many little bits of useful information about trench warfare.

There was practically no work to be done beyond the daily routine of stables and exercise. We used to take the squadron out to exercise every morning from about 9.30 to 11.30. The country was quite unsuitable for any kind of cavalry training, but a few jumps were put up, over which to school the horses.

There was a very fair variety of recreation, considering the circumstances. Two or three enterprising officers in other regiments brought back a few couples of harriers and beagles from leave in England and started hunting the hares. It was hardly an ideal country for the chase, being 90 per cent. plough, and very few jumpable obstacles except dikes and ditches. Still, it was very good fun while it lasted, but the French Government soon brought such pressure to bear against it that the British Commander-in-Chief was forced to issue an order stopping all forms of hunting and shooting. Shooting, however, was kept up under difficulties all through the war, very often at the invitation of the local farmer, but always attended by considerable risk of trouble with the authorities.

Besides hunting and shooting there was polo. The Q.O.O.H. was the first regiment to play polo in France, and though at first they had to play on very rough pastures, and generally only two a side, they got a lot of fun out of it.

The men, and some of the officers, played football.

Altogether, these quiet, rather monotonous days passed pleasantly enough. We were thankful to be left in peace for a time, and did not worry about the future, while we soon grew accustomed to our cramped billets and scarcely noticed the petty discomforts, thinking that any change would inevitably be for the worse.

The whole of our Brigade was inspected by the King on Wednesday, 2nd December. We paraded at 9.15 a.m. and then lined up in an unenclosed field facing the road. We had to stand about from 9.30 to 10 o'clock in a bitterly cold

8

wind. This sort of thing always happens on inspection days. When the King did come, he walked down the road along the whole line, accompanied by the Prince of Wales, Sir John French, General Allenby, and about 15 staff officers. The whole thing was over in five minutes.

The only amusing incident occurred in " D " Squadron. Shoeing-Smith Corporal Betteridge, a very useful member of the squadron and an excellent smith, was more accustomed to his own trade of shoeing horses than to the art of wielding a cavalry sword, whether on the battlefield or on a ceremonial parade. Indeed it is probable that he had not hitherto possessed such a weapon at all, and most certainly had never been called upon to draw it. However, he had to be on parade to meet the King, properly equipped with a sword. Some time before His Majesty was expected the Colonel gave the order to draw swords, by way of practice. Corporal Betteridge drew his gallantly with the rest, but as the flashing blades slowly and reluctantly emerged from their scabbards, the officers and sergeants of " D " Squadron were horrified to observe that the worthy corporal's sword was broken off short in the middle. The Squadron Sergeant-Major sternly adjured him to put it back, thinking that, being in the rear rank, he might not be noticed. But it was too late. The Colonel's eagle eye had at once detected him, and his voice was heard all along the line ordering Betteridge to draw his sword again. So when the King came along, one at least of the swords loyally waved in the air showed signs of fierce conflict with the enemy.

Two days later, on the 4th December, the Commander-in-Chief came to inspect us. The Regiment was drawn up dismounted in a hollow square, in a field by the road, while he made a brief informal address, complimenting and thanking us for what we had done, and encouraging us to look forward to victory. This visit and the little speech were very much appreciated by the men, who did not usually welcome inspections. But this was more of a friendly visit and the men were glad to listen to their supreme commander face to face, which they never did again after 1915.

On the night of Sunday, 13th December, and again on the morning of Friday, 18th December, the Regiment was ordered to be ready to move at short notice, but nothing happened and we continued in billets. These orders were part of the plans for attack carried out, in the first case by the II Corps, in conjunction with the French, against two wooded spurs west and south-west of Wytschaete, and in the second case by the Indian Corps in the neighbourhood of La Bassée. Neither attack was successful.

On the 18th December there was an inter-squadron jumping competition, in which " C " Squadron just beat " D " Squadron.

Christmas Day passed quietly and pleasantly. The weather, which had been perfectly awful for weeks past, cleared up for a few days and was fine and frosty. We heard strange stories of fraternizing in the front lines, of football matches between our men and the Germans, and other adventures, which we scarcely believed at first, but which turned out to be true.

A sergeant's diary records :

Dec. 25th.—Presented with Princess Mary's gift and had a good Christmas dinner.

Dec. 27th.—Left for England on seventy-two hours' leave.

Dec. 31st.—Returned to Noote Boom midnight and found some of the boys had rung the old year out, to some tune.

All this first winter people at home were very generous in sending out presents of every kind to the troops at the front—tobacco, cigarettes, chocolate, socks, mufflers, etc. ; while at Christmas quantities of plum-puddings and other luxuries arrived from friends and relations. Besides Princess Mary's gift, every man in the Regiment received a present from the people of Oxfordshire. Mrs. Dugdale started the idea, and asked for subscriptions from the county, and owing to the generous response, the fund reached nearly £400, and every man got a new set of clothing, besides a plum-pudding for Christmas. The subscribers, great and small, were so numerous that we cannot give their names here, but their generosity and thoughtfulness were very much appreciated by all ranks of the Regiment. Mrs. Bonham-Carter was especially helpful in getting subscriptions, writing many letters, and enlisting many supporters for the scheme. Thus the Adjutant's wife appropriately assisted the Colonel's wife in organizing the provision of comforts for the Regiment overseas.

By the end of the year a good many of the horses were showing signs of mud fever and cracked heels, on account of the impossibility of finding dry standing for them. Many of them hardly ever lay down, as we couldn't get enough straw.

On the first day of the New Year three cases of scarlet fever occurred in " D " Squadron, and four more on the second, followed by other cases from time to time. In consequence of this epidemic the Regiment did not move with the rest of the Brigade, but was considered fit to follow on Wednesday, 13th January, when it marched to a new billeting area round Roquetoire, 17 miles from Noote Boom and 10 miles south-west of Hazebrouck. " D " Squadron was in the hamlet of Cauchie d'Ecques, which the men called " Cosy Dick," nearly two miles from Regimental Headquarters and the other two squadrons, which were all in and about Roquetoire. Captain Gill, however, obtained permission to move the whole squadron on 21st January to La Jumelle, 3½ miles away, where there was a so-called " château " or fair-sized country villa for the officers and ample accommodation for men and horses.[1] " Splendid billets," says Sergeant Stroud's diary.

Meanwhile a party of officers returning from leave had arrived at Noote Boom at midnight on the 13th, to find the Regiment vanished and the billets deserted. Nothing disturbed, they made themselves comfortable in their old billets, fully expecting one of the Regiment's five cars would be sent to fetch them next day. However, morning came and nothing happened, so they resolved to remain

---

[1] H.M. the King stayed at this villa in October 1915.

where they were. Fortunately they had with them a stock
of pheasants and other luxuries which they had brought
out from England for the mess. They paid a visit to " E "
Battery R.H.A., which was still in the neighbourhood, but
could get no certain news of where the Regiment had gone.
The battery commander was gravely shocked by the
irregularity of their proceeding in calmly waiting for a car
to fetch them, and suggested that they should report to
the nearest R.T.O. But officers of the Q.O.O.H. were not
accustomed to travel in slow-moving supply trains and
lorries in those spacious days, and they decided to await
events a little longer. But when the second morning came,
and still no sign of a car, it was felt something must be
done. Besides, supplies were running out. At last, after
a day spent in fruitless inquiries, a car appeared at 5 o'clock
in the evening and took them off to Roquetoire.

On 20th January a case of spotted fever occurred in
" C " Squadron, and the Regiment, less " D " Squadron,
which was outside the infected area, was isolated for ten
days.

Life in these billets was very pleasant. All the horses
were under cover, men pretty well off, and beds for all the
officers and most of the sergeants. Each troop had a mess-
room of sorts and, as one of the men put it, " it's fine to
get your legs under a table again," after eating for weeks
out of a mess-tin balanced on your knees while you squatted
on damp straw.

The country round was charming, all very undulating,
with a succession of ridges and valleys very like part of the
Heythrop country, and full of variety—mostly plough, but
plenty of trees, here and there a covert or a patch of gorse.
Altogether a welcome change from our old billets at Noote
Boom.

The mornings were devoted to troop and squadron
training, especially map-reading ; the afternoons to polo,
football, riding, or going for walks, with an occasional run
in the car to St. Omer or elsewhere ; the evenings to reading,
writing, playing cards, etc. Major Fleming brought a

gramophone out from England, at that time rather a rarity, though afterwards to be found in almost every mess in the British Army. Leave, too, was still in full swing. All the officers had already been twice by the end of January, and some a third time, while all the men, except two or three per troop, had been once.

But alas for the uncertainty of fortune !—we were soon back in the Flanders mud again. At 7.30 p.m. on Saturday, 30th January, we got a sudden order to move early next day. Sunday, the 31st, was very cold and frosty, as we marched back eastwards to billets round Le Verrier, about 2 miles west of Steenwerck, and less than a mile from our old billets at Noote Boom. Here we were moderately comfortable, but the change from the pleasant uplands of Roquetoire to the dreary mud-flats of Le Verrier was depressing, while before us lay the shadow of the trenches.

It had been decided that the Cavalry Corps should relieve the French for a month in the trenches near Zillebeke, 2½ miles south-east of Ypres, each division doing ten days in turn. While waiting at Le Verrier we spent as much time as possible preparing for trench warfare, digging model trenches, practising night attacks, and learning to locate snipers. Here, too, we first practised bomb-throwing, Lieutenant Muirhead, in particular, showing a keen interest in it. These early bombs were not the elaborately perfected Mills bomb of later years, but a very crude and home-made article generally constructed out of an empty jam-tin.

Here the men were for the first time provided with waterproof capes, reaching well below the knee, and there were hopes that we should be able to keep pretty dry in any rain. But, though these capes were undoubtedly a godsend and kept the worst of the wet from soaking through the heavy greatcoats, they wore out quickly, and later issues tended to deteriorate in quality.

The Regiment was still very much under strength, having lost a large number of men by sickness, and received no reinforcements since leaving England, except the 3 officers and 40 men who arrived in November 1914. Troops numbered about 21 instead of their full strength of 33. A whole squadron numbered about 100, instead of 158, but could only put 57 rifles into the trenches, excluding officers, the other 40 men being required as horse-holders, cooks, shoeing-smiths, transport drivers, etc.[1]

On Friday, 12th February, the Regiment paraded *en route* for Ypres and the trenches.[2] The journey was made in London buses, now a regular feature of the roads behind the front. By this time, however, they had been deprived of the familiar advertisements of teas and tobaccos, restaurants and theatres, which had given them so homely and incongruous an appearance in the early days. Now they were quite business-like military vehicles, painted khaki all over. It was our first journey in them, and though we disliked our destination, we thought them preferable to horses in the circumstances. The trenches were said to be very wet and, as we were to be in them for five days at a stretch, we were laden with every conceivable form of protection against the weather, and the party at the rendezvous was a wonderful sight. Perhaps the most complete and remarkable turn-out was that of Captain Gill, which included a heavy " Macdougall " cloak, and a pair of long fishing-waders, with brogues and socks all complete.

[1] The proportion of rifles in the trenches to the whole Expeditionary Force would surprise most people if it could be worked out. Taking the figures just given, we get as many as 43% left with the horses even in so small a unit as a squadron, while, even allowing that every other regiment except the Q.O.O.H. could put 100 men per squadron in the line, we only get 8,000 rifles for the whole Cavalry Corps out of a total of, say, 22,000 all ranks, or little more than one-third of the total strength. And the proportion in the whole Expeditionary Force must have been yet lower, after setting off the Headquarters of Armies and General Headquarters, and the whole vast organization of bases and L. of C. See Mr. Churchill's speech in the House of Commons in May 1916, when he argued that there was an undue proportion of ration strength to fighting strength ; that half the total ration strength of the army was still in England ; that of the half abroad, half fought and half didn't ; that of the fighting half only three-quarters were infantry in the trenches ; and that of every six men recruited at one end, only one rifle appeared over the parapets at the other.

[2] Total fighting strength : 179 all ranks, as against 6th Dragoon Guards, 327 ; 3rd Hussars, 301.

We arrived at Ypres about midnight and went into
billets, one officer per squadron being sent on in advance
to spend the night in the trenches, learn the way about, and
guide the Regiment up next day.

At dusk on Saturday, 13th February, the Regiment
paraded in Ypres and marched through Zillebeke, where it
was met by the officers sent up overnight, past Cavan's
dugout, and up to the trenches, where it relieved the North
Somerset Yeomanry. The Regiment was in the centre
of the Brigade, with the Carabiniers on the right, and the
3rd Hussars on the left. Two squadrons held the front
line, " C " on the right and " A " on the left, with one troop
of " D " Squadron attached. Regimental Headquarters
occupied a small dugout just behind the centre of the line.
The rest of " D " Squadron was in support in good dugouts
cut in the side of a high bank 100 yards or so behind the
front line, and well supported by timber props. There was
a row of these occupied by the squadron, with the Brigadier
and staff in one at the end. The whole sector ran through
a wood much damaged by shell fire.[1]

The regimental diary states that we relieved the North
Somerset Yeomanry " in a very good trench line." So it
may have been from the military point of view. Since our
last visit to the trenches great changes and improvements
in their construction had taken place. Dugouts, traverses,
fire-steps, communication trenches, were now universal.
The trenches were more solidly made, weak points revetted
with timber, and the bottom floored with duck-boards.
But unfortunately, although every endeavour was made to
drain them, the very heavy and constant rains had partially
flooded the trenches in most parts of Flanders, and our
sector was terribly wet, the water standing 4 or 5 feet deep

---

[1] The division was organized for the trenches into two brigades : " A "
Brigade, under Brigadier-General Bingham, consisting of 4th Cavalry
Brigade and 5 squadrons of 3rd Cavalry Brigade ; " B " Brigade, under
Brigadier-General Chetwode, consisting of 5th Cavalry Brigade and 4
squadrons of 3rd Cavalry Brigade. The trench line was divided into two
sections—Right section, held by 7 squadrons in line with 2 in support ;
Left section, held by 3 squadrons in line with 1 in support.

IN THE TRENCHES, FEBRUARY 1915.

GROUP OF OFFICERS, WINTER 1914–1915.
Capt. W. S. Carless, Lt. A. J. Muirhead, Major V. Fleming, Capt. F. A. Gill, Lt. E. H.
Chinnery, Major C. R. I. Nicholl, ————.

in places, especially in the communication trenches. The men were provided with long gum-boots, which they took over with other trench stores from the outgoing garrison. But even so they got very wet. The weather was cold, with some rain.

The Regiment was marvellously lucky, being five days and nights in these trenches without a single casualty, except three or four men with trench feet, whereas another unit in the Brigade lost nearly 30 men killed, sick and wounded.

Various little exciting incidents occurred during our stay in these trenches, but nothing of any importance. We threw bombs and were trench-mortared for the first time. During the last two nights there was some expectation of a German attack and they were reported to be massing on our front. No. 2 Troop, "D" Squadron, was sent up to strengthen "C" Squadron in the front line. The French artillery were behind us and they put down a beautiful barrage on the German lines, the shells skimming just over our heads. The squadron "stood to" from 8.30 p.m. to 2 a.m., but nothing more was heard of the attack.[1]

The enemy kept very quiet all the rest of the time. One day Sergeant Elliott observed some of them walking about in front of their line, apparently collecting firewood, and promptly had a shot at them, whereupon they all ran like rabbits back to their holes.

The two troops of "D" Squadron not in the front line were employed in carrying rations up from Cavan's dugout every night—an arduous and disagreeable job. No one who has not been on a ration party at night can realize what hard labour it is, or how the men hated it, but anyone who has will not forget it. The enormous weights to be carried— heavy boxes of ammunition, biscuits, and bully beef, besides of course each man's own rifle and ammunition, and many other things such as parcels, rum jars, extra entrenching

---

[1] See, however, Sir John French's 6th Despatch, para. iii, where this attack is mentioned as "half-hearted" and "easily repulsed by rifle fire," and the enemy said to have "left several dead in front of the trenches."

tools. etc.—the darkness, and difficulty of keeping touch, the rough ground, pitted with shell holes, the extreme probability of being shelled or sniped or both,—all these combined to make the task thoroughly exhausting, only slightly relieved by much smothered cursing. In general, throughout the war, the men always preferred the front line, where the strain was frequently broken by spells of comparative peace, to the incessant and wearing fatigues of the support and reserve trenches.

The Regiment was relieved by the 20th Hussars at 9.15 p.m. on Thursday, 18th February, and marched back to their temporary billets in Ypres, where they were to be in brigade reserve for the next five days.

Ypres as yet was very little knocked about, at least in comparison with what it was later on, and several shops and restaurants were still open. We spent two days enjoying the little luxuries of billets, and all was well till about 8 a.m. on Sunday morning, 21st February.

" ' Turn out at once '—German attack on 16th Lancers. With groans and curses out we turned and marched up as far as the École de Bienfaisance—or ' Beanfeast,' as the Colonel called it. There we spent the day, while various excitements and alarms kept us wondering whether we shouldn't have to counter-attack !

" But no orders came, except that one squadron had to go up and support the 16th. Poor old Gillo [1] was condemned to lead up ' D ' Squadron to a rather unknown fate. Eventually it turned out that they simply had to hold a bit of trench next to the 16th. So the rest of us were comfortable enough except that we had certain ration- and ammunition-carrying parties to supply, and officers to lead them." [2]

The half of the Regiment thus employed on ration carrying worked till 3 a.m. on the 22nd and then returned by bus to billets near Le Verrier. The other half, consisting of " D " Squadron, two troops of " A " Squadron, and the machine-gun section, was warned to be ready to go up and

---

[1] Captain Gill.   [2] Lieutenant Fleming's diary.

support the 16th Lancers in the front line, and marched off
at 9 p.m., fully expecting to have to counter-attack immediately on arrival.

Part of the trenches held by the 16th had been blown in
by a mine early that morning, 5 officers being killed, 1 died
of wounds, and 4 wounded, besides 49 casualties among the
men. Later in the day a squadron of the 20th Hussars and
a company of French infantry made an unsuccessful counter-
attack, in which they also lost heavily, the French company
commander being killed and three out of the four 20th
Hussar officers wounded. After dark a new line was established 40 yards in rear of the part blown in, thus forming a
small re-entrant. The Germans were either in the mine or
very close to it on the other side.

The squadron and a half of Q.O.O.H. on arrival at the
trenches came under the command of Lieutenant-Colonel
P. Howell, 4th Hussars, commanding the left section. The
men were distributed in a number of little dugouts close
behind the front line, and just before dawn took over the
front line itself. The following order was issued from
Brigade Headquarters :

" S.C.28.   22.2.15.
" 1. It is possible that enemy may have evacuated the
captured trench, but bombs should be thrown into it occasionally and sniping continued.
" 2. A sharp look-out to be kept during night.
" 3. Captain Gill and Captain Egerton will, under the
direction of R.E., sap towards the enemy's trenches. These
saps to form listening or bombing posts. Later the sap
heads will be joined to form an advanced line.
" 4. Dugouts to be prepared in rear of our present line.
" 5. Orderly to be permanently on duty at all telephone
boxes.
" 6. Two troops of Oxfordshire Hussars to remain
equipped and ready to move in support.
" From Lieutenant-Colonel commanding left section.
" Time, 7.20 a.m.
                    " G. F. H. BROOKE, Staff Captain,
                        for Lieutenant-Colonel."

The trenches were fairly dry and ran through a wood some way to the left of, and on higher ground than, those we had held from the 13th to the 18th. " D " Squadron was on the extreme left of the whole British line, Sergeant List being the left-hand man of the British Army. Our men rather enjoyed the novelty of being next the French troops, with whom they fraternized vigorously and exchanged rations. The Frenchmen were much impressed by our plum and apple jam, and gave us sardines and excellent hot coffee in exchange. Our only objection to our allies was that they would persist in firing what seemed indiscriminate volleys in the direction of the enemy trenches. This went on continuously through the night and was rather disturbing without doing the slightest damage to the Germans. On inquiry it turned out that the French company commander was a Major fresh from the École de Guerre, breathing fire and slaughter against the Germans and full of the " spirit of the offensive." One rather gathered that his junior officers and men did not altogether relish his aggressive policy, and would have preferred to keep quiet in the hope the enemy would do the same.

When we arrived at the trenches we were told we should only be wanted for twenty-four hours, but needless to say the twenty-four became forty-eight before we were relieved. The two days passed very quietly, but it was an anxious time. No one quite knew what the Germans would be at, and there was always risk of another mine explosion and counter attack.

However, the time came to an end at last, and we were relieved by the 2nd Dragoons Guards (Queen's Bays) on the evening of Tuesday, 23rd February, and marched back to Ypres, where, after a good meal, we embussed for home, arriving back in our old billets at Le Verrier about 7 a.m. on the 24th. Leave was still open, and a party went off that very evening.

The Regiment had had its usual luck in the trenches, the only casualties being Private R. Dickens, machine-gun section, killed, and 2 men wounded, all on the 22nd.

GROUP OF OFFICERS IN ZILLEBEKE TRENCHES, FEBRUARY 1915.
Capt. F. A. Gill (cap only), Lt. J. Kingscote, Lt. A. W. Keith-Falconer, Capt. A. H.
Hogarth, Capt. Hon. A. G. C. Villiers (above Capt. Hogarth), S.S.-M. J. C. Warren.

GROUP OF MEN IN ZILLEBEKE TRENCHES FEBRUARY 1915

A few days later the following order was issued from Brigade Headquarters.

" The G.O.C. 4th Cavalry Brigade wishes to place on record his appreciation of the work performed by the Oxfordshire Hussars on the night of 21st–22nd February. The work was a tiring, tedious and unexciting one, and the Major-General wishes to make it known to the regiment how much their labours were appreciated. It is desired to add a special word of praise to the 80 (about) men and the machine-gun section who returned to the trenches for a further 48 hours.

(Signed) " C. E. Bingham,

Major-General."

Two drafts had come up while the Regiment was in the trenches, 5 officers and 140 men in all. Second-Lieutenants E. W. H. Allfrey and F. S. J. Silvertop were posted to " D " Squadron, H. G. Page-Turner and J. L. Shand to " C " Squadron, and R. L. Worsley to " A " Squadron.

On Friday, 26th February, the Regiment returned to the Roquetoire area, where it spent another pleasant fortnight doing troop and squadron training, and playing polo, football, etc. It was now up to rather more than full strength, numbering on 6th March 30 officers and 555 other ranks.

Nothing of much interest happened during this period. On the 2nd March, after dinner, we got an order that the Brigade was to hold itself in readiness to move at immediate notice, and next morning at 9 a.m. we got the order to move at 9.30. The reader may imagine our fury and the desperate packing that took place and the wild surmises we made as to our destination. However, after we had been on the march half an hour we were informed that the whole thing was a little joke on the part of the Brigade Office in order to see how readily we turned out. It was really an excellent thing, though we were very annoyed at the idea of leaving when we originally got the order.

About this date Regimental Headquarters first adopted the practice of laying down a daily routine for squadrons. It may be observed that the time-table, which was frequently

re-issued with alterations throughout the rest of the war,
was rarely followed in all its details by every squadron,
not for want of proper discipline, as sometimes alleged, but
rather because of various practical difficulties where
squadrons and troops were much separated. A specimen
is given below :

6.30 a.m.	Réveillé
6.45	Water.
7.0	Stables.
7.45	Feed.
8.0	Breakfast.
9.0	Parade.
12.0	Water and stables.
12.45 p.m.	Feed.
1.0	Dinner.
2.15	Parade.
5.0	Water and feed. Stables.
6.0	Tea.

Of course this routine varied a certain amount. Once or
twice a week the morning was taken up with longer mounted
" schemes," necessitating stables in the afternoon instead
of parade. The afternoon parade was almost invariably
dismounted. Occasionally we did night operations.

Three more officers joined the Regiment at Roquetoire—
Second-Lieutenant F. Weatherby to " A " squadron (after-
wards transferred to " C "), Second-Lieutenant G. V.
Wellesley to " D " Squadron, and Captain H. C. Jagger,
A.V.C., to be Veterinary Officer in place of Captain W. S.
Carless, invalided to England.

On the 4th March General Allenby, G.O.C. Cavalry Corps,
accompanied by about half a dozen Press representatives,
inspected " D " Squadron.

At 3.30 p.m. on the 8th March the Regiment was ordered
to move billets next morning. It was the eve of the battle
of Neuve Chapelle. At 9.30 a.m. on the 9th the Brigade
marched to billets at Bleu, 4 miles south-west of Bailleul,
arriving about midday. Weather cold and dry. Each
squadron occupied three or four small farms within a radius
of about a mile.

The events of the next few days may be described in the words of the regimental diary.

10th March, 7 a.m.—Saddled up ready to move at short notice till 4 p.m. when the Brigade was ordered to concentrate north of Neuf Berquin, and was ordered to return to billets immediately on arrival at point of concentration.

11th March, 7 a.m.—Concentrated at same spot and remained there off-saddled till 4 p.m., when we returned to billets at Bleu in a restricted area.

12th March.—Ready to turn out at one hour's notice. 4 p.m. ordered to concentrate and reached point of concentration at 6 p.m., where we remained till 8.30 p.m., when we returned to billets.

13th March.—Stood to ready to turn out at short notice from 7 to 10 a.m. 11.30 a.m., Brigade ordered to move billets. Regiment returned to area occupied 9th–11th March.

14th.—Rested in billets.

15th.—The Brigade moved to billets in the neighbourhood of Pradelles.

There is little to add to this account. We were bored and uncomfortable, and never got anywhere near the battle. " C " Squadron occupied a farm which they called the " Mad Woman Billet," the owner's wife, who lived in the house, being a certified lunatic. " D " Squadron was more fortunate. When the billeting area was reduced on the 11th, owing to the arrival of three new infantry divisions, regiments were squeezed into squadron, and squadrons into troop, areas. Regimental Headquarters took " D " Squadron's best farm and left the latter a miserable hovel formerly occupied by one troop only. The squadron promptly sent two officers to inspect some apparently unoccupied cottages in the immediate neighbourhood, and presently lit on a splendid billet, 300 yards outside the area. Here they were much better off than Headquarters—always a source of satisfaction.

On the 15th March, as we have seen from the diary, the Brigade moved into billets round Pradelles, a little village 3 miles east of Hazebrouck, on the main road to Bailleul.

The billets were fairly good ; less comfortable than at Roquetoire, but a great deal better than Noote Boom. We were back once more in the dreary Flanders country, but otherwise had not much to complain of.

The rest of the Brigade moved later to billets at Bleu, but owing to an epidemic of measles in " C " and " D " Squadrons the Regiment was more or less in quarantine, and stayed where it was.

It was a good opportunity for cavalry training, and we did numerous " schemes," mounted and dismounted. We amused ourselves by playing polo a bit, and also by hockey, which was first introduced into the Regiment about this time.

Major Fleming got up a sort of *concours hippique*— against a squadron of the 12th Lancers, and " C " Squadron distinguished itself by beating the Regulars. Cavalry patrols, map-reading, wood-fighting, jumping, sword-thrusting, and bayonet exercise filled up our days. Mention must be made of the famous night attack which " C " Squadron did for the benefit of General Bingham and various other Generals. It was a huge success, chiefly owing to the trouble and thoroughness with which Major Fleming had arranged everything, and partly also to Lieutenant Muirhead's trench mortar, or rather " bomb gun," as it was called in those days.

The Brigadier was especially keen on wood-fighting, and each squadron in turn was called on to carry out a practice attack in the neighbouring Forêt de Nieppe. When " C " Squadron's turn came, Major Fleming had all the men drawn up in front of General Bingham and proceeded to give a most Napoleonic lecture on wood-fighting, which greatly impressed the Brigadier ; no one could carry off these things more brilliantly than the member for South Oxfordshire.

" D " Squadron was less fortunate, Private Long being discovered by the Brigadier reading a newspaper under a tree in the midst of the operations.

The following tale is perhaps worth telling. " D "

Squadron was in the habit of parading at 9.30, although the orthodox hour was 9 o'clock. One morning, about 8.45, a message suddenly arrived from Headquarters saying that the Brigadier and Colonel wished to see the squadron at work and directing Captain Gill to meet them with the squadron at such and such a point at 9 o'clock. It was an awkward moment, but Gill was equal to the emergency. He immediately sent word to the Colonel that a scheme had already been prepared for the squadron to carry out an attack in force on a position near the rendezvous indicated in the Colonel's message, timed to culminate about 10 a.m. Unfortunately the Colonel was suspicious and a few minutes later suddenly appeared in the officers' mess. Some were shaving, others were sitting about and smoking, another was still in bed. Only one was fully dressed for parade, and even he was reading the papers. The Colonel was speechless with rage, the squadron leader made what answer he could, while the subalterns preserved a discreet silence. The story of the encounter soon ran round the Regiment, and that afternoon at tea-time officers from the other two squadrons trooped in to hear the full story. The tea-party was at its height, shouts of laughter were echoing through the house, when suddenly in marched the Colonel. Hush fell on the assembly, but the Colonel was almost equally taken aback. He had come prepared to give the squadron a proper " telling off," but the presence of the numerous guests was an unexpected obstacle. Not, however, to Captain Gill, who, fortified by general support, won the day with the remark : " My dear Arthur, what on earth is the good of having parade at 9 when only one person wants it then and 500 want it at 9.30 ! "

We heard a good deal of the 15-inch howitzers which were now being used on our front. It was said that they were only allowed to fire six shells per day, that each shot cost £250, that the explosion was so terrific that several of our men were permanently deafened when one burst in the German trenches 300 yards away, and 126 Germans went mad and had to be taken to a lunatic asylum !

9

Our transport was now reduced to one wagon per squadron, and kits cut down accordingly.

A more serious loss was that of all our motor-cars, the last of which was taken on a final joy-ride to Dunkirk, and stored there.

On the 2nd April Major F. G. Proudfoot, R.A.M.C., joined the Regiment as Medical Officer, Captain Hogarth having gone home sick on the 22nd February.

Ordinary leave had been stopped since the 1st March, and only special leave in cases of real urgency was now granted.

A serious epidemic of measles broke out at Pradelles and depleted our strength considerably. It had, however, one minor compensation, in enabling us to remain in our billets when the rest of the Brigade was turned out and put in a restricted area in order to make room for a division of infantry.

CHAPTER VI

THE SECOND BATTLE OF YPRES

(23rd April—31st May 1915)

ON the morning of Friday, 23rd April, the three squadrons were out training as usual in different parts of the area. It was a fine spring day, and after nearly six weeks in the back area the realities of war seemed a long way off. Suddenly and without warning the Regiment was ordered to turn out as soon as possible. The order was received at Regimental Headquarters at 9.45 a.m., but there was some difficulty in collecting squadrons. Motor-cyclists were despatched to search for them, and by 11 a.m. they were all back in billets, hastily packing up and making other preparations for a move.

Meanwhile, orders were received at 11.15 a.m. for the Regiment to concentrate at Bleu, 4 miles distant, at noon, to move north, but these were countermanded at 11.45 a.m. by an order to join the Brigade at Strazeele as it passed on its way north. At 12.30 p.m. squadrons turned out and the Regiment formed up with its head at Strazeele. Here it halted in the road till 3.15 p.m., while as many as could took advantage of the opportunity to get some coffee and bread and butter in the village. No one, except perhaps Regimental Headquarters, knew what had happened to cause this sudden turn-out, and all sorts of rumours were flying about, some saying that the Canadians had broken through, others that the Germans had done so. We had not yet heard of the gas. We learnt later that the French lines about Langemarck had been heavily attacked—the Germans using asphyxiating gases—and had given way, thus leaving a gap north of Ypres which had to be hastily filled, chiefly by the Canadians. It was this first use of gas which had caused all the trouble.

After a long delay we moved off at 3.15 p.m. and marched

about 3 miles in three hours. All the roads were covered with a continuous stream of troops moving up. We again halted in the neighbourhood of the Mont des Cats and waited in the road till 9 o'clock, when we were sent back 4 or 5 miles to billets at Thieushouk. (" D " Squadron billeted at Caestre.) It was midnight before all the horses were watered and fed.

At 4.40 a.m. next morning, the 24th April, we received orders to turn out at once and concentrate at the Mont des Cats. A heavy attack was in progress. The Germans had crossed the canal and driven back the Canadian left flank. We then marched about 15 miles at a fast trot to Vlamertinghe, which we reached about 9 o'clock. Here we off-saddled and spent the day in a large swampy field about 3½ miles behind the front, where we remained till the following morning. A fairly heavy bombardment was kept up most of the day, but no shells came near us. Weather fine and dry with a cold wind ; rain in the evening.

Late in the afternoon Lieutenant Wellesley, who had been on a machine-gun course at Wisques, arrived in a *civilian taxicab*, which he had hired in the market-place at St. Omer and loaded with two cases of champagne and a large hamper of fresh asparagus. He had wandered far and wide in search of the Regiment. At one point, close to Laventie, a few shells fell some 300 yards in front of the taxi, whereupon the driver stopped his engine and got underneath the car. After considerable persuasion he was induced to come out, but flatly refused to go any farther down that road.

After finally delivering his fare at Vlamertinghe, the taximan departed thankfully to his home beyond St. Omer. He was an elderly man, and probably never got so near the front again.

At 4.30 a.m. next day we were woken up by a heavy bombardment at the front, and at 5 a.m. we saddled up ready to move.[1]

---

[1] The Regiment seems to have been very much below strength at this time, for an officer's letter says : " I have only got one sergeant and twelve men in my troop, i.e. nine rifles dismounted."

We remained standing to till 12.15 p.m., when we were
sent up to dig trenches near Boesinghe, a few miles north of
Ypres and just west of the canal where the gas attack had
first been launched on the evening of the 22nd. We arrived
there at 2 p.m. and dug till dark. There were a lot of
Zouaves in a farmhouse near by, and those who had the
gift of making themselves " aimable " to our allies were
entertained with excellent coffee and red wine.

About 4 p.m. two officers and eight men were sent back
to find billets for the Regiment. After riding 10 miles they
found four farms and made all arrangements, only to get
orders at 9.30 p.m. to return to the Regiment at Vlamertinghe.

That was a bad night for everybody. The Regiment had
returned to its horses about 8.30 p.m., thinking that it was
going back to billets. But no such luck. They marched
to a field about a mile west of Vlamertinghe, where horses
were picketed and left in charge of number three's. The
rest of the Regiment was then turned out to draw rations.
Owing to confusion in the darkness, masses of men, lorries,
and transport everywhere, and other causes, we didn't get
rations drawn till past 3 a.m. We were all cold, tired, and
hungry, having had nothing but bits of biscuit and chocolate
since midday, and no sleep. Towards 4 a.m. we marched
back to Vlamertinghe and went into billets. Here we had
a proper meal and a good sleep till 3.45 p.m., when we were
warned we might be required for the trenches ; but it was
found there was not sufficient room for the whole division,
and our brigade was left in billets for the night, ready
to move at half-an-hour's notice.

An order was issued that not more than four officers per
squadron were to go to the trenches, as the proportion of
officers to men was so much higher in the cavalry than in
the infantry. As we have seen, a squadron at full strength
could bring only 100 rifles into the firing line, while more
often than not it could not muster more than about 50, i.e.
the equivalent of one subaltern's command in the infantry.
To take six officers into action with so small a force, as had
hitherto been the practice, was clearly ridiculous.

We remained quietly in billets till 4.30 p.m. on Tuesday, 27th April. Officers and men were having tea when two or three small shells whistled over " A " Squadron billets and burst about 500 yards away. These were evidently range-finders, for half an hour later much bigger shells were coming over. Everybody ran to move the horses and wagons away. The A.D.M.S. Canadian Division called for volunteers to carry the wounded out of Vlamertinghe church, which was being used as a hospital, to a place of safety, and the whole Regiment turned out and helped to carry close on 200 men nearly a mile to ambulances. Sergeant C. Hyde, of No. 2 Troop, " D " Squadron, was killed, and three men in the same troop wounded, by a shell falling almost on top of them while carrying wounded. Two officers and the Squadron Sergeant-Major buried Hyde in the military cemetery behind the church, while a Canadian Chaplain read the burial service amidst the exploding shells.

Major Proudfoot, the Medical Officer, was also wounded in the leg by this same shell, and invalided to England.

Although Vlamertinghe was so close to the front line, the town had never been shelled before, and was consequently full of civilian inhabitants, whose flight with bag and baggage when the shelling began was a pitiful sight.

Meanwhile the Brigade had been ordered to leave the town and return to their led horses two miles away. The Q.O.O.H., having remained behind to carry the wounded, were the last to arrive at the horse lines, for which they were severely censured by the Brigadier. A few days later they received a special message of thanks from the Canadian Division.

The Regiment had got back to the horse lines about 8 p.m., and two hours later the whole Brigade was ordered to proceed to Potijze and take over a line of trenches there. The Regiment went up under the second-in-command, Major Nicholl, and four officers per squadron, the remainder being left with the horses.

We had to march 8 miles, carrying the usual mass of heavy equipment. The Scots Greys had had 21 casualties on the road the night before, so we expected to get a few shells, which we did, but luckily no one was hit.

We reached the trenches at 3 a.m. on Wednesday, 28th April. They formed the third, or perhaps fourth, line of reserve, known as the G.H.Q. Line, north-east of Ypres between Potijze and Wieltje, so we were only troubled by shells, not by bullets. Seven men were wounded by a shell which burst in one of our trenches.

These were the most extraordinary trenches we had ever been in, and ran through a sort of rest-camp occupied by a battalion of infantry. They were Territorials and had only left England on the 20th April, came into action on the 24th, and had already made two attacks in the open by the 28th. They had been told to dig themselves in and rest here, but they had merely dug open pits with no protection against shrapnel. Soon after daybreak their cooks began lighting fires and the smoke rose in clouds from every corner. Officers and men bustled about above ground all day, without the slightest regard for enemy observation, and caused us a good deal of anxiety. Altogether it was an extraordinary scene, more like a holiday camp than a reserve line. There was terrific excitement in the afternoon when a German aeroplane was brought down by rifle fire in front of the 3rd Hussars. Both aviators were wounded and captured. The infantry opened a violent fusillade, and made a wild rush for the machine when it fell. S.S.M. Warren shot two pigs with his revolver in the grounds of Potijze Château and had them cooked and served as delicacies to his squadron. The change from the eternal bully stew was much appreciated, even by the officers, and nobody stopped to consider what pigs are likely to have eaten on a battlefield.

We remained in the same line till the evening of Thursday, 29th April, when we moved into trenches previously occupied by the Carabiniers. These were a few hundred yards from " Hampstead Heath," as someone had christened our first position, and faced due east. Friday and Saturday were quiet days except for stray doses of shrapnel. We were in the third line of trenches, surrounded on all sides

except for a gap in our rear, so that we could be shelled
either from in front or from either flank. We were, however,
nearer the left or north side of the salient, and most of the
shelling came from that direction. " At night here one
can see the flares from the front trenches literally on all
sides of us, except for the narrow bottleneck to the west."
(Officer's letter.)

Lieutenant Kingscote had a narrow escape on the 30th
April, being hit in the back and knocked over by the cap
of a shrapnel shell. He was sent to hospital and thence to
England and never returned to France again.

Lieutenant Wellesley was hit on the head by a piece of
shrapnel on the 1st May, but did not go to hospital. One
man was also hit on the head by shrapnel from our own
anti-aircraft guns. Otherwise nothing of moment happened
until Sunday evening, 2nd May—except the complete
destruction by shell fire of Major Fleming's sheepskin coat.

Just before 5 p.m. on the 2nd heavy rifle and machine-
gun fire suddenly began on our left, and at the same time a
thick greenish haze was seen coming over the ridge towards
our trenches. This was instantly recognized as the new
German gas, and respirators, which had only been issued that
afternoon, were immediately put on. These respirators
were not, of course, the elaborate gas-masks of later days,
but thick pads of cotton-wool soaked in some mixture
which made the gas more or less harmless. They were fitted
to cover the mouth and nose and fastened at the back of the
head. Some of the infantry from the second-line trenches
came back in a dazed condition. Meanwhile the firing
grew more and more violent, and presently, about 5.15 p.m.,
our line of trenches and all the ground behind the front
line began to be literally plastered with heavy shells. They
burst all round, some within 4 or 5 yards of us, and splinters
of metal and showers of earth flew in all directions. Luckily
none fell actually within our trenches, and the men were all
sheltered to some extent by the earth-works or dugouts
which they had made in the past day or two. At about
5.30 p.m. we were ordered to " stand-to," ready for action

at a moment's notice, it having been reported that the front
line had been broken. This report turned out to be incorrect, and towards 7 p.m. the violence of the bombardment began to abate gradually, and by 7.30 p.m. everything
was comparatively calm again, with not more than the
ordinary intermittent sound of guns and rifles occasionally
firing.

During the whole period of our stay in these trenches
reconnaissances of our front line were carried out daily by
officers of the Regiment.

At 1 a.m. on Monday, 3rd May, the Regiment was relieved
with the rest of the Brigade and marched by a very cir-
cuitous route—to avoid shelling—across fields and by-paths,
back to the horses. The distance as the crow flies cannot
have been more than seven miles, but as we marched it
must have been well over twelve, for we were going the
whole time from 1 a.m. to 6.45 a.m. with only two short
halts of five minutes each. This was a stiff walk for cavalry
untrained for long marches, carrying an enormous weight
of stuff, and the men were very nearly exhausted when they
reached the horses.

The Brigade was led by the Brigade-Major, the Brigadier
returning on a lorry, sent to fetch picks and shovels, but
used by the Regiment to carry all the men's blankets as
well. The loading of these greatly delayed the departure
of the lorry, and as the road was being steadily shelled,
the Brigadier grew more and more anxious to be off. Great
was his indignation when he discovered the cause of the
delay, and next morning official displeasure was made
known in the usual manner. Little it mattered to tired
men, who counted carriage of blankets cheap at the price.

Immediately on arrival at the horse lines at Ouderdom
the Brigade had to ride on another four hours to billets at
Houtkerque, where it received orders that it would have to
move to another area later in the day. The Regiment was
ordered to vacate billets not later than 5 p.m., and marched
by Ledringhem to Wormhoudt, on the Cassel–Dunkirk
main road, where it arrived about 7.45 p.m.

Here we were 18 miles west of Ypres and in very fair billets. We enjoyed five days' rest in fine spring weather, and then marched about 18 miles, passing through Cassel, to billets near Doulieu, getting in about 7 p.m. on the 8th May. Here we stood-to, ready to saddle up and move at short notice, till the 10th, when the order to be ready at short notice was cancelled. The idea was that the 2nd Cavalry Division should co-operate if the attacks at Festubert were successful, but they were not.

Lieutenant Pepper and Keith-Falconer and two men went to hospital with measles on the 11th.

The billets here were very cramped. Most of the officers squeezed into a few tiny cottages, but the men bivouacked in the open. Fortunately the weather was fine, though cold, but Thursday, the 13th, was a day of pouring rain, and the Regiment was ordered to send for tents from railhead.

But at 10.30 p.m. that evening orders were received to be ready to move by bus at short notice, and at 11.30 p.m. further orders came to be at point of concentration for embussing at 1 a.m. on the 14th. The Germans had made a gas attack on the line held by the 1st and 3rd Cavalry Divisions, with a fair measure of success. The 1st Cavalry Division suffered heavy losses, but managed to hold their portion of the line. The 3rd Cavalry Division was driven back, but made a brilliant counter-attack, which restored the line almost as it was before. The Essex Yeomanry particularly distinguished themselves in this counter-attack.

The buses arrived at 2.15 a.m. on Friday, the 14th, and took the Brigade to Vlamertinghe, arriving there about 8 a.m. A cold, nasty wet morning. They spent the day in huts, while the Colonel went up with other officers of the Brigade to see the trenches to be taken over at night.

At 7.5 p.m. the Brigade marched through Ypres to Potijze and took over trenches from part of the 1st Cavalry Division. The Regiment relieved the Bays, putting two squadrons and the machine-gun section in the front line, and one squadron in support. The relief was completed

CAPTAIN GUY BONHAM-CARTER, 19TH HUSSARS, ADJUTANT, QUEEN'S OWN OXFORDSHIRE HUSSARS.

(Taken at Steentje, near Bailleul, December 1914.)

about 10 p.m. and the night spent repairing and improving the trenches, which had been much damaged by shell fire.

That night the Regiment suffered a great loss. As Captain Bonham-Carter, the Adjutant, was returning from the front line to the support trenches about 3 a.m. he was shot in the head by a sniper and died almost immediately. He was buried near Sergeant Hyde in the military cemetery at Vlamertinghe.

It would be difficult to exaggerate the value of Guy Bonham-Carter's services to the Regiment, or the gap left by his death. The Adjutancy of a yeomanry regiment is a pleasant and desirable billet for the Regular officer in peace time, but in war it becomes a position highly onerous and responsible. During all these early months of the war, especially in the difficult days of mobilization and first landing in France, and still more when first in action near Cassel and afterwards in the heavy fighting round Messines, Guy Bonham-Carter had been the Colonel's right-hand man, and the friend and adviser of the whole Regiment. Many in the Regiment did not always take too kindly to Regular Army ways and were inclined to be critical of the professional soldier's methods and ideas, but none ever doubted or criticized our Adjutant, whom all recognized as the best of friends. His military ability, his natural bravery, his cheery laugh, his unfailing kindness to all—these were but a few of the many gifts which won our admiration, our friendship, and our remembrance.

The remainder of the Regiment's stay in these trenches was comparatively uneventful and may be recorded in the following extract from the regimental diary :

15th.—Fairly quiet day except for one hour's shelling during the morning and a little in the evening.

16th.—Very quiet all day. Heavy rifle fire to our right at some distance about 8.15 p.m.

9 p.m.—We had a short spell of shrapnel fire, about ten minutes ; one man slightly wounded.

17th.—Quiet with the exception of a little artillery fire, mainly our guns ; no shell fire near our trenches.

18th.—A foggy wet day ; no shelling to speak of on either side ; trenches falling in a great deal owing to wet and much time put in repairing the parapets.

19th.—Still raining and the trenches in an awful state. Considerably more sniping and fixed-rifle firing after dark, which interfered to some extent with work on the trenches, mainly in support line.

20th.—Bright morning, quiet day, less sniping than the previous day.

21st.—Quiet day, fine and bright, and trenches much improved. Relieved by Royal Irish Fusiliers at 10.30 p.m. and marched back to huts near Vlamertinghe.

A curious incident occurred in these trenches. A man was seen tied up to something just in front of the German trenches and directly opposite our line. Once or twice he raised his arm, as if making a signal, but we never knew whether he was an Englishman or a German put there for punishment ; the distance was too great to be sure, and it was impossible to get to him.

The Regiment rested in the huts till 4.25 a.m. on Monday, the 24th, when it was turned out again. There had been another gas attack all along the eastern part of the Ypres salient and our line had been broken north of the Menin road. A strong north-east wind made the gas fumes felt as far back as Vlamertinghe. The Regiment remained in reserve all day, and at 7.45 p.m. marched up to relieve troops of the 1st Cavalry Division. At 2 a.m. on the 25th they took over a line without trenches at the north-east corner of Zouave Wood.

The line held by the 2nd Cavalry Division ran from a point about three-quarters of a mile S.S.E. of Hooge in a wide bulge eastwards through woods to Hooge Château. From there a gap of a thousand yards existed to the line which the counter-attacking troops had succeeded in establishing east of Witte Poort Farm. The Oxfordshire Hussars held Zouave Wood and had the task of forming two *points d'appui*, or strong-points, facing the gap, one for Major Scott's squadron of 4th Hussars at the T-roads west of Hooge, the other in Zouave Wood itself. They

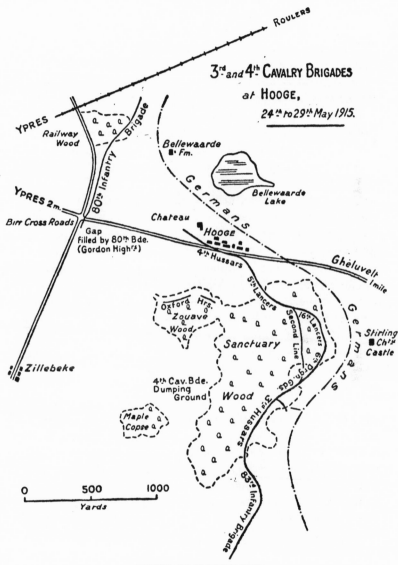

BATTLE OF BELLEWAARDE.

" thoroughly entrenched Zouave Wood, thereby earning praise from General Vaughan." [1]

The 25th passed quietly. After dark a trench was dug connecting the left of the Regiment with the infantry north of the Menin road, and a new strong-point was formed and garrisoned by Captain Gill's squadron at a farm immediately south-west of Zouave Wood and roughly halfway between Hooge and Zillebeke ; it was given the name of Yeomanry Post. At 10.30 p.m. the Regiment, less "D" Squadron, was relieved by the 5th Yorkshires, and went into support close by. Here they remained four days, all quiet, except for sniping. Sergeant Roberts, "C" Squadron, was killed on the 27th.

"D" Squadron was heavily shelled at Yeomanry Post, but held on until ordered to move into trenches near by. On the 27th a troop of R.E. was sent to help them put the post in a state of defence, and the machine-gun section, which had been sent to support the 4th Hussars in Hooge on the 27th, was moved to Yeomanry Post at night on the 28th. On the 29th S.S.M. Warren was wounded in the knee.

At 12.40 a.m. on Sunday, 30th May, the Regiment was relieved by the North Somerset Yeomanry and marched back to Vlamertinghe, where soup was served out, after which the Regiment left in busses for Doulieu at 5 a.m. Here they found the horses, who had not moved since the Regiment went to Ypres on the 13th, and at 8.30 a.m. on the 31st marched to a new billeting area between Wallon Cappel and Bois des Huit Rues, arriving about noon. One officer, Lieutenant Allfrey, slept right round the clock at Doulieu, going to bed immediately on arrival and never stirring till he woke up next morning to find the Regiment moving.

On the 31st May Brigadier-General T. T. Pitman, 11th Hussars, assumed command of the Brigade, in place of General Bingham, who left to take command of the 1st Cavalry Division.

Leave reopened for four officers and sixteen other ranks every four days, for periods of seventy-two hours in England.

[1] 4th Cavalry Brigade Diary.

YPRES, THE CLOTH HALL, 1915

"D" SQUADRON LIMBER.

Captain Gill went to England with measles and sciatica, and the latter became so severe that he was never able to return to France. During the seven months he had commanded " D " Squadron he had been with them every time they went to the trenches, a record not achieved by any other officer.[1] He was succeeded in the command by Captain Villiers.

The casualties during the period from 31st October, 1914, to 31st May, 1915, were : 2 officers and 14 other ranks killed or died of wounds ; 4 other ranks died of disease or accidentally killed ; 3 officers and 42 other ranks wounded ; total casualties to 31st May, 1915: 65.

[1] Captain Fane also had never missed a turn with his squadron, but he was not present when " D " Squadron and half " A " Squadron were sent to support the 16th Lancers at Zillebeke in February 1915.

CHAPTER VII

Loos—Vermelles—The Somme

(1st June 1915—11th November 1916)

The first few days at Wallon Cappel were spent polishing up kit and getting things straight again after three weeks' absence from the horses, after which the Regiment settled down to cavalry training. The billets were good and the weather fine.

Captain G. T. Hutchinson was appointed Adjutant in place of Captain Bonham-Carter, and on the 30th June Major Nicholl went to England to take command of the 2nd line, his place as second-in-command being filled by Major Scott. Major Hermon-Hodge then became O.C. " A " Squadron.

On 1st July seven officers and 200 other ranks were sent to La Clytte to dig trenches and defence works in Kemmel and its neighbourhood, and approximately this number, relieved at intervals, continued work throughout the whole of July and August. Sergeant Elliott (" D " Squadron) and 3 other ranks were wounded by shell fire when returning from work one evening, otherwise there were no casualties.

On 13th July the Regiment moved to a new billeting area round Buysscheure, 4½ miles north-east of St. Omer. Here they were very comfortable, and the country, though flat and somewhat featureless, was pleasant enough in the fine summer weather. A certain amount of training and musketry instruction was kept up, but work, especially mounted training, was naturally restricted by the absence of the digging party, which left the remainder of the men with at least three horses each to look after.

The strength of the Regiment on 28th August was 26 officers, 541 other ranks, and 611 horses. One officer away sick, 2 other ranks and 1 horse below establishment.

IN CAMP BEHIND THE LINES.
(Wallon-Cappel, June 1915.)

OFFICERS OFF DUTY (WALLON-CAPPEL, 1915).
Major R. E. U. Hermon-Hodge, Capt. Hon. A. G. C. Villiers Capt. G. T. Hutchinson

In July Major-General Sir Philip Chetwode was appointed to the command of the 2nd Cavalry Division in place of General Kavanagh, who had himself succeeded General Hubert Gough in April and who now followed his example in taking command of an infantry division. Lieutenant-General Byng had succeeded General Allenby in command of the Cavalry Corps in April.

On 1st September the digging party returned, and regular mounted training was resumed, with frequent brigade and regimental field days, besides the ordinary squadron "schemes." Leave was again stopped about this time, no one knew why, but rumours of an impending attack were abroad.

The twelve officers remaining of those who had sailed with the regiment in 1914 celebrated the anniversary by a dinner at Buysscheure on 19th September, the names of those present being : Lieutenant-Colonel Dugdale ; Majors Scott, Hermon-Hodge ; Captains Villiers, P. Fleming, Fane ; Lieutenants Palmer, Pearce, Keith-Falconer, Muirhead, Chinnery ; Surgeon-Captain Hogarth. Major V. Fleming and Captain Hutchinson were away on special leave.

This summer of 1915, though uneventful, marked another stage in the history of the Regiment, because it afforded the first real opportunity to complete the lessons of early training —interrupted by embarkation—and to reorganize as a cavalry regiment. At Dunkirk the Regiment had been thrown very much on its own resources, and its subsequent experience in the early autumn, though eminently educational, contained nothing of the routine of a soldier's life. Officers and men had continually to think and act for themselves, doing the best they could by the light of nature without time to consider what Cavalry Training or other manuals might prescribe for the changing situations with which they were confronted. The ensuing winter was, in effect, a struggle to preserve the health of men and horses, and to make the best of new and unfavourable conditions of life. The other units which composed the 4th Cavalry

10

Brigade were in similar circumstances, and it was impossible
to reap the full advantage of being brigaded with two
Regular cavalry regiments and " J " Battery, R.H.A.   By
the end of the winter the Regiment had learnt to look after
itself—in some respects the yeomen were perhaps better
qualified than the Regular soldiers to adapt themselves to
novel conditions in a foreign country.   It remained for
the Yeomanry to take full advantage of a summer behind
the lines to become a cavalry regiment in fact as well as
in name.   It may be noted that about this time the name
of Oxford Hussars became the official designation of the
Regiment, not " with intention," but as a more convenient
title than the Queen's Own Oxfordshire Hussars (Yeomanry).

The standard of smartness was brought home to the
yeomen by two visitors from the Higher Command.   The
first was none other than Sir John French himself, Commander-in-Chief of the British Armies in France, who
addressed the 4th Cavalry Brigade, explaining the difficulties of the situation in the Second Battle of Ypres with
which they had been confronted, and complimenting them
for their part in it.   For this purpose it was necessary for
the Regiment (dismounted) to form part of a hollow square,
within which the Commander-in-Chief stood on a G.S.
wagon, and to present arms—both exercises constituting
a somewhat high trial for 500 men, not one of whom had
ever drilled on a barrack square.   The other visitor was
General Kavanagh, G.O.C. 2nd Cavalry Division, who came
to inspect the Regiment, and saw each squadron separately
formed up in its billets.   The yeoman's recollection of
pre-war inspections was that they were at best a tedious
business, turning largely on the correct rolling of the greatcoat, and other points which to the civilian mind counted
little for fighting efficiency.   He dismissed the whole affair
contemptuously as " spit and polish."   It came therefore
as a surprising experience to be convicted of shortcomings
which certainly did impair fighting efficiency—and to see
one man detected by the G.O.C. with a blunt bayonet,
another with a nose-bag which would not hold the feed, and

HALLEBAST FARM, NEAR LA CLYTTE, AT 10 A.M.

THE SAME AT 11 A.M. ON THE SAME DAY.

a third with a spare horseshoe which could not be fitted to
his horse. All this gave food for reflection, and, as one of the
officers remarked, " The Divisional Commander said nothing
stupid all day "—a handsome tribute to the trained soldier
by the civilian, which perhaps marked an unconscious
recasting of pre-war ideas.

The Regiment gained a great deal in every way by the
appointment of Brigadier-General T. T. Pitman to command
the 4th Cavalry Brigade. From their new Brigadier, from
both Brigade Majors (first Major Beddington, and afterwards Major Chance), and from the whole of the Brigade
staff the Regiment obtained unfailing kindness, advice, or
instruction. The Brigadier himself appeared to have a
special understanding of the strong and weak points of the
yeomen, and a happy faculty for making the best of them.
Perhaps any comment on superior officers is improper, but
it may be permitted to say that General Pitman was always
extremely popular in the Regiment.

Though training was handicapped by working parties,
the efforts of squadron leaders accomplished a good deal.
During the periods of work with the digging parties, officers
and men gained fresh experience in the siting and construction of defensive works of a more permanent character
than those which they had previously occupied ; and though
the work was done under the direction of the Corps, the officer
in charge had the advantage of constant and often contradictory criticism from various representatives of the Higher
Command.

In billets the opportunity was taken to improve the
general standard of musketry. A short range was improvised, and by taking small parties at a time the squadron
leaders were able to put their recruits through a systematic
course. Similar training was carried out with bombs and
the " bomb-gun "—not yet dignified by the name of " trench
mortar." A medical officer also visited the Regiment and
gave a demonstration of the protection against gas by smoke
helmets. Men thus protected walked through a trench
filled with gas fumes, and the spectators were impressed—

and relieved—to observe that neither the exponents nor they themselves in the immediate vicinity suffered any ill effects.

For the officers there were various brigade schemes, mainly directed to train squadron and troop leaders for the possibilities of open warfare. In particular the Regiment learnt how to occupy a village and to place the necessary pickets and outpost lines—in the light of experience gained by the cavalry during the retreat from Mons. These lessons were received by the yeomen with interest, but without enthusiasm. To them the prospect of open warfare seemed infinitely more remote now than it did in October 1914, and every visit to the trenches confirmed this impression. It is true that a mysterious operation described as "going through the gap" was sometimes mentioned, generally in a spirit of rather incredulous levity ; and it was understood that cavalry units had actually followed up the advance at Neuve Chapelle, until their presence became an embarrassment to the infantry engaged, and they were withdrawn. But in the Regiment the possibility of advancing through a so-called gap in the German lines, and exploiting the victory, was not regarded as imminent.

One point about active-service conditions which sometimes escapes notice is the importance, perhaps even the necessity, of providing some form of relaxation—mental and physical—for the troops engaged. The tastes of the Regiment were primarily athletic. At Wallon Cappel the Brigadier offered a prize for a long-distance team race of eight representatives from each of the nine squadrons and the battery under his command. In " D " Squadron Major Villiers had once represented Oxford University in the two miles, and knew something of training. In " C " Squadron Major V. Fleming was always an effective and assiduous runner. On the most unlikely occasions in France he was to be found running to keep himself fit—and inducing rather hesitating brother-officers to do the same. At Pradelles he organized a mile handicap for his squadron, and won it himself from scratch. The team race at Wallon

PROGRAMME OF "D" SQUADRON HORSE SHOW.

Cappel was won by "D" Squadron, with "C" Squadron second—a minor triumph for the Territorials. At Buysscheure reasonably good grounds were secured for football and hockey, and polo was resumed—indeed, the Oxfordshire Yeomanry Polo Ground became almost a fashionable rendezvous in July and August. In September "D" Squadron held a successful horse show, followed a few days later by an officers' jumping competition, in which the squadron was just beaten by a squadron of the 9th Lancers. These distractions, alternated with training and digging parties, kept officers and men fit and cheerful, and provided a welcome change from the dreary scenes of the Western Front. The yeomen had also cultivated the friendliest relations with the inhabitants ; volunteers from every squadron helped in the harvest fields, and they felt very much at home.

On Tuesday, 21st September, the Brigade moved billets, somewhat suddenly, the Regiment going into billets in and around Serny, 15 miles south of Buysscheure and 5½ miles south-west of Aire. Here they remained three days, doing a brigade field day on the 23rd. It was still very hot, and lovely weather.

On Friday the 24th we moved on to Heuchin, about 10 miles farther south, arriving there at 10 p.m. The weather now became damp and muggy. However, we were glad to be in a much nicer country, with wooded hills and valleys.

Saturday the 25th saw the opening of the battle of Loos. Great things were expected ; the cavalry were to go through the " gap " ; and Regular officers were talking gaily about being home to finish the hunting-season.

The Brigade was ordered to stand-to from 9 a.m., but did not march till 2.30 p.m., when we set off on a long trek towards the front. It was just beginning to rain. After going about 12 miles, in pouring rain the whole time, we reached the Bois des Dames, 5 miles south-west of Béthune and 12 miles W.N.W. of Loos. Here we bivouacked for

the night. It was still raining hard, and the prospect was
not inviting. We picketed the horses in an open stubble
field on the edge of the wood. The darkness made it
extremely difficult to see what one was doing or where to
put down the picketing lines. Then the horses had to
be watered, which involved taking them half a mile along
an avenue blocked with cavalry and artillery. Eventually,
however, we got all the horses picketed, watered, and fed,
and officers and men were able to get something of a meal,
after which they pulled down a rick of straw and made
themselves as comfortable as they could for the night. The
rain stopped about 8.30 and gave way to a fine mild night.

Next day, the 26th, was a nice day, foggy early, but it
turned cold and windy on the 27th, and it rained heavily
from 5 p.m. on the 28th till the morning of the 29th. On
the 27th we saddled up at 4.30 a.m. and remained standing-
to till 5.10 p.m., when we received orders to off-saddle.
On the 28th we again saddled up at 5.30 a.m. All this
time we were kept on the *qui vive* by the idea of being used.
All sorts of rumours came in ; at one time we heard that
the French cavalry had got through farther south, at another
we thought that we should be off ourselves. But nothing
came of it all, and, as far as the cavalry was concerned, it
was Neuve Chapelle over again.

On the 29th the Brigade moved back into billets, the
Regiment going to Lières, 2 miles west of Lillers. Here
we remained standing-to at two hours' notice.

On October 2nd a working party of 2 officers and 75 men
under Captain P. Fleming was sent to Vermelles to help
clear up the battlefield. Lieutenant Weatherby and four
men were wounded, and the General in charge of the work
(Brigadier-General Wormald, 5th Cavalry Brigade) was
killed. The party returned on the 4th.

On Sunday, October 3rd, the Brigade moved billets again,
the Regiment going to Auchy au Bois, a mile or two farther
west. Here we had quite good billets, but there was
difficulty in watering the horses, as there were no streams
or ponds, and the whole Regiment had to water in one

yard, a lengthy and inconvenient process. The weather
was now wet and cold most days. Auchy au Bois is probably
best remembered, by " D " Squadron at any rate, for the
charms of the lady at the estaminet where Lieutenant
Wellesley had his billet and the sergeants had their mess.

Early on the 14th we moved to a new billeting area at
Mazinghem and Rombly, three or four miles farther north,
but did not stay long.

On Sunday, October 17th, we moved again to Coyecque,
10 miles farther west, and 12 miles S.S.W. of St. Omer,
" C " Squadron going to Delette, a mile or two away. Here
we had splendid billets, in charming country. " Training was
carried on during the month of October as far as circumstances and the state of the ground permitted." (Regimental Diary.) Leave was reopened, but only for one
officer and three men per regiment at a time, though the
number was increased later on. The period of leave was
also extended to eight clear days in England. From now
on to the end of the war one's turn for leave came round
much more slowly than in the early days—about twice a
year for officers and about once in eighteen months for the
men, if they were lucky. Of course there was always a
small number, both of officers and men, who managed to
wangle about twice their just ration regularly every year,
always on the most plausible and seemingly unassailable
grounds.

The weather still continued very wet, with occasional
fine days.

On the 23rd October Lieutenant Muirhead left the
Regiment to take up the appointment of A.D.C. to Major-
General Fanshawe, commanding an infantry division.

There had been a good many changes among the officers,
besides those mentioned in the narrative, since the early
part of the year, and it may be well to deal with them at
this point.

Second-Lieutenant Hall went to England sick in February
1915, and did not come out to France again. Surgeon-
Captain Hogarth rejoined from England in June, Lieutenant

Keith-Falconer and Second-Lieutenant Shand in July.
(Shand was very unlucky. He had had his leg broken by
a kick from a horse playing polo in April and was sent to
England. Sent out again in July, he slipped into a pit
one night when up with a digging party and broke his leg a
second time, within a week of his return to France. After
this the Regiment never saw him again.) Second-Lieutenant Silvertop left to join the Flying Corps on 10th
September. Second-Lieutenant H. E. Evetts joined the
Regiment on 31st July ; Second-Lieutenant G. E. Schuster
on 22nd August ; Second-Lieutenant H. D. Savory on
24th October.[1] Second-Lieutenant Page-Turner injured a
leg while with the digging party in July, and went to
hospital, eventually finding his way back to England. Him
also the Regiment did not see again, though he afterwards
returned to France in the capacity of a Rent Officer.

The full list of officers serving with the Regiment on
31st October 1915 was as follows :

Headquarters :
 Lieutenant-Colonel A. Dugdale (Commanding) ;
 Major J. W. Scott (Second-in-Command) ;
 Captain G. T. Hutchinson (Adjutant) ;
 Lieutenant J. J. Pearce ;
 Lieutenant J. A. Moncreiffe (Machine-gun Officer) ;
 Surgeon-Captain A. H. Hogarth (Medical Officer) ;
 Captain H. C. Jagger (Veterinary Officer).
" A " Squadron :
 Major R. E. U. Hermon-Hodge ;
 Captain H. A. Fane ;
 Second-Lieutenant R. L. Worsley ;
 Second-Lieutenant H. D. Savory.
" C " Squadron :
 Major V. Fleming ;
 Captain P. Fleming ;
 Lieutenant G. H. Palmer ;
 Lieutenant E. H. Chinnery ;
 Second-Lieutenant F. Weatherby.

---

[1] Of these, Lieutenant Evetts was posted to " A " Squadron, but went
to hospital on 21st September ; Lieutenant Schuster to " D " Squadron,
and then to Brigade Headquarters as Intelligence Officer, on 21st September ; Lieutenant Savory to " A " Squadron.

" D " Squadron :
    Captain the Hon. A. G. C. Villiers ;
    Lieutenant A. W. Keith-Falconer ;
    Second-Lieutenant G. V. Wellesley ;
    Second-Lieutenant E. W. H. Allfrey.

On Sunday, 31st October, 3 officers and 100 other ranks
per regiment were sent up from the Brigade to dig trenches
between Ebblinghem and Staple. These trenches formed
part of an elaborate defence system known as the G.H.Q.
line. They were about 20 miles behind the front line, and
were of course never used, as even in 1918 the Germans
never got within five miles of them.

Some officers, in anticipation of a winter in billets, clipped
their chargers this autumn for the first time since leaving
England, but not their troop-horses, and many thought it
better to leave even their own horses with their coats on,
lest, in the event of active operations, they might have to
stand out at nights in wintry weather. But experience
showed that the clipped horses kept their condition better,
and when in later years they sometimes were out at night
in winter, it was wonderful how quickly they grew a coat ;
besides, the officer or his groom between them could generally " snaffle " an extra rug or blanket. Unclipped horses,
on the other hand, grew terrific coats, which made them
sweat excessively whenever they went out, even only to
exercise, and made it impossible to groom them at all
adequately.

There was a great deal of talk at this time about the
cavalry taking over a section of trenches permanently.
Some Generals were said to favour it, others to oppose it.
Quite a number of cavalry officers seemed rather to favour
the idea, partly, no doubt, because people have short memories
and get bored doing nothing, but partly also because a good
many had a sort of feeling that if the cavalry really weren't
any use on their horses, they ought to do a bit on foot. It
didn't do either officers or men any good to be idle in billets
for too long.

The transfer of senior officers—usually the second-in-command—from cavalry regiments to command infantry battalions had already begun.

On Tuesday, 16th November, billeting parties were sent on to a new area about 13 miles farther east, and the whole Brigade followed next day.

The area occupied by the Regiment was about halfway between St. Omer and Boulogne and comprised the villages of Bléquin (Regimental Headquarters), Ledinghem (" A " Squadron, Vieil Moutier (" C " Squadron), and La Calique (" D " Squadron). La Calique was a straggling hamlet standing on a ridge some 650 feet high, 4½ miles west of Bléquin. The road between ran over a bleak expanse of open country, with no hedges and very few cottages and trees. Just north of La Calique the ridge sloped very steeply down to the small village of Vieil Moutier. " C " and " D " Squadrons were thus widely separated from Regimental Headquarters, and " A " was a mile away on the other side, so that the whole area was very scattered. This was inconvenient for Headquarters, and involved long journeys daily for the squadron transport, but was rather welcome to squadrons, who liked being independent. The only drawback for them was the extra work for the transport, but that only affected the S.Q.M.S. and three or four men.

There had been heavy snow on the 16th, and the hilly, lonely countryside looked thoroughly wintry. The billets were not promising at first sight, but the inhabitants were fairly friendly, and after a few days we managed to settle in comfortably.

Major Winston Churchill arrived at Regimental Headquarters on 18th November, but went on at once to G.H.Q. He was then attached to a Guards battalion to gain experience of trench warfare, and was afterwards appointed to the command of an infantry battalion.

On 21st November the Cavalry Corps was organised as a dismounted division ready for use in the trenches, divisional Generals taking command of the dismounted division in turns, and brigade, regimental, and squadron commanders in like manner taking their turn in the subordinate commands.

But it was only a paper organization at present, and did not affect our daily life for some time to come.

For the first week or ten days in the new area the weather continued cold, and there was frost every night. Several days were spent in improving billets and fitting up shelters for horses in the various farms, after which " much work was done training bombers and indifferent shots and some work done with officers' patrols, but more was impossible owing to men being away digging." (Regimental Diary.) Thirty-three per squadron were in fact away, besides men on leave, and the remainder were fully occupied with the horses. The other regiments in the Brigade received 100 dismounted men each towards the end of October, to help look after the horses when the cavalry was employed dismounted, either holding trenches or on working parties, but the 100 for this Regiment, though promised, had not arrived by the end of 1915.

Those officers who had not yet been in the trenches were attached to infantry battalions in the front line for a week's instruction.

Lieutenant H. M. Worsley joined the Regiment on 17th December, having previously held a commission in the Honourable Artillery Company, with whom he had served in France from January 1915 and had been twice wounded. He was at first posted to " D " Squadron, but was transferred to " C " Squadron a few weeks later.

On 24th December the digging party returned to billets for Christmas.

Christmas Day, if less memorable than that of 1914, was certainly more comfortable, and probably more enjoyable. Fifteen turkeys were bought locally for each squadron, out of profits made by the regimental canteen ; plum puddings, one per man, were provided by the people of Oxfordshire ; and there was real English bottled beer.

Sergeant Stroud's horse celebrated Christmas by breaking loose about 8 o'clock at night and galloping off towards Desvres, jumping the railway gates, and staying away for a week before he was found.

The digging party returned to Staple by an unpleasantly early train on the 26th, but the very next day orders arrived for their return to billets, and back they came on the 28th. The High Command had suddenly decided to employ the newly organized dismounted cavalry division in the line, and we were warned to prepare to move in a few days.

Here are the Regimental Orders for the 31st. They may serve as a specimen for some 1,500 others issued under Colonel Dugdale's name during the course of the campaign, and will also give some idea of the amount of detailed work necessary to move even so small a unit as a regiment.

"Regimental Orders by Lieutenant-Colonel Arthur Dugdale, C.M.G., Commanding Q.O. Oxfordshire Hussars.

"30th December 1915.

"*Dismounted Company.*—1. The Oxford Hussars Company of 4th Dismounted Battalion and details for Battalion Headquarters will proceed under Squadron arrangements to Desvres station to-morrow, where Major Hermon-Hodge will assume command of the Company, and will be ready to entrain there at 7.30 a.m.

"*M. Gun Section.*—2. The Machine Gun Section will proceed with its transport to Wizernes, where the B.M.G.O. will assume command, and will be ready to entrain there at 9.30 a.m.

"*Transport.*—3. Transport of Dis. Coy. and Battalion H.Q. will start from Bléquin at 3 a.m. to-morrow and will proceed to Desvres station, ready to entrain there at 5.30 a.m. The limber detailed from 'C' Sqdn. for S.A.A. will proceed independently to Desvres station by 5.30 a.m. O.C. 'D' Sqdn. will detail 20 men under a N.C.O. to join the transport at La Calique at 4 a.m. and assist with loading at Desvres : the 'D' Sqdn. limber detailed for S.A.A. will join at the same time. Rations and forage for 31st inst. will be carried.

"*Horseholders.*—4. Dismounted men from 3rd Hussars and 6th D.G.s will report for duty at Sqdn. H.Q. as detailed and will be available to bring back led horses from Desvres.

"*Returns.*—5. O.C. Sqdns. and M.Gun Sec. will send to orderly room to-night nominal rolls in duplicate of officers and men detailed for duty with the Dismounted Battalion.

" *Stores.*—6. O.C. ' A ' Sqdn. will send 1 N.C.O. detailed
for Dis. Batt. to report to Sgt. Turner at Regtl. H.Q. at 10
a.m. to-morrow : he will accompany G.S. limbered wagon
with West gun and spare stores to be dumped at the *mairie*
at Nielles by 12 noon and taken on by lorry.   This N.C.O
will remain with the stores and West gun until they are
taken over again by the dismounted Company.

" *Maps.*—7. All copies of sheets 36 B and 36 C in possession will be taken with Dismounted Company : a full issue
of maps required will be made subsequently.

" *Equipment.*—8. O.C. Sqdns. and M.Gun Sec. will
arrange that arms, equipment, and clothing to be carried
and worn by men detailed for Dis. Batt. include : rifle,
bayonet, bandolier and 100 rounds S.A.A., waterbottle,
mess-tin, and haversack, rations for 31st and iron ration,
coat (warm), mackintosh, cardigan, leather jerkin, cap-
comforter, spare pair of socks, and waterproof sheet, goggles,
(2) tube smoke helmets : those issued to men left in billets
to be utilized for this purpose, and balance to be made up
with film smoke helmets.

" Platoon commanders must make their own arrangements for a supply of lanterns or candles.

" (*Signed*) G. T. HUTCHINSON,
Captain and Adjutant,
Q.O. Oxfordshire Hussars."

" C " and " D " Squadrons left billets at 6 a.m. on Friday,
31st December, and marched 3 miles to Desvres station ;
Headquarters and " A " Squadron started at 4.30, having
8 miles to cover. Some units in the Brigade had even
farther to go, and must have left billets before four o'clock.

At Desvres the 4th Cavalry Brigade dismounted battalion
came under the command of Lieutenant-Colonel Dugdale,
with Major Webster of the Carabiniers as Second-in-Command, and Captain Hutchinson as Adjutant. Each regiment in the Brigade provided the strength of a company,
and each squadron furnished two platoons, each composed
of 1 officer, 2 sergeants, 4 corporals, and 41 men. A company
numbered 8 officers and 282 other ranks, and a whole
battalion about 900 all ranks.

We entrained about 7.30 a.m. in a thing called a " strategic train," which travelled at an average speed considerably below that of the slowest goods train ever known, and was made up of a few worn-out second-class coaches for the officers and so-called " cattle-trucks " for the men. (Those of us who had travelled in France before the war had often noticed these wagons bearing the inscription " Chevaux 8, Hommes 36," and had always wondered what on earth the second part of it meant, since it was clearly fantastic to suppose that human beings ever travelled in them. Now we knew.) There was, as usual, not enough room, and both men and officers were packed like a bank-holiday crowd. We started at 9 a.m. and eventually detrained at Lillers at 3 p.m., after a long roundabout journey of 50 miles, at an average speed of 8 miles an hour. There were ten buses to convey the battalion to Ligny-lez-Aire, and as each bus could only carry 25 men, 72 per cent. of the party had to walk 7 miles to their billets. This doesn't sound such a very long way, but for men carrying 50 or 60 lbs. of equipment and not accustomed to marching, and who had been on the move since four or five in the morning, it was pretty hard work, and they were very tired when they reached billets at 7 p.m. It rained most of the way.

From the centre of our billeting area at Bléquin to Ligny-lez-Aire the distance as the crow flies is 17¼ miles ; the distance covered by the battalion, 14 miles by road and 52 by rail, total 66 miles ; time occupied, 14 hours. The whole journey by bus could have been done in two hours, or if sufficient buses were not available, we could have ridden it on our horses in four hours.

The Oxfordshire Company was commanded by Major Hermon-Hodge ; platoon commanders were Lieutenants Palmer, Keith-Falconer, Chinnery, Winterbottom, Allfrey, and R. Worsley. Captain Fane and Lieutenant Wellesley were attached to Battalion Headquarters as Bombing Officer and Scout Officer respectively. Lieutenant Savory was Salvage Officer. S. S. M. Warren was Company Sergeant-Major.

The weather was still awful. The New Year came in

with a night of rain and howling wind. On New Year's
Day the battalion rested in billets. On the 2nd it moved
by buses in two parties to Béthune. In the first party were
the Colonel and about ten or a dozen officers from the battalion, who, on reaching Béthune at 11 a.m., went on up to
the support trenches on a tour of inspection. It rained all
day.

In the afternoon the trench-inspection party returned
to Béthune, where the rest of the battalion had arrived.
Not for the first or last time in the war someone had omitted
to make billeting arrangements, and the town was crammed
with troops. However, billets were found at last and the
battalion settled down to enjoy its last night in civilization
for some weeks.

It was the Regiment's first visit to Béthune. At that
time it was universally regarded as the best shopping centre
and pleasure resort in the British Army area ; it was full of
shops and there was hardly anything one couldn't get there.
The town afterwards suffered very heavy damage from the
enemy's long-range bombardment in April 1918.

Next morning (3rd January) we marched to Sailly
Labourse, 4½ miles south-east of Béthune, and spent the day
in squalid billets preparatory to going to the trenches at
night. It was the first fine day for a long time.

At 2 a.m. on Tuesday, January 4th, we marched to the
support trenches near Vermelles, arriving at 5.15. The
3rd Hussars company went into billets (so-called by courtesy ;
really cellars for the most part) at Vermelles, where they
were in support. The Carabiniers went into huts at Noyelles,
and were in reserve.

The trenches occupied by the Q.O.O.H. were known as
Curley Crescent and were altogether superior to anything
we had known hitherto. Even the Zillebeke trenches,
which had so impressed us a year before, were primitive
compared with these.

Battalion Headquarters at Vermelles were in the biggest
dugout we had ever seen. You went down about ten steps
which brought you to a narrow corridor, leading to a kitchen

on the left, and to the officers' quarters on the right.
The latter consisted of the Colonel's private cabin and
the officers' mess on the same level as the kitchen, while
down another flight of twenty steps was the officers'
sleeping-room, containing three bunks and a stretcher.
The rooms were about the size of the cabins on a good cargo
steamer, and the kitchen was as big as many kitchens in
small private houses. There were two pretty good officers'
dugouts, high enough to stand up in, and all the men had
dugouts also. One of the dugouts actually contained a
wicker-work armchair, a luxury very rarely found even in
billets.

A certain amount of shelling went on all day and a little
desultory rifle fire, but nothing of any interest happened.
Our trenches were 800 yards behind the front line, with
which they were connected by a perfect labyrinth of communication trenches, turning and twisting in all directions,
crossed by six other lines, the first of which was the old
German line as it was before the fighting in September 1915.
Behind that were the various old British lines. There were
signboards at most of the crossroads, but even with
their help it was very easy to get lost, especially at night.
In fact the whole sector resembled nothing so much as the
maze at Hampton Court, magnified 100 times, with walls
of chalk instead of shrubbery.

At 1 a.m. on Saturday, 8th January, our company were
relieved by the 20th Hussars and marched back to billets,
i.e. huts at Noyelles, a small village 2 miles behind the front
line, which we reached at 4 a.m. Here we remained in
reserve. Practically the whole battalion was taken each
day for fatigues and digging parties. These parties were
usually out from four or five in the afternoon till any time
between 9 p.m. and midnight, and were thoroughly unpopular. Halfway up to the front line they generally met another
party going in the reverse direction, and as the men were
heavily loaded with rations or ammunition or timber,
passing was a matter of great difficulty and much hard
swearing. Or they would be held up for ages at a cross-

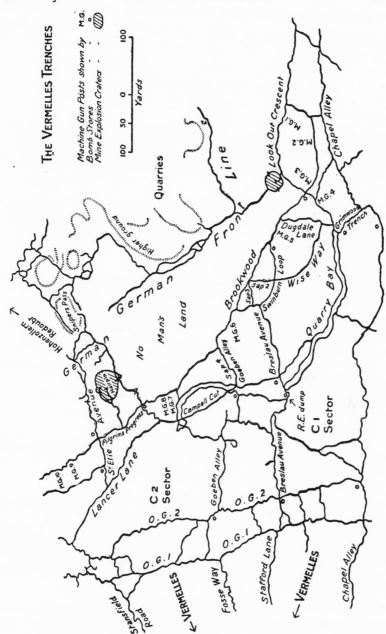

THE VERMELLES TRENCHES

Machine Gun Posts shown by   M.G.
Bomb Stores   -   -
Mine Explosion Craters   -   -

Yards

11

roads in the trench-system, always with the chance of being shelled. However, there were two great advantages about being in reserve, the first being that one was reasonably sure of a good night's sleep, and the second that there were some excellent bath-houses where both officers and men could get a hot bath.

At midnight on the night of January 12th–13th we marched up to relieve the 3rd Cavalry Brigade dismounted battalion in the front line. The Q.O.O.H. took over the right sector, the 3rd Hussars the left, and the Carabiniers were in support. The trenches were very good, mostly boarded, and quite dry. There were no dugouts in the front line, but shelters here and there made of half a dozen stout logs thrown across the trench and covered with plenty of earth, and a sofa-shaped seat for two cut out underneath.

Our first day, Thursday the 13th, was quiet, but bitterly cold, especially at night, and the wind raged down the trenches, but on Friday it got much milder. Nothing of much incident beyond periodical shelling occurred till Saturday the 15th at 11.30, when the Germans started shelling the right of the battalion's line with 5.9-inch shells. It only lasted fifteen minutes, but was rather unpleasant while it did last. Several shells landed very close to the trench, and one fell on the parados and blew in the trench. Luckily no one was hurt, although two men were standing only 2 feet off. All their coats and kits were buried by the explosion, and it was a marvel how they escaped. There was another short period of shelling on Saturday evening, and we were also worried by rifle-grenades.

Much work was done improving the trenches. A new piece of front-line trench called Brookwood Street was occupied, and a second-line trench on the left was in course of construction. There was some shelling, to which our guns replied quickly and efficiently. There were four casualties during the three days.

" Generally during the fortnight that the trenches have been occupied by the Cavalry our snipers have begun to

get the upper hand with the enemy, whereas previous to
this their snipers were very active." (Regimental Diary.)

It may be noted that Lieutenant Wellesley, in the capacity
of Battalion Scout Officer, played a prominent part in
bringing about this desirable change in the situation. He
was awarded the Military Cross for his services, and was,
I think, the first officer in the Regiment to receive this
distinction. Private Muller got the D.C.M.

Each squadron in the Brigade furnished two picked men
as snipers. They formed an independent party working
on its own, with billets in the cellars of some ruined houses
in Vermelles. The snipers worked in pairs and used to take
up their positions in specially contrived posts before dawn,
retiring after dark unless there were some special patrol or
reconnaissance to be carried out by night. This work often
meant lying motionless throughout the day, gazing into
the mirror of a periscope.

We were relieved by the 20th Hussars at 3.15 a.m. on
Sunday, 16th January, and marched to Noyelles, arriving
dog-tired at 6.15. Here we remained five days in
reserve.

On the afternoon of the 16th Lieutenant-Colonel Dugdale
handed over the command of the battalion to Lieutenant
Colonel Webster (newly promoted to command the Carabiniers), and on the same day Major Villiers relieved Major
Hermon-Hodge in command of the Oxfordshire company.

Noyelles was an ugly village, from which all the inhabitants had been cleared out, but it did not get shelled while
we were there, and had not been much knocked about.
Vermelles, on the other hand, was a most "unhealthy"
place, perpetually being shelled, and did not possess a single
house which had not been badly damaged, and only about
two or three with any roof. The church was all in ruins,
the outer walls and the belfry alone partially standing. A
great deal of excitement was caused one night by the sound
of the church bells ringing there. It was investigated by
several officers and men, who vouched for the fact. As far

as I know, no explanation of the mystery was ever forth-
coming, and it was generally attributed to spies.

The battalion returned to the trenches on Friday night,
21st January, leaving billets at 9.15 p.m. and arriving at the
trenches at 12.15 a.m. on the 22nd. We took over the same
piece of line as before, with the Carabiniers on our left and
the 3rd Hussars in support, in Curley Crescent. Immediately after taking over the Carabiniers had a bomb fight at
a place in their line called the Hairpin, which lasted until
4 a.m.

We had good weather, but not such a quiet time as before.
The enemy were very active with rifle grenades and trench
mortars, and our guns retaliated. The first day (Saturday)
our guns shelled the enemy trenches rather heavily, with the
result that the Germans shelled us back for a bit, but not
much damage was done. Sunday morning was quiet till
1 p.m., when suddenly 6-inch shells began to fall on the
extreme right of our line, held by the two " D " Squadron
platoons, under Lieutenant Keith-Falconer. The British
front curved back westwards south of the cavalry sector,
which thus formed something of a salient, and a big
German naval gun lay somewhere on our right, whence it
directly enfiladed the " D " Squadron trench, which had
very few traverses and contained several dangerous long
straight bits. (It should be mentioned that the Q.O.O.H.
were on the extreme right of the cavalry, joining up with the
infantry.) The bombardment lasted for an hour and a half,
quite a hundred heavy shells being fired, and twelve getting
direct hits on the parapet and blowing in the trench in six
places, so that it was only possible to get along it by crawling on hands and knees over the top. The trench on the
left was also blown in in four or five places. During the
bombardment the two " D " Squadron platoons, less four
men left as sentries, were withdrawn into a communication
trench running up to the right flank of their trench. Here
they were fairly safe, as they were broadside on to the
shells, and there were no casualties. After the shelling
stopped, it took the whole of both platoons, with a working

party of twenty 3rd Hussars, till 10 p.m. to repair the trenches. Next day (24th January) the same thing started at 11 a.m. and continued thirty-five minutes. The garrison was at once moved into the neighbouring communication trench,and no one was hit, but the trench was again blown in in five places, in one place so badly that it was literally obliterated, leaving a solid wall of earth for 10 yards where the trench had been. The men worked in reliefs continuously from 3.30 p.m. till midnight, by which time, with the help of a small working party, they had made the trench tolerably habitable again.

During this time the battalion was engaged constructing a new trench behind Brookwood, which in places was being evacuated owing to enemy mine-galleries being reported beneath it. It was patrolled every twenty minutes instead, and the new trench held by the main body. There was also much trench mortar and rifle-grenade activity on the 24th.

The battalion was relieved by the 5th Battalion (Oxford Hussars company by 12th Lancers) at 1.15 a.m. on Tuesday, 25th January, and marched back to the huts at Noyelles, getting in at 4.15 a.m.

The cavalry had now completed about half the period which they were intended to spend in these trenches, and the second half was to be decidedly more strenuous and eventful than the first. This was chiefly due to the mining activities of the enemy, or perhaps it would be more correct to say of both sides. Our own mining or tunnelling companies had been busy for some time in the sector occupied by the 4th dismounted battalion, and had driven shafts deep under No-man's-land towards the German line. Nor had the enemy been inactive. His men could be clearly heard tapping away in shafts and galleries close to our own, and at any moment the opposing miners might have come face to face. However, this did not happen, but several large mines were exploded, as we shall see.

Meanwhile, we have anticipated. The 27th January was the Kaiser's birthday, and it was thought that so great and sacred a day would hardly be allowed to pass un-

celebrated by the anniversary-loving Hun. Every pre-
caution, therefore, was taken against a surprise attack.

At 7 p.m. on the 26th the battalion was " ordered to turn
out at once and march to Vermelles " :

" On arrival it was found that the battalion usually
quartered there in support had been pushed up nearer the
firing line, and that the 4th Battalion was to ' stand-to '
in Vermelles, reserves being brought up from farther back
and quartered in Noyelles." (Regimental Diary.)

There was " considerable shelling by both sides during
the night," and " a German attack was expected but did
not materialize on the sectors held by the 2nd Dismounted
Brigade." (Regimental Diary.)

Next morning, the 27th, the battalion was ordered back
to billets at Noyelles, and the scare was over. The next
few days were spent resting in the huts, cleaning up, and
getting baths, and the rest was much broken by the usual
daily working parties.

The battalion marched at midnight, 30th–31st January,
to relieve the 3rd Battalion in the front-line trenches.
The 3rd Hussars took over the right sector, the Carabiniers
the left, and the Oxfords the support, or old German front
line. During the morning a 60-pdr. trench mortar, supported by a 4.2-inch battery and two R.H.A. batteries,
bombarded the German trenches, but the chief result was
that the " enemy at once retaliated with heavy trench
mortars and did some damage in Elie Avenue." At 10.30
a.m. a band was heard playing in their lines. Nothing
much happened during the rest of the day, beyond some
shelling of our reserve trenches, but at 8.30 p.m. much
firing broke out on our right, afterwards found to be a
false gas alarm. " A night firing scheme was carried out
by our supporting artillery and machine guns, some of the
latter employing indirect fire against the German lines
which were at once lit up by flare lights." (Regimental
Diary.) The mining officer reported the probability of a

mine going up in or near our lines in two or three days'
time.

The 1st February passed without incident, except for
an attempt by German bombers, supported by snipers, to
throw bombs into Brookwood Trench. The Diary notes
that they " got none in."

On the 2nd " an artillery firing scheme was arranged for
the afternoon on the crater in front of the Hairpin . . .
several direct hits were obtained." But " German retaliation with 6-inch and 4·2-inch guns was heavier than
expected." It was the old story ; our men hopelessly
outnumbered in heavy guns and trench mortars, and forced
to rely largely on the R.H.A., always most gallant of allies
and welcome of friends, ready with help in every emergency,
but armed only with 13-pdrs., of little use against the
concrete dugouts and fortified emplacements of the Germans.

At 4 p.m. on the 2nd orders were received at Battalion
Headquarters—

" to take steps to cope with a mine, which it was hoped to
blow up between the legs of the Hairpin, some time during
the night. It was considered essential to do this as soon as
possible as the enemy were known to be sapping toward
us with a view to mining operations."

I cannot do better at this point than quote verbatim the
account of the subsequent operations given in the Regimental Diary.

" 4.30 p.m. Orders were received to be ready for the
mine at 8 p.m. Artillery and trench mortars were warned,
but owing to some mistake Brigade machine guns were not
warned until the very last moment, and . . . had the machine
gunners nearest the mine not heard, by chance only, an
hour or so beforehand, their services (which proved very
valuable indeed) would have had to be dispensed with,
as they would not have had time to prepare their emplacements, etc., and this was most necessary as these guns had
apparently already been marked by the enemy. Arrangements were made to send bombers forward to act as a
covering party and to deny our side of the crater to the

enemy as soon as the mine went up, at the same time
M.G.s were by cross-fire to cut off the enemy from being
able to reach the crater from above ground, and this proved
most successful. Our trench mortars were to bombard the
inside of the crater just behind it and the Hairpin legs at
far end if required. The trench mortars worked very well
and helped very much to silence the German bombers who
tried bombing the left leg of the Hairpin when the mine
went up. The artillery also put up a barrage behind the
crater as soon as the mine went up. . . . The trenches were
cleared 100 yards either side of where it was expected to go
up. It went up at 8.45 p.m., which was exactly the time
ordered. Bombers went forward at once and got on both
flanks of the crater, denying it to the enemy, who started
bombing the left leg of the Hairpin. When it was certain
that the lips and flanks had been made good, Captain
Swinburne, R.E., with 3 platoons 6th D.G.s started digging
saps from legs of Hairpin to one side of the crater and also
connecting the latter with our trenches by a sap running up
between the Hairpin legs, the lip of the crater being not
more then 30 to 40 yards from our main trench at this
point, and the centre sap of the Hairpin only requiring
prolonging about 20 feet to bring it up to the crater on one
side. The enemy started with trench mortars and rifle
grenades as soon as the mine went up, and opened a hot
rifle and M.G. fire along the front for some distance on
either side. They also turned a heavy gun apparently
on the crater, but the shells fell some distance short."

The following extract from a letter supplements the above
description. "We 'blew' last night, and after a rare
scramble our people got on one lip and the German gentlemen on the other. For the next two hours each side threw
bombs frantically into the middle part of the basin (neither
could reach the other), and the whole thing, in the light of
the frantically fired star shells, looked like a huge white
cauldron of boiling chalk. Meanwhile every machine gun
and rifle in the place popped off, amid wild hurrahing of
our men."

After things quieted down the battalion was relieved by
the 5th Battalion, the relief being completed by about

4 a.m. on 3rd February. The Oxfords went into Curley Crescent, the 3rd Hussars to Vermelles, and the Carabiniers to Noyelles. Battalion Headquarters were at Vermelles. Later in the day Lieutenant-Colonel Webster handed over command of the battalion to Lieutenant-Colonel W. T. Willcox, 3rd Hussars, with Major V. Fleming as second-in-command.

For the next five days the battalion was in support, finding the usual guards and working parties, till midnight, 8th–9th February, when they went up to relieve the 3rd Battalion in the front line. The relief was completed by 3 a.m., and the rest of the 9th was a " particularly quiet day. Oxford Hussars had three casualties to grenadiers about 8 p.m."

On the 10th the R.H.A. did good work retaliating to and silencing rifle-grenades and trench mortars which had been annoying us. Otherwise nothing of importance happened.

Another quiet night followed, but about 2.30 p.m. on the 11th heavy shelling began and continued with varying intensity till 5 p.m., doing a good deal of damage to the trenches, but only causing three casualties in our battalion.

" At dusk a mine was blown up by the enemy, . . . accompanied by a heavy bombardment of mine area. Our retaliation appeared singularly inadequate, and the difficulty and delay in getting touch with and support from the howitzers was very noticeable." (Regimental Diary.)

The battalion was relieved by the 5th Battalion at 2.45 a.m. on the 12th, and reached the huts at Noyelles at 4 a.m.

" The battalion was lucky in having few casualties and a comparatively quiet time, but the presence of 4 German mines under or near our parapet compelled the attention of all ranks." (Regimental Diary.)

The 12th February was devoted to rest, baths, and rifle inspection. The 13th, a wet and gusty day, brought more inspections, this time of smoke helmets as well as rifles, cleaning of equipment, and the inevitable fatigue parties.

On the 14th the billets were cleaned up, and at 11.45 a.m. the " battalion paraded and marched to Béthune. . . . Three shells fell near the place of assembly half an hour before our time of departure." The battalion arrived in billets at Béthune at 2 p.m. and remained there for the night. On the 15th they " entrained at Béthune at 7 a.m. on a wet and stormy morning and left for Lumbres at 8.15 a.m., arriving there at 11.15 a.m." Thence they went on to billets by lorry.

We must now retrace our steps for a moment and note briefly the events that had occurred in billets since the departure of the dismounted company on New Year's Eve, 1915. Chief among these were sundry changes among the officers.

The scheme for the employment of the Cavalry Corps as a dismounted division in the trenches had included the provision of 100 additional men per regiment to help look after the horses during the absence of the trench party. Owing to the Yeomanry at that time drawing their reinforcements from a different source and through different channels than the Regular cavalry, the 100 men for our Regiment had not arrived on the 31st December, and the 3rd Hussars and 6th D.G.s each sent us 30 men to fill their places temporarily. However, on the 12th January a draft of 2 officers (Lieutenant W. Pepper and Second-Lieutenant A. C. Rawlinson) and 100 men arrived from England and were distributed amongst squadrons.

On the 15th January " C " Squadron moved from Vieil Moutier to Senlecques, where they were rather more comfortably situated, about 2½ miles south-west of Regimental Headquarters at Bléquin.

During January Major J. W. Scott left the Regiment to take command of the 8th Somerset L.I., and Major V. Fleming succeeded him as Second-in-Command, Captain P. Fleming becoming O.C. " C " Squadron.

The departure of Major Scott deprived the Regiment of one of its most capable and efficient officers. Courage and resource in action, zeal and energy in billets, were but a few among his many qualities. Besides these, he had from the beginning the professional soldier's knowledge and training, which most of us were still painfully acquiring, coupled with the advantage of previous war experience in South Africa. What this meant to the Regiment in 1914 those who were with it then know best, but in 1915 too he did great work, first as a squadron leader, and then as Second-in-Command at Headquarters.

Captain G. T. Hutchinson was appointed Staff Captain, 3rd Divisional Artillery, and was succeeded as Adjutant by Lieutenant F. Weatherby.

Lieutenant G. E. Schuster, who had been our Brigade Intelligence Officer since September 1915, was appointed Staff Captain of a Heavy Artillery Brigade.

Second-Lieutenants J. P. Higgs, H. J. Soame, R. C. Byass, H. H. Smetham, and A. E. MacColl joined the Regiment, Smetham and MacColl being posted to " A " Squadron, Higgs and Soame to " C," and Byass to " D "

Mr. Pearce, the Regimental Sergeant-Major, went to England owing to ill-health, and Squadron Sergeant-Major Collier was appointed R.S.M. in his place, Sergeant Grant becoming S.S.M., " C " Squadron.

Squadron Sergeant-Major Warren was given a commission in the 14th Battalion, Welch Regiment.   He had been thirteen years in the Oxfordshire Yeomanry, and had served with the Australian contingent in the South African War.   Sergeant Tompkins, for the second time, succeeded him as S.S.M., " D " Squadron, having previously filled the post from June to September 1915.

The remainder of February was occupied in cleaning up kit, saddlery, etc., and in troop training, riding school, etc., till a heavy fall of snow on the 23rd February stopped all further training till the 28th, when a thaw set in.   The snow lay very thick and deep, and a fierce north wind drove it in great drifts on the hilly roads, making traffic difficult.

On the 22nd began the battle of Verdun, which chiefly affected us by causing the stoppage of leave.

We read in the Diary that " All men who came out with

the Regiment and have not since been inoculated are being
done in groups of about eight per group at a time. This
rather interferes with training." It is almost incredible,
but true, that inoculation against enteric was not compulsory, at any rate for a very long time, if not for the whole
war. Fortunately cases of " conscientious objectors " were
so rare as to be negligible, not exceeding one or two per year,
and they generally yielded in the end, since it was found inex-
pedient and contrary to public policy to send them on leave
to England.

The Brigadier inspected " D " Squadron on the 23rd
February and " C " Squadron on the 3rd March.

At the end of February the machine-gun sections throughout the cavalry were taken out of the regiments to which
they belonged and grouped together into machine-gun
squadrons. Originally each regiment had one machine-gun
section, under a subaltern, but some time in 1915 the number
was doubled, so that there were now two per regiment, and
two officers. These were now grouped together into
squadrons of six sections, each squadron forming a separate
unit, commanded by a Major or Captain under the immediate
orders of the Brigadier. But, although entirely removed
from regimental control for all ordinary purposes, such as
orders, routine, leave, etc., the members of the new machine-
gun squadrons still retained a connection with their parent
unit, and wore their regimental badge for a considerable
time, until eventually merged into the Machine-gun Corps,
with an entirely separate organization.

Little of interest occurred during March. The Diary notes
" more frost and snow at the beginning of the month which
interfered with training for a short time. Leave reopened
about the middle of the month." Major Fleming made up
some very good squadron schemes, which were carried out
with varying success. Major Villiers introduced an excellent
system of afternoon classes in " D " Squadron, where each
officer specialized in one particular subject, and took each
troop in turn for an hour a week. Thus one officer would
be responsible for musketry, another for bombing, another

for map-reading, another for anti-gas drill, and so on. The scheme worked very well, and the men showed considerable keenness.

Among the amusements at this time may be recalled the " D " Squadron toboggan-run down the very steep hillside between La Calique and the railway. This was great fun while it lasted, but really got too dangerous when the snow hardened, as there was a nasty dip at the bottom of the run which upset nearly everyone. However, nobody was seriously injured.

" Had jumping competitions, tent-pegging and sword drill, mounted squadron and troop training, and had got extra good billets. Some very pleasant evenings spent here, and in some cases sergeants have been known to refuse their breakfast at the mess after a quiet game of brag. And so the month went on ; every day something was done to keep the men fit." (Sergeant Stroud's Diary.)

We lost our medical officer, A. H. Hogarth, one of the last of the old Surgeon-Captains, who went to England on the 22nd February and became D.A.D.M.S. of a home division. (He died in September 1919, as much on active service as anyone, for he had literally worked himself to death during the war. He was a familiar and well-remembered figure in the Regiment in the winter of 1914–15, when he grew a reddish beard to keep out the cold and rode about in his blue cavalry cloak, so that he was once nearly arrested as a spy. But he has a more serious claim to our remembrance and regard, for he did his job and did it well ; was always at hand, in all times of danger and discomfort, to give first aid to sick or wounded, and in billets or on the march was untiring in his pursuit of all enemies to health.)

He was succeeded as Medical Officer by Captain S. E. Whitnall, R.A.M.C.

Second-Lieutenant J. A. P. Whinney joined the Regiment on the 16th March, and was posted to " D " Squadron. He had only left Rugby in the previous July, and was much the youngest officer we had.

Lieutenants Pepper and Palmer were promoted to be Captain.

The Divisional Commander inspected the horses of the Regiment on the 18th March and expressed his satisfaction with their general condition and turn-out.

A good deal of useful mounted training was done between the 15th March and the 15th April, after the snow cleared away, but there were many wet days. As late as the 17th April there were still howling gales, cold and rain.

Hotchkiss guns were first issued to the cavalry in April, and much time was devoted to the instruction of as many men as possible as Hotchkiss gunners and to devising the most efficient method of loading the guns and ammunition on the pack-horses. Two horses per squadron were earmarked for Hotchkiss packs, and the men detailed to lead them probably had as difficult and thankless a task as any in the Regiment. However well the pack was loaded, there was always a chance of something giving, and the whole cumbersome mass falling heavily to the ground, probably just when the Regiment was trotting. Then the pack-leader and one or two of his mates had to fall out and fasten the thing more securely, perhaps in pouring rain, and certainly with much hard swearing, and then trot on for miles, passing other troops or transport all the time, to catch up their proper place in the column. With time and experience trouble with the Hotchkiss pack became rarer, and was more often a sign of unskilful loading, but at best it was a beastly thing to lead on a long march.

Our wheeled transport had long since been cut down to bare regulation minimum—one heavy G.S. wagon and two limbered wagons per squadron—and now the number of officers' pack-horses was reduced from six to four per squadron.

The number of other packs was meanwhile growing alarmingly. A regimental order of the 10th May lays down that—

" In future the establishment of pack-horses per squadron apart from the Hotchkiss rifle, Hotchkiss rifle ammunition pack, and officers' packs will be 8 per squadron. All squadrons have now 4 pack-saddles, three of which will carry pioneer equipment, i.e. 10 shovels, 5 picks, 35 sandbags and dixies on each pack, the remaining pack-saddle will carry ammunition in boxes. The four remaining pack-horses will carry riding saddles, two of these horses will carry ammunition in saddle bags . . . and two reserve rations."

All this tended to reduce both the fire power and mobility of the cavalry, but the apparent loss was fully compensated, as regards fire power, by the greater fighting value of the Hotchkiss rifle, commonly estimated to be worth at least half a dozen rifles, and as regards mobility, by the elimination of wheeled transport from the actual fighting portion of a regiment.

On the 19th April Lieutenant Keith-Falconer left the Regiment and became Intelligence Officer at Brigade Headquarters.

On the same day the Regiment marched to temporary billets at Nordausques, Tournehem, and Zouafques (about 10 miles north-west of St. Omer), for cavalry training in the Second Army area, a big tract of land rented from the French and devoted entirely to training, where one could ride anywhere regardless of crops. The Diary notes that " rain prevented any use of the area till the 25th, after which for the rest of the month the Regiment was engaged each day in squadron and regimental training."

On the 30th April a party was sent to reconnoitre a suggested billeting area round Le Wast, Bellebrune, and Cremarest, and reported most unfavourably, and the Colonel wired to the Brigadier saying " area quite impossible." Two days later a message was received from Brigade Headquarters that—

" billeting area for Regiment would be Escœuilles, Brunembert and Surques, and that the move was to take place on Wednesday, 3rd May, before 10 a.m. Accordingly, on the 3rd May, the Regiment, with the exception of ' A ' Squadron and the Signallers, marched from Second Army Training

area to new billets in Escœuilles and Surques.   ' A '
squadron returned to old billets in Ledinghem. Signallers
returned to Bléquin on account of measles infection."

On the 5th " A " Squadron came to Selles and billeted
there. Headquarters and " C " Squadron were at Escœuilles, and " D " at Surques.

Here we were about 13 miles east of Boulogne, and in
excellent billets. The weather was lovely and the country
round very jolly.

On the 20th May the Regiment paid another visit to the
Second Army training area, " doing a scheme including
trench crossing, wire cutting, trench filling on the way to
bivouac." Here they spent three days, training, doing a
scheme under the inspection of the Divisional Commander
on the 22nd May, and returning to billets on the evening of
the 23rd.

The remainder of the month was spent training ; mounted
work in the mornings, musketry, bombing, physical drill,
and bayonet fighting in the afternoons.

Sergeant Stroud notes in his diary that at Surques in
May they " did some running across country, also went
several times boar hunting, but could not get near enough
to them to have any sport." Private Batchelor notes that
he " had bed " at Surques, from which we may infer that
the men were for the most part comfortable in these billets.
The same diary contains almost daily references to saddle
cleaning in the afternoons. This was, no doubt, in preparation for the Divisional Horse Show, which took place
at Harlettes on the 27th May. " D " Squadron did well,
getting first prize for best limber team, second for best
trained horse, fourth for light-weight horse. " C " Squadron
limber won third prize.

On the 29th May one officer (Major V. Fleming) and 73
other ranks went by motor-lorry to the Ypres salient to
dig and improve trenches.

The Brigadier gave an Old Etonian dinner to all Old
Etonians in the Brigade on Saturday, 3rd June. It was a

HORSE LINES.

THE TROOP COOK.

great success, and much enjoyed by everybody. About half a dozen members of the Regiment were present, including Major Villiers, Captain Philip Fleming, Captain Pepper, Lieutenants Keith-Falconer and Wellesley. (Major Val Fleming, also an Old Etonian, was away with the digging party.)

At midday on the 7th June we heard of the death of Lord Kitchener. Almost simultaneously we got orders for the dismounted battalion to go up to the trenches, and at 5 p.m. they went off in lorries under Colonel Dugdale, and arrived at Reninghelst at 3 a.m. or thereabouts on the 8th. (The cause of this sudden demand for their services was a heavy German attack on the Canadians in the southern half of the Ypres salient.)

The battalion remained in the Reninghelst area eleven days, but took no active part in the fighting, living in huts and standing-to at short notice, " getting what exercise was possible by route marches, which were necessarily short." From the 15th to the 18th digging parties, 150 to 300 strong, were out each night digging trenches for telephone wires.

On the 19th the " battalion returned by lorries to billets in the old area, arriving there about 7 p.m." (Regimental Diary.)

The very next day, 20th June, the whole Brigade left the Colembert area at nine in the evening, and marched all night to Staple, where they billeted, going on again at 9 p.m. next day to the Doulieu area, which they reached about 2 a.m. on the 22nd.

We had spent two very pleasant months in the country near Boulogne, not to mention six winter months as well, broken only by six weeks in the Vermelles trenches and the recent move to Reninghelst, so it was high time for the cavalry to justify their existence again. Still, however much we felt this, we were not particularly pleased to see the old Doulieu country again.

The Brigade was ordered to stand-to ready to move at five hours' notice, and the next few days were devoted to the inspection of packs, the issue of regulations as to the

12

method of carrying various articles, and other preparations for a possible " gap."

The battle of the Somme began on the 1st July, but after the first day or two the news became less and less hopeful, and the " gap " preparations " finally degenerated into a resumption of training, the Colonel, urged on by Val, trying to goad us into a bit more than the usual activity." (Major Fleming's Diary.)

The usual forms of training, patrols, musketry, physical drill, bayonet exercises, etc., were varied by practice in building rafts and bridging canals, and by the stampeding of —— Squadron's horses during field firing one day ; the Regimental Diary records a " surprise turnout of Regiment at short notice ; not well done ; comments to O.s C. squadrons," memories of which probably inspired the remark in Major Fleming's diary, quoted above.

Second-Lieutenant F. Holford had joined from England on the 18th May ; Second-Lieutenant Silvertop rejoined from the Flying Corps on the 6th June ; and Second-Lieutenant R. Lakin arrived with a draft of 13 other ranks on the 9th July.

The weather was moderate, and we were much plagued by mosquitoes.

An event of some importance about this time was the first issue of steel helmets, commonly called tin hats. Extremely unpopular with all ranks on account of their weight and discomfort, they were a valuable protection against shrapnel and flying fragments of heavier shells, and undoubtedly saved many lives. Many a man escaped a dangerous wound at the cost of a slight graze, thanks to his much-abused tin hat.

On the 15th July Brigade Headquarters moved from Doulieu to Bleu, and Regimental Headquarters moved into billets vacated by Brigade Headquarters.

On the 31st July the whole Regiment moved to a new billeting area in and around Morbecque, 2 miles from Hazebrouck.

A few days later a working party of 3 officers and 130

men was sent to Nieppe. There were already 150 men
away on other working parties, so little further training was
possible, except a few special classes for the men and some
tactical rides for officers.

On the 17th August Lieutenant Weatherby broke his
leg while playing polo (the Regimental Diary calls it
" exercising in a field "), and on the 24th Lieutenant Keith-
Falconer rejoined from Divisional Headquarters and took
over the duties of Adjutant.

On the 28th there was a welcome break in the monotony
of life in billets, the Colonel, Second-in-Command, Adjutant,
and squadron leaders attending an interesting demonstration
of a bombardment and attack carried out by the Second
Army School at Wisques. After half an hour's intensive
bombardment, by heavy trench mortars, a great mine was
exploded, leaving a crater 150 yards across from lip to lip,
followed by a hurricane bombardment by other lighter kinds
of trench mortar, and then an assault by infantry.

On the 2nd September the working parties returned
to billets, and on Wednesday, the 6th, the division set off
for the Somme area. The Regiment paraded at 8.20 a.m
and marched 13 miles, entirely on cobbled roads, to Raimbert, a colliery village near Lillers. Here they had good
billets, and next morning at 8.15 resumed their march,
arriving at Eps, a small village in a well-wooded, undulating
country, 9 miles south-west of Raimbert, at 11.20 a.m. We
were now well out of Flanders and glad to be off the famous
" Hazebrouck 5A " map at last.

We left Eps at 7.45 a.m. on the 8th September. Our
road lay through a beautiful hilly wooded country, and, as
on the two previous days, the weather was quite perfect.
After so many weeks of inaction, it was a pleasure to be on
the move again. We reached Caumont, a little village
in a dip in the hills, about six miles south of Hesdin, at
1 p.m., after a march of about 20 miles. Caumont is
situated on a stream with the poetical name of the " Rivière
de la Fontaine Riante," or " River of the Laughing Foun-
tain," and the countryside was pretty, but as a billet its

merits were not great, though pleasant enough for two
nights in summer.

Next day we had a small field day in the morning, practising crossing a defile and capturing guns in position.

Then, on the 10th, we left Caumont at 8.45 a.m. and
marched to Auxi-le-Château, some 6 miles to the south-east,
doing a brigade scheme on the way, and getting into billets
at 1 p.m.

Next day, 11th September, the Brigade moved on again,
making an early start at 6.15 a.m. We had some rather long
halts on the way, and did not reach our billets at Vigna-
court, 10 miles from Amiens, till 1.45 p.m., although the
distance from Auxi was only about 18 miles.

We marched again at 1.30 p.m. on the 12th September,
and reached camp at La Neuville, near Corbie, at 7 p.m.
At La Neuville we picketed the horses and bivouacked in
the open. This was well enough until it started to rain in
the night, and little trickles grew into pools of water on one's
groundsheet, so that most people woke up with a wet
jacket. However, next day thirty-one tents were issued to
each regiment, which improved matters considerably,
though, as each squadron only got six, of which the officers
took one, and the sergeants another, there was only one per
troop at the last, so that many were squeezed out. But they
probably had the best of it as long as it didn't rain ; you
took your choice between fresh air, elbow-room, and the
risk of a wetting, or one-fifteenth share in a tightly closed
bell-tent, a thick atmosphere, and a partial security against
rain. The men grew very skilful in constructing " bivvies,"
made of a couple of groundsheets and a stick or two, and
this was just as well, for, though we did not know it, we
were to spend the next two months with a limited supply
of tents in most indifferent weather.

The move from Morbecque to La Neuville had been the
Regiment's longest continuous march since the war began,
and it may be of interest to note, as an example of the rate
at which cavalry travels, moving comfortably and entirely
without haste, that they had covered about 78 miles in

seven days, or an average of 13 miles a day, with one day's
rest. Of course they can, and did at earlier and later stages
of the war, easily do double, or if necessary even treble,
that distance, and the comparative shortness of our marches
on this occasion was, no doubt, partly due to the necessity
of adjusting our movements and halting-places to the
movements of other troops. And the paramount necessity
of finding water for the 6,000 or 7,000 horses of a cavalry
division is a constant problem for the " Q " staff when a
move is in progress. Grumbling about billets was a daily
occupation for most people, often with good cause, but they
overlooked the difficulties. The 2nd Cavalry Division was
fortunate in its A.A. and Q.M.G., Lieutenant-Colonel A. J.
McCulloch, who always looked after it well.

We were now at last in the Somme country, about a day's
march behind the old front line, but quite double that
distance from the front as it was now after two and a half
months' solid fighting. We knew that another great " push "
was coming off very soon, and that, if successful, it was
hoped to send the cavalry through the " gap," of which we
had already heard so much and seen so little.

At first we thought it rather nice country here—rather
like the Berkshire downs—but later we grew to dislike it
only less than the Hazebrouck flat.

On the 13th and 14th September we did a little squadron
training, and the Colonel and squadron leaders went up to
see the route across the trenches. Six more Hotchkiss
rifles were issued to complete establishment.

Friday, 15th September, we were up betimes, and marched
at 5.15 a.m., reaching camp at Dernancourt, near Albert, at
8.15 ; seven miles in three hours ! Space was very limited,
billets did not exist, and we pitched camp by the roadside.
At ten o'clock the Brigadier explained the situation to
Colonels and squadron leaders. This was roughly as follows :

The Fourth Army (General Rawlinson) was attacking
the enemy defences between the Combles ravine and
Martinpuich, with the object of seizing the quadilateral
Morval–Lesbœufs–Gueudecourt–Flers. The Reserve Army

(General Gough) was attacking simultaneously on the left, and a French corps on the right of the Fourth Army. Tanks were being used for the first time. It was anticipated that the infantry would reach their objective within five and a half hours of zero (6.20 a.m.).

The general plan of operations was to establish a flank facing east, while the bulk of the Fourth and Reserve Armies advanced northwards towards Sapignies–Achiet le Grand–Miraumont, the cavalry covering their right flank.

The Cavalry Corps, which had been broken up in February, had been recently re-formed under Lieutenant-General Kavanagh, and consisted of five divisions, all of which were now concentrated in the neighbourhood, at the disposal of the Fourth Army.

The objective of the 2nd Cavalry Division was Bapaume and the high ground north of it, reconnaissance of the country west of the line Bapaume–Noreuil, and the destruction of the Cambrai–Boyelles railway. The 3rd Cavalry Brigade as advanced guard was to pass Gueudecourt, throw out flank protective detachments, hold high ground, and push forward reconnaissances towards Vaulx, Sapignies, and Ervillers, while the 5th Cavalry Brigade, following the 3rd, was to be prepared to send a detachment to destroy the railway at Achiet le Grand. The 4th Cavalry Brigade was in reserve.

It was an ambitious scheme which came to nothing, the infantry attack not getting as far as was hoped.

From 10 a.m. onwards we stood-to, ready to move at half an hour's notice. Heavy bombardment was heard all day, and aeroplanes were very active. In the evening it turned very cold, and a few tents were issued, but we had to hand them in again next morning, " for fear of their being left behind in the event of a sudden move."

For the next four days we stood-to at one hour's notice. " Patrols were sent to Fricourt, Mametz, and Carnoy," to reconnoitre the route for the cavalry, if required to advance.

The weather broke on the evening of the 17th, and it

rained almost incessantly for several days. The scene of
desolation presented by the horse lines was unimaginable :
a stretch of ground about a mile long by 400 yards broad,
every available inch occupied by horses, with a few dozen
tents dotted here and there, and the whole surface churned
into a state of mud and slush, where men reeled and staggered
as they walked, sinking over their ankles at every step.

The officers were not so badly off. They were wet,
muddy, and uncomfortable, but had good mackintoshes
and at least a partial change of clothing, and were able
to keep their blankets tolerably dry. But the men and
horses were in a pitiable condition. Nearly all the former
had got tents or shelters of some kind, but few had mackintoshes or any change of clothing, and their " British warms "
soon got sodden through. Also it was practically impossible
for them to keep their blankets dry. A rum ration was
issued on the 18th, the mere rumour of which led to an
immediate and universal outburst of song throughout
the camp.

As for the horses, they looked and were miserable.

Tents had been reissued after the first day. Inside any
one of them, straw, blankets, boots, mackintoshes, mirrors,
helmets, rifles, etc., lay about in confusion most of the day,
after a compulsory tidying-up for inspection by an officer
every morning.

A divisional scheme in conjunction with aeroplanes had
been arranged for the 20th, but had to be postponed owing
to weather conditions, and took place on the 21st instead.

On the 20th September " A " Squadron moved camp
about a quarter of a mile, to a drier piece of ground, and on
the following day the remainder of the Regiment did the
same. The " D " Squadron officers were much annoyed
at having to vacate an enormous wooden hut which they
were occupying. They accordingly formed the idea of
taking it with them. The posts were all loosened, and at a
given signal 90 men lifted the hut bodily out of the ground
and carried it half a mile to where a position had been prepared for it in the new lines.

On the 25th September we stood-to at one hour's notice
from 12.35 p.m. to 8 p.m.

For the next seven weeks we remained under canvas in
the mud, waiting to go through the " gap " which was
never made. Danger there was none, except one night
when an " aeroplane dropped bombs round the camp about
9.15 p.m., one bomb killing one 3rd Hussar and wounding
three, and killing 12 and wounding 13 horses." (Diary,
25th September.) Discomfort there was a great deal;
boredom there was even more.

The boredom was relieved by occasional visits to Albert,
where men looked at the gilt Virgin suspended face down-
wards in the air on the top of the ruined church tower. It
was commonly said that when she fell the war would come
to an end, but as a matter of unromantic fact she was
finally dislodged some time in the great German offensive
of 1918. Others said that she had been carefully secured in
position by French engineers. Anyway, it was a striking
spectacle. Albert had no other attractions, and was an
" unhealthy " spot, much searched by shell fire.

There were several cages full of German prisoners near our
camp. Some of our officers got into conversation with
them. Some had been on the Eastern Front, and said the
fighting in the west was much worse, particularly the shell
fire. Asked what their cavalry was doing, they said they
worked in the fields and rode their horses, and didn't go
into the trenches. (This was not strictly true, for German
cavalry regiments were occasionally identified opposite our
line ; but a British infantryman would probably have given
a very similar answer about our cavalry.) They said they
were very well fed in their army. They were all dirty and
unkempt, but not more so than might be expected of men
recently captured.

Then there were the new tanks, which we sometimes
saw, and which naturally were objects of great interest.

A great deal of useful work was put in training, the ground
providing good opportunities for brigade and regimental field
days on a large scale, besides ordinary squadron schemes.

And, of course, after no long time, the inevitable working parties were called for. The first of these was sent up on the night of the 3rd October, and others followed later at frequent intervals. The majority were not permanent, but returned after the work had been done. They generally had about ten or twelve miles to go, riding across country the whole way, to avoid blocking the roads. They were supposed to use the famous " cavalry track," so called, which rapidly became an almost impassable sea of mud. More bad language was heard on these hideous night journeys than on most other occasions of the war ; rain, wind, darkness, utter weariness, horses floundering hock deep in the mud, officers struggling to make out the way by the light of an Orilux lamp and a wet map flapping in the wind, men trying to keep touch, and at the end of several hours' riding, a march on foot carrying rifles and tools, and finally only an hour or two's work before they were ordered back to the Regiment. That was the usual programme.

Some officers made private expeditions to the battlefield round Delville and Trones Wood and elsewhere, and were vividly impressed.

" The whole ground is so utterly torn up by shell fire that there is no single piece of ground between the shell holes broad enough for a single horse to walk on. . . . There were boots with feet in them, helmets with heads in them, half-buried corpses, dead men lying on their backs with their arms stretched out, their faces so blackened with congealed blood that at first sight one took them for black men. The blue-black-purple colouring of their faces and the ' grinning ' look of their bared teeth if seen in a picture would have been condemned as exaggerated and unreal." (Officer's letter.)

The Diary notes that the weather during October was " very bad, particularly towards the latter end of the month, when work was quite stopped. The first week of November also was very wet and windy, no training possible."

The following officers were serving with the Regiment on 31st October 1916 :

Headquarters : Lieutenant-Colonel A. Dugdale (Commanding), Major V. Fleming (Second-in-Command), Lieutenant J. J. Pearce, Lieutenant A. W. Keith-Falconer (Acting Adjutant), Lieutenant H. E. Evetts (Signalling Officer), Lieutenant J. L. Goldie (Quartermaster), Captain S. E. Whitnall, R.A.M.C. (Medical Officer), Captain H. C. Jagger, A.V.C. (Veterinary Officer).

"A" Squadron : Major R. E. U. Hermon-Hodge, Captain H. A. Fane, Lieutenant L. Winterbottom, Lieutenant R. L. Worsley, Second-Lieutenant H. H. Smetham, Second-Lieutenant A. E. MacColl. (*Note.*—Captain Fane was away sick for a few weeks at the end of October.)

"C" Squadron : Major P. Fleming, Captain G. H. Palmer, Lieutenant E. H. Chinnery, Lieutenant F. S. J. Silvertop, Lieutenant H. M. Worsley, Second-Lieutenant A. C. Rawlinson, Second-Lieutenant H. D. Savory, Second-Lieutenant H. J. Soame, Second-Lieutenant F. Holford.

"D" Squadron : Major Hon. A. G. C. Villiers, Captain W. Pepper, Lieutenant G. V. Wellesley, Lieutenant E. W. H. Allfrey, Second-Lieutenant R. C. Byass, Second-Lieutenant R. Lakin, Second-Lieutenant J. A. P. Whinney, Second-Lieutenant C. T. Hardy.

On the 6th November General Chetwode came to say good-bye to the Brigade, on leaving the 2nd Cavalry Division to take up a command in Egypt. He was succeeded by Major-General W. H. Greenly.

The autumn was now so far advanced, and the weather so awful, that it had for some time been evident that the cavalry could not be usefully employed on the Somme. Men and horses had been living in the mud for fifty-four days, and though their discomforts were trifling compared with those of the infantry in the trenches, the combination of discomfort with inaction, and the feeling that one was doing nothing to help win the war and apparently serving no useful purpose, had become depressing. Officers and men were more " fed up " than perhaps ever before or after during the war. Moreover, they were likely to deteriorate in efficiency if they remained idle in the mud much longer.

At first there had at least been the advantage of abundant opportunities for mounted training on the wide spaces of the Somme country, especially after harvest time. But, as we have seen, no training of any kind had been possible since about the 20th October, and the horses were rapidly losing condition from standing out in the wet. Good grooming was difficult in any case in the incessant rain, and was rendered more so by the perpetual absence of men away on working parties. So there was general satisfaction when the Division received orders at last to return to billets, although many reflected uneasily that once again the cavalry were marching back from the battle with never shot fired or sword drawn in help of the infantry.[1] The little we had done had been but hewing of wood and drawing of water.

The Regiment left camp at 9.15 a.m. on the 8th November, after a day and a night of pouring rain, and marched about 12 miles to Bussy, where they arrived at 2.15 p.m. and went into bivouac. From there we marched next day at 7.45 a.m. past the outskirts of Amiens to Belloy-sur-Somme (16 miles), arriving at 1.15 p.m. and going into billets for the first time for eight weeks. We left at 9 o'clock the following day and marched 17 miles to Caours, where we arrived at 2.30 p.m., " after a most enjoyable march through beautiful country."

We continued our march at 9.30 a.m. on the 11th November, and reached our final destination at Vaulx (17½ miles) at 2.10 p.m.

The date has no special importance, and only a coincidence attracts attention to it now. No one knew that " half-time " was already over, and though another long holiday was just beginning for the cavalry, there was no interval for the infantry and no official declaration of the score. The war had become so much a matter of routine that it was difficult to imagine any other form of existence. Men dimly recalled the days before the war, more vividly

---

[1] This is not true of all the cavalry ; at least one regiment had been in action for a time, and there were a few casualties in all. But it is broadly true of the general feeling of most cavalry officers at that time.

the eager days of 1914, the elation and excitement of first
going into action, fought their old battles and played their
old parts again, but few cared to think too closely of the
future. Vaguely one longed for peace as for a time when one
might reasonably hope to live and could make plans for the
future without a sense of tempting fate. The wiser did not
think, but lived for the present. One thing only seemed
certain. Victory could not come without a break-through
on a far greater scale than any yet attempted, and pro-
portionately greater casualties. So it seemed best to enjoy
what pleasant things might come one's way, rare intervals
of leave, pleasant rides about the country, football, good
billets while one had them, and the constant society of one's
friends.

The Regiment, which some wit had nicknamed " the
agricultural cavalry " in 1914, had changed greatly in the
past two years. Already in 1915 staff officers and regular
officers were beginning to admit its equality in value with
the Regular cavalry, though they might qualify the implied
compliment by the reflection that the Regular cavalry was
no longer what it was in 1914. Still, all questions between
professional and amateur eliminated, there can, I think, be
no denial that the Regiment had considerably increased in
efficiency since its first appearance at the front. Then it
possessed certain distinctive qualities, which have already
been sufficiently enlarged upon in an earlier chapter, but
it necessarily fell below the high standard of the pre-war
Regular cavalry in some points. Two examples, in which
there had since been marked improvement, may be quoted.
The first is musketry. Everybody knows the amazing
brilliance and accuracy of the " Old Army " in this respect.
The Regiment was very patchy on the range when war began;
it had some very good shots, but the general standard of
performance was very unequal, which is hardly surprising,
considering the little time devoted to practice. As a result
of constant effort after mobilization, both in England and
in France, it had reached a very fair degree of skill by the
end of October 1914, but there was still much room for im-

provement. Men occasionally let off rifles when they
were not intended to, while fire-control and accurate range-
finding were not the strong points of all the officers. By the
end of 1916 enormous progress had been made in all branches
of musketry, and in addition a proportion in each troop had
been trained as Hotchkiss gunners.

A second very notable improvement had taken place in
what, for want of a more comprehensive term, may be called
" march discipline," though really going beyond the more
limited meaning of that phrase. In the early days a sudden
turnout was apt to result in squadrons assembling at all
sorts of different places and at every time except the right
one, and though commonsense generally put matters right,
the regimental rendezvous was not always a scene of military
order. But by the summer of 1915 the Adjutant could rely
on squadrons moving to a given place at a given time with
the punctuality of a Regular unit. Indeed by 1916 they
did it better than some Regulars.

In minor matters too, there had been all kinds of changes
towards a more military and professional standard. The
men had long since learnt to salute in a proper style and on
the proper occasions, whether mounted or on foot ; the
orderly-room had been entirely reorganized under Captain
Hutchinson's adjutancy, and an orderly room clerk [1]
appointed, so that orders were now issued and returns
collected with a regularity unknown in 1914–15 ; a signalling
section had been formed under a trained signalling officer,
and an efficient telephone service maintained between
squadrons and Regimental Headquarters ; approved sanitary measures were strictly supervised and enforced ; men's
kits and equipment constantly inspected and kept up to
date by squadron and troop officers, who were held responsible for reporting deficiencies. Only perhaps in the matter
of horsemanship was there not much room for improvement
on the 1914 standard ; and that standard was generally well
maintained.

[1] Sergt. Turrill ; in more peaceful days assistant engineer to the Cor-
poration of Oxford.

If some at times regretted the change from the informal, somewhat happy-go-lucky soldiering of 1914, the disappearance of some old friends and the arrival of strange faces among officers and men, and—what was more serious—the gradual falling-off in the supply of suitable officers, if something had been lost of the all-round high character, intelligence, and initiative in the non-commissioned ranks, there can be no doubt that the Regiment had gained much in the more strictly professional parts of military efficiency.

CHAPTER VIII

ARRAS—GILLEMONT—CAMBRAI

(12th November 1916—20th March 1918)

THE middle of November saw the Regiment comfortably installed in permanent winter billets, Headquarters and " D " Squadron at Vaulx, " C " Squadron at Le Ponchel, and " A " Squadron at Willencourt, all within a mile or two of each other and of Auxi-le-Château, a pleasant market-town where we did our shopping. But the prospect was less bright on the evening of our arrival. Regimental Headquarters were all right, indeed better off than they had ever been before, so far as officers were concerned, as they had got a very good château entirely at their disposal. Of the rest, " A " Squadron were very well off, and " D " Squadron made themselves pretty comfortable after a few days. But " C " Squadron were unlucky, and drew the worst billet, La Neuville, a tiny hamlet in the " A " Squadron area, where they spent six uncomfortable days, with their horses in the open, until the persistent efforts of Major V. Fleming practically forced Brigade Headquarters to give the Regiment the village of Le Ponchel.

The year closed uneventfully, and the Diary disposes of the last six weeks in a single sentence :

" The remainder of the month and the whole of the month of December has been devoted to getting comfortable in billets, clipping horses, cleaning all kit and equipment, followed by winter training consisting of equitation, skill at arms, musketry, signalling, twelve new signallers being trained, map reading, scouting, etc."

On 20th November Mr. Collier, the Regimental Sergeant-Major, had to go to hospital in England. He had almost completely lost his voice, and though he seemed quite

177

confident that he would get right and come out again, he died of consumption in June 1917.

During the first eighteen months of the war he had been a pillar of strength to " C " Squadron, and a constant help and support, first to Major Nicholl, and then to Major Val Fleming, his squadron leaders, who always thought very highly of him. His promotion to be R.S.M. in February 1916, at the same time as Major Fleming became Second-in-Command of the Regiment, was a serious loss to his old squadron, but he never forgot his old friends there and always took a special interest in their welfare and efficiency. The perpetual office work at Headquarters was not much to his taste ; his greatest wish was for real cavalry fighting and a chance to use his sword, failing which, he was happiest in the front trenches. If perhaps he seemed rather stern and grim to those who did not know him well, especially to young officers and men, he was always popular with the sergeants and respected by the senior officers. He was a fine soldier and a brave man.

Squadron Sergeant-Major Matheson, Royal Scots Greys, was appointed Regimental Sergeant-Major in his place.

Second-Lieutenant E. G. Howarth joined from England on the 27th November, and was posted to " D " Squadron. Lieutenant Chinnery went home on leave on the 11th December, fell ill, and was sent to hospital. After a long period of illness and convalescence he was sent before a medical board and invalided out of the service in June 1917. Second-Lieutenant Byass went to hospital with a dislocated elbow on the 26th December, was sent to England, and did not return again to France.

The country round Vaulx and Le Ponchel was very jolly—rolling hills and pretty valleys. We had some grand walks and rides.

Ten or twelve miles from our billets was the village of Crécy, where the English defeated the French in 1346. The battlefield, like most others, was just a stretch of bare ploughed fields without hedges, and has probably changed little in appearance since the fourteenth century.

A BAD BILLET.
(Near Ypres, 1915.)

VAULX CHÂTEAU.
(Regimental Headquarters, November 1916—February 1917.)

Leave reopened, at first for very small numbers, afterwards increased. All the men who came out with the
Regiment had had two leaves, and the May 1915 draft were
now going for the first time.

Some time in December the sergeants of a squadron of
the Scots Greys came over and had a shooting match with
the " D " Squadron sergeants and " got properly beat and
so they did in the evening." (Sergeant Stroud's Diary.)

Christmas Day was celebrated in the traditional manner :
sports in the morning, turkeys and plum-puddings for dinner,
and a concert in the evening.

On Tuesday the 26th the officers had a regimental dinner
at Vaulx Château, at which we mustered twenty-three all
told. Thanks largely to the inspiration and energy of Major
Val Fleming, and to the excellent arrangements of the
Quartermaster (Lieutenant Goldie), it was a tremendous
success. This was the first occasion on which all the officers
had dined together since they left St. Omer in October
1914, and it was also the only attempt at a regimental
dinner, properly so called, between July 1914 and June
1919.

On the 31st December Lieutenant Pearce left the Regiment and became officers' riding instructor at the Third
Army School at Auxi-le-Château.

The strength of the Regiment at the end of the year
was : officers 31, of whom 4 were away sick ; other ranks
585, including the dismounted party of 89 ; horses complete.

All through December the weather had been getting
steadily colder, and there had already been snow. With
the New Year came bitter frosts and more snow, lasting
well into February.

On the 7th January 1917 the Brigade supplied a pioneer
battalion for railway construction at Savy, halfway
between Arras and St. Pol. " Pioneer battalion " was
merely a glorified name for a digging party, one-third being
found by each regiment in the Brigade. Major Fleming
was in command of the battalion, and Captain Pepper in
command of the Oxford Hussars company, the Regiment

13

providing 10 officers and 240 men in all. The only noteworthy incident was a wagon-load of shells catching fire
and the contents exploding. No record remains of what
actually happened, but Major Fleming was specially thanked
in Corps Orders for his work at the time.

For the next two months the Regiment remained in
billets " with about two men to five horses, and classes of
instruction and training were carried on as far as circumstances would permit." (Regimental Diary.)

A Divisional School was opened for the purpose of instruction in the various branches of cavalry training and tactics.
There were three courses, each lasting three weeks, and three
officers per regiment attended each course. The object
was to train present and future squadron leaders, and all
squadron leaders, seconds-in-command, and senior troop
leaders were sent in turn.

Captain Whitnall, the Medical Officer, left in January
and was succeeded by Captain F. A. Grange, R.A.M.C. ;
Second-Lieutenant C. H. Bottomley joined the Regiment on
the 21st January and was posted to " C " Squadron ;
Second-Lieutenant Savory left the Regiment on the
12th January.

Major Villiers relieved Major V. Fleming in command of
the pioneer battalion on the 9th February.

On the same day Major Nicholl and Lieutenant Weatherby
returned from England, the former after twenty months
in command of the second line. Their return involved
considerable re-shuffling of officers. Major Nicholl resumed
his former position as Second-in-Command of the Regiment ; Major V. Fleming went back to command " C "
Squadron, displacing his brother Philip, who became
second-in-command once more, and reverted to the rank of
captain ; Captain Palmer, from second-in-command of
" C " Squadron, became a troop leader again ; Lieutenant
Weatherby resumed his duties as Adjutant, displacing
Lieutenant Keith-Falconer, who, however, remained at
Headquarters as Assistant Adjutant and Intelligence Officer.

Leave to England was again stopped on the 9th February

for all below the rank of Lieutenant-Colonel, on account of
the congestion of traffic on the railways. By way of compensation, leave to Paris was easy to obtain, and now began
to become rather fashionable, at least for officers. As long
ago as Christmas 1914 Captain Gill had taken his leave in
Paris, and Lieutenants Weatherby and Wellesley had also
been there more than once during the war, but only now did
it become at all usual. Later some of the N.C.O.s and men
also went.

On the 28th February the Brigade moved to a new
billeting area. Regimental Headquarters and two squadrons
(" A " and " D ") went to Vron, 18¾ miles west of Vaulx,
and halfway between Abbeville and Montreuil on the main
Paris–Boulogne road, while " C " Squadron went to Les
Hallots, a little hamlet near by.

Vron is a large village, clean and prosperous, and the
billets were very good, by general consent about the best
we had had so far ; also the nearest to the sea that we had
ever been, about 7 miles off. " C " Squadron had again
drawn what they thought much the worst billet, but, though
it did not appear promising to begin with, they eventually
settled down and were quite comfortable. So everybody
was happy—except perhaps the officers who had just
returned from leave in Paris and found even the best billets
unendurable for a time.

The country round was very low-lying and our billets
were only 35 feet above sea-level. There were very big
woods, where " C " Squadron were, full of wild boar and
other animals, including a few foxes.

Nothing much happened during March. Second-Lieutenants B. H. Matthews, W. B. Riddell, D. H. Williams,
and S. B. Wood joined the Regiment on the 4th, and
Lieutenant Evetts went to hospital on the 21st. On the
6th the pioneer battalion returned, and on the 25th a
working party of 2 sergeants, 2 corporals, and 38 men under
Second-Lieutenant Holford was sent to the forward area
near Arras, where they lost two men killed by shell fire on
the 29th.

Towards the end of February the Germans began to evacuate their positions on the Somme, and by the middle of March they were in full retreat all along that sector of the line. We were all rather wondering whether we should be moved up in pursuit, but no orders came, and we were merely kept very busy training—principally troop and squadron work, with musketry instruction and Hotchkiss rifle drill, occasional regimental and brigade schemes and staff rides.

On the 17th March the final for the Dugdale Football Cup was played off, No. 2 Troop, " D " Squadron, beating No. 3 of the same squadron by 1 goal to 0, amid great enthusiasm. (The cup had been won by No. 2 Troop, " C " Squadron, the year before.) And among other amusements at this time many will remember the famous " D " Squadron concert and *tableaux vivants* on the 8th March, with Adam and Eve, Peeping Tom and Lady Godiva as the chief features of the bill. The Colonel was present, and is said to have been much shocked.

The long frost had come to an end late in February, but the weather still continued desperately cold right up to the end of March.

Training continued till the 5th April. On the previous day the dismounted party was sent to railhead ; Lieutenant Winterbottom was evacuated to hospital, and did not return to the Regiment again ; three other junior officers were sent back to the Base, there to remain as reinforcements ; and orders were received to move billets on the 6th. Next day these orders were cancelled, and on the following day (April 6th) fresh orders came to move on the 7th.

At 9 a.m. on Saturday, 7th April, the Regiment moved 24 miles to billets at Bealcourt, near Auxi-le-Château, having previously dumped a good deal of superfluous kit at Vron in order to lighten the transport for action. Everybody knew there was going to be another attempt at a " gap," and of course we were assured it was bound to come off this time. But repeated failures had somewhat dulled enthusiasm. Still, most people tried to be hopeful.

On the 8th April, Easter Sunday, at 1 p.m., the Regiment moved to huts at Pas, 7 miles east of Doullens—rather a tiring march, only 15 miles, and nearly seven hours in doing it. Heavy transport was left at Bealcourt. Up till Sunday night the weather had been fine, but it began to rain again early Monday morning (9th April) and turned to sleet and snow. On arrival at Pas, orders had been received for one squadron to be attached to the 3rd Cavalry Brigade, and " A " Squadron (Major Hermon-Hodge) was detailed for this duty.

The battle was timed to begin at 5.30 a.m. on the 9th, on a front of nearly 15 miles from Croisilles, south-east of Arras, to Givenchy-en-Gohelle, south-west of Lens. The attack was entrusted to the First Army (General Horne) on the left, and to the Third Army (General Allenby) on the right. The main objective on the left was the Vimy Ridge, on the right Monchy-le-Preux hill, but apart from the gaining of ground, one purpose of the operations was to draw enemy forces from other parts of the front, notably from Champagne, where the French were preparing a large-scale offensive for the 15th. If the Third Army captured Monchy-le-Preux, it was intended to attack and capture part of the Hindenburg Line between Arras and Cambrai.

The Cavalry Corps was disposed as follows : three divisions to the Third Army, one to the First Army, and one in G.H.Q. reserve. The 2nd Cavalry Division was allotted to the Third Army, and was to move on the right, with the 3rd Cavalry Division on the left. The prospective area of operations by these two divisions lay south of the river Scarpe, where the front was crossed diagonally by the rivers Cojeul and Sensée. The 2nd Cavalry Division was ordered to secure as its first objective a line on the right bank of the Sensée River from Fontaine-les-Croisilles (inclusive) to Vis-en-Artois (exclusive), and, on relief by infantry, to advance to its second objective, the line Riencourt-lez-Cagnicourt (exclusive) to the high ground north-west of Villers-lez-Cagnicourt, as far north as the Arras–Cambrai road. Detachments were to be pushed forward to

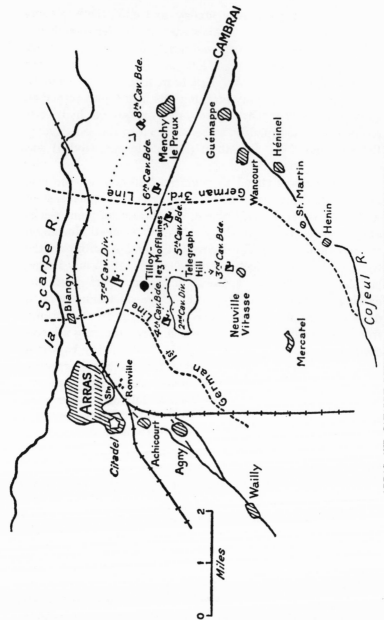

ARRAS, 2ND CAVALRY DIVISION AT THE BATTLE OF THE SCARPE, 1917.

the line of the Canal du Nord. It was emphasized in Orders
that the enemy was to be pursued with the utmost vigour,
every endeavour made to turn his retirement into a rout,
and in the event of success the pursuit pressed to the
utmost limit of the strength of men and horses. " When
we do start it must be understood we go all out." (2nd
Cavalry Division message to Brigades, 9.10 a.m., 11th April
1917.)

But before these objectives could be even hoped for,
much less attained, it was essential that the German third
line astride the Scarpe should be broken, and the villages
of Héninel, Wancourt, and Guémappe, in the Cojeul Valley,
captured. Not till the third day of the battle was Monchy
taken, and even then the line Héninel–Wancourt–Guémappe
was still resisting strongly at 11 a.m. Hopes of breaking
it ran high for a time, and the leading cavalry brigades were
ordered to be ready to push forward immediately it was
possible for them to cross the Cojeul. But at 2.15 p.m.
there were still conflicting reports about Wancourt, and,
though General Greenly was told by Third Army Headquarters that it was in our hands, he did not believe it, and
sent patrols to find out the true state of affairs. They found
the enemy still in possession, and the Division was presently withdrawn, all hopes of further cavalry action being
abandoned.

But we anticipate, and must return to the Regiment,
which we left at Pas on the eve of the battle.

At 9.30 a.m on Monday the 9th orders were received for
the detached squadron to report immediately to the 3rd
Cavalry Brigade, and at 9.50 further orders came for the
rest of the Regiment to be ready to move at one hour's
notice. At 10.5 " A " Squadron left camp to report to the
3rd Cavalry Brigade, and at 10.15 the Regiment was ordered
to be at the brigade concentration point at 11 o'clock. We
moved off at 10.45, just as the snow stopped and the sun
came out. We were the last regiment of the Division. An
officer who was sent on as liaison officer to Divisional
Headquarters had to ride by the whole of the column and

did not reach the head till 2.30, which gives some idea of the length of a division on the road. The Regiment arrived at the position of readiness, near Tilloy-lez-Mofflaines, 2 miles south-east of Arras, at 4.45 p.m., but meanwhile the two leading brigades (3rd and 5th) had been sent forward along the cavalry track to follow up the infantry advance, which was reported to be going very well. (The " cavalry track " ran eastwards from Arras towards Wancourt, south of the Arras–Cambrai road.) " It was really quite exciting to see them going off with their Brigadier leading." For a moment, indeed, it looked as if the cavalry were going through at last, and hopes ran high.

" It was really almost like leaving covert at the beginning of a hunt, but we only got on a mile or two, and hadn't even seen any Boches, when we came to a check, owing to the infantry being held up by the last line of defence. This turned out to be the end of the day's proceedings. We hung about where we were till 8.15 p.m., when we got orders to go back to billets. We hardly got shelled at all." (Officer's letter.)

The Brigade returned to Wailly, 3 miles south-west of Arras, for the night, Major Hermon-Hodge's squadron remaining with the 3rd Cavalry Brigade in bivouac north-east of Wailly.

" We had a terrible march back to billets. . . . We had not started ten minutes before a terrific storm of rain came on, and it became as black as ink. We had to ride back across country along the cavalry track, with continual checks and stops and blocks and sudden moves on, with a blinding rain, tired horses, and trenches, pits, and wire to stumble into if you once got off the track or lost touch with the man in front of you, whom you could hardly see. We only had four or five miles to go, and took four hours. Got one filthy ruined house for a billet, but very glad of it." (Officer's letter.)

" Pegged horses out in a field, snowing hard, no rugs for horses, lot of men had to sleep behind their horse, owing to

such a small place and the Division occupying it. Several
men went to hospital sick." (Sergeant Stroud's Diary.)

Next morning (10th April) nothing happened till 1.50
p.m., when we got orders to move up again to the position
of readiness near Tilloy, which we had occupied the previous
day. Moved off at 3.15 and reached position at 4.30.

" We heard that we were probably going on, as the
opposition which had held us up the day before was now
reported by the infantry to be giving way. Two brigades
were therefore pushed on to the next position of readiness
about a mile behind the German front line as it existed on
Sunday. Our Brigade was held in reserve in the same
position as Monday, behind a ridge which had been the
German front line." (Officer's letter.)

The Brigadier went up on foot to the top of the ridge,
where one could see the village of Wancourt a mile or so to
the front lying in a hollow. The question was—who was
in it ? British or Germans, or both ? From the ridge, too,
could be seen the two other brigades advancing. They
had remarkably few casualties, only one or two chance
shells falling among them. But one of those few shells
caught a troop of " A " Squadron (still attached to
the 3rd Cavalry Brigade), and killed Sergeant Price (as
brave a man and as good an N.C.O. as any squadron ever
had), wounded two other men, and killed three horses. As
the others rode forward, Price, dying, called out : " Good
luck, No. 2 Troop."

The Brigadier watched the two forward brigades take up
their position, and send out patrols, and then sent word
back to the Divisional Commander to say that he proposed
to move his brigade up to the next position as soon as the
leading brigade moved on. Just at this moment a blinding
snowstorm came on and lasted for about an hour. But
at 7 p.m. the leading brigades were still in the same position.
We could not make out through our glasses what was holding
them up, but it turned out afterwards that some of the
villages ahead of them were still in possession of the enemy,

and the infantry situation was still obscure. The Divisional Commander decided that nothing further could be done that day, but gave orders for the Division to be in position again by 5 a.m. next day. We then withdrew to Arras, where we arrived at 8.45 p.m., watered and picketed the horses, and billeted ourselves in cellars.

We were up soon after three on Wednesday morning (11th April), and moved off at four to the brigade concentration point, and thence to the position of readiness near Tilloy, which we reached at 5.30. It was bitterly cold. There had been a sharp frost the night before and the ground was rocky hard. In addition to the frost a very cold wind blew fiercely all day. Between six and seven the 5th Cavalry Brigade was rather heavily shelled and 300 horses killed. At 12.30 p.m. our Brigade was sent up to relieve them near Monchy-le-Preux, and " A " Squadron rejoined the Regiment from the 3rd Cavalry Brigade. The tactical situation had become more or less stationary. At 3 p.m. General Greenly got orders to withdraw the whole Division to the billets they had occupied on the night of the 9th–10th. About 4.30 it began to rain hard, and then turned to snow. We reached our billets at Wailly about 6 p.m. Heavy snow was falling, everybody was more or less wet and cold, the horses were in a pitiable condition of cold, hunger, and fatigue, and the streets were flowing with liquid mud 6 or more inches deep. Also there were no billets except houses in a varying degree of ruin, hardly any with a whole roof, many with none at all.

The Commanding Officer had fortunately accumulated a good reserve ration of rum, which by his orders was now issued and served in the men's tea, whatever their creed about drink might be. It was much appreciated and did much more good than if it had been issued when received in billets at an earlier date. The Quartermaster did not want to issue it for fear the other regiments might be jealous, to which the Colonel replied : " Damn the other regiments ; I have carried that ration to be used when really required." And well used it was.

At 10.30 a.m. next day (12th April) the Regiment was

ordered to parade at the brigade concentration point at noon, whence we marched back to the huts at Pas, and arrived at 4.50 p.m., never having gone out of a walk. Here we found the heavy transport, and had a more comfortable night than for some days past.

The battle of Arras was over, as far as the cavalry were concerned. It had been an extremely trying time for both men and horses. The Division lost 394 horses killed, wounded, or missing, and 274 died of exhaustion ; total 668. The Brigade lost 76 killed, wounded, or missing, and 61 died of exhaustion ; total 137. Of these the Regiment had 14 killed, wounded, or missing, and only 2 died of exhaustion ; total 16. The high hopes of the first day had not been realized, and the battle had been at best but a partial success. The cavalry as a whole had not been able to do much, but some regiments, particularly in the 3rd Cavalry Division, had some stiff fighting.

The Regiment stayed in the huts at Pas for the next eight days, moderately uncomfortable in a sea of mud, but glad to have a roof over its head. On April 20th the billeting area was extended, and the majority of the Regiment moved into farms and cottages, the remainder into a better set of huts.

During the month reinforcements kept coming up in small numbers ; 26 other ranks and 29 horses from the base, and 3 officers and 79 other ranks rejoining from the dismounted party.

During the first three weeks of April the weather was very bad—frost, snow, and very cold winds. In consequence the horses had a very bad time. Spring being very late, there was very little grass, but every advantage was taken of what there was for grazing, and during the last week of the month the horses began to improve. Forage, which in March had been reduced to 4 lb. of oats and hay daily, owing to submarine losses and other difficulties, was now increased to 12 lb. each of oats and hay and 2 lb. of bran.

" The horses of the Regiment were inspected by the Corps Commander on the 22nd and he expressed satisfaction generally with their condition under the circumstances.

He was very strong on grazing and very little work."
(Regimental Diary.)

On the 29th April the Regiment was saddened by the
news of Lieutenant-Colonel Scott's death. He was killed
on the morning of the 23rd by a chance shot while leading
his battalion (8th Somerset Light Infantry) in an attack on
Greenland Hill, east of Arras.

At the very end of April the weather at last became quite
spring-like, beautifully warm and sunny. The first ten
days of May were a pleasant interval. There was nothing
much doing in the way of training ; the horses were taken
out to graze most days. We had just begun to wonder how
much longer we were going to remain in these billets when,
about the 9th or 10th of May, the rumour got about that
we were going to the Péronne area, to hold what was
supposed to be a very quiet sector of the line. And, sure
enough, on Saturday, 12th May, at 8.15 a.m., the Brigade
moved some 15 miles south to Villers Bocage, on the main
Doullens–Amiens road. Next day, at 7.45 a.m., we went
on to La Neuville, near Corbie, 12 miles distant. It was
an intensely hot day, and many were glad of a bathe in the
swiftly flowing Ancre that afternoon. Monday, the 14th,
at 8 a.m., the Brigade marched another 10 or 12 miles south-
east to Harbonnières. Here there were signs of war, and
the billets were less good. The village had been far behind
our line until a few months earlier, and the inhabitants
were only now beginning to return. On the following day
we marched at 7 a.m. to Hamelet, near Roisel, 5 or 6 miles
east of Péronne. This was a 21-mile trek, and we did not
get in till 2.30 p.m. The first part of the march was through
an absolutely devastated country, with hardly a stick or
stone standing, and all the ground ploughed up by shells and
the marks of troops. Then—soon after crossing the
Somme—we suddenly emerged into what looked just like
an English countryside, with hardly a sign of war, and quite
deserted by troops. It was our first view of the district
evacuated by the enemy in March without fighting, and

consequently spared the destruction of battle. The ground
not having been cultivated, grass had grown everywhere,
and gave the country quite a different aspect from that of
the ordinary French agricultural landscape. Small woods
and villages enclosed by trees were dotted here and there,
and as the trees were all in leaf, everything looked peaceful.
But whenever one passed through a village one found all
buildings burnt to the ground and everything destroyed.
In Tincourt there was a gigantic mine crater evidently
blown up by the Boche before leaving.

On our arrival at Hamelet we were glad to find Major
Val Fleming already there to welcome us. He had gone
home on special Parliamentary leave about ten days before,
and had started back from London on the 13th May.
Arriving at Pas late that night, he found the Regiment
gone and the huts deserted, and spent the next forty-eight
hours feverishly pursuing us in borrowed motor-cars.

We bivouacked in a field that night. The weather
immediately began to change, and next day was very cloudy.
Then it started to rain in earnest ; luckily some tents had
been issued just in time.

We heard that the Regiment was to take over the Gillemont Farm area, and we gathered that it was not altogether
the " cushy " sector that we had been led to expect.

It had been arranged that " C " Squadron was to take over
Gillemont Farm first, with " D " Squadron in support at
Lempire, and " A " in reserve at St. Emilie. This was to
be for five days, and then " C " were to come back to St.
Emilie, and " D " were to take over Gillemont.

After the first night in bivouac at Hamelet, " C " Squadron
had orders to go up to Lempire that night (16th May),
to take over the support position. Major Fleming and
Lieutenant Worsley went up to Gillemont during the day
to look round the position, and came back looking much
more serious than when they started.

The " C " Squadron officers to go up were Major V.
Fleming, Lieutenant H. M. Worsley, Lieutenant F. S. J.
Silvertop, and Second-Lieutenant C. H. Bottomley. Silver-

top and Rawlinson tossed up who should go, and it turned up for " Chops."

Squadron Sergeant-Major Grant and Squadron Quarter-master-Sergeant Maisey were the two senior N.C.O.s. The strength of the squadron was 4 officers and 105 men.

The afternoon before they went up was spent in getting everything ready, inspecting rifles and smoke helmets, arranging about bombs, ammunition, rations, and so forth. Major Fleming was always wonderfully thorough about that sort of thing, just making the difference between having a first-class fighting force and an indifferent one.

They paraded (dismounted) in the rain at 6.30 on a miserable evening (16th May), and started for their 4-mile march to Lempire, where they were all put into various billets—cellars, remains of stables, and bits of shelters. Here they came under the command of Lieutenant-Colonel W. T. Willcox, 3rd (K.O.) Hussars, commanding the left sub-sector of the Brigade front.

On the next day, the 17th, Major Fleming and Lieutenant Worsley again made a personal inspection of the position and defences at Gillemont Farm preparatory to taking over from the infantry that night. The squadron was ordered to parade at 9.30 p.m., ready for the trenches.

At seven the same evening " A " and " D " Squadrons (dismounted) left camp at Hamelet and marched up to Templeux-le-Guérard and Lempire respectively. Lempire is a small village about a mile west of Gillemont, and Templeux-le-Guérard another village a mile south of Lempire. Both were in ruins, but a good many houses were still standing, in a more or less demolished state, and in these, and particularly their cellars, the troops were billeted. The support squadron (" D ") was employed each night from 8 p.m. to 4 a.m. improving and fortifying a defensive position in a sunken road just outside Lempire.[1]

---

[1] " A " Squadron officers were Major Hermon-Hodge, Lieutenant R. L. Worsley, and Second-Lieutenant Smetham. " D " Squadron officers were Major Villiers, Lieutenant Keith-Falconer, and Second-Lieutenant Whinney. Sergeant Elliott was acting S.S.M. and Corporal Drake acting S.Q.M.S.

Before going further with the story we must briefly explain the situation and the nature of the ground in this part of the front. Both were something altogether new in our experience.

To begin with there was no continuous line at all, such as we had been accustomed to on all our previous excursions to the trenches since the first days of November 1914. Here there was only a chain of posts and entrenched positions, separated from one another by fairly considerable stretches of open ground. These gaps in the line were patrolled at night, but there was nothing to prevent substantial bodies of troops coming through and cutting off one or more of our posts. As a matter of fact, nothing of this sort occurred, but there were strange tales of small parties of two or three soldiers setting off on a message or other duty from one post to another and never being seen again. And certainly two officers of " D " Squadron, taking a stroll outside Lempire during the first night, with a view to familiarizing themselves with the way up to Gillemont, very quickly got off the track and began walking round in circles ; only the stars and a compass saved them from the Hun.

The cavalry were organized as follows. The Cavalry Corps was relieving the III Corps on the front between the Omignon River and Epéhy-Peizières. The 2nd Cavalry Division was relieving the 42nd Division on the front from Hargicourt (exclusive) to Peizières (inclusive). The front was divided into four sub-sectors, B.1, B.2, B.3, B.4. The 4th Cavalry Brigade, with the 12th Lancers and 20th Hussars, were to take over B.1 and B.2, and to be called Pitman's Brigade. The 3rd Cavalry Brigade, with the Scots Greys, were to take over B.3 and B.4, and to be called Bell-Smyth's Brigade. Pitman's Brigade held the right sector of the divisional front from Hargicourt (exclusive) to Lempire (inclusive), a distance of rather over 2 miles. One machine-gun squadron (12 guns) was allotted to each brigade. B.1, the right sub-sector, was held by the 6th D.G.s, with the 12th Lancers in support. B.2, the left sub-sector,

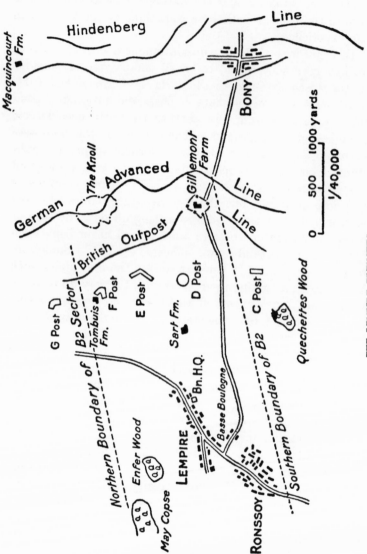

THE LEMPIRE TRENCHES.

under Colonel Willcox, was held by the 3rd Hussars, with
the 20th Hussars in support at Lempire. Gillemont Farm,
forming part of B.2, was held by one squadron of Oxfords,
with one in support at Lempire and one in reserve at St.
Emilie. The Scots Greys were in brigade reserve. Headquarters of the left sub-sector were at Lempire and Brigade
Headquarters at St. Emilie.

The defences on the front consisted of an outpost line ;
the main line of resistance known as the Green Line ; the
Brown Line and Brown Support Line. The Green and
Brown Lines each consisted of a series of mutually supporting
posts, the intervening ground being defended by wire and
the cross-fire of machine guns. The scheme of defence laid
down that, (a) in the case of local attacks, the outpost line
must be held, and in the event of the enemy penetrating
into any portion of it he must *at once* be counter-attacked
and ejected ; while (b) in the case of attack by the enemy in
force, the Green Line must be held at all costs, and "troops
holding the outpost line will do everything possible to delay
and break up the enemy's attack." Patrolling of No-
man's-land was to be undertaken actively every night, and
our patrols were to be stronger than those of the enemy.
One or two men in every patrol were told off to secure
identifications. For the first five or six days we were to
aim at getting to know the ground and the position of any
enemy advanced posts. Sub-sector commanders were to
prepare plans for raids and counter-attacks.

A Cavalry Corps Instruction, dated 14th May 1917, said :

" The policy laid down by the Army for the front held by
the Cavalry Corps is that a defensive attitude must be
adopted owing to the wide extent of front which has to be
held. In such a case a wide No-man's-land is of advantage
as opposed to advancing our trenches as near as possible to
those of the enemy when an offensive is contemplated. In
order to obtain a wide No-man's-land, a very active and
offensive attitude is imperative all along the front, so as to
prevent the enemy pushing forward his advanced line and
posts close to our front system."

14

Gillemont Farm was an important and rather isolated tactical point in the outpost line, and " a dangerous post " (Brigade Diary). The surroundings are as typical as any of Picardy, that part of France over which armies have fought and marched and camped ever since the days of Julius Cæsar two thousand years ago. It is a bare, bleak country of rolling, windswept uplands, sparsely populated and very lonely in time of peace. The farm stands near the western edge of a broad ridge or narrow tableland, 450 feet above sea-level, sloping gently westwards towards Lempire, much more steeply eastwards towards Bony. The comparatively steep slopes on the eastern side gave the Germans splendid cover from observation, where they could move freely, unseen except from an aeroplane. On our side, on the other hand, every movement was visible to German observation posts, until one reached the communication trench leading from the road to the farm ; this was accurately registered by the German gunners, and consequently afforded little comfort, if they chose to shell it. Fortunately they did not often do so, except during a raid. (It may be added that, though it was the middle of a hot May, this communication trench was ankle deep in water. Troops soon learnt to avoid it whenever possible.)

The farm had originally been an ordinary typical French farm, perhaps rather smaller than the average in this part of the country, surrounded by the usual outbuildings and ring of trees. The buildings were all in ruins now, and formed the No-man's-land between us and the enemy, in which listening posts and patrols crawled breathlessly and stealthily in the night watches. Our position consisted of a semicircular-shaped trench on the western side of the farm, with the two horns of the crescent running into the trees round the farm. At the end of the southernmost horn a small fire trench formed a T with the top facing the farm buildings. In front of this was a listening post. The disposition of the troops was no doubt altered from time to time to meet the varying exigencies of the situation, but in general, at any rate at first, squadron headquarters were in a dugout in

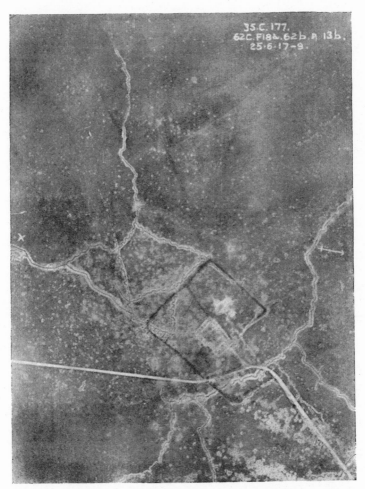

AEROPLANE PHOTOGRAPH OF GILLEMONT FARM.

the centre of the main trench, two troops were in the main trench, more or less in reserve, one troop in the right-hand T-shaped trench, and one troop on the left wing, facing half-left rather than straight to the front. Some distance to the right or south of the farm ran the second-class road from Lempire to Bony, on which there was a feeble barricade, but no post, picket, or sentry, so that it was easy enough to walk straight through to the German lines, or vice versa. Beyond the road was a Carabinier post. To the left or north of the farm was a fairly wide stretch of open country before one reached the nearest 3rd Hussar post, with which it was difficult to keep touch.

The existing situation at Gillemont Farm at the time of " C " Squadron's arrival was that on several occasions the Hun had raided the place, and on each occasion he had succeeded in getting in. The probability was that he would try again, but one thing was certain—that Major Fleming would never let his squadron be turned out of the position. Friends who saw him on his return from his preliminary tour of inspection observed that he looked unusually grave and serious, and it was evident that he foresaw a hard time ahead.

" C " Squadron left Lempire at 9.30 p.m. on the 17th and marched up to Gillemont Farm, where they took over from the infantry about midnight.

As usual in the trenches, an astonishing number of returns were called for daily, and the list of those required from the commander at Gillemont is a fair specimen of the amount of " office work " to be done in the front line.

(1) Situation Report, by runner, twice daily, 6 a.m. and 5 p.m.

(2) Report of work done during past twenty-four hours.

(3) Report of work to be done during next twenty-four hours.

(4) Casualty Report.

(5) R.E. Requirements.

Besides these, which were all rendered daily, there were

also a " Scheme of Defence " and a " Scheme of Routine " to be prepared and submitted to Headquarters on taking over.

The first night passed uneventfully. Major Fleming, accompanied by Sergeant Bull, carried out a valuable reconnaissance of the ground in front of his position, and his report is quoted below. (*Note.*—Code names were used for the various units while in the line. Thus " Will " means Headquarters ; " Val," " C " Squadron ; " Child," " D " Squadron, and so on.)

V.F. III. 18.V.17. 9.30 a.m.   VAL H.Q.   WILL.

Situation Report. Midnight 17/18—10 a.m. 18.V.17. Relief complete without incident 12.30 a.m. Night quiet— a few rifle grenades thrown short in Farm by enemy. Enemy scout started firing flares from enemy edge of Farm, stopped by our bomb and rifle fire. At dawn enemy working party came under our long-range rifle fire. 9.-9.30 a.m. Valley and commun. trench shelled by whiz-bangs. Between 2 and 3 a.m. Lieutenant H. Worsley and a corporal patrolled plateau N.E. of Farm. They found the enemy working on a continuous wired line corresponding roughly to line shown on aeroplane photographs, following roughly contour line 140 north and south of Gillemont. Judging from the sounds the enemy were making dugouts. They were able to [get ?] within 30 yards of the trench about 145 N. of Gillemont and could see plainly owing to the numerous flares sent up by the enemy.

At 4 a.m. I went out with a sergeant and found the ruins of the Farm quite clear of the enemy. I was able to get far enough down the sunken road leading to Bony to see the enemy working on a continuation of the line observed by Lieutenant Worsley. Owing to the dim light I cannot guarantee that this line is wired throughout, but parts of it were. Owing to being fired upon by an enemy sentry I returned to the Farm buildings and worked down the southern side, and was able to observe what was *apparently* the end of the wired portion of the enemy line behind Gillemont Farm. I saw three enemy in a wired sap at the extreme S. end of the line.

There were a large number of more or less continuous

enemy trenches running along the S.E. side of the valley through A.13.c. and A.19.a. but I could not see any enemy working on or holding them, nor could I see any wire.

I left my return rather late, and owing to the light and the observation from Bony was only able to instal one pair of snipers in the Farm, but they are in a position on the extreme enemy edge of the ruins from which they could stop any small parties or individuals from entering the Farm, and they are supported by converging fire from my forward right and left posts on the edge of the farm enclosure.

This evening I hope to establish two forward posts on the enemy edge of the Farm buildings, possibly one of them with a Hotchkiss.

I have ordered all my troops, posts, and snipers to avoid any offensive action pending the consolidation [? of the position] and to confine themselves to keeping the enemy out of what we have got.

I should be glad of an R.E. opinion this afternoon on the question of consolidating and connecting up the forward edge of the Farm.

VAL FLEMING, *Major, O.C.* " *C* " *Sqdn., O.H.*

On Friday, 18th May, everything was very quiet, except for a short period of heavy shelling in the afternoon, in which, however, only one man, Private Roads, was killed.

" In general, however, everything seems extraordinarily peaceful compared to the trenches we have formerly occupied. To begin with, one can stand up in the trench and survey the surrounding country, not with impunity, but with a certain degree of safety. At any rate, it is not certain death to show oneself within a mile of the line, as it used to be. Secondly, the whole country is green with grass everywhere, and trees are growing as usual, which is quite unlike the olden times." (Officer's letter.)

There was a great deal of work to be done : deepening saps to posts, strengthening posts, strengthening parapets, wiring, improvement of fire steps, draining communication trenches, improving squadron headquarters, etc. Most of this had to be done at night, to avoid observation, and the R.E. materials required were considerable. On one day alone the following were asked for :

> 100 sandbags ;
> 500 yards barbed wire ;
> 30 pairs wiring gloves ;
> 50 wire screw posts ;
> 50 sheets corrugated iron ; and
> 100 feet 4″ × 2″ : all most urgent.

From Major Fleming's " Orders in the Event of an Attack," issued at 4 p.m. on the 18th, we take the following :

" *Sniping posts* delay attack by rapid fire as long as possible. Post leader sends back a man immediately attack develops, with all information, and falls back himself on his strong-point.

" *Strong-points* . . . resist at all costs. Support furnished without further orders as follows . . . [Details omitted.]

" *S.O.S. signals* . . . not to be sent up without direct orders from O.C. Sqdn.

" No attention to be paid to casualties until attack has been repulsed."

" A " Squadron (in reserve) moved this day from Templeux-le-Guérard to St. Emilie, about a mile behind Lempire.

Next day, Saturday, the 19th, Gillemont Farm was shelled with gas shells, and the garrison had a trying time. By his reports (quoted below) Major Fleming obviously felt that the storm was brewing, and at his request a troop of " D " Squadron [1] was sent up to Gillemont, and a troop of " A " Squadron [2] sent up to take its place in support at Lempire.

V.F.XI. 19.V.17. 2 p.m. VAL H.Q. WILL.

Situation Report No. III. 3 a.m.–3 p.m. 19.V.17. My first post in Farm was approached by about ten enemy at 2 a.m. On being fired on at short range they ran away. Otherwise night quiet except for two half-hours of enemy

---

[1] No. 1, under Sergeant Sansom.

[2] No. 4, under Second-Lieut. Smetham.

H.E. shelling on farm buildings.   A few bombs were thrown
at left sniper's post at dawn.

From 8.30 a.m. persistent though not very heavy shelling
of farm buildings and support trench by enemy guns of all
calibres, from 5.9 to rifle grenades.   About eighty gas shells
were burst in forward post area.   Enemy trench mortar fired
about 12 rounds during luncheon interval.

Our own 18-pdrs. and 4.5s dropped a number of shells into
and behind my localities about 10 a.m. (time not guaranteed).
No casualties known of.

Owing to gas shells no work possible except among left
Troop.   Owing to lack of sleep it will be difficult to remain
here longer than four days, i.e. each two troops have forty-
eight hours in advanced posts and snipers' posts.   I am
reserving the fifth troop for supports and working parties.

My dispositions for to-night will be as per plan and
accompanying notes,[1] unless any change unknown to me is
necessitated among snipers' posts.   If so, I will advise you.

Reference to your personal letter, I am still in visual touch
with KIRB'S left post, but have not yet received map
reference his left locality's H.Qrs. asked for in my wire
V.F.1.   Would you be so kind as to notify KIRB's left and
your " E " and " D " Posts that I shall not require M.G.
support until S.O.S. signal is sent up.   It may be given then
without further request from me.

VAL FLEMING, *Major, O.C. " C " Sqdn., O.H.*

No shelling 1.30–2.30 p.m.

Saturday evening was calm and still, and all shelling had
died down.   The weather had improved, and the last day
or two had been warm and sunny.   The usual working party
from " D " Squadron went out at dusk, but for some reason
or other returned to Lempire earlier than usual, and was in
billets by midnight.   Up at Gillemont all was quiet.

But the shelling began again, and at 1 a.m. on the 20th
May Major Fleming replied to an inquiry from Headquarters :
" My squadron holds its locality."   Then later :

No. V.F.XV.   Date 20.V.17.   Time 2.30 a.m.
Situation Report No. IV. 3 p.m.–3 a.m. 19.V.17.   All quiet
3 p.m.–7 p.m.   Thence to 9 p.m. gradually increasing

[1] Omitted.

shelling by heavy enemy H.E.s thickened towards 9 p.m. by trench mortars and gas shells.

This was the last message received from Major Fleming. Suddenly the storm broke. Almost exactly at 3 a.m. the Germans began a hurricane bombardment of Gillemont Farm with heavy guns and trench mortars, which lasted about half an hour. Presumably most of the squadron took what shelter they could in the rather inadequate trenches, and practically all we know of this period is that at some moment —the exact time is not known—Major Fleming was going up from his squadron headquarters to the right-hand sector of the line, and that about ten yards from the front line he probably met Silvertop, and a shell landed on the trench and killed them both instantaneously. No one saw them killed, but the bodies were found lying on the top of the parapet, from which it has been supposed that they climbed out of the communication trench with the intention of taking a short cut to the troop in the advanced trench on the right. The time was probably about 3.30 a.m.

The Diary merely says :

" 3.30 a.m. After artillery preparation the enemy attacked the Farm and was repulsed with loss by our barrage and rifle fire. Two prisoners were captured. During the bombardment Major V. Fleming and Second-Lieutenant Silvertop were killed by a shell ; 3 O.R.s also killed by shell fire and 5 wounded, of whom one died during the day. Major Villiers took his Squadron part way up in support and himself went through the enemy barrage to find out the position, and finding the attack had been driven off, remained in command of ' C ' Squadron and sent his squadron back."

For his services this day Major Villiers received the D.S.O.

The three men killed were Privates G. N. Buswell, J. Lovejoy, and C. White ; all of " C " Squadron. Private L. G. Gillett, " D " Squadron, died of wounds.

An unofficial account says :

" It began with a tremendously heavy bombardment with every kind of shell at about 3 a.m. About 3.30 two companies (i.e. anything from 250 to 500 men) attacked a ruined farm, which forms a sort of outwork just in front of the right of our position, and which we hold with part of our force. One of the two attacking companies never got near the farm, being held up by machine-gun fire. The other one, however, according to all reports, came on several times to within about 50 yards of our forward trench, but was driven off each time. The whole thing died away soon after 4 o'clock. Two prisoners, who had taken cover in a shell hole just in front of our lines, and couldn't get back, were spotted and captured an hour or two later, amid immense enthusiasm."

The following messages were sent by Major Villiers from Gillemont Farm :

I

To O. C. WILL.

Sender's Number   Day of Month
      A.V.5   20

Telephone broken stop VAL FLEMING killed stop the position seems all right except for very heavy shelling which is not so great now stop I left squadron at barricade and receiving no message came on myself and sent for squadron but am sending it back to wait close to barricade stop am staying here myself leaving Keith-Falconer with squadron stop a few casualties.

From A. Villiers, *Major*.
Time 4.12 a.m.

II

To Lieut. Keith-Falconer
      CHILD

Sender's Number   Day of Month
      A.V.6   20

Take squadron back to sunken road except N.C.O. and eight men from No. 4 Troop, " A " Squadron, whom I want here to work on trenches stop if nothing happens before five fifteen send squadron back to billets except No. 2 Troop stop send this note on to Colonel Willcox stop VAL and SILVERTOP killed stop send " A " Squadron's nine men by communication trench stop position seems all right except for heavy shelling.

From A. Villiers.
Time 4.30.

III

To O.C. WILL.

Sender's Number
A.V. 7

Day of Month
20

Very heavy bombardment by shells and trench mortars beginning between two-thirty and three AAA A few Germans came forward but were driven back with some casualties AAA The trenches have been blown in but are being repaired AAA It seems to have been the Germans' intention to raid the post AAA The shelling was exceptionally severe both in the trenches and communication trench AAA CHILD waited at barricade and I came on to find out situation stop I first sent to bring them nearer but on further investigation I sent them back again to wait by barricade and then later on back to billets stop I have taken ten men from CHILD to replace casualties stop MAJOR FLEMING and LIEUTENANT SILVERTOP killed instantaneously by shells stop other casualties about six details later stop.

From A. Villiers, *Major*.

Time 5.25.

IV

To O.C. WILL.

Sender's Number
A.V.9

Day of Month
20

" C " Squadron do not wish to be relieved to-night AAA I will stay up with them AAA Two Hotchkiss rifles are out of action completely AAA Can you get two Hotchkiss rifles from Hermon-Hodge as I would prefer to keep my squadron's rifles ready for to-morrow or in case of having to come up in support AAA Machine guns would be invaluable AAA Do you think that you could get us one machine gun at least AAA The barricade is undoubtedly the best place for support squadron to go to AAA It is difficult to say definitely but the general opinion is that our artillery support was satisfactory AAA The Germans were in larger numbers than I thought at first and there is no doubt that they had a considerable number of casualties as they were fired at from many directions at close ranges AAA The G.O.C. said he would arrange for R.E. officer with working party to work up here to-night AAA Will discuss work to be done when R.E. officer comes round this morning as the G.O.C. said he would AAA I hope very much that Phil Fleming is not sent up here to take over as Worsley and I can manage all right and the N.C.O.s and men are full of go and very pleased with repelling the attack AAA There are two officers' and two men's bodies to bury. Please arrange for our ration party to take them back to-night AAA One body is too smashed to move AAA We do not want a lot of visitors to-day please and if anybody comes up we should like them to come up the communication trench.

From A. Villiers, *Major*.

Time 8.15.

These messages and Major Fleming's reports give a far more vivid and far more truthful impression of what actually happened than any subsequent narrative pieced together after the event. Reading them, one sees, first, the squadron arriving and taking over from the infantry ; then the squadron leader going out the very first night to see for himself what the enemy was doing ; finding considerable activity, wiring, digging, etc. ; being fired at by an enemy sentry in the grey dawn and returning home over No-man's-land almost by daylight ; the urgent demand for more wire and sandbags ; the steady and ominous increase of enemy shelling ; one feels an unexpressed foreboding of attack ; then silence. There is a gap, and Major Villiers' messages take up the story again. The situation is well in hand ; confidence is unshaken ; the " men are full of go and very pleased with repelling the attack."

It seems certain that the Germans never really looked like capturing the position. They had probably counted on the heavy preliminary bombardment putting the garrison out of action altogether, or at least driving them below ground and so stupefying them as to give the attackers an easy walk-over. It seems to have been the policy hitherto not to hold the Farm against attacks in any force, but to let the raiders in and rely on driving them out afterwards, if they did not go voluntarily. The stubborn defence put up by " C " Squadron, after the death of their commander, and with the two remaining officers fully occupied with their troops and unable to exercise any general control, must have come as an unpleasant surprise to the enemy.

No greater blow could have befallen the Regiment than the death of Major Fleming. Beloved by his many friends, worshipped by his squadron, admired and respected by all, he was a most gallant officer, a born leader of men. Deriving authority from his own ability and merit, being also a man of notable courage, he was able to control men freely by strength of character and personal example rather than by force of military discipline. Having everything at home to make life good, he set it aside utterly to serve his country. For he was by no means one of those, happy in their generation, who love fighting for fighting's sake ; to him it was all thoroughly distasteful, and in quiet times behind the line he was never tired of descanting on the utter weariness of the whole thing. And yet he might so easily, and with perfect justification, have obtained a responsible staff appointment, in which he would not only have been reasonably safe and comfortable, but would also have done good and valuable work for the country. For his intellectual abilities were considerable, well above those of many staff officers. But that was not his way ; he recognized the importance of staff work, and the need of able men to do it well. Only it just wasn't his ideal of service.

He was noted also for a complete understanding of his duty, and for great energy and self-discipline in its performance. He never spared himself, and he expected the same of others. It was typical of him that after a long day reconnoitring a position, or doing some other job, he would return to billets thoroughly tired and immediately set to work studying plans for the morrow, writing orders, interviewing the sergeant-major, or inspecting billets, stables, etc. Thoroughness was his motto in all things, and he never left to others work that he could possibly do himself. Witness one of the last exploits of his life, the already-mentioned reconnaissance in front of his position at Gillemont Farm. Nine squadron leaders out of ten would have sent a subaltern or sergeant to do the patrol and report, and no one would have thought the worse of them for doing so. Major Fleming went himself.

MAJOR VALENTINE FLEMING, D.S.O., M.P.

He did not always suffer fools gladly, and could not en-
dure the slacker, of whom there were few in his squadron ;
they generally found it convenient to change their habits.

The Regiment lost in Val Fleming not only a brave and
capable officer but also a character of singular charm and
attraction. Those who knew him best perhaps remember
him chiefly as the staunchest and truest of friends, the
gayest and brightest of comrades ; they recall the athletic
figure with the long, quick stride and the keen, eager face,
the laughter and talk full of shrewd thrusts which enlivened
good days and bad, merry evenings in billets, wet and
anxious nights in trenches. He left a gap that could not
be filled, a memory that could not be forgotten.

Silvertop, too, we all liked very much, and he was much
missed, especially in " C " Squadron. It seemed a strange
irony of fate that, having left the Regiment in September
1915 to join the infinitely more dangerous service of the
Royal Flying Corps, he had returned to us unscathed, only
to fall in a chance raid on an isolated post.

The two officers and the four men who died with them
were buried in the little cemetery at St. Emilie, one of the
few which have been left undisturbed by the War Graves
Commission, prettily situated behind a small chapel or
shrine, planted with a few trees and hedges, looking out over
the wide open spaces towards Epéhy.

We must return to the story. Monday, the 21st, was a
quiet day. " D " squadron relieved " C " at Gillemont at
11 o'clock that evening, " A " going up in support to Lempire
and " C " to reserve at St. Emilie. Monday night was very
quiet, but rain set in immediately after " D " Squadron's
arrival, and continued uninterruptedly until about midday
Tuesday. The trenches were soon in a frightful state,
inches deep in mud and water. There were no proper
dugouts ; only a few shelters covered with mackintosh
sheets. The four days to the evening of the 25th passed
quietly, the rain stopped, and the weather was mild and
warm. There was a good deal of artillery activity for a

quiet part of the line, but rifle fire was almost non-existent.
" D " Squadron were shelled from 1.30 to 2 a.m. on the
23rd, and also for an hour or two on the 24th, but no damage
was done. There was a violent bombardment of the
trenches on their right for half an hour one night, but no
attack. There were intervals of absolute quiet.

But this otherwise peaceful and uneventful time was
marked by one terrible accident. At 12.30 a.m. on the 24th
May Lieutenant Keith-Falconer went out with Sergeant
Gare to visit the listening posts, which were about 50 yards
in front of the advanced trench on the right. When
within about 10 yards of them they were suddenly challenged,
in English, and Gare, who was leading, quietly gave the
password. Almost immediately one of the sentries fired
and shot Gare through the right lung. He was just about
to fire again when the other sentry, Private Newell, knocked
the rifle out of his hand. Meanwhile Gare was already
unconscious, and died while being carried back to the
advanced dressing-station.

The whole squadron was very much upset at such a
shocking accident. Unfortunately these accidents were
only too common in the war ; another regiment on our right
had two men shot in the same way that week ; but this was
the first and only one that occurred in the Oxfordshire
Yeomanry. Being on listening post is jumpy work except
for the strongest nerves, and the man responsible in this
case was quite a young lad, who had evidently lost control
under the strain. He was completely exonerated by a
court of inquiry.

" Poor Gare was an admirable fellow in every way, of
magnificent physique and bearing, strong as a lion, as smart
as a Guardsman, very brave, and an excellent troop sergeant,
very much liked by all ranks in the squadron, especially the
men in his own troop. He was a corporal in the Bicester
troop before the war, and was promoted to be sergeant in
November 1914. He had been Wellesley's troop sergeant
since June 1915." (Officer's letter.)

" A " Squadron relieved " D " at 10 p.m. on the 25th.

" D " went into reserve at St. Emilie, and " C " moved up to support at Lempire. The weather was gorgeously hot. On their journeys to and from the trenches and elsewhere in this area people noticed that a considerable number of trees, especially fruit trees, had been cut down by the Boches during their retirement in the spring, and many others not cut down had been gashed all round the stem deep enough to kill them in a year or so. This particularly spiteful and vindictive example of German " frightfulness " made a special impression on our men, agriculturists who understood the value of such things and resented their senseless destruction.

On Saturday, the 26th, there was " some shelling and activity with trench mortars and rifle grenades," in the course of which Lieutenant R. L. Worsley and 3 other ranks were wounded. Worsley was hit by shrapnel in several places, but was able to walk 2 miles back to the dressing-station. During the next two days there was more shelling of the front line ; one man was killed and two wounded. Major Hermon-Hodge was very slightly wounded and remained at duty.

On the 29th " C " Squadron relieved " A " at Gillemont, " D " went up to support at Lempire, and " A " came back into reserve at St. Emilie.

The 30th was a " quiet day, 2 men wounded in Gillemont; ' A ' squadron of Royal Scots Greys relieved ' D ' Squadron at Lempire during the evening, ' D ' went into reserve at St. Emilie and ' A ' into Divisional Reserve at Villers Faucon." (Regimental Diary.)

Next day, the 31st, the whole Regiment was relieved by the Scots Greys, squadrons marching back to camp near Brusle independently. " C " Squadron, which had 10 miles to go, did not get in till between two and three in the morning of the 1st June.

The Regiment spent the next fifteen days in Corps Reserve, less a dismounted party of 80 under Second-Lieutenants Holford and Matthews, who were at the Quarries near Templeux-le-Guérard, working on the so-called " Brown Line." For the rest the time passed pleasantly enough ;

the camp was well situated in the centre of great rolling grassy uplands, dotted here and there with spinneys and clumps of trees. The general appearance of the countryside was not unlike the Berkshire downs. The horses were all looking pretty fat and well now, having had a good rest and plenty of grazing. The weather was glorious, and there was fairly good, though rather shallow, bathing near by in the little river Cologne. An officer's letter says : " For the most part everything is very quiet, and one might almost forget there was a war, were it not for the occasional sound of a gun in the distance and the frequent passage of aeroplanes overhead."

On the 4th June Major Nicholl, Major Villiers, and Lieutenant Keith-Falconer went to an old Etonian dinner near Péronne, at which General Rawlinson, commanding the Fourth Army, presided. There were about 130 present altogether, including General Greenly and General Pitman. We still mustered six Old Etonians in the Regiment, but three of them—Captain Fleming, Captain Pepper, and Lieutenant Wellesley—were away.

During this interval of rest a certain amount of " training " was carried out, especially practice with rifle grenades. Nor were the Regiment allowed to forget they were still cavalry, and each squadron did at least one mounted " scheme " for the Brigadier's inspection. Saturday afternoon, 9th June, there were Brigade sports, mostly of a comic or semi-comic description, such as obstacle races, potato races, etc., attended by the Corps, Division, and Brigade Commanders, and by most of the officers of the Brigade. There were about fifteen events altogether, of which " D " Squadron won the mounted wrestling, mounted and dismounted tug of war, and the potato race, while " C " Squadron won three other events. So the Regiment did pretty well. On the 10th June the Brigadier presented Military Medal ribbons to four men of " C " Squadron who distinguished themselves at Gillemont on the 20th May.

Further scope for activity was provided by agricultural work. We read in a sergeant's diary, under date 6th June, that parties were "sent round to old farms and villages to find any farm implements that would do for hay-making. Plenty of grass in the district." A large quantity of hay was saved in this way, and the men rather liked the work, a welcome change from the interminable digging and training.

On Friday, 15th June, the Regiment sent a "trench party" of about 300 men, under Major Hermon-Hodge, to relieve the 5th Lancers in divisional reserve at the Quarries near Templeux-le-Guérard. From here they sent working parties of 2 officers and 160 men each night to work on Gillemont Farm. Major Nicholl relieved Major Hermon-Hodge in command of the party on the 17th June.

Life at the Quarries was not unpleasant, if perhaps a little monotonous ; both officers and men were reasonably comfortable in tents, tin shanties, and dugouts ; work was regular, but not too strenuous, and for the first week at any rate there were no disasters. Many of the huts and shanties were decorated with roses and other wild flowers, any quantity of which were to be found growing in the ruined villages in the neighbourhood. The weather was now grillingly hot. Private Batchelor's diary for the 19th June contains an interesting account of some impromptu and rather original sports.

"Walked into the village for a bath and got some strawberries and red currants in gardens. Races after tea. Competitors had to run 50 yards, drink a mess-tinful of beer, undress, run back and light a cigarette, and run back and dress and then run to starting-place. Winner, J. Boyles. *Cook's Race.* Run 50 yards, light a fire, cook an egg, eat it, and run back to starting-point. Winner, Taylor, 15 francs and a bottle of whisky."

That same night the working party was heavily shelled at the barricade on the road to Gillemont Farm, while carrying timber, and had to give up work for the night and return to the Quarries. The following night there was a "working party as usual, very quiet on front, do not like it so quiet." (Sergeant's diary.)

15

But nothing serious happened until the night of June 21st–22nd. We sent out our usual working party of 160 men with two officers (Whinney and Soame) at 9.15 p.m. on the 21st. At 1 a.m. on the 22nd the Germans began a violent bombardment of Gillemont Farm with heavy guns, trench mortars, and rifle grenades, and after about half an hour made an attack on the position, which appears to have been partially successful ; at any rate the garrison was withdrawn from the fire trenches commanding the right and left fronts and the approaches to the main communication trench, where squadron headquarters were situated. Unfortunately our working party, which was of course in no way responsible for the defence of the post, was out wiring in front of the line—

" and were not warned of the withdrawal of the garrison. ' A ' Squadron on the right suffered severe casualties from shell fire, which was unavoidable, but ' D ' Squadron on the left side, on withdrawing according to orders, found the Boche in possession of the trench and about 20 of them were either killed or taken prisoner. Total casualties : 1 Officer, Second-Lieutenant J. A. P. Whinney, and 10 O.R.s killed ; 12 O.R.s, of whom one died in hospital, wounded. One Sergeant and 8 O.R.s missing, believed prisoners of war." (Regimental Diary.)

No detailed accounts by eye-witnesses of this disastrous episode exist, or, if any do, they have not come into my hands. Even at the time survivors gave confused and contradictory accounts of what had happened. Apparently the " D " Squadron party at any rate was caught under the barrage and cut off from the trenches. They took what cover they could by crouching in the numerous shell holes all round the position. Curiously enough, in spite of the violence of the bombardment, few, if any, of the casualties seem to have been caused by the barrage, probably because the weight of this fell on the trenches behind the working party. It was when the barrage ceased and the attack began that most of the trouble occurred. Some were killed

outside the trench ; Second-Lieutenant Whinney was one
of these. It is supposed most probable that he was making
for the trench, and in the darkness stumbled against some
wire, and was shot while caught up in it. Three or four
other men were killed here, in front of the line ; the body
of one of them (Private Shayler) was found hanging over
the wire, rifle in hand, facing the enemy.

Whinney was one of our most promising young officers.
We had all got to like him very much, and he was one
of the three or four best troop leaders in the Regiment.
We all felt very sorry about him. He was such a bright,
cheery lad, full of life and energy and gaiety, and only
twenty.

Meanwhile, the majority of the party seem to have made
their way back to the trenches, which they found full of
Germans. Several jumped in right amongst them unawares,
and were immediately surrounded and seized ; Sergeant
Hepworth was one of these. (He was one of the best of
our sergeants, much missed in his squadron for the rest of
the war.) Others were more fortunate, and got through
after various adventures ; some saw the enemy in time to
shift their course and avoid them ; others were lucky in
jumping into parts of the trench unoccupied by the enemy.
One man (Private Bailey, hereafter known as Bayonet
Bailey) managed to escape after being three times bayoneted,
twice clubbed on the head with a rifle butt, and left for dead.
What was left of the party got back to the Quarries about
4 a.m.

On the evening of the 27th June the Regiment relieved
the 5th Lancers in Gillemont Farm. " D " Squadron,
under Lieutenant Wellesley, held the farm itself ; " A "
Squadron, under Captain Fane, was in support in the sunken
road outside Lempire ; " C " Squadron, under Captain
Palmer, was in reserve at the Quarries. The whole was
under Lieutenant-Colonel E. T. Cook, 20th Hussars, commanding the left sub-sector, with headquarters at Lempire.
The Brigade was under General Pitman, with headquarters
at St. Emilie, as before.

The defences of the Farm had been considerably re-organized and improved since the Regiment's first tour of duty. New fire trenches had been dug, and the whole of the front properly wired; also a large dugout, 20 or 30 feet deep, had been made in the centre of the position to accommo-date squadron headquarters and serve as a report centre. Most important of all, two strong posts, specially armed with machine guns and Hotchkiss rifles, had been established on the left wing, which had been a weak point with no adequate defences at our first coming, six weeks before. Each of these posts was now held by a troop, while the old " Farm post " on the right was now held by two troops instead of one.

" D " Squadron held the Farm for three days, during which it rained very heavily, " water above shoe-tops." But they had a very quiet time.

On the evening of the 30th " A " Squadron relieved " D " at Gillemont, " C " going up to support in the sunken road and " D " coming back to reserve at the Quarries, where they arrived at 3 a.m. on 1st July, having had singular good fortune during their three days at Gillemont. Most of them were still asleep when at 11.45 a.m. that same morning a chance shell landed right on a dugout occupied by Corporal Blelock and three men, killing them instantly. Blelock was a man of iron nerve; no danger ever ruffled him; a good brain and a clear head, quick to grasp essentials; and he could be trusted always to act with determination and common sense if left on his own responsibility.

The same shell caused severe shell-shock to Second-Lieutenant Riddell, sleeping in the adjacent dugout, and he was removed to hospital in a state of prostration.

While " A " Squadron was holding Gillemont, " C " Squadron carried out a very successful raid on the German trenches, in which Second-Lieutenant A. C. Rawlinson and four other ranks were wounded. Full details are contained in the following report by the Brigade-Major :

REPORT BY 4TH CAVALRY BRIGADE OF RAID
    CARRIED OUT BY " C " SQUADRON, OXFORD
    HUSSARS, AT 12.30 A.M., 4TH JULY.

The hour of zero was 12.30 a.m., 4th July. The preliminary bombardment was short and intense ; it was
started at 12.30 a.m. 4th July, and lifted at 12.35 a.m.,
at which hour the two parties " B " and " E " were due to
enter the trenches.

" B " Party consisted of 2 N.C.O.s and 15 O.R.s.
" E " Party consisted of 1 officer, 1 N.C.O., and 15 O.R.s.
The above numbers included signallers, R.E.s, etc.

Both parties had to crawl forward ¼ of an hour before
zero to positions of readiness opposite their objectives ; and
as the guns opened advanced forward against the enemy.

To take the action of each patrol in detail :

" B " PATROL

As the patrol moved forward the leader found the wire
in front of the enemy's first trench uncut. The two R.E.
men with the torpedo at once blew the wire up (it was only
one knife-rest thick) and the party crossed the trench ; it
was 3 feet deep and blown in. Here they dropped a flanking
party to watch their right flank ; and then advanced
towards the second trench. They found our bombardment
had destroyed the enemy wire and they entered the trench
without difficulty. The leader of the party here ordered
two of his men to return to the first enemy trench which
they had crossed, and these two men on their way back
found seven of the enemy behind the hedge. A bombing
fight ensued : two of the enemy were killed, and four ran
towards the farm and were lost ; the last, however, showed
fight, and had to be shot ; this was done, and he died
within a minute or two before anything could be got out of
him. The remainder of the patrol moved on and passed
round the island, where they found two dead men on the
right-hand side ; they also found a small dugout—it was
empty except for one man's kit. A German was also seen
down one of the trenches ; but he ran away at once. Away
on the right a party of about twelve Germans was seen, but
before they could be taken on, a trench-mortar bomb landed
in the middle of them and they vanished.

As much damage was done to the enemy trenches and wire
as was possible, and as time was now up, the party returned

with the kit they had found, unmolested and without casualties. They were lucky enough to find that the enemy had laid out his kit as for an inspection ; this rather lightened their task of obtaining identification. It seems possible that the garrison were about to be relieved, and were waiting to march out.

" E " PATROL

The trench-mortar fire, which was trying to cut the wire in front of this party, fell rather short, and at first hampered their movements to some extent. They found the German wire uncut ; and the R.E. brought forward a Bangalore torpedo ; it failed to explode. A second was brought up ; it exploded and also detonated the first ; an excellent gap in the wire was the result. While all this was going on, the enemy bombed and fired at the patrol, the second-in-command and four men were hit.

In spite of the enemy fire at close range, the remainder carried on.

The gap made, the patrol entered the trench ; the officer in command was now wounded. The command then devolved on a young Lance-Corporal [1] who took charge, reorganized the party, and continued the raid with determination. About seven or eight Germans ran down the left of the trench ; two Oxford Hussars chased them, but the enemy got out of the trench where it was blown in and ran across country. The trench was searched, but no live enemy found.

The patrol now advanced towards the second trench. They were, however, held up by wire, which was uncut. Their time was now up and they therefore had to withdraw. This was successfully accomplished. All the wounded were brought back and the rest of the patrol returned, bringing with them some enemy kits.

The total casualties were 1 officer and 5 O.R.s wounded.

The enemy's retaliation was not heavy, and all those taking part in the raid were safely withdrawn to reserve area.

Our bombardment slowly died down after zero plus 20 mins.

(*Sgd.*) F. Nicolson, *Captain,*
5*th July* 1917.   *Brigade Major, 4th Cavalry Brigade.*

[1] R. W. Hawken.

Colonel Cook, commanding the sector, wrote the following letter to Lieutenant Palmer, commanding at Gillemont :

" I have been asked to convey to you the entire satisfaction of the Divisional Commander at the manner in which last night's raid was carried out. He considers it to have been highly successful and all the information required was gained. Will you please convey the above to all officers and other ranks concerned ?

" I should like to take this opportunity on my own behalf of congratulating you, Lieutenant Rawlinson, Sergt. Butler, and all other ranks, on the splendid way in which you carried out your mission. The whole raid was organized in a manner which I could not have believed possible, taking into consideration the short time available. The foresight, skill, and dash were beyond praise, and I should like you to tell your men that their action throughout was worthy of the best traditions of the British cavalry. The required identifications were obtained ; unluckily there were no live Germans to make prisoners, but that is the fortune of war. I very much regret the casualties you sustained, but I trust that the wounded are all doing well and wish them a complete and rapid (though not *too* rapid to keep them out of Blighty) recovery.

" Lieutenant Rawlinson's wound was particularly unlucky, but I gather it, happily, is not serious.

" I take this opportunity of tendering to you my heartiest thanks for the splendid way in which you have carried out your orders in the spirit and in the letter, and I should like your men to know how proud I am to have had the Oxfordshire Hussars under my command."

E. T. COOK,
Lieutenant-Colonel, 20 H. *Comdg. Sub-sector* C.2.

The flow of information was well maintained. With the raiding party went a man carrying a field telephone and a coil of cable, which he unrolled as he went along. This cable was connected with a telephone in Lieutenant Palmer's dugout, and at each successive stage in the raid the officer in charge reported progress to squadron headquarters. As Lieutenant Palmer sat listening to these reports, he simultaneously repeated them down another telephone to

Colonel Cook, and the latter in his turn passed them on to Brigade, and thence to Divisional and Corps Headquarters. At 11.30 p.m. on the evening following the raid (4th July) " C " Squadron, under Lieutenant Palmer, relieved " A " Squadron in Gillemont Farm. They had not been there two hours when, at 1.20 a.m. on the 5th, they were very heavily bombarded with trench mortars, the bombardment being followed by an attack on both sides of the Farm about 1.45 a.m. The enemy made three determined attempts to enter our trenches, but were driven off each time. We lost four men killed, including Sergeant Bayliss, one of " C " Squadron's very best N.C.O.s, and Private Podbery, one of the four men who had received the Military Medal a few weeks before for gallantry in the first attack on Gillemont Farm on the 20th May.[1] Another man died of wounds, eight men were wounded, and the trenches were very much knocked about. The Divisional Commander expressed his great appreciation of the gallant conduct of the squadron in holding the position throughout an exceptionally heavy bombardment. There is no doubt they did very well.

The whole Regiment was relieved by a battalion of the 106th Brigade on the night of the 6th–7th July. Gillemont Farm was bombarded during the relief, and " C " Squadron had one man wounded. The horses were sent up to meet them halfway, and the last squadron (" C ") got back to camp near Brusle at 4 a.m. on the 7th.

For the next four days the Regiment remained in camp, cleaning up and training. During the absence of the trench party two officers had left the Regiment : Captain H. C. Jagger, A.V.C., Veterinary Officer, to be A.D.V.S., 1st Cavalry Division (24th June), and Second-Lieutenant R. Lakin, to be A.D.C. to the G.O.C. 6th Cavalry Brigade. From the nature of his duties Captain Jagger has not appeared as much in this history as the great part he played in the life of the Regiment merits. He had won himself an almost unique position as well by his admirable efficiency

---

[1] Another of the four, Private Macey, was killed with Corporal Blelock on 1st July ; see p. 214.

as by his personal qualities ; he was the friend of all, from Colonel to Private, and our pleasure at his well-deserved promotion was mingled with keen regret at his departure. It may also be mentioned here that his connection with the Regiment dates back to the South African War, in which he had served as Veterinary Officer with the Yeomanry.

The Regiment had now been seven weeks in what we may call the Gillemont " area," of which about five had been spent either in the front line at Gillemont Farm or in Divisional Reserve, supplying working parties every night. The actual time during which the Regiment held the Farm itself was twenty-three days. During that period there were three organized raids, one by ourselves and two by the Germans, besides almost daily bombardments ; in addition there was a serious enemy raid while we were in reserve, in which our working party was involved, as already stated. The net result in casualties was : 3 officers and 23 other ranks killed, 3 other ranks died of wounds, 3 officers and 32 other ranks wounded, 9 other ranks missing, 1 officer and 4 other ranks in hospital with shell-shock ; total casualties : 78 all ranks, including 7 officers.

Gillemont Farm has always been remembered with special interest by those of the Regiment who were there. For them it is almost the chief landmark in the middle years of the war. The fighting was little more than an affair of outposts ; the place a tiny pin-point in the Allied line, not marked on any but the largest maps. The Farm was an isolated post, rather important in this particular sector ; little outside support could be hoped for, and any squadron holding it knew it must rely entirely on its own grit and resolution to resist an attack. The casualties, the sharp and sudden raids, the comparative novelty and independence of the situation, all combined to stamp it on men's memories, so that they came to associate the Regiment with the place in a way one never did with an ordinary piece of trench line.

On Thursday, 12th July, the Regiment left camp at Brusle and began the move back to a more peaceful area. The first day's march was to Cappy, a little village on the

Somme between Péronne and Amiens, about 16 miles west of Brusle. Here there were no billets, the village being just on the edge of the devastated area, and we bivouacked in a pleasant spot in a chalk ravine, in glorious summer weather. The great feature of our stay at Cappy was the bathing. Close by below a mill in the Somme there was a stretch of beautifully clear running water which made a perfect bathing place. We read in Private Batchelor's diary : " Bathed in river. Swimming horses. Bert Lines came off and had a ducking. White wine and new potatoes for supper."

Next day we marched 14 miles, and reached Bonnay, 9 miles north-east of Amiens, at midday. Here there were quite nice billets and good bathing in the Ancre. Here also leave reopened, and twelve men from the Regiment were sent off rejoicing.

On the 14th the Regiment moved on 17 miles to Orville, near Doullens. Here there was more bathing, in the Authie, but rather muddy.

Next day, 15th July, we completed our journey by a short march of 5 miles to Lucheux, 5 miles north-east of Doullens, having come 52 miles from Brusle in four days, travelling gently in the hot sunny weather.

Lucheux is a charming little town, with very nice woods all round. There are a few remains of what must have been a magnificent old Norman castle, destroyed many centuries ago. On its site there is another castle, dating from the fifteenth century, which was then (1917) being used as a hospital for officers suffering from shell-shock. More important than ancient monuments, however, were the excellent billets for officers and men. The Regiment was about 12 miles from the rest of the Brigade, as it had been found impossible to squeeze it into the allotted area. So we did not expect to stop there more than a day or two, but in the end we stayed a fortnight.

Training and musketry were now the order of the day, and nothing of much interest occurred, except the 2nd Cavalry Divisional Horse Show at Frévent on the 28th July. The Regiment was moderately successful, winning first prize for

limbered wagon teams with the " D " Squadron team (for
the second year running), and second prize for heavy-weight
troop horses. " C " Squadron limber won second prize—
also for the second year running.

About this time an announcement appeared in the
Gazette that Major Hermon-Hodge and Major Villiers relin-
quished their temporary rank and reverted to Captain.
The Colonel was much annoyed, because as a matter of fact
Major Hermon-Hodge should have been confirmed in his
rank as Major, to fill the vacancy caused by Major Fleming's
death. Then it was doubtful whether Major Scott's place
had ever been filled, so that it was believed Major Villiers
was entitled to it. However, no one outside the Military
Secretary's office at the War Office has ever been able to
understand the method by which these things are done.
One of the two officers concerned was very indignant and
stoutly refused to remove the crown from his shoulder-
straps, a resolution in which he was firmly supported by
the Colonel, and which was justified by his reinstatement
not very long afterwards.

On Sunday, 29th July, the Regiment moved 14 miles to
Fillièvres, in the valley of the Canche, 6½ miles south-east
of Hesdin. Regimental Headquarters, " A " and " C "
Squadrons, were at Fillièvres, and " D " at Galametz, a mile
away. At the end of August " D " Squadron moved to
Aubrometz, a mile from Fillièvres, on the Frévent road.

The billets here were quite comfortable, and the country
pretty, with trout-fishing in the river Canche, so we had
rather a pleasant time for the next two months. The
weather was very wet in the early part of August, but
improved towards the end of the month, and became quite
good in September.

Soon after our arrival at Fillièvres we heard the good news
that Sergeant Hepworth and all the other men missing on
the 22nd June, except two, were prisoners of war in Germany.

Lieutenant A. E. MacColl rejoined from England on the
7th August, accompanied by five new officers—Second-
Lieutenants G. H. S. Boas, C. B. Fish, H. Hodgson, L. Dove,

and V. H. Bicker-Caarten, the three last-named from the Bedfordshire Yeomanry (second line). MacColl went back to his former squadron, " A," and the others were distributed as follows : Boas to " A," Hodgson to " C," Dove and Bicker-Caarten to " D " ; Fish returned to the Base.

On Sunday, 12th August, there were regimental sports, and on the 15th August an inspection of the Regiment by the Brigadier. The next event worth noting was a highly successful Cavalry Corps Horse Show held near St. Pol on the 1st September. This was quite the biggest thing of its kind since the war began, and attracted officers from all parts. Unfortunately it was rather spoilt by the weather, which was cold, windy, and cloudy, with sharp squalls of rain in the afternoon. " D " Squadron won second prize in the class for limbered wagon teams. The most interesting event of the day was the officers' jumping, which was won by Captain Geoffrey Brooke of the 16th Lancers, with his two chargers, " Alice " and " Combined Training." The rest of the jumping was bad, on the whole, which was perhaps only natural, as the course was a stiff one, and officers at the front did not usually get a chance of having first-class jumpers. Some Indians gave a rather remarkable display of trick riding. Among the vast crowd of spectators were the Commander-in-Chief, innumerable major and minor Generals, and nearly everybody one knew from Oxfordshire : Lieutenant-Colonel Walter Hodgson (G.S.O.1, 5th Cavalry Division), Major Philip Hunloke (G.S.O.3, First Army), Captain Sir Algernon Peyton (11th Hussars), " Parson " Gibbs (Chaplain, 10th Hussars), Major Frank Gore-Langton (Coldstream Guards), Major Jagger (A.D.V.S., 1st Cavalry Division), Captain the Earl of Leven and Melville (Royal Scots Greys), and many others.

On the 16th September 32 other ranks were sent to the Base to reduce the Dismounted Party to 30. Many men being away on special agricultural leave, the remainder of the nominal 70 were kept. On the 23rd 4 officers and 115 other ranks were sent off on a working party to build light railways, but returned eleven days later.

Lieutenant Wellesley caused some amusement by his involuntary failure to return from leave, and his subsequent adventures. Having sent all his uniform to the tailor to be cleaned he went off to Scotland and did not return to London till after closing hours on the day prior to the expiration of his leave. The tailor failed to deliver his uniform, and there was no means of getting it before the leave train left next day. However, Wellesley was determined not to be defeated. He therefore arrayed himself in ordinary civilian clothes and a soft felt hat, with a Burberry as the only available sign of his military standing, and thus attired, presented himself at Victoria Station. Most people would hardly have got any farther ; indeed, the majority would probably never have got so far. However, somehow or other, in the crowd and confusion, Wellesley managed to slip through the barrier, and on to the train unobserved. All now went well till the train reached Folkestone, where he immediately found himself held up by the Embarkation Officer, who absolutely refused to allow him on the boat. More than this, he evidently regarded him with considerable suspicion, and, after addressing a number of searching questions, ordered him to return to London and report forthwith to the War Office. On his way back to the railway station Wellesley noticed that he was being closely shadowed by detectives. He had some doubt how his story would be received at the War Office, but, much to his surprise, they merely asked how long his uniform was likely to remain in the hands of the tailor, and, being informed, promptly said he had better take another five days' leave. This unexpected windfall so astonished Wellesley that he asked how it was that, if extensions of leave were so readily obtainable, officers did not more frequently find means of getting stopped at Folkestone by the Embarkation Officer, whereupon he was told that his was the first case of its kind which had ever occurred, and that, were they to become more frequent, it would probably become necessary to handle them in a different manner.

On the 6th September General Greenly came to see the

Regiment at work. He was with us from 9.30 to 12.30, and spent an hour with each squadron. Each carried out various little displays, e.g. mounted and dismounted attacks on a position, firing at targets with rifles and Hotchkiss guns, physical drill, etc.

A skill-at-arms contest for all officers of the Brigade took place on the 15th September. Second-Lieutenant Dove, one of our new officers and an old Regular sergeant-major, won, and Major Hermon-Hodge and Captain Weatherby were both among the first ten. There were four events : tent-pegging with a lance, dummy-thrusting with a sword, rifle shooting and revolver shooting (the two latter dismounted).

About this time Captain Fane became rather seriously ill with pleurisy, and eventually had to go to hospital on the 16th September, very much against his will, and to the regret of everybody else. He looked so bad when he left that many of us gravely doubted whether we should ever see him back with the Regiment in France. However, he reappeared in a remarkably short space of time, long indeed before he was fit to do so.

Captain Keith-Falconer returned to " D " Squadron as Second-in-Command on the 17th September, in place of Captain Pepper, who had succeeded Captain Fane as Second-in-Command of " A " Squadron.

All this time mounted training was being carried on, and, in addition, Hotchkiss gun classes, bayonet and bombing practice, map-reading, etc. Lieutenant-Colonel Ronald Campbell, from the School of Musketry, kindly came over and gave an interesting lecture on the art of bayonet fighting. Otherwise the training had no special features worth noticing; just the usual troop and squadron schemes, with an occasional regimental or brigade day.

On Monday, 8th October, the Brigade moved billets to an area round Eps, about 14 miles from Fillièvres and 5½ miles N.N.W. of St. Pol. (It will be remembered that we had spent a night here on our march to the Somme in September 1916.) The Regiment had the village of

Eps and the adjoining hamlet of Herbeval. The Diary says :

" Got in before it rained, but from about 5 p.m. it rained almost continuously till the 11th, when it took up and though the weather became much colder it was fine. Stabling in the area for not more than 150 horses, and altogether things very uncomfortable."

The Diary so rarely breaks into comment on comfort or discomfort that one would think that these particular billets must have been specially awful, the more so as Sergeant Stroud's diary calls them " shocking " billets. But I believe that in reality the very bad weather made them seem worse than they were. As a fact, the officers were quite well off, and the men not at all badly off when they had settled down ; it was the unfortunate horses which suffered, and that was almost entirely due to the rain, which reduced their lines to a quagmire. However, the Regiment was presently given another village, Hestrus, which enabled it to spread itself considerably and get nearly all the horses under cover.

On the 11th Lieutenant Boddington, Duke of Lancaster's Own Yeomanry, who had been attached to " C " Squadron since July, left to join an infantry battalion. Two days later Lieutenant Holford was ordered to report to First Army Headquarters for employment with Artillery Horse Lines.

The third Battle of Ypres, or Passchendaele, as it was sometimes called, had now been going on for over two months, and there had been some idea that the cavalry might possibly be used. The 1st Cavalry Division had recently been sent up to the Ypres–Hazebrouck area, and our move from Fillièvres was at first thought to be a preliminary to following them up north, there perhaps to take part in the fighting. However, nothing came of it, and on Friday, 19th October, the Brigade set out on a three-day march to the south.

The first stage (16 miles) was to Rebreuviette, a village on the Frévent–Arras road. At this point Second-Lieutenant Bicker-Caarten and 67 other ranks were sent off on a working party, to build huts for the cavalry in the Péronne district, where it was freely rumoured we were going to spend the winter, holding a sector of the trench line. The fact that the huts were actually being built seemed to lend truth to the rumour.

Next night the Regiment stopped at Bonneville and Montrelet (15 miles), two villages between Doullens and Amiens, and on the third day (Sunday, 21st October) they marched 22 miles and came to an area embracing Oresmaux (Headquarters, " A " Squadron, and half " C " Squadron), Grattepanche (two troops of " C " Squadron), and Estrées-sur-Noye ("D " Squadron), about 9 miles south of Amiens and 53 miles due south of Eps.

We were now farther south than we had ever been before. The billeting was difficult, as there had never been British troops here before, and no warning of any kind had been given to the local " Maires " that any troops were coming. However, everybody soon got settled down, and all the horses were under cover within a day or two. On the whole these were good billets, and I think most of those who were with the Regiment at this time must have pleasant memories of their stay there. The weather was reasonably good and the surrounding country attractive; wide, open spaces of undulating ground, with here and there a wood or a valley to break the monotony. Training was continued as far as possible, but with so many men away on working parties it was impossible to do a great deal. At any rate, it was limited to troop and squadron work, which most people preferred to brigade or regimental field days. So there was plenty of leisure, spent in jolly rides and walks, sometimes galloping down a hare, much football, and an occasional visit to Amiens. This was the time of year when the harvest had been got in and one was able to ride freely across the stubble fields, and the four miles across country from Oresmaux to Estrées made a very pleasant morning's ride.

Considerable excitement was aroused amongst the good folk of Estrées through Major Villiers shooting an inhabitant in the head while practising with his revolver. Fifty francs and a bottle of champagne compensated for the wound, which was not serious, but the fact that the wounded man was seventy years of age, unarmed, and a Frenchman, must not be allowed to detract from the accuracy of the shooter.

On the 24th October 33 more other ranks were added to the working party, and on the 25th Lieutenant R. L. Worsley rejoined from England. With him came four new officers : Second-Lieutenants A. S. Ingram, T. A. Mason, W. J. Mason, and H. C. Reed. Early in November Major Hermon-Hodge went home for the winter to be Instructor to the 2nd Cavalry Reserve Regiment in Ireland. Captain Pepper now took command of " A " Squadron.

About this time began the great disaster to the Italian Army at Caporetto, when they were driven back hundreds of miles, many thousands were killed and thousands more surrounded, and it looked for a time as if all Italy might be overrun. It soon became known that British and French troops were being sent to reinforce the Italian front, and people began to wonder whether any cavalry would be sent. The name of Italy suggested sunshine, and I think a good many felt they would rather like to go there, at any rate for the winter.

Private Batchelor gives an interesting account of a conversation which he had with German prisoners on a hospital train on November 17th :

" Reached Havre at 5.30. German prisoners on train. They said that Russia was finished and admitted Austria no good without German aid. They thought Italy would be finished soon and the war would be over in the summer. German army had plenty of food and then the prisoners and lastly the civilians. Can't believe this. He did not fear America, as Germany and her allies had 15 million men, but he was glad he was a prisoner all the same. Spoke broken English and thought of coming to England after the war, but he will find his mistake, I hope."

The secret of our coming attack at Cambrai had been well kept, better than any previously. Though it had been decided on for a long time past, nothing leaked through

16

till about the 10th November.   No doubt the story of the
huts being built near Péronne for our accommodation while
holding a trench line helped materially to put us off the scent.
However, the truth was evidently becoming known, for on
the 12th November the following entry appears in Sergeant
Stroud's diary :   " Rumours of a stunt at Cambrai."

The Regiment marched at 10.15 a.m. on Friday, 16th
November, to Cappy (25 miles), the little village on the Somme
where we had stayed a night on our way back from Gillemont
in July.   It was a slow march, with several long halts, and
we did not get in till 8.15 p.m. and then spent an hour and a
half watering the horses and getting the lines down in the
dark.

The Regiment left Cappy at 4.20 p.m. next day, and,
marching through Péronne, reached a camp of huts at
Tertry (17 miles) at 9.30.   The horses were stabled in long
tin-roofed sheds without sides.   We stayed in this camp
" drawing extra rations, etc., etc., ready for gap operations,"
till 2.15 a.m. on the 20th, when we moved up 10 miles to the
north "to a position of readiness near Villers-Faucon,
arriving there after watering about 7 a.m."

The situation was as follows.   The Third Army (General
Byng) had attacked at 6.20 a.m. with six divisions on a
front of 6 miles from east of Gonnelieu to the Canal du
Nord opposite Hermies.   The main purpose was to gain
possession of Bourlon Ridge, the capture of which would
turn the enemy defensive lines south of the Scarpe and
Sensée Rivers and expose his communications to our
artillery.   It was further necessary to establish a good flank
position to the east, in the direction of Cambrai, but the
capture of Cambrai itself was not aimed at.   Two features
distinguished the battle from all the big attacks which
preceded it :   there was no great artillery preparation lasting
many days before the battle, and thus far greater secrecy
was preserved ;   and secondly, tanks were used on a far
greater scale than ever before, 360 being used on the first
day.   An essential requisite for complete success was speed ;
if the main objectives—particularly the crossings over the

Canal de l'Escaut at Masnières and Marcoing and the
enemy's last line of defence on the Masnières–Beaurevoir
line—were not gained in forty-eight hours, the enemy
would have time to bring up his reserves.

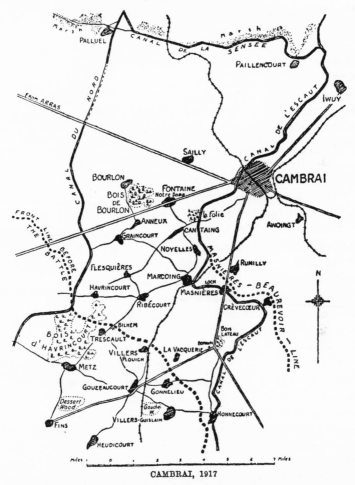

CAMBRAI, 1917

Five divisions of cavalry were available. (Though one
was detached from the Cavalry Corps and attached to an
Infantry Corps, its task remained virtually unchanged.)
In the event of complete success by the infantry within the
specified time, three cavalry divisions would pass through

the gap and sweep right and left of Cambrai, destroy the enemy's communications, and act as a screen to the advance of the infantry. The 1st Cavalry Division was to move west, the 2nd and 5th east, of the Canal de l'Escaut. The two latter were to isolate and swing past Cambrai, then turn westwards, and seize the passages of the Sensée at Paillen-court and Palluel.

So much for the plan. In practice it did not materialize, and though the infantry met with considerable success, piercing the enemy lines to a depth of 4½ miles and taking 5,000 prisoners during the day, they did not achieve that complete success which was necessary before the cavalry could fulfil their mission.

The Regiment remained near Villers-Faucon, ready to move at any moment, from 7.30 a.m. till 11.50, when we got orders to saddle up, and moved off with the rest of the Division at 12.20. We moved up by very slow stages to a little beyond Villers-Plouich, about 7½ miles south-west of Cambrai. Here we came to a definite halt at 4 p.m.

Meanwhile, two squadrons of cavalry from another division ahead of us had crossed the Canal de l'Escaut during the afternoon, but at six in the evening Masnières and the Masnières–Beaurevoir line were still held by the enemy, the main bridges over the canal were broken, the existing crossings were narrow and still under fire, and it would have taken a long time for any large body of cavalry to cross, even if there were no opposition. It was therefore decided to withdraw the cavalry, and orders to this effect were issued to the 2nd Cavalry Division at 6.30 p.m. A rare muddle then ensued. The order never reached the Division till 2 p.m. next day, but they heard of it through their liaison officer with the 5th Cavalry Division in the middle of the night, and got under weigh about one in the morning, only to be met by an officer from Corps Head-quarters sent to cancel the order and turn them back. However, the 4th Cavalry Brigade was saved from this confusion by getting the original order direct through the 5th Cavalry Division about 8.15 and acting on it forthwith.

It was an awful march. After saddling up with great difficulty in the dark, we got started at 9.20. We took about an hour to cover the first quarter of a mile. All the roads were congested with every kind of traffic, wheeled, mounted, and dismounted, and after going about half a mile the leading squadron (" D ") got cut off from Regimental Headquarters by transport cutting in between. The night was pitch dark, the country so disfigured that roads and other landmarks were quite unrecognizable, and the horses had had no water since 6 a.m. However, we managed to find some watering-troughs and puzzle out our way home, arriving at Villers-Faucon in fragments, Regimental Headquarters at 2 a.m., " D " Squadron and half " C " at 4.15, and the remainder between 6 and 7 a.m. on the 21st.

Captain Fleming met with a nasty accident during the night. The flash of a big gun firing close by terrified his mare, already maddened by the traffic, and plunging sideways she fell back on him in a deep pit by the roadside. He was severely injured and was sent to hospital, and thence to England, nor was he able to return to the Regiment in France until September 1918. Captain Palmer now took command of " C " Squadron.

The rain, which always seemed to attend any British forward movement (Loos, the Somme, Arras—only the last was snow), set in on the afternoon of the 20th, and continued on the 21st and 22nd. The horse lines, and all around them, were a sea of mud. We stood-to at short notice but nothing happened. On the morning of the 23rd we were told that we were going back to the huts at Tertry next day. However, orders were received at 3.45 p.m. to saddle up at once, and at 4.45 we moved to Equancourt (7 miles N.N.W.), arriving about 9.15. Mercifully, it was a fine night, and we bivouacked in a rather nice sheltered valley.

Next day, the 24th, the Regiment stood-to at half an hour's notice all the morning—

" With fresh orders issued and cancelled every half-hour

till 1.15 p.m., when the Brigade was ordered to move to
Dessart Wood in its own time. Arrived there at 3.45 p.m.
Patrols ordered to reconnoitre route to cross-roads south-
east of Metz to guide Brigade in the dark if required.
Lieutenant Howarth detailed." (Regimental Diary.)

Dessart Wood was about a mile and a half east of our
previous night's bivouac. On arrival we heard that we
were likely to be turned out at two the next morning, so
everybody had an early meal and went to bed soon after
seven o'clock. It was not a very cheerful evening. The
wind had been cold all day, and during the night it became
a gale with frequent heavy rain-squalls. All kinds of
gloomy and ominous rumours were afloat about the operations contemplated next day.

The fighting of the first two days had fallen short of
complete success. We had not got Bourlon Ridge, and
enemy reinforcements had now come up. The question
for the Commander-in-Chief was whether to continue the
battle or not. The decision was to some extent forced on
him by the fact that, having got so far, we could not stay
where we were. We must either go on, or withdraw altogether
and give up most of our gains. A further consideration was
Italy. By continuing the attack opposite Cambrai we should
help to draw off German forces from that front. So it was
decided to go on, and the second phase of the battle for
Bourlon began on the morning of the 23rd. But on the
evening of the 24th the ridge was still uncaptured.

The 1st and 2nd Cavalry Divisions were now placed at
the disposal of the IV Corps, and at 7 p.m. on the 24th
orders were issued for the 2nd Cavalry Division to move up
to the Flesquières area early next morning, ready to exploit
any success gained by the infantry.

The attack staged for the morrow was to be carried out
on a narrow front by only two battalions and 24 tanks ;
the objectives were strictly limited to a depth of 800 yards ;
and the enemy were reported to be in good heart, and very
strong in machine guns.

The G.O.C. Cavalry Corps directed that, if the infantry

were unable to make a gap, the cavalry were to try to make one themselves, but that not more than one brigade was to be used dismounted for this purpose.

Réveillé was at 5 a.m. on Sunday, 25th November. It took the men the best part of an hour and a half to saddle-up in the dark and rain and wind. Over and over again the gale would lift the neatly folded blanket off the horse's back while the man was stooping to pick up the heavily loaded saddle and hoist it into position. Then was a man heard to pray : " O Gawd, do play the bloody game." It was impossible to get the fires alight, so nobody had any breakfast except cold " bully " and biscuit. (There was one exception. An enormous mail arrived just as we were starting, containing, among other things, a bottle of sherry for the officers of one squadron, who promptly drank it, an excellent substitute for early-morning tea.)

Lieutenant H. M. Worsley was sent off at 6 a.m. as liaison officer with the infantry brigade attacking in Bourlon Wood, and Lieutenant G. V. Wellesley as liaison officer with 40th Divisional Headquarters at Havrincourt.

At 6.30 a.m. the " Regiment marched with Brigade to high ground north-west of Ribécourt in full view of the Boche." (Regimental Diary.)

" All the horses were shivering when we moved off, and altogether it was one of the most unpleasant mornings I have spent out here. . . . The rain stopped and the sun came out, but the wind was bitterly cold." (Officer's letter.)

At 8.30 a.m. our infantry were holding a German trench north of Bourlon village, with a gap along the western outskirts of the village. Tanks and infantry were still occupied in " mopping up " Germans in the village. It was agreed by the commanders concerned to advance north-wards from Bourlon village, either with infantry, if any available, or with a dismounted brigade of the 2nd Cavalry Division, and under cover of this dismounted advance every endeavour would be made to push a mounted brigade through the gap formed. But General Greenly, commanding the 2nd Cavalry Division, made it clear that he did not intend to attack unless (1) the whole of Bourlon village was in our hands by 1 p.m. ; (2) the existing gap in the west of the village was closed by the infantry.

It was soon found that no infantry were available for the attack, and our Brigade was detailed for the duty.

However, at 11.45 a.m. information was received that the enemy had counter-attacked and were now established in the northern part of Bourlon Wood, whereupon General Greenly telephoned to the Corps Commander that mounted action was no longer possible, to which the latter agreed and cancelled the order to attempt it. By 2 p.m. Bourlon village was definitely lost to the enemy, and at 2.15 p.m. it was decided to form the Division into a dismounted brigade under Brigadier-General Pitman to reinforce the troops in Bourlon Wood, and at 4 p.m. the brigade so formed was placed at the disposal of the 40th Division.

The led horses were sent back to Dessart Wood, where the horse lines were now feet deep in mud and water. This marks the end of the offensive period of the battle and the beginning of the defensive.

The dismounted battalion formed from the 4th Cavalry Brigade, and called the 4th Battalion, was commanded by Lieutenant-Colonel Dugdale, with Major Du Pre, 3rd (K.O.) Hussars, as second-in-command, and Captain Weatherby as Adjutant. Captain Palmer commanded the Oxfordshire company, with Lieutenant MacColl as second-in-command and Lieutenants Soame, Bottomley, and Howarth in command of the " A," " C," and " D " Platoons respectively.

They spent the night in Flesquières, and at 2 p.m. on the 26th were ordered to move at dark to relieve the infantry in support trenches south-west of Graincourt. The relief was completed at 10.30 p.m. The snow had turned the trenches into slimy ditches 6 inches deep in liquid mud.

At 10.45 a.m. on the 27th the 4th Battalion was ordered to move up to the sugar factory on the Bapaume–Cambrai road, 1½ miles S.S.W. of Bourlon village, and was heavily shelled on arrival there at 1 p.m. At 3 p.m. they were ordered to relieve the infantry in Bourlon Wood, immediately south-east of Bourlon village, and to come under the orders of the G.O.C. 185th Brigade, 62nd Division, which had now relieved the 40th Division. The relief was completed shortly after midnight.

The line taken over faced north-west. Trenches were practically non-existent, so a line of troop posts was rapidly dug and the position made secure. The headquarters of all three battalions of the dismounted brigade, together with two infantry battalion headquarters, were together in a chalet in the centre of the wood. The whole brigade was heavily shelled throughout the night and all next day. Gas-masks were worn almost continuously.

The 4th Battalion was relieved after dark on the 28th, and the Oxfords marched back to Flesquières. At 11.30 a.m. next day they were ordered back south to Ribécourt, where they met the led horses and returned to Dessart Wood, arriving there between 5.30 and 7 p.m.

On Friday morning, 30th November, the Regiment was fully expecting to be sent back to huts for a rest, but it was to be disillusioned. Those who were in the horse lines about 10.30 that morning were surprised to see a lot of men and transport streaming back from the front towards them. At first they thought it must be troops that had just been relieved, but they didn't seem very orderly in their march, and when some of them got nearer it was seen that they were mostly detached groups of stragglers. Some officers asked the first group that passed what was happening, and they said it was a retirement, and that the Boche was coming on fast and had already reached a village about 2 miles away. They at once warned their men to stand-to and very soon they got orders to saddle up. (We learnt afterwards that the enemy had attacked with large forces at both sides of the base of our salient and broken the line at Gonnelieu.)

At 12 o'clock we moved off towards the front, in support of the 5th Cavalry Brigade, but did not go far. We hung about with our horses till 4 p.m., when we were moved up

round the west side of Gouzeaucourt, a village reached by
the enemy in the morning and since then retaken by the
Guards. Here we hung about again till 6.30, when we went
back to Dessart Wood for the night, getting there about
8.30.

It had been an unpleasant sight to see British soldiers
retiring that morning. It is true that most of them were
working parties and not actually fighting troops, but still
they were British soldiers and should have risen to the
occasion and turned at bay.

On arrival at Dessart Wood the Regiment was ordered
to be saddled up ready to move at 6.30 a.m. next morning.
All the following day (1st December) they remained standing-
to, saddled up, ready to move immediately, till 2.30 p.m.,
when orders were received to off-saddle, but to be ready to
move at half an hour's notice. At 2 p.m. Lieutenant Dove
was sent with a patrol to find out the situation on the front
of the 20th Division in the neighbourhood of Gouzeaucourt.
At 3.30 p.m. warning was received that a working party
would probably be required that night, and an hour later the
party in question, consisting of 3 officers and 140 men from
each regiment, was ordered to be at Brigade Headquarters
at 5.15 p.m.

The Diary notes that Lieutenant Evetts went to hospital
this day (1st December). Poor Evetts was most unfortunate,
having been regularly sent to hospital two or three times a
year ever since he first came out in 1915, though always as
keen as mustard.

Luckily the weather had improved since the dreadful
25th November, and the Regiment was well off for food and
tents. But, except for one or two officers who managed to
get a bath on the 22nd, hardly anyone had had his clothes
off since the 16th November. Feet were icy cold all day,
because boots had been thoroughly wetted and there was
never a chance to let them dry. Socks were wet every
night, but the veteran campaigner never takes them off,
so that they get beautifully warm and dry in the blankets
during the night. If you take them off, as some people do,

not only are your feet colder during the night, but your socks are still wet in the morning. This usually sounds incredible to people who have never slept out of doors, but it is doubtless well known to most soldiers and sailors, and is worth noting by any youthful warrior who may chance to read these pages.

To return to our story. The Regiment stood-to all day on the 2nd December. At 6.30 p.m. an order was received that the Brigade would probably have to find a dismounted battalion to go into the line on the night of the 4th–5th.

Next day, the 3rd, there were more " alarums and excursions." Thus :

" 6 a.m. Ordered to ' stand-to ' at half-hour's notice not saddled up. 9.30 a.m. Ordered to be ready to saddle up at a moment's notice. 4 p.m. Working party ordered for work during the night. 4.30. Order received for Dismounted Company from Regiment to be ready in case required and working party to ' stand-to,' one or other being required. 6.40. Working party ordered to parade at 7.15 p.m." (Regimental Diary.) Sergeant Stroud's diary adds : " 6.40 p.m. Working party paraded and went up to dig a new line of trenches taking trenching tools with pack ponies. Going up we passed a divisional dump belonging to a division that had been cut off when the Boche broke the line on 30th November. Our men being very hungry, as they were on short rations, helped themselves. We loaded our pack ponies with loaves, bacon, sugar, etc., and sent them a short way back to camp, so as to miss any officer or guard that might be connected with the dumps ; we were well stocked for a few days."

The 4th December was a repetition of the previous days. That is to say, we stood-to all day, but nothing happened.

Ever since the 20th November, and still more since the 30th, there had been a great deal of bombardment most of the day and night. At Dessart Wood we were about 3 miles behind the front line.

The weather turned bitterly cold on the evening of the 1st, and for the next few days it was impossible to keep warm.

The 2nd Cavalry Division was called on to relieve the 1st in the front line in Gauche Wood, just east of the railway between Epéhy and Gouzeaucourt. The Regiment provided a company under Captain Pepper, with Captain Keith-Falconer as second-in-command, and Lieutenants Allfrey, Williams, and Mason, with platoons of 65 men from each squadron. The 3rd (K.O.) Hussars provided Battalion Headquarters.

The party paraded at 4 p.m. on the 4th and reached the trenches (some 4 or 5 miles away) at 8 p.m. Weather cold and frosty. The Oxfordshire Company was in support with Battalion Headquarters, the other two companies being in the front line, about 400 yards farther on. They had a very comfortable time, as the support trench was really a sunken road, which had been fitted up with tin huts and shacks. They were shelled a certain amount, but had no casualties.

Notice was received next day (5th December) that the trench party would be relieved about 7.30 p.m. and should be expected back at Dessart Wood at 10 p.m. Actually, as was usually the case, the operation was carried out about two hours behind schedule time, and the party got back about midnight, ground frozen iron hard.

Next morning (6th December) the whole Division began its move back out of the war area. Cambrai had failed to fulfil expectations, as had all the preceding attempts at a " gap." Loos, the Somme, Arras, and now Cambrai, all seemed to have had much the same result ; great expenditure of blood and iron and human energy, with very little to show for it. The war of position still went on unchanged. Nevertheless, although Cambrai had been a disappointment in many ways, especially to those who had been most sanguine, it had had more elements of success, and had been less of a disappointment than the earlier battles. Just as Arras had been a step forward, though a disappointingly short one, so Cambrai also was another step. For the first time the infantry had made a real " gap " and some of the cavalry had really got through the enemy lines. But, as

usual with all these attacks, everything had turned on the
first day or two ; after that the battle degenerated into a
series of attacks and counter-attacks, standing-to and
turning-out, orders and counter-orders, blood, slush, cold,
wet, and weariness.

The first day's march was to Boucly (8½ miles), the second
to Hamel (24 miles), along the great Roman road which runs
as straight as an arrow for nearly 40 miles, from Amiens
almost to St. Quentin.   One passed through village after
village so completely destroyed that in more than one case
it was impossible to recognize the site even by the few stones
lying about which were all that remained of the works of
man.   A large and prominent notice-board with the name
of the village was the only proof to convince the sceptical
and reassure the officer trying to read his map.   In one or
two villages, however, a few rough white shanties had been
run up and tenanted by the indomitable French peasants,
who little by little began to creep back to their ruined homes
and even, where possible, make forlorn efforts to till the
ruined soil.   Nor did they forget the chance of a little
commerce, and in at least one place an old lady was doing
a flourishing trade in buns and biscuits and soft drinks and
coffee.   It was not to be for long.   Some 3½ months later
you might have seen them wearily trundling their belongings
westwards again, swept away by a greater devastation
than any they had yet seen.   But we anticipate.

The other feature of this road was—and is—the endless
succession of dead trees bordering both sides, so gaunt,
stark, and uncanny that many an otherwise war-worn
troop-horse, habitually regarding motor-lorries, caterpillar
engines, and the fire of monster guns with the utmost contempt and indifference, could by no inducement be persuaded
to keep near these ghostly trees, but persistently shied
away on to the slippery tarmac.

On the third day (8th December) the Regiment completed
its journey, marching another 21 miles to Lœuilly, 11¼ miles
S.S.W. of Amiens.   Here they found billets with all kinds
of luxuries, beds, and even electric light.   All three squad-

rons were billeted in Lœuilly, while Regimental Headquarters established themselves at Wailly, a little village close by. However, the next day (Sunday, 9th December), all arrangements were upset by Regimental Headquarters, who, dissatisfied with their billet at Wailly, decided to migrate to Lœuilly and evict one of the squadrons there. The lot fell on " D " Squadron, who moved out to Wailly, not without a strong feeling of dissatisfaction and some bitter comment. Nor were they alone disturbed. Both the other two squadrons were also obliged to rearrange their area a good deal in order to accommodate Headquarters.

" D " Squadron's new home at Wailly turned out to be satisfactory enough for the officers and sergeants, and not too bad for the men. The two really serious drawbacks to it were, (1) the very indifferent accommodation for the horses, (2) the fact that not more than three troops could be squeezed in, the remaining troop being in a farm a mile away. But these billets as a whole were good, both in Lœuilly and Wailly, and the inhabitants more friendly and accommodating even than usual, so that many members of the Regiment look back with pleasure on the few weeks they spent there. The surrounding country was singularly remote, lonely, and primitive, but very pleasing and restful.

Hot baths and a complete change of clothing for the first time for twenty-five days restored some sense of comfort to the men, and steady grooming did much the same for the horses.

On the 12th December Captain Pepper went to hospital, and on the 17th Captain Fane returned, much to everyone's surprise and delight. He had left us in September a very sick man indeed, whom one hardly dared hope to see again before the summer at the earliest. But Captain Fane took a lot of stopping when it was a question of getting back to the Regiment, and the hospital had yet to be found that could hold him for long.

In the big woods near Wailly were wild boar, and one or two grand boar shoots were organized by the sporting peasants of the neighbourhood, to which some of our sergeants were pressingly invited. That *la chasse* was forbidden in France during the war seems to have made little difference to the natives here ; perhaps they had special permission to kill boars as destructive enemies to agriculture. But with our men it was different. The French Government and High Command had made such repeated complaints to British General Headquarters about hunting and shooting by British officers that it had become necessary to issue the most severe orders against such offences. Consequently, the chase, though still indulged in whenever possible, was attended with serious risks, which none but a few thought worth while. However, the resourcefulness of the yeoman was once again too much for authority on this occasion. Clad in a spare suit belonging to their village host, with ancient bowler hats on their heads, Sergeant-Major Tompkins and Sergeant Elliott, and no doubt other enthusiasts, sallied forth on the great day and mingled with the native sportsmen, undetected by the prying eyes of A.P.M.s and military policemen. History does not record whether they shot anything—I rather believe not ; but several of the Frenchmen did their best to shoot one another. However, whatever the sport, it was at least an interesting experience and a satisfaction to have outwitted authority.

The Division was now ordered to take over a line of trenches east of Péronne, and at noon on the 19th December the " Regimental Dismounted Party under Captain A. W. Keith-Falconer paraded to proceed by lorries to Salœuel for night. H.Q. of 4th Dismounted Cavalry Brigade found by Q.O.O.H. less second-in-command found by Carabiniers."

On the 21st December notification was " received that Captain F. A. Grange, R.A.M.C., attached to Q.O. Oxfs. Hrs., had been awarded a Military Cross for gallant conduct while the Battalion was in Bourlon Wood." On the 30th Captain Pepper rejoined from Hospital, and on the 31st 20 O.R.s arrived as reinforcements. The Diary notes that the " weather during the month was very cold and very trying for men and horses while in Dessart Wood. Hard frost and snow from 16th to end of month."

We must now record the movements of the dismounted party. A letter says :

"We left billets at 12 noon to-day, and marched to Regimental H.Q., which we reached at 12.30. Here we should have been met by lorries, but of course they had been sent to the wrong place, and we did not get off till 2.20. We had a desperately cold journey, but fortunately it was not far, and we reached our billets at 3 o'clock."

The party comprised the following officers : Lieutenant-Colonel A. Dugdale, in command ; Major S. R. Webster, 6th Dragoon Guards (Carabiniers), Second-in-command ; Captain F. Weatherby, Adjutant ; Lieutenant J. Paton, 6th Dragoon Guards, Signalling Officer ; Lieutenant E. G. Howarth, Intelligence Officer ; Lieutenant H. H. Smetham, Bombing Officer ; Captain F. A. Grange, R.A.M.C., Medical Officer ; Captain J. L. Goldie, Quartermaster. These made up Battalion Headquarters. The Oxfordshire Company was commanded by Captain Keith-Falconer, with the following officers : Lieutenants Hodgson, Williams, Mason, and Bicker-Caarten, and Squadron Sergeant-Major Tompkins. The other two companies were supplied by the 6th Dragoon Guards and 3rd Hussars respectively, and each company contained 180 men, the total strength of the battalion being about 600 all ranks. The battalion formed part of the 2nd Cavalry Dismounted Brigade, commanded on this occasion by Brigadier-General Charles Campbell, of the 5th Cavalry Brigade.

Réveillé was at 4 a.m. on Thursday, 20th December, and the party entrained about 6.30 at Saleux station, 2 miles south-west of Amiens. The train left at 7.40 and arrived at Roisel, 43 miles from Amiens, in a little over four hours. "The thermometer being somewhere near zero and the train unheated we had a coldish journey." (Officer's letter.) From Roisel they marched 4 miles to a camp of huts at Vendelles, where they were in reserve.

Next day they paraded at 8.30 a.m. and marched 3½ miles to Cote Wood, just west of the little village of Villeret

and 3¾ miles due east of Roisel. Here they took over the
support line from a battalion of the North Staffordshire
Regiment, the relief being completed at 11.15. At 1.15
p.m., " not having sufficient accommodation for men in
support line 3rd (K.O.) Hrs. were ordered to return to
Vendelles till material could be found to make shelters."
(Regimental Diary.)

The Oxfords and one squadron of the Carabiniers were
placed in the support line, and two squadrons of the Carabiniers were held " at call of O.C. 5th Brigade in front line."
(Regimental Diary.) Liaison was established with the 5th
(Dismounted Cavalry) Brigade at the " Egg," a sheltered
recess behind the front line forming their headquarters.
The support line was about 1,500 yards from the front line.

The cold was very great ; all the ground iron-hard and
covered with snow.

This support line in Cote Wood was more or less a " resting " place ; there was no stand-to in the morning, and men
were allowed to take their boots off at night. In fact, the
officers of the infantry battalion which we had relieved had
been in the habit of sleeping in their pyjamas, a practice
which was thought altogether too risky by our officers,
besides much too cold. But the latter actually had their
valises with them, a thing never before known in the trenches.
The fact is, this was a very quiet bit of the line, and was
looked upon by the infantry as a sort of holiday resort, after
the battle of Cambrai. This was not unnatural, but such
a view had its dangers. Three months later this was to be
the scene of the greatest of all German attacks, and the
whole of the Cote Wood support line and far beyond it was
overrun on the first day.

The 4th (Dismounted) Brigade spent five uneventful days
in support. Working parties of from 150 to 300 strong
were sent up every day and sometimes got shelled. There
were one or two casualties, but nothing serious.

The last day at Cote Wood was Christmas Day. Plum-
puddings were issued with the day's rations, but otherwise
bully beef formed the main part of the Christmas menu, and

17

naturally festivities were out of the question. This was the first Christmas which any of the Regiment had spent in the trenches, so no one could complain, or did so. Indeed, now that it is over, most of those who were there are probably rather glad to have spent at least one Christmas in the trenches.

However, the officers seem to have done themselves pretty well, judging from the following note in one of their letters :

" We had a sumptuous Christmas dinner—soup, tinned herrings, a pheasant, some beef, an excellent ration plum-pudding lit up with burning rum, and sherry, burgundy, and brandy to drink. . . . It was an awful night out, and a lot of snow fell, but inside our hut we were as warm as toast."

At 6 a.m. on the 26th December the leading regiment " paraded and marched to relieve 5th Brigade in the front line." The Oxfords, however, were not required to move till two or three hours later, and so did not have réveillé till 7 o'clock. They took over their sector of front at 12 noon. The 3rd Hussars were on the right, the Carabiniers in the centre, and the Oxfords on the left. It was a very bright morning, and the relief ought to have been completed two hours earlier.

The trenches were very good on the whole ; beautifully dry owing to the hard weather, and well provided with dugouts and shelters. " Company " Headquarters was in a most palatial and commodious dugout some 40 feet deep, in the support trench. Here the commander of the company or regimental party lived, with his second-in-command, sergeant-major, signallers, servants, and other satellites, entirely shut out from daylight, burning a minimum of eighteen candles a day, that only allowing of one alight at a time in the mess, one in the signal office, and one in the kitchen. As the ration issued was only about eight per day, the rest had to be bought privately—if obtainable, which they hardly ever were. Luckily the Oxfords had brought up a private store.

" Battalion " Headquarters was at the " Egg," about half a mile behind " Company " Headquarters.

The front line was about 400 yards in front of " Company " Headquarters, with which it was connected by a deep winding communication trench, now quite passable in the frosty weather, but unbelievably deep going when wet. The whole " company " was required to hold the front line, the nearest supports being two " platoons " or dismounted squadrons of the 3rd Hussars, which formed the battalion reserve. There was no telephone from " Company " Headquarters forward to the front line, and the only means of communication was by runners, of whom there were always two in the Headquarters dugout. But one realised that in the event of a big attack telephone wires would be cut and runners killed by the barrage, so that communications would have to look after themselves ; in other words, practically cease to exist. (This was what actually happened in most parts of the line broken in the great attack of March 1918.)

Talking of runners, one may perhaps recall a little story to the credit of a young private [1] in " D " Squadron. He, with another man from " C " Squadron, had been detailed as runner, a job which, though unpleasantly dangerous in an attack, was a pretty soft one in ordinary trench life. Instead of having to stand awake as sentry in the front line every other hour through the night, and probably work improving the trenches most of the day, besides being so stiff with cold or sodden with wet that he couldn't sleep when he did get a chance, the runner at Company Headquarters had a comparatively luxurious time. Living most of the day in a warm dry dugout, having no " fatigues," and no sergeants to hustle him, except perhaps the sergeant-major, who was generally too busy with " returns," and having really very little to do, beyond an occasional message to take, or a walk round the front line behind the Company Commander once every three or four hours, he had a job altogether rather envied by many private soldiers. How-

[1] Hancock (?)

ever, it evidently didn't appeal to our young " D " Squadron friend, who within twenty-four hours of his new duty was already pining to get back to his troop in the front line. It was an easy matter to find a substitute, for, as the officers' cook said in withering tones when he heard of the runner's request, " Well, all I can say is, if you don't know a good job when you've got one, there's others wot does."

It was very cold in the front line, but the men got a certain amount of warmth and rest in the dugouts. Hot thick soup was brought up in food containers at midnight and midday, and was very good and hot, full of gobbets of fat floating about in it, which might have turned the stomach at any other time, but now was all to the good. Hot tea was similarly brought up at 8 a.m. and 5 p.m., and rum was issued every night.

The military situation hereabouts was very quiet at this time. The five days which the dismounted party spent in the front line were hardly more eventful than those in support. The following extracts from the Diary show this :

" 26. Went round the line, inspecting defences. Very quiet. 27. 2.30 a.m. Went round the line, very quiet night. 28. 10 a.m. Went round the line with G.O.C. 2nd Dismounted Cavalry Division. A regular blizzard blowing and trenches filled with driven snow. Villeret Lane and Railway Support heavily shelled till 1 p.m. Offence by our guns asked for, otherwise very quiet. Snow fell till about 10 p.m. 29. A beautiful bright cold morning after a very quiet night, visibility good and German aeroplanes very much in evidence. Enemy threw 265 shells in forty-nine minutes between Spade Lane and Club Trench. Very little material damage. No casualties. 30. Very quiet night. A raw cold day. A little shelling from 2 to 3 p.m. between Club Trench and the Egg. 31. Very quiet night. A small silent raid during the night by the troops on our immediate left front found .the German front-line trenches unoccupied. Some shelling between Club Trench and the Egg during the morning. Our guns were asked to retaliate and shelling ceased. Otherwise all was very quiet."

An officer writes :

" We were 5 days 16¼ hours in the line, during which time we did not have a single casualty except one very slight wound, nor, I think, did either of the other two companies in the battalion. I have never been in such a quiet sector before. . . . At night you hardly hear a shot fired, except by the machine guns, who have to fire from time to time to keep their guns from freezing."

The Battalion was relieved by the 3rd Cavalry Brigade at 4.30 a.m. on New Year's Day, 1918, the Oxfords being relieved by the 5th Lancers. One squadron (or platoon) of the Oxfords went into the line at Hetty Post, while the other two squadrons went into support about a mile behind the front line, where they relieved the Royal Scots Greys. The rest of the Battalion went back into reserve at Vendelles.

Our company was relieved by the 3rd Hussars at 6 p.m. on the 3rd January and marched back into reserve in the huts at Vendelles.

On the 5th January Lieutenant-Colonel S. R. Kirby, 6th Dragoon Guards, with his Headquarters, took over command of the 4th Cavalry Dismounted Battalion from Lieutenant-Colonel Dugdale, and on the same day Major Villiers took over command of the Oxfordshire Company from Captain Keith-Falconer, a proportion of the other officers, non-commissioned officers and men being relieved at the same time. Major Nicholl accompanied Colonel Kirby's Headquarters as Second-in-Command.

At 8.30 p.m. on the 6th January, the Battalion left the huts at Vendelles and marched to the intermediate or support line at Cote Wood. For the previous forty-eight hours it had been desperately cold, with a hard frost at night. Towards evening it clouded over and the wind shifted round to the south. It still remained pretty cold, however, but at 8.15 it suddenly came on to rain heavily, and continued for several hours. It took the Battalion an hour and three-quarters to get up to the trenches. The roads were like glass, as the rain had not had time to melt the ice and snow. The Battalion had to walk about 2 miles an hour the

whole way, and even then people were slipping about all
over the place. Next morning the trenches were a scene of
sodden and squalid misery. Not a man had got a dry
stitch on him, and even if their dugouts were not dripping
with water (which most of them were), nearly everybody
had got wet the night before, and those who had not very
soon did so by rubbing up against the slimy sides of the
trench.

For the next five days the Battalion remained in support,
each company taking turns as "inlying company," and
working parties, averaging 100 per company each day, for
repairing trenches, dugouts, and gunpits.

On the 11th January the Battalion relieved the 5th Cavalry
Brigade Dismounted Battalion in the front line, the Oxford-
shire Company taking over from the 20th Hussars in Railway
Trench, where they were in support to the rest of the
Battalion. The relief was complete by 10.50 p.m.

The trenches here were in a very bad state and had to
be pumped out twice a day.

This second tour in the line was rather more eventful than
the first. A great deal of time was spent draining and clearing the trenches, but besides this several useful patrols were
carried out, and one raid. Some details of these may be
taken from the Regimental Diary.

At 5.30 p.m. on the 12th one officer and two men left our
trenches and proceeded to Bank Trench, where they heard
two of the enemy walking along a trench from the opposite
direction, meeting, and holding a short conversation, then
moving off in opposite directions again. This recurred
after an interval of five minutes or so. Smoke was seen
in the trench as if coming from a dugout. The patrol
returned at 7.30 p.m.

At 6 p.m. on the same day an officer and two men of the
2nd Field Squadron went out from the centre sector and
inspected the wire, which was reported as very good, with
the exception of one place at the northern end where the
outer belt was weak, and there was only one bit of con-
certina wire on the enemy's parapet.

Next day (13th January), at 6 p.m., a squadron of the Carabiniers was withdrawn from the line to Hesbécourt for the purpose of being trained to carry out a raid. This squadron was replaced in close support to the front line at "Thompson's Rest" by a squadron from the 3rd Cavalry Brigade.

At 6.30 p.m. on the same day 1 officer and 30 other ranks left Railway Trench to examine the enemy wire in front of Bank Trench. Noise was heard, and it was thought an enemy working party was working on the wire. Our party then proceeded to return, but ran into the enemy wire; one rifle shot was fired from Bank Trench and the officer was very slightly wounded; some bombs were thrown and one man also slightly scratched. Both officer and man remained on duty. At 11 p.m. the patrol returned.

The next few days were quiet, and were entirely occupied in drainage and clearance of trenches and strengthening of wire.

The "silent" raid on the enemy's trench known as Bank Trench was fixed to take place at 2.40 a.m. on January 17th, and was carried out by 2 officers and 40 other ranks of the Carabiniers.[1] The party left our trenches in two parties, as follows: Right party, 1 officer and 32 other ranks; Left party, 1 officer and 8 other ranks. The left party entered Bank Trench just over the entrance to a dugout. One German was just coming out of the dugout as the party entered the trench. This man they captured and proceeded to withdraw immediately. The right party proceeded very slowly owing to the enemy lights and snipers, and did not enter the trench, as the signal for their return was given on the arrival of the prisoner in our trench. There were no casualties.

That evening (17th January), between 7.30 and 8.40 p.m., the Battalion was relieved by the Dismounted Battalion of the 3rd Cavalry Brigade, the Oxfords being relieved by the 4th Hussars. They then withdrew to rest at Hesbécourt,

---

[1] Two men of Q.O.O.H. took part, the Carabiniers being found to be two short at the last moment,

one company (Carabiniers) being detached to hold Hetty Post.

At 6.30 p.m. on the 19th the Oxfords relieved the Carabiniers at Hetty Post, and remained there till 6.30 p.m. on the 21st, when they were relieved by the 3rd Hussars. They had no adventures there, and their brief tour of duty may be related in the words of Sergeant Stroud's diary :

" Had quiet time while in the post, with the exception of Lieutenants Allfrey and Reed, who went out on the front without passing a message along. Corporal Huckerby had already his Hotchkiss trained on them, when someone recognized Allfrey, otherwise it would have been a fateful day."

The Oxfords had a bad march back to Hesbécourt, owing to the limbers following them across country instead of going by road. Some parts of the way the men had to push the wheels, as the mules could not draw their load, and a sergeant said some of the language used turned the air blue.

On the 23rd, at 7.30 p.m., the Battalion once again returned to the support line at Cote Wood, where they relieved the 5th Cavalry Brigade's Dismounted Battalion. Our company took over from the 20th Hussars. The usual working parties were required daily and nightly ; otherwise nothing worth mentioning happened, and they were finally relieved by the Mhow Brigade between 5.30 and 7 p.m. on the 27th (Oxfords relieved by Central India Horse), and marched back to Roisel, where they were accommodated in tents for the night. Next morning they entrained at 10.30 a.m. for Saleux, where they were met by lorries and conveyed to billets.

Little of interest had been happening back in billets with the horses. Practically the whole of the men's time was taken up grooming and exercising the horses, of which there were seven to every two men, including sergeants.

We were nearing the end of our stay in this pleasant country south-west of Amiens, the remotest, and in many ways the nicest, area we had yet been in. Although the

Regiment was there for nine weeks, less one day, the great majority of officers and men were away in the trenches or at divisional and other schools for more than half that time.

At 8 a.m. on the 8th February the Regiment set off for Devise, in the devastated area, about 6 miles south-east of Péronne. It was a very long march—40 miles—and it is difficult to credit the statement in the Regimental Diary that they arrived at 1 p.m.—an average speed of 8 miles per hour without halts !

At Devise they took over the camp occupied by the Jodhpur Lancers, and the next nine days were mainly spent in fatigues, cleaning camp, and repairing and adding splinter-proof banks round the huts.

A new source of danger and annoyance to troops in camp had recently developed. This was the greatly increased bombing by enemy aeroplanes, and measures had to be taken to guard against it. Trenches were dug a few feet from the side of the huts and the earth from the trench heaped up against the wall of the hut. Of course nothing could protect one from a direct hit, but these banks of earth kept out flying splinters from a bomb bursting near by.

It was very cold, but fine weather. Considering the circumstances, we were not too badly off here at all. Officers and men were in good huts, and fairly comfortable ; and the horses were quite decently stabled.

On the 12th Second-Lieutenant C. S. Jennings joined the Regiment, and was at first posted to " D " Squadron, but not long afterwards became Signalling Officer at Regimental Headquarters. On the 15th there was a practice alarm at 7 a.m. We were all on parade and ready to move off in about three-quarters of an hour, long before the rest of the Brigade. On the 17th the Corps Commander presented medal ribbons after divisional church parade at Devise. On the 23rd Lieutenant A. C. Rawlinson rejoined from England, after seven months' absence wounded. About this time Sergeant Raynham, " D " Squadron, was appointed Squadron Sergeant-Major, " C " Squadron.

From the 18th to the 28th squadron, regimental, and

brigade training was carried on. We went out from 9.15 to 11.15 every morning. At first it was chiefly troop drill, as both men and horses had got rather rusty during the long period in which training had been impossible. But the ground was so hard from frost that it was often difficult to do anything except at a walk.

On the 28th February the Regiment was ordered to send a billeting party to Ennemain, as the Brigade had to move next day into the 12th Lancers' area. This order was received at 1 p.m., but two hours later was cancelled by another order to prepare for an attack and be ready to move in fifty minutes.

However, the attack never took place, and at 9.30 a.m. next day the Brigade marched to its new area at Ennemain, where it was very crowded. The Diary notes : " Snow and frost and much discomfort owing to lack of proper watering arrangements."

On the 3rd March the 4th Dismounted Brigade paraded at 1.30 p.m. to march to Vermand to be in reserve for one night and take over a line of posts on the night of 4th–5th. Major J. J. Dobie, 3rd (K.O.) Hussars, was in command, Major Villiers Second-in-Command, and Captain Goldie Quartermaster. Captain Fane commanded the contingent from the Regiment. Approximately 70 men per squadron were sent up, leaving one man to four horses behind. " Snow all gone and some rain."

On the 4th there was " more snow in the early hours but rain after middle day." (Regimental Diary.)

On the 11th the trench party returned after a very quiet time, the only casualty being one man wounded.

On the 13th the Brigade moved again, this time to Grandru, a small village 4¼ miles E.N.E. of Noyon. Brigade and Regimental Headquarters occupied the few billets available, and the rest were in tents, with horses in the open. Fortunately the weather began to improve soon after their arrival.

On the 16th Lieutenant MacColl rejoined from hospital and on the 17th Lieutenant Hardy went to hospital with appendicitis. On the 20th Second-Lieutenant Reed was sent to the Base as Bombing Instructor for reinforcements. On the same day Mr. Matheson, the Regimental Sergeant-Major, left to join a cadet school, preparatory to taking a commission in the infantry, and was succeeded by Squadron Sergeant-Major Heather, from the 20th Hussars. As it turned out, Mr. Matheson, who might reasonably have looked forward to five or six months' peace soldiering at a cadet school in England, was given his commission within a few days of leaving the Regiment. As he wrote shortly after, he found himself back at the front again almost immediately, a full-fledged officer, complete with " pack, pip, and platoon." He was killed in action a few days later.

On the 20th a working party of 55 other ranks from " A " Squadron, under Captain Pepper, with Lieutenants R. L. Worsley and H. H. Smetham, left for Condren, 9 miles east of Grandru, in the marshes of the Oise, and on the extreme southern sector of the British line. Here there was excellent duck shooting, and Captain Pepper immediately sent an express messenger back to the Regiment for his gun. But men, not ducks, were to be shot next day, and rifles wanted more than shot-guns.

As far as scenery went, Grandru was about as nice a district as we had yet visited, and, though living in tents, we spent a fairly pleasant week there. Noyon, where there was an excellent restaurant, good shops, and baths, was a great attraction, and there were besides some delightful rides in the woods. Here, then, we may leave the Regiment for the moment, on the eve of the great retreat.

CHAPTER IX

THE GERMAN OFFENSIVE

(21st March—3rd August 1918)

FROM now onwards the story becomes more difficult to trace and loses much of the personal detail to be found in earlier chapters. In much of the fighting for the rest of the war the Regiment was frequently split up into squadrons or composite parties, and but rarely employed as a complete unit. There were exceptions to this, notably in the fighting of August 1918 and again in some later stages of the campaign ; but in many instances either a single squadron was detached for some quite independent mission, or, as in the period immediately before us, cavalry regiments were broken up and used piecemeal in a series of composite parties. The narrative will show how this came about, but it will also show the difficulty of piecing together any consecutive story, while yet giving to each separate party its fair share of treatment.

At the end of the last chapter we left the Regiment in billets, or rather in bivouac, at Grandru, not far from Noyon. For weeks past there had been talk of the impending German offensive, but no one outside the higher circles of the staff had any real knowledge of what was going to happen. Since that time it has been made clear in more than one published account that those in authority knew very well what the enemy were preparing, even to the exact date and place. Of this, however, we knew nothing beyond what strong and persistent, but vague, rumour supplied. And I think it would be true, or not far from true, to say that at this period of the war most people, certainly most of those who had been on the Western Front for any length of time, had become utterly callous to rumour of any kind. It provided something to talk about in the mess, but nothing more. For three and a half years we had heard so many and so conflicting prophecies of victory and defeat, of advances and retirements, of " gaps " and " pushes," British or German, most of which had proved entirely incorrect, if not always quite baseless, that nothing short of a direct order could now disturb us. No one worried about anything except the date of his next leave, and how and why some other fellow had wangled himself in a turn or two ahead on the roster.

Nevertheless, it must be noted that at this time the Allies in general, and the British Army in particular, were relatively weak compared with the Germans. Their strength had been much reduced by the heavy and unsuccessful offensives of 1917, and the drafts sent out from England were inadequate both in quality and quantity. Moreover, the Government at home, yielding to pressure from the French, had forced Sir Douglas Haig to take over more line south of St. Quentin, and we now held 125 miles of front with less strength than when holding only 110 miles a year earlier. The Americans, though nominally at war for nearly twelve months, had not yet arrived in sufficient numbers to be of any use, and the few that had arrived were still training far behind the line. On the other hand, the Bolshevik Revolution in November 1917 and the subsequent collapse of the Russian Armies had enabled the Germans to withdraw large forces from their Eastern Front. As a result, " by the 21st March the number of German infantry divisions in the Western theatre had risen to 192, an increase of 46 divisions since the 1st November 1917." Of these 192 German divisions, 68 were in line against 33 British, of which three were cavalry, equivalent (dismounted) to at most one infantry division. We were therefore definitely on the defensive.

As mentioned at the end of the last chapter, a working party of 3 officers and 55 other ranks had been sent to Condren on the 20th March. The process of disintegration had thus begun. At 10 p.m. that night the Regiment received orders to prepare for an attack, and to be ready

at one hour's notice as from 6 a.m. next morning, the 21st.
The overture was about to begin.

That same evening we got the London newspapers containing the notice in the *Gazette* that S.S.M. Wise and Tompkins were to be Second-Lieutenants in the Regiment, a well-deserved promotion which pleased everybody. The former had served in " A," the latter in " D," Squadron since the beginning of the war, and each was now posted to a troop in his own squadron.

Sergeant Shrimpton was appointed S.S.M. " A " Squadron, and Sergeant List S.S.M. " D " Squadron.

At 4.30 a.m. on Thursday, 21st March, an intense hostile bombardment opened and spread rapidly over the whole British front from La Fère nearly to Arras. The bombardment was accompanied by a thick fog, which greatly helped the enemy. It prevented our men seeing the attacking forces till close upon them ; it prevented their S.O.S. signals being seen and it obscured the vision of our artillery and machine gunners. The brunt of the attack fell on the Fifth Army, under General Gough, holding the extreme right sector of the British line and linking up with the French at or near Barisis. The Cavalry Corps was in reserve to the Fifth Army.

At 10.30 a.m. the 2nd Cavalry Division was ordered to form a dismounted brigade, the 4th Cavalry Brigade forming a battalion under the command of Lieutenant-Colonel Dugdale, with Major Webster, 6th Dragoon Guards (Carabiniers), Second-in-Command ; Captain Weatherby, Adjutant; Lieutenant Howarth, Intelligence Officer ; Second-Lieutenant W. J. Mason, Bombing Officer; and Captain Goldie, Quartermaster. The regimental (company) commanders were Captain Fane, Oxford Hussars, with Captain Palmer, Second-in-Command, Lieutenant Allfrey and Second-Lieutenant Williams, platoon commanders ; Captain Bagnell, 3rd Hussars, and Captain Hermon, 6th Dragoon Guards. Each regiment in the Brigade furnished 250 other ranks, except the Oxfords who, having already a large part of one squadron away on a working party,

SERGEANT ELLIOTT AND SERGEANT RAYNHAM.

S.S.-M. TOMPKINS.

only mustered about 195. The whole Battalion was thus something under 700 strong, excluding Headquarters.

The Battalion was ordered to embuss at the cross-roads at Appilly, and arrived at Viry-Noreuil at 1.30 p.m. At 2.45 p.m. they were placed under the command of the G.O.C. 18th Division, two companies less one squadron (platoon) with one machine-gun section being ordered to report to the G.O.C. 55th Brigade at a quarry near Liez. The 6th Dragoon Guards company and two machine-gun sections were held in divisional reserve 1½ miles W.N.W. of Liez.

The Battalion (two companies and one machine-gun section) set off at once to 55th Brigade Headquarters, carrying machine guns, Hotchkiss rifles, and ammunition, besides ordinary fighting kit. On arrival at 6 p.m. Colonel Dugdale reported to the Brigadier, who ordered him to send one company to hold the line about three-quarters of a mile north of Liez while the infantry went forward to assist the retirement of the forward posts, and one to Fort Liez for the same purpose. The Oxford Hussars were detailed for the former duty, the 3rd Hussars for the latter.

The Oxfords took over their allotted sector without incident, and all went well till about 2.15 a.m. on the 22nd when a heavy bombardment began. Six men were killed and eight wounded, and at least one platoon seems to have been in danger of being cut off and surrounded. However, they succeeded in extricating themselves and getting back to Battalion Headquarters, after wandering about in the fog for an hour and a half. Among the killed was Sergeant H. V. Drake, of " D " Squadron, one of the best N.C.O.s in the Regiment, greatly missed.

On the way up to Fort Liez the 3rd Hussars were fired at by our own infantry holding a defensive flank facing S.S.E. of Fort Liez, but managed to stop their fire without sustaining any casualties.[1] At 8.40 p.m. the line on the right flank of Fort Liez gave way, and the fort being reported captured, the 3rd Hussars were ordered to return to the

[1] The right of their line having been threatened, the infantry thought they had been outflanked by the enemy.

quarry. On arrival there it was found that the fort was still holding on, and the 3rd Hussars were again sent up in support.

Elements of infantry, 3rd Hussars, and Oxfords retired during the night, and all units that could be collected were withdrawn over the canal, and the bridge near Liez blown up at 6.30 a.m. on the 22nd. At 8 a.m. the Battalion assembled according to orders at Francs Bois Farm and began to put it in a state of defence. An hour later, however, Colonel Dugdale, finding the farm to be nothing but a shell-trap and an impossible position to hold with the force at his disposal, withdrew the Battalion to the eastern edge of the Bois de Frières and began to dig a line of strong points facing east.

At 11.30 a.m. orders were received from the 55th Brigade to send two companies to establish a line of posts 500 yards east of the south-eastern corner of the Bois de Frières, and to relieve any details of infantry found there. The Oxfords were sent to the right, the 3rd to the left, while the 6th Dragoon Guards remained on the edge of the wood. These positions were taken up about 1 p.m., and the two companies held on in face of local attacks till relieved about midnight on the night of the 22nd–23rd, when the Battalion was placed under orders of the 43rd Brigade, 14th Division. A long night march followed.

At 6 a.m. on the 23rd they arrived at the western edge of the village of Faillouel and took up a position facing east. (It being impossible to carry the machine guns and Hotchkiss rifles and ammunition from the Bois de Frières, limbers were asked for and the guns and ammunition left under a guard. By some mistake the limbers went to the wrong place, and the enemy breaking the line at this point, some of the guns were taken over by infantry and the guard, and the remainder rendered useless. The Battalion was therefore without machine guns or Hotchkiss rifles for the rest of the operations.)

At 11 a.m. the Oxfords were sent to the 5th Cavalry Battalion, under Major A. C. Little, 20th Hussars, and

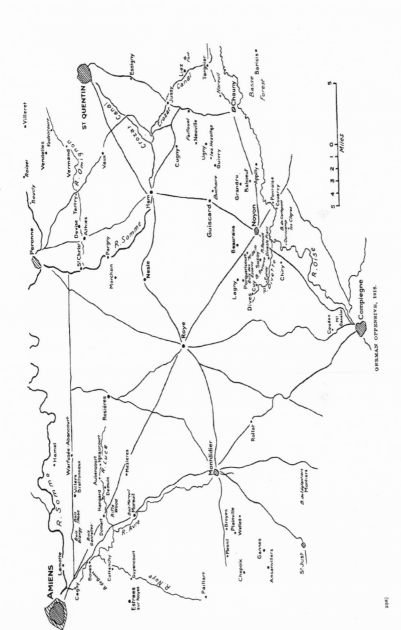

GERMAN OFFENSIVE, 1918.

AMIENS

ST QUENTIN

Peronne

Noyon

Compiègne

Montdidier

Roye

Chauny

Ham

Guiscard

Nesle

5 4 3 2 1 0   5
Miles

[307]

ordered to counter-attack and re-take the line of the canal south of Jussy. The projected counter-attack was, however, not undertaken, owing to the left flank having given way. The Oxfords were then ordered to take up a position in a sunken road a mile south-west of Jussy, which they held while the infantry retired and took up fresh positions. (A staff officer was seen firing a field gun over open sights single-handed.)

About 1 p.m. " a message came through that a French division were concentrating in Ugny to take up a line from Ugny to Cugny, and that we were to fight a rearguard action to delay the enemy till the French were in position." The 6th Dragoon Guards and 3rd Hussars, with elements of the 5th Cavalry Battalion and numerous stragglers, took up a position facing north and covering Faillouel village, the line being later extended on the right by infantry, with a defensive flank to the north-east.

" All this time the infantry in front were coming back and the enemy appeared to be trying to turn our right flank, as numbers of them were seen crossing our front from left to right at long distances, but at times within rifle fire, when they were dealt with."

About 2 p.m. large bodies of Germans in column of route were seen going along the valley from Flavy in the direction of Cugny. Our left flank being turned, a retirement was ordered, first, to the eastern edge of Bois de Genlis, and later, through the French infantry who were taking up a line through Bois de Genlis from in front of Ugny towards Cugny, to billets in La Neuville-en-Beine. Posts for the night for local protection were established in conjunction with the 5th Cavalry Battalion.

The Regiment's losses on this day were 7 killed, including Sergeants E. E. Hall and H. Kidman, and 46 wounded, including Captain Fane and Second-Lieutenant W. J. Mason. Captain Palmer was also wounded, but remained at duty. Sergeant Hall and Sergeant Kidman, both of " C " Squadron, were men of exceptional character and ability, who had

18

served the Regiment well. Hall had been acting S.S.M. for a time, and Kidman had done specially good work at Gillemont in 1917.

(The son of a well-known hunting farmer near Banbury was wounded during the morning, and asked Major Little the way to the nearest dressing-station. Major Little replied that he knew of no dressing-stations, " but," he added, pointing towards the west, " that's the way to the sea, and that's where we shall all be very soon, if we go on at this rate." The man thanked him for the information and said, as he turned to go, " I hope I shall be there to see you win the Bicester point-to-point next year, sir." It so happened that Major Little did win the Bicester point-to-point just twelve months later, and shortly after the race a young farmer came up and tapped him on the shoulder. It was the lance-corporal of the year before, come to congratulate him on his success and to remind him of their last meeting.)

Next day, the 24th, the Battalion stood-to at 5.30 a.m. An hour later they were ordered to W.11.b,[1] where they remained till noon, when they were ordered to retire to the farm " des Grands Beines "[2] and report to Staff Officer, 14th Division.

On arrival at the farm they were shelled, and dug themselves in on the right of some French troops holding what was now the second line. Here they remained till ordered to retire to Bouchoire at 3 p.m. At 4.30 they arrived at Bouchoire cross-roads, which were immediately shelled. At 5.30 they were ordered to Crissolles ; at 6.15 they arrived at Rimbercourt, where they waited nearly an hour ; at 9 p.m. they reached Crissolles and there got orders to march at 11 p.m. to Beaurains, where they were to meet the led horses.

Note.—" The lesson to be learnt from this phase of the operations would appear to be that it is no use keeping the cavalry as a ' mobile reserve ' if the moment the battle begins they are taken from their horses and conveyed up in motor-buses and thus rendered immobile. Numerous

---

[1] 2 miles west of La Neuville.   [2] 500 yards south-west of W.11.b.

instances occurred when the Brigade, had their horses been near, could have been used for dismounted action or even as cavalry mounted in certain instances. Patrols could also have been used to get in touch with other units and prevent the position being as obscure as it was ; and further, if horses had been there, the men would not have been tired out by long marches, carrying in one of them machine guns and Hotchkiss rifles and ammunition. The machine guns and Hotchkiss rifles would not have been lost. The infantry would not have become so demoralized had cavalry been employed to act with them." (Regimental Diary.)

The following account by Lieutenant Allfrey supplies some vivid details and gives an admirable picture of the battle as seen by a platoon commander and his men.

21st–25th March

21st March

11.00 a.m.   Left Appilly cross-roads in motor-lorries.

12.30 p.m.   Arrived in support of 18th Infantry Division at Viry billet for night.

1.30 p.m.   Great confusion, arrival of G.O.C. 14th Infantry Division, who says we are supporting wrong part of front, and we ought to be supporting the 14th Division at Liez. Are ordered to leave all spare kit (blankets, British warms, etc.) at Viry.

2.8 p.m.   March to Liez, man-handling Hotchkiss and machine guns and ammunition ; men very tired.

8.30 p.m.   Explain to N.C.O.s rough idea for counter-attack to take place that night to try to rescue Buffs, who have been surrounded since 2 p.m.

8.40 p.m.   Plans changed ; explain to N.C.O.s that counter-attack is off, and we are to help Queen's Surreys hold on till 5 a.m. 22nd March, when everyone is to retire west of Crozat Canal.

9.0 p.m.   FOG. " D " Squadron split up as follows : No. 4 Troop under Lieutenant Williams go to " A " Company.

Nos. 1 and 3 Troops under Captain Palmer go to " B " Company.

No. 2 Troop under self go to " C " Company.

9.30 p.m.   Arrive and report to Lieutenant in command of " C " Company Queens.

9.45 p.m. Three officers of " C " Company cut as to who is to take 20 men and try to rescue party of Buffs, last heard of at 2 p.m. by carrier pigeon, already then surrounded by Germans. All officers agree that the attempt is bound to fail, and call the idea murder, but one goes.

9.50 p.m. Am ordered to hold trench 300 yards in advance of company, and am given 7 men and 1 Lewis gun as well as 14 men I have.

9.50–12 p.m. All quiet ; post Lewis gun on right of trench, Hotchkiss on left, leaving Corporal Page and Privates Ayers and Hunt to protect rear as company commander does not know where Germans are, so may be attacked from any direction.

22nd March

2.15 a.m. Germans start to shell position heavily. Both Sergeant Drake and self fail to find either Privates Payne or Freeman or the Lewis-gun team (all on right of line). Former never heard of again ; the latter got away, and I heard next day that they are safe.

2.30 a.m. Private Bayliss killed, Sergeant Drake, Private Claridge badly wounded, Private . . . slightly wounded.

2.35 a.m. Order retirement along trench to Corporal Page ; fail to take Private Claridge with us, owing to his being too heavy to carry.

2.40 a.m. Two infantry guides say they can guide party to " C " Company.

2.40–4.0 a.m. Lost in fog.

4.0 a.m. Find Battalion H.Q. ; arrive with " C " Company Commander and 25 other ranks. Am told it is impossible to try to bring in either Sergeant Drake or Private Claridge.

Fog clears—

7.0 a.m. Men very tired ; ordered to dig trenches just west of canal near Liez. Work under these conditions impossible, so leave infantry Major and labour company to do work, same Major killed here next day defending place.

9.0 a.m.–12.30 p.m. Sleep in wood. Except small party who wire outside of wood.

1.0 p.m. Regiment (" C " and " D " Squadrons) leave wood to go to billet at place half-mile west of Vouel.

1.30 p.m. Arrival of 3rd Hussars going in same direction.

1.45 p.m. We see through field-glasses fight going on in Tergnier.

1.50 p.m. Order to load 5 rounds and fix bayonets.

2.0 p.m. Arrival of Captain Fane, who says that Germans have driven back 3rd London and have crossed at Tergnier. Orders us to form a firing line in grass field ; sends to tell Colonel Dugdale of situation.

2.0–11.30 p.m. Remain in field.

Fog.

11.30 p.m. Infantry Colonel tells me two French divisions will relieve us that night.

12.0 midnight. " C " Company of Queen's Surreys relieve us.

23rd March

12.30 a.m. Ordered to leave Hotchkiss guns in wood ; never seen again.

12.45–5.0 a.m. March.

5.0 a.m. Arrive half-mile west of Faillouel.

5.0–7.0 a.m. Sleep on road.

7.0 a.m. Attempt to cook breakfast.

7.5 a.m. Orders to put fires out.

Fog clears.

9.0 a.m. Ordered to march ; situation very obscure.

9.30 a.m. Attached to 5th Cavalry Brigade under Major Little.

9.35 a.m. Ordered to attack railway quarter-mile south of Jussy.

9.45 a.m. Infantry between Flavy and Jussy retire.

9.50 a.m. Receive orders from Major Little to retire.

10.0 a.m. Retire. Shouted orders from Captain Fane not to retire. Left of squadron obeys ; but, owing to noise and distance, right of squadron fails to hear and continues to retire. Result utter confusion.

10.10 a.m. Captain Fane hit. Sergeant Stroud hit. Private Boyles killed. Others hit (probably Private Howkins).

10.15 a.m. Line reformed east of Faillouel. Captain Palmer in command of about 350 men ; left flank in air, Germans seen preparing for attack ; nobody with more than 20 rounds of ammunition.

10.30 a.m.   Am sent to report state of defence to Major Little.

11.0 a.m.   Major Little tells me it is impossible to get any ammunition and orders me to tell Captain Palmer to retire further to Faillouel, saying the right of the line will retire also.

11.30 a.m.   Private H. Hicks hit.   I return only to find that infantry Colonel has retired with 300 of Captain Palmer's force, forcing him to retire with those left.

11.30 a.m.–12.30 p.m.   Fail to find Captain Palmer.

12.30 p.m.   Am ordered by infantry Colonel (complete stranger) to collect men with him on Faillouel–Villequier–Aumont road.

1.0 p.m.   Arrival of Major Cheyne, 16th Lancers, and Sergeant List, with about 15 men of " D " Squadron.

2.0 p.m.   Major Cheyne decides, against wishes of infantry Colonel, not to support the French, who have arrived by now.

2.0–3.30 p.m.   Major Cheyne offers his services with 8 officers and 80 other ranks to 150th Infantry Brigade (General S. Jackson) at Villequier–Aumont, who orders us to hold roads from Villequier–Aumont to Chauny until the French have time to take over.

3.30–4.30 p.m.   Decide where to hold.

4.30 p.m.–3 a.m.   Hold position with the French holding front line 700 yards due east.   All quiet.

24th March

3.0–6.0 a.m.   March to rejoin cavalry at Cailllouel.

6.0 a.m.–2 p.m.   Rest at Cailllouel.

2 p.m.   Start to rejoin division at Bailly.

4.0 p.m.   Ordered to support the French and hold Appilly Château.

4.30 p.m.–4 a.m.   Hold Appilly Château.

25th March

Rejoin 2nd Cavalry Division at Bailly.

It is clear from the above account that the dismounted party had had a very wearing time during the four days

from the 21st to 25th March, as hard a time perhaps as any
in the Regiment's experience since the battle for Messines
in 1914. We must now turn back to the morning of the
21st and see what the rest of the Regiment had been doing.
And first as to the working party under Captain Pepper.
They were at once transformed into a fighting force, under
General Cator, and used to support the infantry, but no
written account has been preserved of their doings. Captain
Pepper and a few men were wounded.

During the 21st and 22nd the rest of the Regiment
remained at Grandru with the horses, in a state of preparedness, ready to move at short notice. There was a strange
unreality in the still peaceful atmosphere of the place, with
a terrific battle raging only a few miles away. The continuous roar of the bombardment and the pitiful sight of
refugees on the Noyon road were the only evidence of war.

At 3 p.m. on the 22nd a composite mounted squadron
was formed from brigade details, one troop from the
Regiment under Lieutenant H. H. Soame, the squadron
forming part of a composite regiment under Major Bonham,
Royal Scots Greys. This force was to assist the infantry
retiring from Ham.

At 11.30 a.m. on the 23rd March the led horses and
transport of the Brigade were ordered to move from Grandru
to bivouac near Pontoise, whence they moved to Bailly at
1 p.m. next day. On the way there, orders were received
to send horses to fetch the dismounted party, the remainder
to go on to Bailly. Here they got billets of a sort in some
huts. The dismounted party, having met the led horses
somewhere east of Noyon, rode *via* Noyon and Pontoise to
Bailly, where, as already related, they eventually arrived
in the small hours of the 25th.

The Regiment was not, however, reunited, for already,
at 4 a.m. on the 25th, and before the return of the dismounted
party, another composite regiment of six squadrons
(mounted) had been formed under the command of Lieutenant-Colonel E. T. Cook, of the 20th Hussars. The con-
tribution of the Regiment to this new mixed force is not

precisely stated in the diary, but Captain Weatherby was in command of two troops of the Oxfords and one troop of the 5th Lancers. We shall refer to their movements later.

At 11 a.m. on the 25th yet another composite regiment was formed from brigade details under Lieutenant-Colonel W. T. Willcox, 3rd (K.O.) Hussars, and concentrated at Pontoise. Major Villiers commanded the Oxfordshire squadron in this force.

The remainder of the brigade details, now reduced to about one man per ten horses, passed a hectic night at Bailly on the 25th–26th March, saddling and off-saddling the horses half a dozen times, and standing-to ready to move all night.

Already at 11 p.m. on the 25th the " B " Echelon (i.e. the heavy transport) had been moved to an area south of Compiègne, and at 8 a.m. next morning the led horses and " A " Echelon marched to the same bivouac. Before they started, however, their man-power was reduced once more, and a (very) mixed force of some 150 men, drawn from all units in the Division, was sent under Captain Keith-Falconer to report to General Pitman at Chiry, on the Noyon–Compiègne road. This left the led-horse party almost manless and the horses were moved southwards, roped together like beasts going to market, with about two men per troop, one at each end, to control them.

During the march of the led horses the following incident occurred. As the column was proceeding along the road to Compiègne, they overtook a crowd of infantry stragglers, who had got separated from their units and were plodding along, no one perhaps quite knew where, but still hoping to arrive somewhere. A brilliant idea struck Colonel Dugdale. " Any of you fellows like a ride ? " he said, and in a few minutes they had all clambered up safely on the backs of the many riderless horses. One man in particular climbed on a horse behind the saddle, which was piled up with blankets, and finding no chance of sitting on top of the bundle, seated himself on the horse's quarters, but this was disallowed. After continuing at a walking pace for some time, the Colonel thought he would try a trot, but this was too much for our infantry friends and the rest of the march was completed at a walk. On arrival in camp late in the day they were doubtless a little sore in places but none the less pleased with themselves. One Lancashire lad, after dismounting stiffly, and standing well back from his charger, gazed at him with a look of deep admiration, and said : " Well, when aa gets back to Battaalion, aa'm for the traanspoort."

The following account of the operations of Captain Weatherby's mounted squadron, forming part of the composite regiment under Colonel Cook, is taken from the Regimental Diary.

25th March

5 a.m.   Ordered to concentrate at Vauchelles.

2 p.m.   Moved to Lagny. There formed dismounted divisional trench party and ordered to Mericourt over the canal by Catigny. Stopped at Catigny owing to further German advance and ordered to take up a line over the canal facing Chevilly.

5.30 p.m.   Ordered to return to Lagny and ride to southwest of aerodrome at Catigny. On arrival came under heavy machine-gun fire. Dug a line with right on Catigny road, left in touch with 5th Brigade. Sent a patrol to canal by Catigny.

11 p.m.   Ordered to take up a new line on Roye–Noyon road. On arrival there sent a patrol to get touch with Canadian Brigade on right but failed to do so. Horses left about 1,000 yards behind.

Midnight 25th–26th.   Ordered to return to horses and march to Lassigny–Dives road.

8.30 a.m.   Troop of 5th Lancers sent to 3rd Brigade and replaced by Lieutenant Soame's troop.

10.30 a.m.   Ordered to seize and hold Charbonnaux Farm. 6th Dragoon Guards to occupy farm with one troop. Oxford Hussars with one troop (Sergeant Butler) in close support, one troop Oxford Hussars (Sergeant Elliott) to right flank, where they dug in and got touch with 5th Lancers. Lieutenant Williams's troop (Oxford Hussars) took up position on left of Sergeant Elliott's troop and dug in. Whole line under a good deal of machine-gun and shell fire. Led horses of Brigade also heavily shelled.

4.30 p.m. Owing to left flank being turned, ordered to retire from the left. Successfully accomplished with few casualties in spite of heavy machine-gun fire from both front and left flank. Mounted and retired through belt of fire. Took up new position facing Plessis. Heavily shelled while mounting. Held position facing east from village till ordered to withdraw. Enemy kept on making strong flanking movements with which our small force was unable to cope.

6 p.m. Ordered to retire. Mounted and marched through Dives under heavy shell fire to Thiescourt. Halted in woods at this place.

9.30 p.m. Ordered to Elincourt. Arrived there 11 p.m.

27th March

8.30 a.m. Ordered to rejoin Regiment at Jonquières. Second-Lieutenant Williams sent with patrol to report to Divisional Headquarters at 7.15 a.m.

The third composite mounted force, under Colonel Willcox, of which one squadron was commanded by Major Villiers, left Bailly at 11 a.m. on the morning of the 25th March and marched up to Pontoise, where it was concentrated under the order of Brigadier-General T. T. Pitman, who was then commanding the various mixed forces of the whole Division, the Divisional Commander being away temporarily commanding the 14th Division. Colonel Willcox's force does not seem to have been actively engaged on this day.

Next morning they were reinforced by what remained of the brigade details, about 50 men in all, and about 11 a.m. on the 26th they were hurriedly moved up from Chiry to Dives-le-Franc, 5 miles west of Noyon. Owing to the suddenness of the movement and the haste with which it was carried out, there was no time to give explanations, and most people had little idea of what was going on, though it was vaguely understood that they were going to support some unit in difficulty. (Actually the plan was to get in touch with the French, who were taking over the line here, and to hold a position on their right, until more of their troops arrived to relieve us.) Shortly after the arrival of our men at Dives they got a sudden order to line a high ridge north of the village. Riding forward, they dismounted for a time under fairly sharp rifle fire and marched up to the ridge, while the horses were hastily trotted back under cover. (This, by the way, was one of the very few occasions during the war on which this operation, so often practised in peace-time training, was ever carried out under fire in the open, as one imagined it before the war. Previous experience had been mainly confined to dismounting a trench party on the road several miles behind the line.)

Major Villiers' squadron spent the rest of the day and the following night on the ridge, where they dug themselves in and resisted all attacks until relieved at dawn next day—27th March. They suffered severe bombardment at times and were perhaps fortunate in not having more casualties than they did. A squadron of the 3rd Hussars close by had a very rough time.

Having been relieved, the whole of Colonel Willcox's force marched back to Chiry, where they found the horses, which had been sent back there in the middle of the night. After an hour or two spent in getting the men and horses fed, they set off southwards along the Noyon road to rejoin the rest of the Brigade, led horses, etc., at Jonquières, some miles south of Compiègne. Here the whole Brigade, less one or two detached parties still out on patrol, was reassembled after a week's dispersion in various composite forces, at first dismounted, then mounted, most of which had at some time or other been engaged in hard fighting.

" Throughout the whole of the fighting in this area very gallant work was done, both mounted and dismounted, by units of the 2nd and 3rd Cavalry Divisions . . . in support of our own and the French infantry. The work of the mounted troops, in particular, was invaluable, demonstrating in marked fashion the importance of the part which cavalry have still to play in modern war. . . . Without the assistance of mounted troops, skilfully handled and gallantly led, the enemy could scarcely have been prevented from breaking through the long and thinly held front of broken and wooded ground before the French reinforcements had had time to arrive." [1]

More news of the battle had trickled through by now, and people had been startled by the extent of our losses. The whole Somme country had been overrun, and all the old familiar landmarks of 1916–17 were now in enemy hands. Péronne had fallen on the 24th, Noyon on the 25th, Albert on the 26th, and by the evening of the 27th the Germans were within 12 miles of Amiens.

But the disaster had one good effect. Men who in calmer times were most frequently heard scoffing at the incapacity of Governments and Generals, and had even talked of the folly of going on with a war promising no end and no hope of victory, were now silent. Everybody felt and knew that we had taken a bad knock, but for that very reason there could be no more talk of peace, no choice but to fight to the end.

At Jonquières we were promised two or three days' rest and refit, but this idea was soon dispelled. We spent one blessed night in decent billets, but early next morning, about 4 a.m., the Adjutant [2] appeared in the officers' mess with the unwelcome news that we were to saddle-up at once, ready to move at 6 a.m. The Germans were reported to have broken a wide gap in the line near Montdidier, and we were to go and stop it. I don't think most of us got even this much information all at once, but bits of it filtered gradually through during the day.

It was now the 28th March, exactly a week since the opening of the great attack. We were ordered to march at 6.45 a.m. All day we rode northwards, mostly across country, through open fields, for once happily regardless of crops and *dégâts*. The Colonel seized the opportunity to

---

[1] Official Despatches.

[2] Lieutenant A. C. Rawlinson was now Acting Adjutant, *vice* Captain Weatherby, temporarily commanding " A " Squadron.

MAJOR-GENERAL T. T. PITMAN, C.B., C.M.G.

Commanded 4th Cavalry Brigade, 1915–1918, 2nd Cavalry Division, 1918–1919.

do a little regimental drill as we went along, forming and reforming squadron column, column of squadrons, line of troop columns, and other formations, opening out into extended order and closing up again, all to the sound of the trumpet. Few officers had any idea of the different trumpet-calls, and relied mainly on close imitation of those in front of them. The commander of the leading squadron was forced to use his wits and guess, unless he was lucky enough to have a trumpeter of his own to act as interpreter.

Another difficulty on this day was the absence of maps. At Jonquières we had been farther south than ever before, and so great a retreat never having been anticipated, there were naturally no maps to issue. So the Staff Captain was reduced to buying up the few and inadequate maps obtainable in the nearest town, and the supply of these did not go far.

During the morning the Regiment heard that their Divisional Commander, Major-General W. H. Greenly, had broken down under the strain and overwork thrust on him while temporarily commanding the 14th Division. For several days and nights during the recent fighting he had never left his post, issuing orders and directing operations continuously without a moment's rest or sleep. He had commanded the 2nd Cavalry Division since November 1916, and there was great regret everywhere at the news of his breakdown.

He was succeeded by Brigadier-General T. T. Pitman, who was by now quite an old friend of the Regiment, having commanded the Brigade since June 1915.

The day of the 28th passed pleasantly enough. Though the march was long and the pace fast, and the prospects something more than doubtful, men felt refreshed by even one night's rest in quiet billets, and it was always good to be on the move and on a horse, instead of sitting in a dirty trench. Though we had been going in the wrong direction for the past seven days, there was always hope that the tide would turn. And it was more interesting than any phase in the war since 1914. Moreover, the weather had been wonderful, a succession of beautiful warm spring days, with only one short cold interval about the 26th.

After riding for seven hours, with but few halts, the Brigade halted at last at Chépoix, close to the main Paris–Amiens railway, at 2 p.m. For the last few miles they had closely followed the line of the railway, and one saw with relief an occasional locomotive on the move, though no sign of ordinary passenger traffic. At least this vital and familiar line of communication, this link with home and civilization, was still intact.

On arrival at or near Chépoix, the Regiment halted by some brick kilns near the railway, and presently there came the reassuring news that the Germans had been turned back and we were no longer required to fill the gap. So at 3 p.m. we were sent into billets for the night at Gannes.

Gannes is a pleasant little village about a mile west of the Paris–Amiens railway, on which it has a little wayside station through which the great continental expresses now thunder half a dozen times a day. Then, however, on this 28th March, it was undisturbed by all but a passing locomotive from time to time. The village was almost bare of inhabitants. Almost, but there was at least one aged old couple who preferred to face the possible, and at that moment rather probable, arrival of the enemy, rather than risk by flight the entire destruction of their property. For that was the fate of the refugees. Their houses were ransacked from top to bottom by the first troops who arrived, not by those of the enemy only. In this case the French had already been in the village and had cleared out much of its contents. Not only had hay and straw for the horses, bread, chickens, and wine for the men, been taken freely, but the wardrobes and cupboards of most of the houses had been systematically plundered of everything of any value. Much of what remained was strewn about the floor, women's clothes and Sunday finery, children's boots, family portraits and other little treasures. The taking of these things was loot, which every soldier must condemn. But it was hard to keep men, worn with seven days' bloodshed, hunger, and weariness, from taking what seemed certain otherwise to fall into the hands of the Germans. The view of the French *poilu* was that the Boche would very likely be here in a day or two, so it was no use leaving anything for him to plunder. I am afraid that our men helped themselves to a good deal in the way of eatables, especially chickens and the contents of the village grocer's shop, such as remained after the French had gone through them. Even some of the officers made use of a bottle or two of wine which they found lying about in their mess. All this probably sounds very shocking to the civilian mind, or even to the staff officer who has never been farther afield than G.H.Q. And no doubt it is very reprehensible to eat someone else's chickens and to drink someone else's wine, but—these men had been on the edge of hell for several days and had every expectation of being there again within a day or two ; the stuff they most wanted was there to their hands, abandoned by its rightful owners ; in all probability the Boche would have it before long if they did not. So they took it, and none may rightly blame them except those who have been similarly tempted and have resisted ; certainly not the armchair moralist at home.

The great danger of loot is drink. If once the men get at the liquor, they are soon out of hand and terrible excesses may follow. Happily this did not happen at Gannes.

Everybody that night had a good meal and the prospect of a good sleep in a comfortable billet. And at about 9 o'clock everyone was supremely content with life.' It was not to be for long. At that hour orders arrived from Brigade Headquarters for a dismounted party of 300 men under Major Nicholl to report to the 56th French Division at Broyes to garrison the defences of that place. The party was made up of 100 men from each regiment in the Brigade ; Lieutenant Rawlinson went as Adjutant, and Captain Keith-Falconer commanded the Oxford Hussars company. They first rode to the neighbouring village of Plainville, where they arrived about 1 a.m. and spent some time wandering about in the dark before finding the hovels in which they were to billet. They were then ordered to relieve the French battalion holding the defences of Broyes at 2 p.m. next day—29th March—and some time in the early morning they marched up to the latter place, where Major Nicholl interviewed the French commander and obtained instructions as to what was required of him. The French General and his staff were extremely courteous and highly efficient ; at any rate they impressed our officers very favourably by the rapidity and clearness with which they explained the situation and issued their orders, while the much smaller number of staff officers at a French Headquarters was a notable point of contrast with our British practice.

The village of Broyes was fairly full of French troops and not far behind the outpost line. Although quite untouched by shell fire, it had been cleared of civilian inhabitants and the houses thoroughly ransacked, as at Gannes. The rôle of Major Nicholl's force was to be in support or reserve, and it seemed likely that they would be chiefly employed in the familiar work of digging trenches, which at present were few and scanty. However, it all came to nothing in the end, for at 2 p.m. they were ordered to rejoin their own Brigade at Tartigny, en route for Chaussoy. On arrival there they found that the Brigade had gone on to Estrées-sur-Noye, where they at last overtook it.

Meanwhile the rest of the Brigade, after a full night's sleep and a morning spent in bathing themselves, grooming their horses, cleaning their rifles, and polishing up their kit and equipment in general, set off from Gannes at 2 p.m. on the 29th greatly refreshed. They marched northwards and were told they were going to spend the night at Estrées-sur-Noye, 8 or 10 miles south of Amiens, where " D " Squadron had been billeted in November 1917. The prospect of squeezing a whole brigade into a village which was known to have been somewhat cramped even for a squadron was not altogether reassuring. However, the prospect fell short of the reality.

On arrival at Estrées some time in the late afternoon the

Brigade found the village already crammed full to the last inch with divisional troops, ammunition columns, A.S.C. units, etc. etc. So, having watered the horses, not without difficulty, in one small pond by the road, the whole Brigade pushed on in the growing darkness to the next village, Sains-en-Amienois, a mile or two farther up the Amiens road. This also was full, so there was nothing for it but to go cn to bivouac in the Bois de Boves. Here they eventually arrived at 11 p.m., and were told to be ready to move at 5 a.m. next morning. By the mercy of Providence it was a fine mild night. Just before " getting down to it " we heard the news that Foch had been appointed Generalissimo of the Allied Armies on the Western Front.[1]

On the 30th March the Regiment moved on again to Bois l'Abbé, where it arrived about 11 a.m., and remained all the rest of that day and the following night. Steady rain set in soon after they got there and continued for many hours, making everything very wet and muddy. Little groups of men sat about huddled under trees, while the cooks performed miracles with fires kindled from damp sticks and produced dixie after dixie of black sugary tea. The Regiment spent the night in some discomfort.

The 31st March was a " quiet morning," bright and sunny. Overdue letters and newspapers arrived. These were the first English papers seen since the battle began, and they revealed appalling losses on our front. The Germans had swept on irresistibly at all points, in overwhelming superiority of numbers ; the worn French and British Armies stood on the edge of disaster ; no Americans were there to help them. The Regiment was ordered to saddle up at 12.50 p.m. and moved at 2.45. The enemy was reported to have broken through and to be advancing towards Thennes, and we rode at a great pace across country in that direction, passing through a most violent thunderstorm on the way. The rain fell in torrents and the wind blew a hurricane ; we halted and faced the other way till it passed over. Few

---

[1] The decision to place Marshal Foch in supreme control was actually taken at Doullens on the 26th March.

19

knew where we were heading for or what we were going to do, but the pace at which we were moving seemed to spell mischief. The whole Brigade finally halted in a valley north-east of Thézy, where it waited till 5 p.m., when a dismounted party was formed in readiness to take over a piece of line for the night if required. Meanwhile, it was rather unpleasantly shelled for a time, little damage being done, however.

We must pause here for a moment to explain the circumstances which led up to the present situation. Amiens was gravely threatened, and the Fifth Army had sent an urgent call for the cavalry on the morning of the 28th March. Hence our forced marches on the 28th and 29th. " On the night of the 29th our infantry were holding a line from Moreuil along the south edge of Moreuil Wood, through Point 104 to Demuin." [1]

Shortly after 7 a.m. on the 30th March the enemy was reported in Moreuil Wood, and the 2nd Cavalry Division was ordered—by telephone—to " cross River Avre at once and move south-east across the river Luce and clear up the whole situation in the wood and secure the line as far as Moreuil." [2]

We need not follow the details of the fighting on the 30th and 31st, in which the 4th Cavalry Brigade was not engaged. The rest of the Division re-established the line, with severe losses, and held it till relieved by the infantry at 2.30 a.m. on the 31st. Eleven hours later, at 1.45 a.m., the situation was again " reported to be unsatisfactory," the infantry were seen retiring from the wood, and the enemy advancing in large numbers north of it. General Pitman then ordered the 4th Cavalry Brigade " to proceed to Thennes and to co-operate with the 8th and 20th Divisions to restore the situation." This brings us to the point at which we broke off the narrative.

[1] Pitman, " The Operations of the Second Cavalry Division (with Canadian Cavalry Brigade attached) in the defence of Amiens, 30th March –1st April," *Cavalry Journal*, vol. xiii, No. 50, pp. 360–71, vol. xiv, No. 51, pp. 48–64.

[2] Moreuil is 12 miles south-east of Amiens.

"The Carabiniers and one squadron 3rd Hussars were moved up to fill the gap between the left of the 3rd Cavalry Brigade and the infantry at Hourges," while the remainder of the Brigade was formed into a dismounted party under Lieutenant-Colonel Willcox, 3rd (K.O.) Hussars. The Oxford Hussars contingent was made up as follows : Major Villiers, in command ; Lieutenants Allfrey, R. Worsley, and MacColl ; S.S.M. Raynham and 126 other ranks.

The situation " was far from satisfactory." The infantry " had been dribbling back in twos and threes throughout the day, and by the evening the Germans had taken the whole of Moreuil Wood and Rifle Wood, except the north-eastern corner of the former. . . . On the left the 20th Division had been driven back to Hourges Village and to Hangard, which was held by a company of French. . . .

" To the north the 1st Cavalry Division had dug themselves in on a strong line running north and south in front of Hamel Village. To the south of them the Australians carried on the line to Hangard Wood, where elements of at least three infantry divisions were gradually being withdrawn and collected, there being very little fight left in them. The 3rd Cavalry Division had by this time arrived in the Avre Valley, and it was obvious that if Amiens was to be saved, the only thing to do was to throw in the remainder of the cavalry, drive the Germans back, and endeavour to hold on until fresh troops arrived." [1]

The following account of the operations of Colonel Willcox's force is taken from the Regimental Diary :

ACTION OF 3RD HUSSARS AND OXFORD HUSSARS NEAR HOURGES ON THE 1ST APRIL 1918

(Ref. Map 66e and 62d)

The led horses of the two Regiments with a mounted reserve of three troops of " A " Squadron 3rd Hussars had been left near Thézy [2] on the evening of the 31st March and a dismounted party of two squadrons 3rd Hussars and the Oxford Hussars was formed.

[1] Pitman, " The Operations of the Second Cavalry Division in the Defence of Amiens."

[2] 2 miles west of Thennes.

The dismounted party marched *via* Domart to a farm 1,000 yards north of that village.

One troop of " A " Squadron, 3rd Hussars, joined the dismounted composite Regiment, while " C " Squadron,

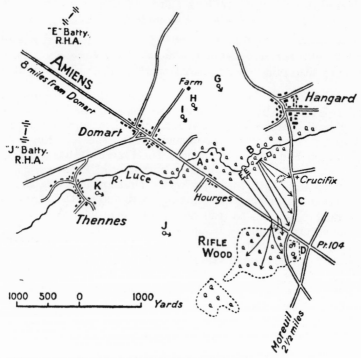

CAPTURE OF RIFLE WOOD BY THE 2ND CAVALRY DIVISION, 1ST APRIL 1918.

A 1st Wave, 4th Cavalry Brigade, Assembly Point.
B 1st Wave, 4th Cavalry Brigade, Jumping-off Point.
C 1st Wave, 4th Cavalry Brigade, Objective.
D 1st Wave, 4th Cavalry Brigade, Machine Gun Squadron.
E 2nd Wave, 5th Cavalry Brigade, Jumping-off Point.
F 3rd Wave, Canadian Cavalry Brigade, Jumping-off Point.
G Five Guns, 5th Machine Gun Squadron.
H Five Guns, 5th Machine Gun Squadron.
I Eight Guns, Canadian Machine Gun Squadron.
K Three Guns, Canadian Machine Gun Squadron.

3rd Hussars, was ordered away to reinforce the 6th Dragoon Guards.

1st April

3 *a.m.* The composite Regiment, consisting of two squadrons 3rd Hussars and three squadrons Oxford Hussars,

was warned to take part in a counter-attack of the 2nd
Cavalry Division on Rifle Wood just south-east of Hourges,
which had been captured by the Germans.

6 *a.m.* The troops for the counter-attack assembled on
the southern bank of the river de Luce, the 4th Cavalry
Brigade Composite Regiment being north of Hourges just
east of the bridge.

7 *a.m.* All commanders met in Domart, where the orders
were gone into. There was not time for any reconnaissance
of the ground.

The wood was to be attacked from the north in three
waves. The first wave was to seize the second-class road
from the north-east corner of the wood where it forms a
T with a road to Hourges and consolidate along its line to
the T road-junction south of Hangard. The second wave
was to follow and form strong-points on the north-east face
of the wood. The third wave was to go through the wood
and clear it and consolidate along its eastern and southern
faces, where it would be relieved by the 6th Dragoon Guards.

The troops forming the counter-attack were :

First wave : 4th Cavalry Brigade Composite Regiment
composed as above ;
Second wave : 20th Hussars ;
Third wave : Canadian Cavalry Brigade.

Zero was to be at 9 a.m., previous to which artillery and
the divisional machine guns were to bombard the wood.

The 4th Cavalry Brigade Composite Regiment, dumping
their British warms at the assembly point and leaving their
spare officers there, worked east through the trees south of
the river to near the walled garden, just west of which was
selected the jumping-off point. The advance up to this
point was screened from the view of the Germans in the
wood. The going was boggy. Along the edge of the trees
to Hourges were a few tired infantry.

From the edge of the trees the ground sloped gradually
up to the first wave's objective, and being devoid of cover,
except at one point—a bank—the advance was in full view
of the north-eastern face of the wood which commanded
the approach from its hill side. There was a little dead
ground just before reaching the right of the objective.

The commander of the first wave had been told he could
start any time after 8.45 a.m., the actual moment depending

upon what advantage the ground gave him in his approach to his objective.

To reach the above-mentioned bank the advance had to move across open ground in full view of the wood. The attack therefore could get no nearer its objective than the jumping-off point selected.

The configuration of the ground did not lend itself to any covering fire. Covering fire, however, was provided by the divisional machine guns on the other side of the river.

As the hostile fire was expected to be chiefly in enfilade from the wood and not from the Regiment's objective in front, it was decided to make one continuous advance—the only check being at the bank by the left of the line—and not a succession of rushes, as covering fire to a flank was not practicable ; and considering that the operation was the outflanking of the wood, a bold, steady, and determined advance without a check would undoubtedly rattle the Germans in the wood.

The attack was formed thus :

Left.	*Right.*
3rd Hussars.	Oxford Hussars.

1st Line.   Bayonets with scouts in front.
2nd Line.   Hotchkiss on flanks, bayonets in centre.
3rd Line.   Support and consolidating party with tools.

The points of advance given were :
Right : North-east corner of the wood.
Left : A crucifix at the T-road on left of objective.

Four guns of 4th Machine-gun Squadron followed in rear of the right.

At 8.50 a.m. the second and third waves had not arrived, but it was decided to start off, for the following reasons :

(1) To take advantage of the British bombardments of the wood ;

(2) To reach the objective before the German barrage was put down ;

(3) That the capture of the objective on the left of the wood by the first wave would so rattle the Germans in the wood that the advance of the second and third waves on to the wood itself would be greatly facilitated.

The men were told that the Commander-in-Chief laid very great importance on the success of the counter-attack, and that he expected the 2nd Cavalry Division to recapture the wood.

At 8.56 *a.m.* The attack jumped off, and as the first line appeared in the open a very heavy machine-gun fire opened from the wood, and a German S.O.S. went up from the wood. After passing the bank a certain amount of rifle fire came from the front of the left of the attack, but the heaviest fire was from machine guns in the wood in enfilade.

At 9.10 *a.m.* The first wave reached its objective and commenced consolidating. The left half of the objective was found to be a sunken road.

On the left the Hotchkiss rifles immediately got into action at a range of 500 yards against Germans retiring from " scrapes " on the side east of the objective, and also on the hostile machine gun marked on the sketch.[1]

On the right a Hotchkiss rifle of the 3rd Hussars which had got out of touch and joined the Oxford Hussars did considerable execution against Germans leaving the wood. The valuable work done by the Hotchkiss rifles of the Oxford Hussars and the four guns of the 4th Machine-gun Squadron have been reported direct by the officers commanding those detachments ; they did great execution. Some German machine guns behind some heaps just north-west and north of Point 104 were engaged by the Hotchkiss rifle.

The second and third waves shortly after reached the wood, and the German barrage was put down.

A report was sent to H.Q. at Hourges of the capture of the wood. The infantry in front of Hangard were in touch with our left.

11.30 *a.m.* A German concentration was taking place on the ridge east of the captured objective. A report was sent to H.Q. at Hourges and artillery fire prevented any further development.

12.45 *p.m.* " C " Squadron 3rd Hussars joined the Regiment from its duties with the 6th Dragoon Guards.

For the remainder of the day hostile artillery heavily shelled the wood and behind the sunken road, and German aeroplanes flying very low attacked repeatedly with machine-gun fire.

During the afternoon a very large German concentration took place south of the wood, but it was dispersed by artillery and machine guns.

[1] Not printed.

Inniskilling Dragoons and 7th Dragoon Guards reinforced the wood.

The cavalry were relieved by the 14th Division during the night. The relief commenced in the wood and finished on the left, where the 3rd Hussars were relieved by the 7th Battalion Rifle Brigade at 12.30 a.m.

Intelligence.—The wood was held by the German *19th Division*, while the German *208th Division* had its left on our left objective. The *208th Division* had received orders on night of the 31st to take Hangard.

The *2nd* and *3rd Battalions* of the *74th Regiment* (Hanover) were in the wood, with the *1st Battalion* in reserve.

Thirteen machine guns were taken in the counter-attack and 23 prisoners passed through the 2nd Cavalry Division.

Casualties : Major Villiers, Lieutenants R. Worsley and MacColl, wounded ; 12 other ranks killed, 47 wounded, and 1 missing. Among the wounded were Sergeants A. Hawtin and J. Johnston ; both died in hospital.

The following personal account of the operations by the commander of the first wave (Major Villiers) supplements the information given in the Regimental Diary.

" About 2 p.m. on the 31st March the Regiment went from the B. de Blangy to a position near the main road about half a mile north-east of Thézy. After waiting there nearly an hour a dismounted party was called for.

" The party consisted of 4 officers, 120 other ranks, including 7 Hotchkiss rifles.

" We were told to follow the 3rd Hussars to Domart, where we should find the 4th Cavalry Brigade Headquarters.

" We went through Domart which was being shelled, and finally halted on the main road half a mile north-west of Domart. The 3rd Hussars and 4th Field Ambulance were in the same place.

" The ambulances and men were in full view from Rifle Wood, and there was a considerable number of infantry moving up and down the main road, but there was no shelling.

" We waited on the roadside until after dark, when Colonel

Willcox sent to ask if we could go up to the big farm where Brigade Headquarters was. We were told that we could go to this farm, and this enabled us all to have a very good night and also all our pack ponies got watered and fed.

" About 4.30 a.m. I was sent for by Colonel Willcox and the plan of attack explained to me.

" We were told to get under cover near Hourges before dawn.

" It was getting light then and by the time the men were coming through Domart it was quite light, but no attention was paid to us or to anyone else who was moving about.

" We put the men behind some bushes in marshy ground in C.3.b,[1] and I sent Allfrey to try to find a way to a jumping-off place in C.4.d, while Clarke and I went to meet General Seely at 7 a.m. in Domart.

" The C.O.s, squadron leaders, etc., of the various units were all there, and it was past 8 a.m. before General Seely had finished.

" The position and strength of the Germans was obscure, and Colonel Brooke came in just at the finish of the interview and said that our line on the right was considerably farther back than was imagined.

" Colonel Willcox was told that his brigade was to be at their objective at 9.3 a.m. and that he was to choose his time of starting, so as to arrive at that time.

" The right of the 4th Brigade objective was the southeast corner of the wood in C.11.a and the left of the crucifix and cross-roads in C.5.a. The 20th Hussars were to come up on our right about 200 yards behind us, and the Canadians were then to go through to the far side of the wood.

" Colonel Willcox, Clarke, and I went back to where the two Regiments were waiting.

" Allfrey was able to show us the way to a ditch at the edge of a field with a row of trees along it from which we could start the attack—this position was in C.4.b.

" Whether it was possible for the Germans to see us or not, they never disturbed us in any way, although directly the attack began they shelled this area very heavily, and I think that this shows that they must have seen us concentrating for the attack, but were unable to get the guns on to us in time.

" The Regiments were in line along this ditch, and it was

[1] The map references are to the large-scale trench maps (not reproduced).

easy to point out to everyone the corner of the wood which
was to be the right boundary of our objective.

" It was about 8.45 a.m. when the Regiment arrived at
this ditch, and as we were due to start at 8.53 a.m. there was
very little time to go into any details.

" I decided that ' A ' Squadron should go first under
MacColl, ' D ' Squadron about 15 yards or so behind under
myself, ' C ' Squadron under R. Worsley was to be about
the same distance behind ' D ' Squadron and was to be
responsible for bringing up all the tools.

" Each squadron was to have their Hotchkiss rifles on the
right of the line to try to return the fire which we expected
from our right flank.

" We had no idea whether there were any Germans on our
direct front, and we imagined that fire from the wood would
be our chief trouble.

" The distance to the corner of the wood was about 600
yards, and there was a bank about halfway where we intended
to take a breather.

" The front of the Brigade objective was nearly 1,000
yards.

" Our Regiment advanced on a front of less than 150
yards. For the first 40 yards or so we were not shot at, but
then we were fired at, as we had expected, from the wood.

" Batches of Germans could be seen running to their
position on the edge of the wood, and we did a good deal of
firing at them with rifles.

" Three of the Hotchkiss rifles also fired at them during
the advance, though it was difficult to re-form the teams,
which had all suffered casualties, during the actual
advance.

"When we got near the corner of the wood, the Germans
could be seen running away from some of their machine
guns, and we entered the wood at the cross-roads in C.11.a
and pushed some men along the edge of the wood to try to
cut off the Germans whom the other waves were going to
attack.

" This corner of the wood was rather heavily fired on
from the direction C.12, and we also fired a good deal of
ammunition at Germans who were clearing off over the
sky-line several hundred yards away.

" I talked to two prisoners, both of whom said that there
were three companies in the wood, but that they had lost

heavily the day before, and that the companies were very
weak.

" One of them said that he doubted if his regiment would
be strong enough to make an immediate counter-attack.

" They both seemed absolutely ignorant about the situation of their reserves except that they were not in the wood
—one said that the only thing that he knew was that his
regimental headquarters was in a château. In the afternoon in the dressing-station a German Red Cross orderly
told me that they had suffered very heavily the day before
from machine-gun fire, and that all their officers were
casualties—personally I never saw any officers and I do
not know if anyone else did.

" We tried to deepen some pits which our infantry had
made, but of course digging in a wood is always a difficulty
and there was a good deal of hostile firing at the edge of
the wood. Captain Armstrong sent up some R.E.s, who
began to make a strong-point not far from the corner of
the wood where it touches the main road.

" It was not long before a good many wounded Canadians
came back and they said that their line was very thin and
they suggested the possibility of a counter-attack.

" Goldsmith, of 12th Lancers, came up with 45 men, and
they went to a position where they could support the
Canadians in case of need.

" The German shelling began to cause casualties, and no
doubt they spotted the movement of troops up and down
the road to Domart.

" We saw a battery of German guns firing ; their positions
must have been, I think, north-west of Aubercourt.

" In the course of the morning the 6th Dragoon Guards,
3rd Hussars, 7th Dragoon Guards, and Inniskillings came
up—the Canadians being relieved.

" *Tools*.—We had hardly sufficient tools when we arrived
at the objective, and some arrangements should have been
made to bring up a pack pony in case the attack was
successful.

" *Consolidation of the Position*.—We had orders to consolidate the position immediately we got to it. As I have
said above, there was a difficulty owing to the roots of the
trees.

" I am inclined to think that we kept too much on the
edge of the wood, and that some casualties would have been

avoided if more trouble had been taken by the men to keep still and out of sight.

" *Hotchkiss Rifles.*—The difficulty of replacing casualties is a very real one.

" In one squadron which started with three Hotchkiss rifles they suffered as follows :

" No. 1 Gun—No. 1 was killed before going 150 yards and No. 2 was wounded. Private Timms picked up the rifle and took the tool-bag from No. 2.

" No. 2 Gun—No. 1 was wounded at once, dropped the gun ; No. 2 went to pick up the rifle and was killed ; another man picked up the rifle and carried it till the objective was reached.

" No. 3 Gun—No. 1 was badly wounded after going 100 yards. No. 2 was wounded (and has since lost a leg) and started to go back with the tools. Lance-Corporal Watson took the tools from him ; and when the officer gave the order for the Hotchkiss rifle to come into action and return the fire of the Germans (i.e. after we had advanced about 250 yards), Corporal Watson joined up with Private Timms and they fired 12 strips before they had to cease firing owing to the advance of the Canadians.

" They got a box of ammunition from a fellow in ' C ' Squadron which formed the third line.

" I am sure that this fire from the Hotchkiss rifle checked the fire from the enemy, but it is difficult to provide in advance for all the teams being knocked out and it was only because these two men realized at once what had happened and what was required that the rifle was got so satisfactorily and so promptly into action.

" When squadrons are not very strong in numbers it is dangerous to tell off too many men as spare files for the Hotchkiss for fear of overweakening the line in the event of Hotchkiss rifles being used for covering fire or some similar job.

" Another difficulty is the taking off the tools from dead or wounded men during an advance.

" It would seem advisable to arrange for at least two Hotchkiss rifles per squadron to be brought up immediately on arrival at the objective, and a larger issue of tools would be an assistance.

" In the other two squadrons the teams suffered as follows :

" ' *A* ' *Squadron*

No. 1 *Troop Gun.*—No. 1 died of wounds on reaching
    objective.
    No. 2 wounded crossing the open.
No. 2 *Troop Gun.*—No.1 wounded on reaching objective.
    No. 2 wounded on reaching objective.
" The 2 Hotchkiss rifles worked well all day and were
brought back in the evening.

" ' *C* ' *Squadron*

No. 1 *Troop Gun.*—Damaged by a man falling on it just
    after the start.   Nos. 1 and 2 wounded.
No. 2 *Troop Gun.*—No. 1 wounded in the open.
    No. 2 wounded in the wood.

" I cannot express any opinion about our machine-gun
or artillery barrage, but I am quite certain that the Germans
in the wood didn't expect the attack so quickly and that this
element of surprise was of the greatest possible value ;
it prevented them strengthening the garrison in the wood and
enabled us to advance some way before getting severely
shot at."

The whole operation was very successful, all the objectives being gained and held for the day against enemy
counter-attacks which were partially broken up by artillery
fire.   The Divisional Commander (General Pitman) says :

" The attack was carried through with dash and gallantry,
and reflected the greatest credit on all ranks, especially
when it is considered that the Division had been in action
since 21st March, during which time they had suffered very
heavy losses and not had time for rest or refitting." [1]

The following telegram was received from the Commander
of the Fifth Army (General Rawlinson) :

" I am anxious to express to the 2nd Cavalry Division
my admiration and warmest thanks for their successful
counter-attack this morning, and I congratulate all ranks
most heartily on their brilliant achievement.   I fear they
have suffered heavily, but their victory has been invaluable
at this critical juncture."

[1] " Operations of the Second Cavalry Division in the Defence of Amiens."

The Commander-in-Chief telegraphed :

"Convey my congratulations to the 1st, 2nd, and 3rd Cavalry Divisions on the good work done during the recent operations."

The remainder of the Regiment, with the led horses, had been brought back during the previous night to the Bois de Gentelles, where they spent the day of the 1st April. During the night of 1st–2nd April they were sent to fetch the dismounted party back from near Domart, arriving back with them at Bois l'Abbé about 4.30 a.m. on 2nd April.

At 3.30 p.m. that day we were ordered to saddle up and move to billets at Lamotte-Brébière, not far from Amiens. Moved at 5 p.m., as horses had just gone to water when the order came in.

Here we remained three days and four nights, " horses all out, a few men under cover and some in tents." Squadron Sergeant-Major J. J. List, " D " Squadron, joined " D " Squadron officers' mess on the evening of the 2nd, news having been received of his promotion to Second-Lieutenant. He was a substantial addition to the strength of the squadron's officers ; never was promotion more welcome or deserved, and never was anyone promoted from the ranks to a commission in his own squadron a more efficient or more popular officer.[1] Sergeant G. H. Elliott was appointed S.S.M. in his place.

At 8 a.m. on the 6th April the Brigade marched from Lamotte-Brébière, passing north of Amiens by St. Vaast-en-Chaussée and St. Ouen to an area round Eaucourt, Cocquerel, and Francières, within easy riding distance of Abbeville. Regimental Headquarters and two squadrons billeted in Cocquerel and " D " Squadron in Longuet. Next day, the 7th, 167 other ranks arrived as reinforcements from various yeomanry regiments and the 2nd Reserve Cavalry Regiment, and were divided between squadrons, bringing

---

[1] After surviving the whole war, he married and settled down to farm at Black Bourton. Here, with tragic suddenness, he died of pneumonia, after three days' illness, in January 1924, at the age of thirty-seven, greatly mourned and lamented by all his old comrades.

the Regiment up to strength. Lieutenant Evetts rejoined from hospital.

These 167 reinforcements were a queer lot at first, and officers and sergeants talked gloomily together of the prospects of ever making soldiers of them. Many were the hard words used of the officers in charge of the reserve depots in Ireland, where they mostly hailed from. They seemed to know very little of what a soldier most needs to know on active service. They might be able to shoot—that remained to be seen ; but they certainly had no idea how to look after themselves or their horses. And yet, so infinitely more valuable is the briefest glimpse of active service than a lifetime on the barrack square, within a fortnight of their arrival, and before they had yet been under fire, they were becoming quite handy. They were for the most part good but very raw material, and we were fortunate in still having a fair nucleus of the old Regiment left on which to graft the new stock. Thus the old tradition was kept alive.

The Regiment was very crowded owing to the presence of " J " Battery and the 4th Machine-gun Squadron, as well as our own " A " and " C " Squadrons, in the not very large village of Cocquerel. Pressure was relieved on the day following arrival by the battery and machine-gun squadrons moving to another area, and the Regiment proceeded to spread into the area evacuated by them. " Started trying to clean up, etc., but much difficulty owing to not having received any issue of cleaning stuffs." (Regimental Diary.) Squadron and troop leaders spent much of their time in the melancholy duty of writing letters of condolence to relatives of men killed in the recent fighting.[1]

On the 9th April Brigadier-General C. Rankin was appointed to command the 4th Cavalry Brigade in succession to Major-General T. T. Pitman.

On the same day the Regiment, less " D " Squadron, was ordered to move by 10 a.m. on the 10th to Francières, in

---

[1] The total casualties in the Regiment during the twelve days ended 1st April were :—Officers wounded 7 ; other ranks killed 29 ; died of wounds 3 ; wounded 96 ; missing 2. Total 137.

order to make room for Brigade Headquarters at Cocquerel, where General Rankin had had his headquarters for the past three months.

Second-Lieutenants Pollock and Surtees, 1st County of London Yeomanry, were posted to the Regiment, and joined from the Base.

At 5 p.m. on the 9th there was a conference of commanding officers at Brigade Headquarters. The Regiment was reported complete in men, about twenty horses short, and much equipment, mainly Hotchkiss rifle-ammunition carriers, still deficient. Officers numbered twenty-four, including Captain Wellesley and Second-Lieutenant Wise on leave.

At 9 a.m. on 10th April Regimental Headquarters and " A " Squadron moved to new billets at Francières, " C " Squadron remaining at Cocquerel and " D " at Longuet.

Scarcely had the move been completed when at 12 noon came the order to stand-to ready to move at an hour's notice. Up in the north, unknown to us, the enemy had begun his great attack on Ypres the day before and had already won startling success. Reinforcements were urgently called for, and now our line in the south had been somewhat restored and Amiens seemed safe for the moment, the cavalry were free to be sent post-haste to meet the new danger.

At 2.15 p.m. orders were received at Regimental Headquarters for the head of the Regiment to be at the brigade rendezvous, a mile and a half away, at 2.30 p.m.! (The brigade orderly's motor-bicycle having broken down en route had delayed the message.) This of course was impossible, and the Regiment, half full of raw recruits as it was, did creditably in moving off at 3.10. " D " Squadron, by the way, scored by getting the order a good half-hour before Regimental Headquarters, the brigade cyclist having to pass through their village en route. Even so, they had but a slight margin to play with, the saddling-up process being the longest on record in the previous history of the squadron. The new draft, though bursting with willingness, were next door to useless, and the sergeants and few old hands left had to do everything. Sergeant Huckin is credibly reported to have personally saddled four horses besides his own.

The Brigade marched to an area round Le Ponchel, and there billeted, the 3rd Hussars and Oxfords being in the village itself. This, as may be remembered, had been the happy home of " C " Squadron from November 1916 to February 1917, and did not seem so comfortable now when occupied by two whole regiments. Still, we squeezed in well enough and were glad to spend the next day in billets, only disturbed by an order to stand-to at an hour's notice.

On the 12th April at 12.15 p.m. the Regiment was ordered to saddle-up at once. Moving off about half an hour later, we reached Serny at 9.30 p.m. and went into billets. Here, also, old memories were revived and old acquaintances renewed, for the Regiment had stayed here three nights on the way to the battle of Loos, two and a half years before. Since then the village had been occupied by all sorts and conditions of troops, including of late the Portuguese, for whom the villagers had formed no great respect. They seemed genuinely pleased to see their Oxfordshire visitors again.

At 11 p.m. that night we were ordered to saddle-up ready to move at 6.30 a.m. next day, 13th April. At 9.15 a.m. ordered to off-saddle and stand-to at an hour's notice. At 11.45 a.m. ordered to saddle-up at once and pass brigade rendezvous at 1.30 p.m. A dismounted party of 200 per regiment was ordered to be ready if required. Just before 1 p.m. an officer's patrol under Second-Lieutenant Tompkins was ordered to find out the situation (1) east (?) of Merville–Hazebrouck road ; (2) south-east of Haverskerque. Meanwhile the Brigade marched to La Belle Hôtesse, arriving there at 4.30 p.m. and moving on to Sercus at 5 p.m. The 3rd Hussars were detailed as duty regiment and sent to Papote, a mile or two east of Sercus and near the Forêt de Nieppe, in close touch with the Australian infantry. The remainder of the Brigade bivouacked at Sercus, with orders to be saddled-up by 7 p.m. Horses were kept saddled-up all night.

20

At 6 a.m. next morning—14th April—the whole Brigade moved to a position of readiness near Papote, where they spent an eventless day. At 7.30 p.m. they were relieved by the 5th Cavalry Brigade and returned to Sercus.

For the next fortnight the Brigade remained at Sercus, most of the men and all the horses out, and the officers lucky to be squeezed six in a room. The monotony was only varied by daily orders to stand-to at short notice, and by an occasional turn as duty regiment with one squadron at Papote. All this time violent fighting was reported not far ahead, and a summons to action was hourly expected, but the infantry stood their ground, and no call was made.

On the 15th Second-Lieutenant C. Pates, formerly a sergeant in " C " Squadron, joined the regiment from the North Somerset Yeomanry and was posted to " C " Squadron. On the 18th Echelon " B " rejoined the Regiment—usually a sign of relaxing tension in the battle. Captain Pearce rejoined from the Third Army School, but did not stay long with the Regiment, leaving a week later to take up an appointment as Instructor at the Cavalry Corps Equitation School at Cayeux.

At 9.30 a.m. on the 27th the Regiment moved to Le Croquet, and thence on the 29th to Audincthun, beyond Coyecque. Here they were somewhat cramped, but otherwise not uncomfortable, and settled down to training in earnest, chiefly Hotchkiss-gun classes, musketry, and mounted work.

From Audincthun the Regiment moved yet again, marching at 6.30 a.m. on the 5th May to Attin, near Montreuil, where they arrived at 1.15 p.m. Here they found the area " in a very dirty condition after use by Portuguese troops," and the next two days were spent in cleaning up billets. Once this operation was completed, however, Attin was found to be a decidedly good billet. " C " and " D " Squadrons were close to Regimental Headquarters, and " A " Squadron was at a hamlet called La Paix Faite—name of happy omen—about 2 miles away.

On 8th May Major Villiers rejoined from England and

resumed command of " D " Squadron. On the 14th Major
Hermon-Hodge rejoined from Ireland, where he had been
Instructor to the 2nd Reserve Regiment of Cavalry for the
past six months, and resumed command of " A " Squadron,
Captain Weatherby remaining with him as second-in-command. On the 17th Second-Lieutenant B. S. Harvey, North
Irish Horse, and Second-Lieutenant J. Dixon, 3rd 1st County
of London Yeomanry, joined the Regiment, and Second-
Lieutenant B. H. Matthews rejoined from hospital. On the
25th Captain Goldie went to hospital. " The weather was
fine during the month and intensive training was undertaken." The intensive training included as an occasional
variation an expedition to the sands at Le Touquet, where
regimental drill was carried out to the sound of the
trumpet.

During May the Germans developed great activity in
bombing Etaples from the air, and for some time their
machines passed over the 4th Cavalry Brigade almost nightly,
sometimes dropping a bomb or two *en route*, but only once
doing any serious damage, and that not to the Oxfords.
The month was also notable for the arrival of large bodies of
American troops in the area for training, the first we had
yet seen ; also by the news one day of another great German
attack, in the south this time. Alarming reports reached
us of tremendous enemy successes ; the Huns were said to
be within 40 miles of Paris, and nothing seemed to stop
them. However, stopped they were, and, though we did
not know it, stopped for good. They had shot their last
bolt.

Meanwhile Paris leave was still open, though, the Germans
being very near Amiens, all trains went by a roundabout
route, and people found themselves travelling from Abbeville
to Le Tréport in the process of getting from Etaples to Paris.
As the trains conscientiously stopped at every station,
however small, the journey took anything from eight to
twenty-four hours.

Perhaps the greatest merit of Attin as a summer billet
was the bathing in the little river Canche. In peace-time

it would probably not have been thought ideal, for the water
was muddy and the current strong. But in spite of these
minor drawbacks, it was a joy and a godsend to all ranks in
the hot summer weather, and the banks were thronged with
bathers every evening. Inter-squadron swimming races,
with bookies and sideshows complete, were organized on
Sunday afternoons, and were highly successful, thanks
largely to the energy of Captain Wellesley.

In June " the weather was fine and much good work was
done in training." In a divisional musketry competition
No. 2 Troop, " A " Squadron, beat the 3rd Hussars team
by over 100 points, and reached the final, in which, however,
it was beaten by the 5th Lancers by 20 points, with the
20th Hussars third. " Unluckily Hotchkiss rifle jammed
owing to two faulty rounds, and thus 70 rounds were not
fired."

" A War Saving Campaign was started on 4th, the C.O.
giving short lectures to H.Q. and Squadrons on the duty,
necessity, and advantages of subscribing to war loan in one
form or another. The C.O. offered a prize of £5 under the
following conditions, frs. 10 to the troop that raised the most
money each week and frs. 100 to the troop raising the most
in the month, provided that not less than £500 was subscribed. Major the Hon. A. G. Villiers, D.S.O., kindly offered
a prize of frs. 50 to the sergeants' mess that subscribed the
most, provided that not less than £200 was subscribed.
Officers' and sergeants' subscriptions not to be included
for the C.O.'s prize. Towards the end of the month the C.O.
offered a further prize of frs. 50 to the troop that had the
highest percentage of subscribers all ranks.

" About 3,000 certificates were sold during the month,
bringing in nearly £2,300.

" No. 1 Troop, ' C ' Squadron, won the prize first week
with 110 certificates.

" No. 2 Troop, ' C ' Squadron, won the prize second
week with 224 certificates.

" No. 1 Troop, ' A ' Squadron, won the third week with
535 certificates.

" No. 4 Troop, ' D ' Squadron, won the fourth week with
202 certificates.

" No. 1 Troop, ' A ' Squadron, won the competition with
666 certificates.

" H.Q. Sergeants' Mess won Major Villiers' prize of 140
certificates.

" The percentage prize was divided among the 4 troops
of ' C ' with 100 %.

" Average certificates purchased, over six per head.
' A,' 1,007 ; ' C,' 791 ; ' D,' 768 ; H.Q., 375 ; Sergeants'
Mess, 345, included in squadrons." [1]

The few Old Etonian officers left with the Regiment—
Major Nicholl, Major Villiers, Captain Keith-Falconer and
Captain Wellesley—attended the annual 4th of June
dinner, held this year at the Hôtel de France, Hesdin.

On the 27th June Captain Keith-Falconer and Captain
Weatherby left the Regiment for a six weeks' course at
the newly established Cavalry Corps School at Varengeville,
near Dieppe. On the 30th Captain Fane returned from
England and rejoined " A " Squadron as second-in-
command.

After an interlude of nearly ten weeks' rest and training
at Attin the Regiment received orders on the 13th July that
the Brigade would move eastwards next day. Accordingly
the Regiment paraded at La Paix Faite at 9 a.m. on the 14th
and marched to Vieil-Hesdin and Fresnoy, where it arrived
at 3 p.m. and billeted for the night. They left at 1.15 p.m.
next day and marched to new billets at Magnicourt-sur-
Canche, arriving there at 6 p.m. Here they were kept as
G.H.Q. reserve at twenty-four hours' notice, and this
continued till the 22nd, when the Brigade marched back, the
Regiment being billeted for the night at Fillièvres. On
the 23rd the Brigade marched back to its old area, the
Regiment returning to Attin and La Paix Faite as before.

There is little indication of what the Regiment thought
about the war and its prospects at this time. Private
letters and diaries, never very abundant, have now dried
up altogether. But if one may for a moment trust one's
memory, there was beginning to be abroad a new feeling of

[1] Extract from Regimental Diary.

hope and confidence. Foch was making himself felt in the second half of July, and for the first time since March we seemed to be on the offensive and, what is more, to be winning ground ; the fact that the cavalry had not been called on for upwards of three months was in itself a good sign of the state of our front ; people who had been on leave brought hopeful reports from home. One day Mr. Winston Churchill—then Minister of Munitions—dropped down from the sky in an aeroplane, on his way to G.H.Q. at Montreuil, and lunched with Regimental Headquarters ; he, too, needless to say, was full of optimism. Altogether, things began to wear a more cheerful look. And yet it would be rash to generalize overmuch. There were still many, both officers and men, particularly old stagers of 1914–15, who had been caught so often and so bitterly by tales of " gaps " and " pushes " and being home for Christmas, that they never could believe anything again. For them you could put no limit to the war, make no hopeful prophecies. " True, the war must end some day," they would grudgingly admit, " but that's not to-morrow nor yet awhile, and anyway, the cavalry are for it first, so remember that, young fellow ; we've heard it all before."

CHAPTER X

The Advance to Victory

(4th August—11th November 1918)

At the beginning of August the air was still full of rumours. Our line had held pretty securely for four months now. Fresh reinforcements had come out from England to the tired infantry, and the cavalry—officers, men, and horses—had been fattened up for the fight by a long period in good billets, with plenty of time for steady training and recreation. There was much talk of a " push " on a big scale and, though no one knew where, certain indications pointed towards Amiens. This city, with its pleasant memories of good food and good wine, good beds and good shops, had long ceased to have any attraction, had indeed become forbidden ground, searched day and night by the German guns, in imminent danger of that fate which had already befallen Albert and Péronne, Ypres and Arras, Reims and Noyon, and many another town and city of France. From the military point of view its position was all the more serious in that it was a railway junction of capital importance, the fall of which would destroy our existing system of communication and vitally endanger our Army. It was evident, therefore, even to the humblest strategist in the ranks, that a blow to free Amiens must be struck at the first opportunity. Further confirmation came from stories that Foch was concentrating reserves of French troops behind Amiens and from accounts of vast numbers of labour battalions employed building new railways in that neighbourhood. All pointed to Amiens. Still, no one knew. The secret was well kept.

But everyone did know that an attack of some sort, somewhere, some time, was very much in the air and bound to come off before long. An attack by us this time, be it noted, in which, too, cavalry was to be employed on great scale, if all went well. The line had already begun to move, and in the right direction. A fortnight ago, on the 18th July, Foch had turned what seemed at first sight the beginning of a fresh German attack on the 15th July into a brilliant French success. For several days after the enemy had been in retreat. This was on the Marne front, where the Germans had made their third great advance of the year in May. Was it really, as some said, the beginning of the end ? or was it, as so often before, but a mere temporary turning of the tide ? None knew.

So no one was greatly surprised when on the 3rd August orders came to move next day. At 9.20 p.m. on the fourth day of the month and fourth anniversary of the war the Regiment set out on the road to Vron, some 20 miles to the south, arriving some hours after midnight. Here, for the fourth time this year, they found themselves among old friends, in the good billets of February–March 1917. But there was little time to linger now, and after a pleasant day's rest they were off again at 9 p.m. on the 5th, marching to Millencourt, where they remained next day in billets. At 9 p.m. on the 6th they marched to Tirancourt, " a very slow march," says the diary. Next day, or rather night, at 11 p.m. they marched through Amiens to the forward rendezvous near Glisy, where the Brigade arrived about 5.30 a.m. on the 8th, off-saddled and awaited orders. Zero hour was at 4.20 a.m. and the battle had already begun.

We have seen how the German attack on the 15th July had been turned into an Allied success. This

" effected a complete change in the whole military situation. The German Army had made its effort and had failed. The period of its maximum strength had been passed, and the bulk of the reserves accumulated during the winter had been used up. On the other hand, the position of the Allies in regard to reserves had greatly improved. The fresh troops made available during the late spring and early summer had been incorporated and trained. The British Army was growing rapidly. . . ."

It was therefore decided (at a conference held on the the 23rd July between Foch, Haig, and Pétain) that the time had come for us to take the offensive and to press the advantage already gained in the counter-attack on the 18th July. The "objectives on the British front were the disengagement of Amiens and the freeing of the Paris–Amiens railway by an attack on the Albert–Montdidier front," while the French and American Armies were "to free other strategic railways by operations farther south and east." These were definite and strictly limited objectives, but if successfully attained, they were to be followed by an attack on the Hindenburg Line from St. Quentin to Cambrai and the

"vital lateral communications running through Maubeuge to Hersin and Mézières by which alone the German forces on the Champagne front could be supplied and maintained." The German Armies in Flanders would then "find their communications threatened from the south." [1]

For the battle of Amiens 13 infantry and 3 cavalry divisions were assembled, together with 400 tanks, 2,000 guns and innumerable aeroplanes, the whole under General Rawlinson, commanding the Fourth Army.

The rôle of the cavalry was to push through the leading infantry as soon as an opening occurred and endeavour to reach the outer defences of Amiens. From there they would move south-eastwards in the direction of Roye and Chaulnes with the aim of cutting the enemy's communications and helping the operations of the French on our right.

There was a thick mist on the morning of the battle. The cavalry were to advance on a two-division front, the 1st Cavalry Division on the left, the 3rd on the right, and the 2nd in reserve. The attack began well and the leading cavalry brigades moved off close behind the infantry. Soon after seven o'clock the 2nd Cavalry Division moved slowly on *via* Cachy to Hangard Wood, where it halted

---

[1] Official Despatches.

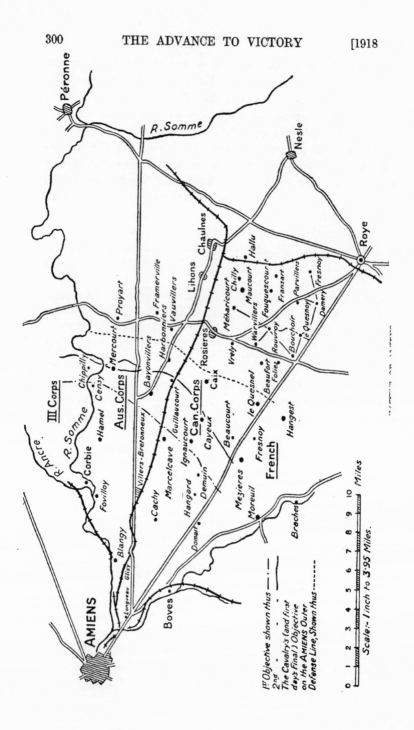

till 2.15 p.m. Reports showed that the battle was going extremely well and both the leading cavalry divisions were in action.

At 2.15 p.m. the Cavalry Corps commander, hearing that the 3rd Cavalry Division was held up at Beaucourt, ordered General Pitman to send two brigades forward to capture the ridge south of Caix. The 3rd and 4th Cavalry Brigades moved off immediately, the 4th leading. They advanced about 5 miles, trotting and cantering, on a two-regiment front, well extended, the Oxford Hussars leading on the right.

The Regiment crossed the river Luce at Caix, galloped the ridge and took Point 95, 1,000 yards south of Caix, without opposition.

The Division then attempted to push on eastwards, but the line Beaufort–Warvillers–Vrély–Rosières was strongly held by the enemy and further progress was impossible.

About 5 p.m. the Regiment was ordered to proceed to the valley north of Caix, as the enemy were reported to be massing for a counter-attack from Rosières-en-Santerre. Here they remained till 9.30 p.m., when they were ordered to withdraw and bivouac in a valley near Harbonnières.

" Arrived there about midnight all very tired." [1]

Meanwhile, the main attack had been very successful everywhere. By nightfall the infantry of the Fourth Army had advanced 5 miles on a front of 11 miles, and had taken over 13,000 prisoners and between 300 and 400 guns. The French also had done well on our right, had reached the Amiens–Roye road, and had captured 3,000 prisoners and many guns. The enemy was thus caught on two fronts.

It had been a good day for the cavalry. The two leading divisions had captured well over 1,000 prisoners, besides guns and other war material. One regiment (5th Dragoon Guards) captured a whole train full of reinforcements, taking 600 prisoners, a complete hospital staff, and 3 batteries

_____
[1] Regimental Diary.

of artillery. Our Division, being in reserve, had little chance of such spectacular booty, but did much useful work nevertheless ; for the first time in the war the Regiment was able to move rapidly across open country against a beaten enemy.

During the night it was decided that the cavalry should make a further advance next day, without waiting for the infantry to break through. This scheme, which originated at Cavalry Corps Headquarters, or perhaps higher up, was thought rather ambitious by those who were to carry it out, and so it proved. Shortly before 7 a.m. patrols reported that the enemy were holding the Vrély–Le Quesnel line in force, and that a mounted scheme was not yet possible. The original orders were therefore cancelled, and the 1st and 2nd Cavalry Divisions, with two battalions of whippet tanks, were told to follow up the attack of the Australian and Canadian Corps and exploit their success.

Meanwhile, the Regiment had saddled-up at 6.15 a.m., breakfasted, and moved at 8.50 to the valley west of Caix, arriving there about 9.30. Here they remained for six hours, during which time all the horses were watered, and off-saddled for three-quarters of an hour, one-third at a time.

The infantry attack progressed favourably, and some units of the 2nd Cavalry Division had stiff fighting, but our Brigade was in divisional reserve and took little part in it. At 3.45 p.m. the Regiment moved up to within a mile W.S.W. of Vrély and remained there till dark, when it moved to bivouac half a mile farther west. "A" Squadron were bombed on their way to this spot, having stayed a few minutes after the other squadrons finishing their tea. S.S.M. Shrimpton was killed—a most valuable N.C.O. and a very great loss to the Regiment ; S.Q.M.S. Chaundy and four men wounded, and about a dozen horses killed or wounded.   "D" Squadron were also badly bombed just as they were dismounting to put down horse lines.

Next day, 10th August, the Regiment saddled-up at 7.30 a.m. and moved to another bivouac near Caix, where they off-saddled and watered.

At 1 p.m. the Division received verbal orders to saddle-up at once and move forward. An infantry division had reported that resistance was broken and that the enemy were fleeing demoralized in all directions—a piece of information which proved entirely false. The 2nd Cavalry Division was told to push forward and capture Nesle, 15 miles ahead of its present resting-place. They moved off at once, with the 4th Cavalry Brigade leading.

The Brigade was ordered to proceed by a southerly route *via* Warvillers–Rouvroy–Parvillers–Fresnoy–Gruny. On arrival at Rouvroy it was heavily shelled.

The Regiment was ordered to take Hattencourt. Fouquescourt was reported to be held by the Canadians, but the advanced guard of the Regiment, a troop of " C " Squadron, was fired on before reaching the outskirts, and it was found that the information was entirely wrong, and that we had not even a footing in Fouquescourt. The Regiment then attempted to turn the flank by Fransart and thus get to Hattencourt, but owing to wire and trenches it was still impossible to move cavalry in that direction. So the Colonel eventually sent patrols under (1) Lieutenant Howarth to find out if Hallu was in our possession ; (2) Second-Lieutenant Hunt to find out if we held Chilly. " C " Squadron remained for the time at the cross-roads south of the " c " in Maucourt.

The two other squadrons and Regimental Headquarters were about 2½ miles farther west of " C " Squadron. Here they came under heavy shell fire ; Captain Fane was very badly wounded, two men killed, two very badly wounded, and about six more or less slightly wounded. Major Hermon-Hodge, who was in command while the Colonel had gone forward with the leading squadron for personal reconnaissance, decided to move the Regiment back behind the Vrély–Rouvroy road. Meanwhile, the Colonel, finding that " C " Squadron could not do any good where they were, ordered them to rejoin the rest of the Regiment about 5 p.m. The Regiment remained behind the Vrély–Rouvroy road till 8 p.m., when the Brigade was ordered to go to the Vrély area to bivouac for the night. They watered and fed the horses on the way there, and got into bivouac about 10 p.m.

At 11.30 a.m. on the 11th the Brigade was ordered to go back to the quarry near Caix. At 3 p.m. they marched back to Courcelles, and remained there in rest, grazing, cleaning up, and salvaging. Captain Fane died in hospital of wounds received the previous day, and was buried at Mézières, near Amiens.

This was a heavy loss to the Regiment.

Horatio Fane was a real out-and-out Oxfordshire man, and all his interests were centred in the county. He was passionately fond of hunting, and many will remember him out with the Bicester, riding any sort of horse at the nastiest and ugliest of fences. He had joined the yeomanry two or three years before the war, and was desperately keen on that too. The war gave him his true profession. He was one of those, rare probably in any army, but most of all in a civilian army, who get some real pleasure and value out of fighting in itself. Not that he did not feel the sadness of it and the loss of friends and comrades—two of his own brothers were killed, one before and one after himself—but he liked the excitement and adventure, and being himself absolutely fearless really enjoyed a scrap. After the battle of Loos, when the Regiment, after four days of discomfort and inaction in reserve, was at last ordered back to billets, many openly expressed their delight. But Horatio was greatly dejected, saying bitterly and scornfully that we should never win the war by sitting still in billets.

Only the day before he died, a friend said to him as they rode together after the retreating enemy, " Well, Horry, that's the sight you have always longed to see ; you ought to be a happy man to-day ! "

Not only was he superlatively brave, he was also a thoroughgoing regimental officer, whose whole heart and soul were wrapped up in his regiment and his squadron. Few officers were ever so beloved by the men, not only in his own squadron but throughout the Regiment. His outspoken humour and vigorous language, his love of sport, his fellow-

CAPTAIN HORATIO FANE, M.C.
(In the Zillebeke trenches, February 1915.)

feeling with the yeomen and farmers of the county, his sturdy contempt of things and persons he didn't like, especially of everything pretentious and insincere, all combined with his courage to make him the idol of the non-commissioned ranks.

Nor was he any less beloved by his brother-officers, or indeed by the whole neighbourhood of Bicester. He was a splendid fighting officer, a gallant sportsman, and a sterling friend.

The battle of Amiens was over. The large captures of the first day's fighting had been increased, and by the end of the battle reached the figure of 400 guns and 22,000 prisoners taken by the Fourth Army alone, not reckoning those captured by the French on our right. We had pushed the front back—speaking roughly—to the old Somme line of 1916, and our front now ran from not far west of Roye (where we joined the French) through the western outskirts of Bray-sur-Somme to the western edge of the town of Albert and thence north to Arras. The main object of the offensive —the disengagement of Amiens and the railways centring on it—had been successfully achieved. And, apart from these material gains, the morale of the German troops, hitherto buoyed up by hopes of victory and an early peace, was terribly shaken ; they had lost the initiative and were now thrown definitely on the defensive.

However, by the 13th August they had been strongly reinforced, and it became necessary to break off the battle and seek an opening elsewhere.

This was found north of the Somme, and the first objective was to be the Albert–Arras railway. After that, the Third Army, under General Byng, was to attack on a front of over 30 miles and endeavour to turn the old Somme line from the north.

But we anticipate.

On the 15th August the Brigade marched west to the La Chaussée area, the Regiment going into billets at Tirancourt. On the 16th at 3 p.m. they were warned that the

Brigade would have to move that night, and at 8.30 p.m.
they left Tirancourt. After a long night march they came
to Le Ponchel and billeted there. Next day, about 5 p.m.,
they moved by squadrons to Raye-sur-Authie.

The next few days were marked chiefly by domestic details.
On the 18th Echelon "B" rejoined the Regiment, an event

BRITISH BATTLES DURING THE ADVANCE TO VICTORY.

seemingly of trivial import, but actually of vital interest at
the time to everybody; no one had seen it for a fortnight,
and its arrival meant—for the officers at least—fresh supplies
of underclothing, soap, candles, matches, tobacco, chocolate,
books, writing-paper, etc. etc. For the men, I fear, it
meant less, since they were supposed to carry all their
worldly goods—and very few they could be—on their much-

enduring horses. Nevertheless, from recollection of the eager crowds which always gathered round the wagon on these occasions, I am inclined to suspect that the sergeants, and some even of lower rank who were " in with " that all-important official, the Squadron Quartermaster-Sergeant, managed to squeeze a good many items of unauthorized personal kit into sundry dark corners. The aforesaid-S.Q.M.S. also had a mysterious and jealously guarded box, the contents of which were supposed to be as laid down in the Field Service Pocket Book and other official publications ; there is, however, reason to believe that it did in fact contain much else besides : to specify further would perhaps be indiscreet.

On the 19th August the C.O. left the Regiment on a month's leave to England, and Major C. R. I. Nicholl assumed command. Lieutenant C. E. Venning, Devon Yeomanry, joined for duty with the Regiment and was appointed Intelligence Officer.

On the 20th Captain Pepper rejoined from England, after being wounded in March. Lieutenant Matthews, who had been wounded on 8th August, left for England.

At 10 p.m. on the 20th the Regiment received orders to be ready at one hour's notice from 5 a.m. next day. One officer (Captain Pepper), with four orderlies, was ordered to be ready to report to Cavalry Corps Headquarters for liaison duties at the same hour.

No further orders were received till 4 p.m. on the 21st, when they were warned to be ready to move about 8 p.m. They did not actually assemble till 9.30 p.m., and then marched to Humbercourt, arriving there at 4.15 a.m. on the 22nd. Then more waiting and hanging about, while news and rumours of the battle filtered through, till 7 p.m., when orders were received to stand-to from 6 a.m. next morning. Again followed more inaction till 4.45 p.m. on the 23rd, when orders were received to parade at 5.45. They then marched to Basseux, arriving there at 9.30 and bivouacking for the night. At 3.30 a.m. on the 24th they were ordered to parade at 5 a.m. and marched to the valley

21

south of Adinfer, where they arrived at 7.30 and off-saddled.
At 10.15 they moved forward to a position of readiness
north-west of Ayette, off-saddled, watered, and fed. At
6 p.m. they saddled-up again and moved back to Basseux
for the night. Next day, the 25th, they were again woken at
3.15 a.m. and ordered to parade at the eastern exit of
Bailleulval at 6 a.m., whence they marched to Humbercourt,
arriving there at 8.40 a.m.

These details make tedious reading and were no less
tedious in performance, but they must be briefly chronicled.
The Regiment was rapidly getting bored. Though not
thirsting for glory, it was quite ready to fight, if and when
required, and would have welcomed the opportunity of
mounted work, but this perpetual marching and counter-
marching, on roads congested with traffic, bivouacking and
packing up again in the small hours of the morning, standing
and waiting the livelong day for orders that never came—
this did no one any good and reminded many of the long-
past days of Neuve Chapelle and Loos or the more recent
but similar experiences of Arras and Cambrai. Was this
to be yet another flash in the pan ? Were we never to go
through the " g " in " gap " ?

The battle had begun at 4.55 a.m. on the 21st, in a thick
fog. (Curious how fog was a feature of three great attacks
in 1918, on the 21st August as on the 8th August and the
21st March.) The preliminary attack on the line of the
Albert–Arras railway was successful, and on the 23rd the
full force of the Third, and part of the Fourth, Army was
thrown into the battle, on a front of 33 miles. At first
all went well, and the infantry had reached the Arras–
Bapaume road by nightfall on the 23rd, but they had been
much troubled by ugly nests of machine guns and increasing
use of mustard gas, both of which caused many casualties.
The enemy's resistance in fact was stiffening and his defeat
was not going to be such an easy task this time as in the
battle of Amiens.

We left the Regiment at Humbercourt on the morning of
the 25th. At 1.30 p.m. they were warned for duty with the

VI Corps as Corps Cavalry, and at 3 p.m. they were ordered to report to the 2nd Division at Douchy-les-Ayette by 8 p.m. to relieve the 15th Hussars.

By this order the Regiment was temporarily removed from the Division and Brigade in which it had served so long— three years and nine months—but it was understood that the change was not to be permanent, and indeed certain administrative details still served as a link with the Brigade. For all tactical purposes, however, it was completely severed from it till the last two days of the war. It should be noted that ours was not an exceptional case ; all the cavalry regiments, at least in the 2nd Cavalry Division, were treated in the same way, and placed at the disposal of different infantry corps.

The explanation of this is that the moment the war became one of movement every unit in the Army, from corps down to platoon, began screaming for mounted troops to help them—their previous opinion of their uselessness having suddenly changed. It was therefore decided to break up the 2nd Cavalry Division in order to supply the wants of the screamers. The Cavalry Corps, consisting of the 1st and 3rd Cavalry Divisions, was kept intact for the bigger operation.

The Regiment arrived at Douchy at 8.15 p.m. on the 25th in a heavy thunderstorm. The Liaison Officer (Captain Pepper) was ordered to report to 2nd Division Headquarters for orders.

On the 26th August orders arrived that six mounted men were to be sent to the 2nd Division, and a similar number to the 3rd Division, for despatch-rider duties. " A " Squadron found both parties. At 3.20 p.m. next day the Regiment was ordered to billets at Humbercamp, and arrived there at 5.40 p.m. On the 28th, at the ghastly hour of 2.15 a.m., it was ordered to send half a troop to the 6th Tank Battalion (Whippets) at Monchy-au-Bois by 8 a.m. that morning. A sergeant and 16 other ranks from " C " Squadron were sent. On this day, too, the diary once again records the return of Echelon " B " to the Regiment, a sign, some thought, of a lull in the advance. They were to be undeceived.

On the 30th Major Nicholl left for England on special leave, and Major Hermon-Hodge assumed command of the Regiment. Captain Weatherby took command of " A " Squadron.

At 5.30 p.m. that evening the Regiment was ordered to relieve troops of the 20th Hussars at the 3rd and 62nd Divisional Headquarters next day, also a troop for duty with " Corps Cage," that is, the place where prisoners of war were kept till they could be passed down to the regular prisoner-of-war camps. " C " Squadron found the men for all these duties, and also relieved the twelve " A " Squadron men on duty as despatch riders.

These last days of August ran out in warm lovely weather while the infantry, south of Arras, continued to press the enemy, in spite of steadily increasing resistance by his rearguards, chiefly machine gunners. Our men had hard fighting. The French entered Roye on the 26th August and Noyon on the 29th. On the same day that Noyon fell, the New Zealand Division drove the enemy out of Bapaume, while the Australians did the same for Péronne on 1st September. Meanwhile, our advance was spreading northwards. The First Army had retaken Monchy-au-Preux, familiar to the cavalry in April 1917, while farther still to the north, in the Lys Valley, the Second Army too was joining in the fray. Early in August the Germans began to withdraw here and there. Merville was the first to fall, on 19th August. On the 30th our troops entered Bailleul, and by the evening of the following day they were at Noote Boom and on Mount Kemmel. We were beginning to get our own back again.

On the 1st September orders were issued for an attack on the Drocourt–Quéant switch of the Hindenburg Line. This was to be carried out by four corps, among which was the VI, to which we were then attached. Of the four divisions in the Corps, the 3rd and 62nd were detailed for the attack, while the Guards and 2nd, with " the Corps

Cavalry Regiment," as we were officially described in operation orders, were in corps reserve. The objectives of the VI Corps included Morchies for the 62nd Division, Lagnicourt for the 3rd Division. The 62nd Division was on the right, the 3rd on the left.

At 6.30 p.m. on the 1st the Regiment received orders to be ready to move at one hour's notice after 6.30 a.m. on the 2nd.

At 6.30 a.m. on the 2nd the Regiment was ordered to report to the Headquarters of the 62nd Division at Ervillers. They arrived there at 11.20 a.m. and were at once ordered to move forward to 187th Brigade Headquarters, ready to exploit any success. At 12.30 p.m. they arrived at a point just east of Mory, where the Divisional Commander ordered them to remain, as the enemy were counter-attacking. An hour later they were ordered to return to billets at Humbercamp, and arrived there at 5.30. At 6.30 p.m. they were ordered to report to the 2nd Division at Ervillers at 7.30 a.m. on the 3rd, with one squadron, and to send another squadron to relieve the 12th Lancers (attached XVII Corps) near Hénin-sur-Cojeul.

The day had gone well, in spite of the fact that we had not been called on to exploit the hoped-for success. The main objective—the Drocourt–Quéant switch and the complicated trench system at its junction with the Hindenburg main line—had been captured, after hard fighting, by the Canadian and XVII Corps. The attack by the 62nd Division had begun favourably, but about midday their advance was held up by counter-attacks. In the evening the 2nd Division was ordered to relieve the 62nd, and the Guards to relieve the 3rd, both to be prepared to continue the attack in the direction of Morchies and Lagnicourt respectively.

The 2nd Division plan of attack was as follows : The 6th Brigade (right) and the 99th Brigade (left), each with one machine-gun company, were to attack the Beugny–Lagnicourt ridge west of Morchies, and if possible make a further advance to the Beaumetz–Louverval ridge ; the

5th Brigade was to be in divisional reserve. The attack
would be made under a creeping barrage, and three Mark IV
tanks were allotted to the 6th Brigade with the special
object of dealing with Maricourt Wood, which was full of
German machine guns. " A " Squadron of the Oxfordshire
Hussars and six whippet tanks were to be in corps reserve,
ready to exploit any success. " Zero " hour was to be at
5.20 a.m.[1]

Probably on account of the capture of the Drocourt–
Quéant switch, the enemy withdrew his line during the night,
and the 2nd Division met with little opposition when they
attacked next morning.

At 5 a.m. " D " Squadron, under Major Villiers, moved off
to report to the 2nd Division, with advanced Regimental
Headquarters under Major Hermon-Hodge. At 8 a.m.
" A " Squadron, under Captain Weatherby, moved off to
report to the XVII Corps.

At 8.30 a.m. " D " Squadron moved up to report to the
6th Brigade Headquarters at Maricourt Wood and were
ordered at noon to act as advanced guard to the Brigade
towards the Canal du Nord, working on a front of 4,000
yards.

Major Villiers gives the following account of the day's
work.

REPORT BY O.C. " D " SQUADRON, OXFORDSHIRE HUSSARS,
    ON OPERATIONS OF THE 3RD SEPTEMBER, WHILE ACTING
    IN CO-OPERATION WITH 6TH INFANTRY BRIGADE.

The Squadron spent the night 2nd–3rd September at
Humbercamp and was ordered to report at 7.30 a.m. on
the 3rd inst. to 2nd Division at Ervillers.

The distance *via* Douchy where the horses were watered
was about 14 miles.

After feeding at Ervillers, the squadron moved to Maricourt Wood (about 1,900 yards west of Morchies), having
sent on two officers to report to G.O.C. 6th Infantry Brigade,
whose brigade had been ordered to take over the whole

[1] Here, as elsewhere in this chapter where the 2nd Division is mentioned,
I am considerably indebted to Mr. Everard Wyrall's *History of the Second
Division.*

divisional front and to advance to the ridge north-west of Hermies.

The infantry were said to be holding the line from Beaumetz-les-Cambrai to the Beetroot Factory in J.9.b,[1] and were going to continue the advance at 1 p.m.

It was arranged with the G.O.C. 6th Infantry Brigade to send patrols to (a) Boursies, (b) Doignies and Demicourt, (c) Hermies, which would report back to the crucifix in J.13.a. The rest of the squadron would be kept together to operate as soon as the enemy had been located.

There was no information at all as to the position of the troops of the 5th Division on our right, and the Guards Division on our left was not so far forward as the 2nd Division.

The patrols reported Boursies and Doignies unoccupied by the enemy and said that they had seen some infantry on the high ground east of Boursies, but as they had passed none of our infantry they thought that they might be English—they were, of course, Germans.

The patrol to Demicourt went straight down the road through Doignies into Demicourt. They caught one prisoner in the sunken road between Doignies and Demicourt, and they also caught another in Demicourt, but had to shoot him as the N.C.O. in charge saw in the village a body of Germans which he estimated to be between 40 and 60, and had to clear off at once.

The patrol to Hermies crossed the railway south of Beaumetz and saw several hundred Germans retiring towards Havrincourt Wood—they were shot at by machine guns on trying to approach Hermies.

All the patrols reported back to the crucifix, and I think that the Brigade must have got the information before 1.30 p.m.

Meanwhile the squadron was brought into the valley in J.11.

A small patrol which endeavoured to approach Demicourt from the direction of Boursies had three horses killed by machine guns from houses in Demicourt.

The situation was now that Demicourt and Hermies had Germans in them, and there were also some machine guns in K.7.b.

At 3.15 p.m. a patrol reported that the Grenadiers were

[1] The map references are to the large-scale trench maps (not reproduced).

in a trench about J.5 Central, and it also saw a few Germans entering the eastern edge of Boursies.

Previous to this some tanks had come up and passed through the south part of Demicourt and also through Hermies. Two patrols, which were pushed on behind these to clear up the situation in the two villages, found enemy machine guns still holding Demicourt and covering the western approaches to it, but reported Hermies clear.

One troop was immediately sent to occupy Hermies and another to try to take Demicourt.

Except for considerable shelling, this was accomplished without difficulty, the enemy withdrawing from the north and east parts of Demicourt as the attacking troop approached.

These two villages having been occupied, Hotchkiss rifle posts were immediately established on the high ground between the enemy and the villages.

The infantry relieved the troop at Hermies half an hour later, but did not take over from that at Demicourt until about 7.30 p.m.

Meanwhile a patrol, pushed forward east of Hermies to clear up the situation between that village and the canal, had been heavily fired on and there were a considerable number of the enemy west of the canal, when the squadron received orders to concentrate at Morchies at 6 p.m.

(This concentration was carried out, the troop at Demicourt being left to follow on when relieved by the infantry.)

Patrols had got into touch with the 5th Division about 500 yards south-west of Hermies.

The German artillery was very active shelling any parties of more than two or three horsemen when they went over any of the ridges.

There was a good deal of wire about and it was quicker and easier to move on the roads, though for a small force like a squadron the country was not unsuitable.

By the time the squadron had arrived back at Vaulx-Vraucourt the horses had covered between 40 and 45 miles —they had been on the move since 5 a.m. and had been saddled-up all the time, having no water since 6.30 a.m. This coming on top of a 35-mile march the previous day was rather a severe trial for them.   (Report ends.)

This was an interesting day's work for " D " Squadron and they were able to render useful service to the infantry of the 6th Brigade, for whom they fulfilled two of the principal rôles of cavalry in the war, viz. affording protection as advanced guard and providing information of the enemy by means of reconnoitring patrols, besides also maintaining touch with our own troops on the flanks. Second-Lieutenant Hunt and 8 other ranks were wounded during the day ; also both Major Villiers' chargers. During the 36 hours ended 9 p.m. the 3rd September the whole squadron (including the fully loaded pack ponies) had covered 84 miles, and many of the officers' horses and those of patrols had done from 100 to 110 miles in the same period.

The Regiment, less "A" Squadron temporarily attached to the XVII Corps, remained in bivouac at Vaulx-Vraucourt till 2 p.m. on the 6th September, when they were ordered to concentrate at Behagnies for training. They reached their new bivouac at 4.30 p.m. Here they settled down for a while in tents and rough shelters of wood and scrap-iron— no real comfort, but pleasant enough in the fine autumn days. It was a strange sensation to be camped out in that waste land of broken iron, rusted wire, and churned-up earth, where less than a month ago the enemy had lived secure behind his lines, and where all was now still and quiet. The noise of the battle had passed on and left all this land desolate and without habitation.

On the 9th September one troop of "D" Squadron was sent to 62nd Divisional Headquarters for despatch-rider duties.

On the 10th Captain P. Fleming rejoined from England, after ten months' absence on account of injuries received in November 1917.

On the 21st "A" Squadron rejoined the Regiment at Behagnies. Preliminary orders were issued by the VI Corps for an attack by the Third Army in conjunction with operations to be undertaken by the First Army at a date to be notified later. Arrangements were made and orders prepared for issue at the appointed time to various parties to be detailed as despatch riders, etc. Meanwhile training continued.

Next day arrangements were made for the Regiment to be rationed by the VI Corps instead of by the 2nd Cavalry Division.

During our stay at Behagnies the weather had changed for the worse and been rather indifferent, except on the 24th, which was a beautiful day. Training continued.

We have now reached the eve of the great battle of the Canal du Nord. But before embarking on the Regiment's share in this operation, we must make a rather wide digression.

The successes achieved by the British Army up to the end of August, briefly described a few pages back, had indeed been remarkable. But for the most part they had but won back ground which we had held for a year in 1917–18. It still seemed quite probable that winter would find us much as we were before the 21st March 1918. But great things happened in the second half of September.

On the 15th September Austria and Germany made overtures for peace, but they were not accepted. On the same day began the Allied offensive against the Bulgarians on the Salonika front ; ten days later an armistice was requested, and the Allied terms were accepted on the 30th. It was a dramatic event, and the news had a magic effect on our troops and our people at home. One felt it as the first definite tangible sign of the end. Towns and prisoners and guns and ships had been captured by both sides for four years past without any apparent effect on the war and without bringing either side nearer to the inevitable breaking-point. But when whole nations began to fall to pieces and capitulate without conditions, then indeed there seemed ground for hope. If one fell away, others would surely follow.

Nor were we disappointed. Four days after the Balkan offensive had begun, the British Army in Palestine started on its amazing career of success. At that date it was lying some 12 or 15 miles north of a line drawn from Jericho westwards through Jerusalem to Jaffa and the sea. Allenby had a magnificent force of cavalry, but this is not the place to describe its exploits. While the infantry drove the Turks back a dozen miles on the first day (19th September), the cavalry rode 40 miles forward in less than two days and cut off the retreat of nearly the whole of the Turkish forces. By the 22nd, 25,000 prisoners and 200 guns had been taken and counted, which numbers had risen three days later to 45,000 prisoners and 300 guns. On the 25th our troops had reached and passed the Sea of Galilee, and Damascus fell on the 30th. But we must not follow this fascinating campaign further. The Turks had taken a smashing knock, but they were not quite beaten yet. We must return to our own unit on the Western Front. That, after all, was where Germany had to be beaten.

The battle of the Canal du Nord had as its main objective the completion of that breach in the Hindenburg Line which had been opened with such success on the 2nd September. It was a big undertaking. Foch had arranged with Haig for three other simultaneous operations on other sectors of the front : one by the Americans on the Meuse, another by the French in Champagne and the Argonne, and a third by the Belgians at Ypres. But the British attack on the Canal du Nord was likely to be the most critical of the three. Here the enemy defences were at their strongest. Moreover, success here would have a moral effect in Germany of almost unequalled importance. Public opinion there had been led to stake the safety of the nation on the supposed impregnable strength of the Hindenburg Line, and if this went, German morale would go with it.

The First and Third Armies were to begin operations with an attack by 14 divisions on a 12-mile front from Gouzeaucourt on the right to the neighbourhood of Ecourt St. Quentin, north of the Arras–Cambrai road, on the left. The attack was to be preceded by an intense bombardment along the whole front of the First, Third, and Fourth Armies, beginning on the night of the 26th–27th September, and followed by an extension of the attack by the Fourth Army, when the First and Third had achieved their primary objectives. Fierce fighting was expected.

The VI Corps plan of attack was for the 3rd Division on the right and the Guards Division on the left to attack under cover of a creeping barrage, supported by the 62nd Division on the right and the 2nd Division on the left. When the two leading divisions had advanced as far as possible, the 2nd and 62nd were to pass through them, " drive the enemy across the Canal de l'Escaut, and capture Rumilly, and the high ground south of the Faubourg St. Paris (south of Cambrai)." [1] The attack was to be supported by tanks.

Here are the orders for the Regiment, issued on the 26th September :

Very Secret   26.9.18.

Q.O. OXFORDSHIRE HUSSARS
ORDERS FOR Z DAY

Order No. 386.

1. Captain Fleming and Lieutenant Howarth will report to their respective advanced Divisional Headquarters by 8 a.m.

2. 2 Troops " D " Squadron will move to a position of readiness—J 34—by noon.

3. 2 Troops " C " Squadron will move to a position of readiness in J.9. by 11 a.m.

4. Headquarters, 3 troops " A " Squadron, " A " and " B " Echelons, will remain under VI Corps orders.

5. All tents and trench shelters will be struck and handed in to Squadron stores before troops leave present camp, and in any case not later than 10 a.m.

N.B.—This does not include those required for personnel of " B " Echelon and led horses.

In the event of a forward move, as many trench shelters and tents as can be carried will be taken on " B " Echelon.

Any tents and trench shelters which cannot be carried will be returned to VI Corps H.Q.

6. " A " 1 Echelon will be under the command of S.S.M. Raynham ; " A " 2 Echelon will be under the command of R.Q.M.S. Thompson.

7. Rear Headquarters Echelon " B " and led horses will be under Second-Lieutenant H. Tompkins.

8. Ration lorries will be at C.19.d.1.1, and can be moved

[1] Wyrall's *History of the Second Division.*

from there to refilling points to be detailed later. Mule
wagons will be ordered to this point.

FOR GUIDANCE.—Each subsequent day lorries will be
found at the previous day's refilling point.

Z DAY 27TH.   Zero Hour 5.20 a.m.

Watches, at least two per squadron, will be synchronized
at Regimental Headquarters at 8 p.m. Y. day.

(Sgd.) H. F. WISE,
Second-Lieutenant & Asst. Adjutant,
Q.O. Oxfordshire Hussars.

On the 26th September " A " Squadron sent one troop to
relieve a troop of " C " Squadron on duty at the prisoners-
of-war cage. " C " Squadron sent one troop to the Guards
Division and one to the 2nd Division, and " D " Squadron
sent one troop to the 3rd and one to the 62nd Division, for
duty as despatch riders.

At 9 a.m. on the morning of the 27th two troops of " C "
Squadron, under Captain Fleming, left to report to the
Headquarters of the Guards Division, the leading division
on the left sector of the Corps front ; while at the same time
two troops of " D " Squadron, under Lieutenant Howarth,
left to report to the Headquarters of the 3rd Division,
leading on the right sector. The above troops were to be
ready to exploit any success and were to await orders near
Hermies. At 4.20 p.m. they received orders to bivouac near
Hermies.

The preliminary bombardment had been the most
terrific yet known in the war, and in some places the German
front-line system is said to have been cut off from all
communication with its supports, rations, and ammunition.
The attack had started very well, but not sufficiently so
to permit of using the cavalry. Casualties in the infantry
had been heavy.

Next day, the 28th, the Colonel received orders at 11.30
a.m. to move the rest of the Regiment (seven troops) up
to Hermies and to be ready to support whichever division
broke through. They reached Hermies at 3 p.m. During

the day a patrol of " D " Squadron was successful in locating a machine-gun post, and also the left of the 42nd Division.

As a result of the day's fighting the 62nd Division on the right had captured Marcoing and crossed the Canal de l'Escaut, and the 2nd Division on the left had reached and held Noyelles, on the west bank of the canal, with two companies pushed out on the east bank.

Having bivouacked for the night near Hermies, the remainder of the Regiment received orders at 11 a.m. on the 29th to proceed to Ribécourt. There they stood-to all day till 5.30 p.m., when they returned to the quarry just south of Hermies.

There had been more hard fighting by the infantry during the day, and the 2nd Division (left) had forced its way over the Canal de l'Escaut, under intense shell and machine-gun fire, but the resistance was too stubborn and the pace too slow for cavalry to be of any use.

At 5.30 a.m. on the 30th the Regiment moved up to Ribécourt and returned to Hermies at 3 p.m. At 5.45 a.m. Lieutenant Smetham with two troops of " A " Squadron was in position to act as advanced guard to the 185th Brigade, having received orders to this effect the previous evening. There was no real opportunity for cavalry action, and the leading parties were heavily fired on by machine guns and also shelled. The leading troop had two men killed and five wounded and six horses killed or wounded.

Little ground had been gained on the Corps front that day. The enemy was too strongly placed in Mont-sur-l'Œuvres and Rumilly, which he was holding with many machine guns.

At 6 a.m. on the 1st October the Regiment moved up again to Ribécourt, stood-to there all day, and returned to Hermies in the evening. But though the Regiment did nothing, the day had been an important and successful one for the Corps. Early in the morning the 2/Oxford & Bucks (part of the 2nd Division) made an attack, but were held up by German machine guns in Rumilly, Mont-sur-l'Œuvres, and elsewhere, and suffered heavy casualties. But in the evening (6.30 p.m.) the 2nd and 3rd Divisions simultaneously attacked Mont-sur-l'Œuvres and Rumilly. Both places were swarming with machine guns and put up a determined resistance, which was, however, overcome by the dash and gallantry of our infantry.

The Hindenburg Line was now finally broken. Some of the Third Army were in the western outskirts of Cambrai, while the First Army was threatening it on the left. On our right, too, the Fourth Army was doing well and so pressing the enemy that he was forced to give up St. Quentin to the French on the 1st October. At the same time the Second Army, together with the Belgian Army, had attacked on the 28th September on a 23-mile front, and in four days had captured—among other successes —Dixmude, the whole of the Houthulst forest, all the heights east of Ypres, and cleared the left bank of the Lys from Comines southwards. Only on the right of the Allied line was success not complete. This was the flank and pivot of the German position and was thus of vital importance to the enemy, who must either hold or surrender or be destroyed. The attack was entrusted to the Americans on the right and to the French on the left, from north of Verdun to east of Reims. Unfortunately the Americans, who at first advanced more rapidly than the French, failed to keep up the pace and were presently held up while the French passed on beyond them. As a result of the check to the Americans, the Germans were able to send strong reinforcements to the Cambrai front, thus throwing the chief weight of their resistance on the British.

We may note in passing that the twenty-four-hour clock system was introduced in the British Army on the 1st October. The danger of confusion between " a.m." and " p.m." was swept away, and with it all the muddling complication of the time between twelve and one o'clock noon or midnight. There had always been discussion and argument whether, for example, a quarter past twelve in the middle of the day should be described as 12.15 a.m. or 12.15 p.m. or 0.15 p.m.

12.15 a.m. was indeed generally ruled out, although the mere fact that it could be discussed or suggested was itself a danger. But between 12.15 and 0.15 the contest waxed hot. Habit, and the general custom of railway time-tables, led the majority to support the former, but a minority, backed by the formidable authority of the Colonel, had always stood stoutly for the 0.15 practice. However, all these doubts and disputes were now set aside, and henceforth every minute of the twenty-four hours required four figures for its description. Thus, one minute after midnight would be written as 00.01, seven minutes to one in the afternoon would be 12.53, and one minute before midnight would be 23.59. This overdue reform effected an enormous simplification in the work of writing orders, messages, etc. For the purpose of this book, however, the old practice of " a.m." and " p.m." is retained, as being more usual and readily understood in ordinary life.

At 7 a.m. on the 2nd October the Regiment moved up to Ribécourt and returned to camp at Hermies at 2 p.m., repeating the performance next day, but returning to camp four hours earlier. At 9.45 a.m. on the 2nd Major Villiers, with three troops of " D " Squadron and one of " A " Squadron, proceeded to Marcoing, where he came under the orders of the G.O.C. 8th Brigade.

On the 4th October the Regiment stood-to at one hour's notice till 12 noon. At 2 p.m. " A " Squadron relieved the four troops serving as despatch riders with the two leading divisions, thus leaving the Regiment with two complete squadrons for offensive operations.

On the 5th October, at 10.40 a.m., they suddenly received orders to proceed forthwith to Ribécourt, whereupon they saddled-up and moved, but on arrival at Divisional Headquarters found they were not required, and so came back to their camp at Hermies at 2 p.m.

Winter-time came into force at midnight of the 5th–6th. The Regiment remained in camp all day, and received preliminary orders for an attack on the 7th, later postponed till the 8th.

" It was rumoured in the early afternoon that the Central Powers had asked for an armistice, and this rumour was confirmed as such by VI Corps order in the evening warning the troops to beware of enemy attempts to fraternize. Continental *Daily Mail* of Sunday morning in camp about 20.00 has confirmed the rumour." [1]

On the 8th October the final phase of the battle for Cambrai began. On that day the Third and Fourth Armies attacked on a front of 17 miles from Sequehart, 7 miles north-east of St. Quentin, to just south of Cambrai. The French on the right and the First Army on the left extended the attack on the south and north respectively. The VI Corps captured the villages of Seranvillers, Forenville, and Niergnies, not without hard fighting, and pushed into the southern outskirts of Cambrai. During the following night (9th) Canadian patrols entered Cambrai from the north, and by nightfall next day the whole city was in our hands, our troops were established 3 miles east of it, and others of them were within 2 miles of Le Cateau. The German "infantry became disorganized, and retired steadily eastwards." [2]

On the first day of the battle the Regiment had repeated the now usual routine of moving up to Ribécourt at 7 a.m., staying there all day, and returning to Hermies at 3 p.m. The process was becoming wearisome.

However, on the 9th October, after moving to Ribécourt as usual at 6.30 a.m., "D" Squadron received orders to move forward to Seranvillers, the remainder to Marcoing Copse. At 10.45 Regimental Headquarters and "C" Squadron followed "D" to Seranvillers, while "D" Squadron sent two troops to Wambaix, and two more to Wambaix Copse, pushing forward patrols towards Cattenières and Estourmel under orders of the Guards Division. At 4 p.m. the Regiment withdrew to bivouac for the night near Seranvillers. Here they emerged from the devastated area into cultivated country again and found at least one house complete with

[1] Regimental Diary.   [2] Official Despatches.

22

roof, etc.—the first for many weeks. Next day they saw
the first civilians, some left behind by the enemy, although
he was still driving most of them back to the rear as he
retreated.

At 7.30 a.m. on the 10th " C " Squadron sent two troops
to the 1st, and two troops to the 2nd Guards Brigade,
pushing out patrols towards Quiévy and St. Hilaire. Two
men were wounded. The following account is taken from
the Regimental Diary :

The first patrol was ordered—

" 1. To find out the line held by the infantry on their
immediate front. 2. To ascertain if St. Hilaire was held
by the enemy. This patrol, under Lieutenant Hodgson,
sent back a complete and accurate report of their first
mission, after which they scouted first the eastern and then
the western edge of St. Hilaire, satisfied themselves that the
village was not held and reported this to the Brigadier.
The whole of this work was completed under an hour. On
the same day a further patrol, under Sergeant Peaker, was
sent to find out if the railway south and south-east of St.
Aubert was held by the enemy. This patrol, which started in
pouring rain, making map-reading very difficult, had orders
to leave St. Vaast on their right and make straight for their
objective. Passing by St. Vaast the patrol was fired on,
but taking advantage of the ground they managed to get
within 400 or 500 yards of the St. Aubert–St. Python railway,
when they were heavily fired on by machine guns and rifles
from the railway and saw about 50 of the enemy on the
railway. This patrol was fortunate in not suffering any
casualties, and reported to G.O.C. 2nd Guards Brigade.

" On the same day the front line of the 1st Guards Brigade
ran along the Bevillers–Avesnes road with their right on
Bevillers and their left on the above-mentioned road where
it cuts the Boussières–St. Hilaire road. The 1/Irish Guards
were held up by a machine-gun nest at the Y Roads south
of the E in Quiévy (Valenciennes 1/100,000). Corporal
Bird and 5 men were sent to find out—

" 1. If the machine guns had retired, and if so—

" 2. To push on to the Quiévy–St. Hilaire road, and if
he met with no opposition—

" 3. To enter Quiévy from the north-east.

" Corporal Bird returned in 23 minutes and reported no opposition up to the Quiévy–St. Hilaire road, but in entering the village of Quiévy they were fired on by two machine guns from the first house. They cantered back along the ridge overlooking the north-west of the village, but failed to draw any further fire.

" The information was of the utmost value to the G.O.C. 1st Guards Brigade."

At 4.30 p.m. " C " Squadron withdrew to bivouac at Seranvillers, and " D " Squadron moved up to Carnières.

At 6 a.m. next day Regimental Headquarters and " C " Squadron moved to Carnières, and " D " Squadron to Boussières, pushing out patrols towards St. Vaast and St. Aubert under orders of the 3rd Guards Brigade. At 4 p.m. " D " Squadron returned to Carnières.

At 4.30 a.m. next morning, 12th October, one troop of " C " Squadron moved forward to St. Hilaire, the rest of the squadron remaining in camp at one hour's notice until 1 p.m., when they moved up to join their advanced troop. At 5 p.m. one troop of " D " Squadron moved to St. Hilaire, and " C " Squadron withdrew to bivouac at Carnières.

On the 13th, at 7 a.m., the remainder of " D " Squadron moved up to St. Hilaire, pushing out patrols to St. Python. At 4 p.m. one troop of " C " Squadron moved to St. Hilaire, and " D " Squadron withdrew to bivouac at Carnières.

But these details become wearisome. The Regiment, less one or two troops with infantry Divisional Headquarters, and one squadron detached for duty as despatch riders and escorts to prisoners of war, remained in bivouac and billets round Carnières till the 23rd.

A word should be said of the VI Corps Club. I don't know whether other corps had clubs of their own ; perhaps some did ; certainly none had better than the VI Corps. Moving continually forward with the Corps, at a safe distance from the front line, but not too far back to be out of reach of the fighting troops when in rest, it was a godsend to tired officers. It consisted of a large marquee, and one or two smaller ones near by. Comfortable armchairs and a large selection of newspapers were provided ; meals were to be had by passing officers, and camp beds by those stranded late at night on their way to or from England ; above all, one could get one's hair cut there, cleanly, efficiently, and in comfort. It was of course impossible to provide anything on so elaborate a scale for the men, but for them also baths, cinema shows, pierrot troupes, and other sources of comfort and amusement travelled permanently in the wake of the Corps. Things had changed indeed since 1914.

During these days the advance in the north had been continued with even greater success than in the previous attack on the 28th September. On the 15th October the Second Army entered Menin, and by the next day they were beyond Courtrai. Ostend, Lille, and Douai fell on the 17th, Zeebrugge and Bruges on the 19th, and by the 21st the combined British and Allied forces in the north had advanced to the Scheldt and driven the German right flank off the sea-coast.

Meanwhile, farther south, on the front of the Third Army, the British had reached the western bank of the river Selle on the 13th. Here they paused for four days, while their now greatly lengthened communications were reorganized. The next objective was—

" the forcing of the Selle positions and the attainment of the general line Sambre et Oise Canal–west edge of the Forêt de Mormal–Valenciennes. This advance would bring the important railway junction at Aulnoye within effective range of our guns." [1]

The battle of the Selle began on the 17th October with an attack by the Fourth Army south of Le Cateau, and by the French south of the Fourth Army. The Germans resisted fiercely, but by the evening of the 19th they had been driven across the Sambre and Oise Canal at all points south of Catillon.

At 2 a.m. on the 20th the Third Army, with one division of the First Army, attacked the line of the Selle north of

[1] Official Despatches.

Le Cateau. Here, too, the enemy put up a stiff defence, especially between Solesmes and Haspres. However, all our objectives on the high ground east of the Selle were eventually captured after hard fighting. But this was only the first part of the battle. The main operation, designed to win the general line from the Sambre and Oise Canal past the western edge of the Forêt de Mormal to the neighbourhood of Valenciennes, was timed to begin at 3.20 a.m. on the 23rd October, and was entrusted to the Third and Fourth Armies. The leading divisions in the VI Corps were to be the 2nd (on the left) and the 3rd (on the right), and the Oxford Hussars were to provide two troops to each for communication and patrol duties. The Corps was to attack on a front of about 2¼ miles, with three successive objectives, the third and final objective for the day being a line running from just west of Beaudignies to just south of Bermerain. The attack was to be renewed on the 24th, the objective for that day being fixed at a line just short of the Avesnes–Le Quesnoy–Valenciennes railway.

The attack was everywhere successful, and by nightfall on the 23rd all objectives had been attained on the Corps front. But the north bank of the Ecaillon, a small river flowing straight across the Corps front and about a mile beyond the third objective, was still held by the enemy, as also were the villages of Beaudignies and Bermerain.

At 10 a.m. on the 23rd the Regiment moved to St. Python, and during the afternoon " A " Squadron sent patrols to Beaudignies and Bermerain to reconnoitre the crossings of the river Ecaillon, which had been swollen by rain and was found to be deeper than expected.

The attack was resumed at 4 a.m. next day. The morning was fine and dry. Our infantry crossed the Ecaillon without much opposition, wading through water up to their waists. At 6.15 a.m. the Regiment moved up from St. Python to Vertain, and thence to Escarmain, " D " Squadron sending on patrols to Ruesnes. At 8.30 a.m. the Regiment moved to the neighbourhood of Ruesnes, " D " Squadron again pushing out patrols, which, however, were unable to get

beyond the village.   At 2 p.m. the Regiment was withdrawn
to billets at St. Python, none being available in Vertain or
Solesmes.

The following note on the work of the patrols is taken
from the Regimental Diary :

" 24th October.   Lance-Corporal Huckerby was sent from
the outskirts of Escarmain to find out (1) if the bridge over
the Ecaillon was possible and in what state it was, and if so
to push on towards Ruesnes to find out the position.   He
carried out his two missions with the greatest speed and
found the bridge in good repair and the infantry just entering
Ruesnes.

" On the same day Corporal Stockford carried out an
important reconnaissance south-east of Ruesnes, keeping
touch with the positions on the right of the 9th Brigade and
sending back valuable information.

" On the same day Lance-Corporal Hunt having received
orders to push forward towards the Valenciennes–Le Quesnoy
railway, his patrol came under heavy machine-gun and rifle
fire on attempting to pass south-east of Ruesnes.   He,
however, contrived to get round under cover of a small copse
and brought back most valuable information.

" On the same day Corporal Tompkins took a patrol to
reconnoitre the enemy's position north and north-east of
Ruesnes.   On reaching the Le Quesnoy road he came under
heavy machine-gun fire, but knowing that the infantry
behind him were not in touch with the troops on their left,[1]
he pushed forward to the north of the village and ascertained
the position and informed the troops on the west of the village
of the position on their flank.   During this reconnaissance
he located an enemy battery firing at close range into the
village."

At 9.30 a.m. next day, the 25th October, the 2nd Division
received reports that the enemy had withdrawn from the
Le Quesnoy–Valenciennes railway in front of our present
line, and their leading battalions were at once ordered to
push on and secure it.

---

[1] The 2nd Division, with which we were working, advanced 4,000 yards
during the day, but the troops on their left failed to keep pace with them.
Their left flank was thus exposed to a depth of 2,500 yards.   (See Wyrall's
History of the Second Division, vol. ii, p. 686.)

At the same time the Regiment was ordered to move from
St. Python to Escarmain, and there come under the orders
of the G.O.C. 8th Brigade, 3rd Division.   An hour later they
moved forward to the neighbourhood of Ruesnes, " A "
Squadron going on to La Belle Vue Farm, whence—

" Lieutenant Smetham was sent with his troop to seize
La Croisette and the high ground overlooking Villers-Pol,
the infantry line at the time being along the railway.   He
seized and consolidated the position a mile in front of the
railway and handed over the line to the infantry at dark." [1]

At 4 p.m. the " A " Squadron posts were relieved by the
infantry, and the squadron withdrew to Escarmain, while
" D " Squadron remained in bivouac south of Ruesnes.   As
an illustration of the uncertainty of the Germans' exact
position it may be noted that an officer sent to look for a
suitable bivouac near Ruesnes tried to billet in a village
full of Germans.   Other officers had similar experiences
during this period.

The battle of the Selle was over.   Our troops had advanced
6 miles between Ors—just east of Le Cateau—and Valenciennes, in spite of swollen streams, thick woods, and much
machine-gun fire, had reached the edge of the Forêt de
Mormal and the Avesnes–Le Quesnoy–Valenciennes railway,
had captured 20,000 prisoners and 475 guns.   The Germans
were losing heart, and tales were told of their slipping out
of the ranks, changing into civilian clothes, and trying to
pass as inhabitants.

On the 26th October Ludendorff resigned.

The last six days of the month were days of comparative
rest and preparation for the next great assault.

At 7 a.m. on the 26th " D " Squadron sent out two patrols
from La Croisette to ascertain (1) whether the bridges over
the Rhonelle were intact, (2) whether La Folie Farm was
held by the enemy.   The first patrol found both bridges
broken down, but the river fordable in one place ; this

---

[1] Regimental Diary.

patrol was fired at from Villers-Pol.[1] The second patrol found La Folie Farm held by the enemy.

At 8.30 a.m. " A " Squadron moved up from Escarmain to " D " Squadron's bivouac near Ruesnes, where they remained till the following day. At 1 p.m. " D " Squadron withdrew to billets at Escarmain.

Next day, the 27th, at 3 p.m., " A " Squadron also withdrew to billets at Escarmain, where the whole Regiment, less " C " Squadron detached for duty with Corps Headquarters since the 15th October, remained concentrated till 1 p.m. on the 29th. During the night of the 28th–29th they were shelled, losing six horses killed and nine wounded.

On the 29th the Regiment, less details detached and one troop of " A " Squadron left at Escarmain " for tactical purposes," withdrew to Boussières, where baths for the men were arranged, and all the rest of the time devoted to cleaning saddlery, etc., etc.

We were now in a country with something like decent billets for all ranks. For three months we had lived in a devastated desert where huts and shanties roughly put together with bits of broken iron and torn sacking, and perhaps an occasional tent or two, were the best that could be hoped for, even far behind the line. Now at last we had reached villages scarcely, if at all, touched by shell fire. Here and there a house would be destroyed, but it was the exception, not the rule. Not only the officers, but the men too, slept with whole roofs over their heads.

But we scarcely hoped for victory yet. The war had lasted so long that we had almost forgotten what peace was like. Besides, it was tempting fortune to look too far ahead. And then, if one did think about it seriously, surely there was every prospect of another winter campaign ! True, the Germans had taken a bad knock and we had made an advance such as we had never dreamed of before. But

---

[1] This place was not captured till the night of the 3rd–4th November, after hand-to-hand fighting by the Coldstream Guards, who had already met with considerable opposition before they could cross the Rhonelle. (See Headlam, *Guards Division in the Great War*.)

this did not make a victory, men argued, with a keen recollection of the much-trumpeted German " victories " of previous years, and their spectacular, startling, and triumphant advances which yet led to nothing. So it was commonly believed that the enemy would retire in good order to a shorter defensive line on the Meuse and there dig in for the winter. Perhaps the end might come in 1919, with luck. Moreover, this view was strengthened by the steady resistance of the enemy, the continuance of machine-gun opposition, and the orderly method of his retreat. There were plenty of prisoners, yes, but there were plenty of fighters too. As for the Higher Command, they had buoyed us up with false hopes so often before, ever since 1914, that we had long since ceased to believe them. But they were right this time.

For Germany's difficulties were increasing. Her allies were falling away. Turkey had signed an armistice on the 30th October. Austria was on the verge of collapse ; her army of many races was rapidly breaking up, her capital was starving, even her ally Hungary refused to supply any more food, and on the 27th she asked President Wilson to send through Sweden what was practically an offer of surrender. On the same day she suffered a smashing blow in Italy from the British and Italian troops under Lord Cavan ; her army scattered in disorder, and on the 3rd November she too signed an armistice.

Germany was now left alone, and at the same time the right wing of the Allied Armies began to advance with startling speed on the Meuse, eventually reaching Sedan on the 7th November, cutting the enemy's lateral communications and forcing him to retreat in the centre.

But the success of the Allied right wing would scarcely have caused so complete and swift a collapse of the German centre without the hammer blow delivered by the British Armies in the battle of the Sambre.

" By this time " (i.e. by the end of October) " the rapid succession of heavy blows dealt by the British forces had had a cumulative effect, both moral and material, upon the German Armies. The difficulty of replacing the enemy's enormous losses in guns, machine guns, and ammunition had increased with every fresh attack, and his reserves of men were exhausted. . . . Though troops could still be found to offer resistance to our initial assault, the German infantry and machine gunners were no longer reliable. . . . If her Armies were allowed to withdraw unmolested to shorter lines, the struggle might still be protracted over the winter. The British Armies, however, were now in a position to prevent this by a direct attack upon a vital centre, which should anticipate the enemy's withdrawal and force an immediate conclusion." [1]

The capture of Valenciennes was an essential preliminary to the final battle. So on the 1st November three corps of the First and Third Armies attacked on a 6-mile front south of the town, forced the line of the Rhonelle and entered Valenciennes on the 3rd.

On the 4th November the First, Third, and Fourth Armies attacked on a 30-mile front from Valenciennes to Oisy on the Sambre. The VI Corps sector was, roughly speaking, in the centre. The 2nd and 3rd Divisions, which had been the leading divisions in the battle of the Selle, were relieved by the Guards and 62nd Divisions. Maubeuge was the ultimate objective.

It rained during the night of the 3rd–4th November, and there was a thick fog at zero hour (6 a.m.) next morning. The Regiment remained in billets at Boussières till the 4th November. At zero one troop of " C " Squadron moved to the neighbourhood of Pont de Buat for duty with " C " Company, 6th Battalion, Tank Corps. An hour later the Regiment, less details detached, moved to near Ruesnes ; one troop of " C " Squadron went to La Folie Farm, under orders of 62nd Division, while another, working with the 2nd Guards Brigade, pushed patrols towards Frasnoy. At 2.30 the Regiment, which had moved forward during the morning, withdrew to billets at Ruesnes.

At 6.30 a.m. on 5th November Lieutenant Soame, with

[1] Official Despatches.

one troop, reported to the G.O.C. 185th Brigade (62nd Division) at La Belle Maison, south-west of Frasnoy. He was ordered to push through the infantry and try to ascertain if Bavisiau (about 2½ miles south-west of Bavai) was held by the enemy, and if not, to push on to Obies. He got into the outskirts of Bavisiau, from which he sent a message back to the G.O.C. 185th Brigade, saying he had been fired on from the west as he approached, but had been able to get into the southern outskirts of the village and was pushing on to Obies. It does not appear whether he got there. Private J. B. Cross was killed, while trying to capture two Germans in Bavisiau. He was the last man of the Regiment killed during the war.

At 7.30 a.m. on the same day another troop of " A " Squadron, under Second-Lieutenant Wise, reported to the G.O.C. 3rd Guards Brigade at La Flaque Farm. They were sent to find out if Amfroipret was held by the enemy, and if not, to push on towards Bermeries and Bavisiau. They were fired at from different houses in the north-west outskirts of Bavisiau and reported the village held by the enemy, which in fact it was, although Lieutenant Soame had successfully passed through the southern end of it and gone on towards Obies, as we have seen.

Meanwhile, the remainder of the Regiment had moved at 10 a.m.—

" to Frasnoy, and later, on information received, proceeded in the direction of Bavisiau with the idea of billeting there, but the information turning out to have been too optimistic and Bavisiau still partly in enemy occupation, it withdrew to billets in Gommegnies and Frasnoy." [1]

It was not till next day that Bavisiau was really in our possession.

The roads were blocked with advancing troops and traffic, and were made still more impassable by the continuous heavy rain which had now set in ; they were also completely destroyed by mine craters in many places. A further

[1] Regimental Diary.

obstacle to progress was the very enclosed nature of the country we were in now, much more like England than the open lands between Amiens and Cambrai. This enclosed country was a machine-gunner's paradise, of which the enemy took full advantage, and much delay was caused by machine-gun fire.

It may be noted here that the advance of the VI Corps, which in the battle of the Selle had been in a north-easterly direction, had now swung almost due east, in conformity with the main movement of the Army, which was now directed against the line Avesnes–Maubeuge–Mons.

After another night of pouring rain the advance was resumed at 6 a.m. next day ; still raining. One troop of "A" Squadron reported to the 185th Brigade Headquarters at Le Cheval Blanc (south-east of Gommegnies) and one troop of "C" Squadron to the 3rd Guards Brigade Headquarters at Le Bracmart (north-east of Gommegnies), both troops sending out patrols on their respective fronts. During the day the line was further advanced, and established east of Mecquignies.

The 7th November began with a repetition of the now daily routine of patrol work, one troop of "A" Squadron going to the 2nd Guards Brigade at Amfroipret at 8.30 a.m. and another of the same squadron to the 186th Brigade at 9 a.m. At 2 p.m., however, three troops of "C" Squadron under Captain Fleming were sent to Locquignol (in the very centre of the Forêt de Mormal) to report to the 38th Division (V Corps). Regimental Headquarters remained at Frasnoy ; "A" Squadron Headquarters at Gommegnies.

The following message was received on the 7th :

Urgent Operations Priority.

Handed in at F.C.O. Office 11.30, received 11.40.
To Oxford Hussars.
G86.

Should an officer bearing a flag of truce present himself at any part of the British front he will be conducted to the nearest Div. H.Q. and the fact notified by Urgent Opera-

TIONS PRIORITY telegram to Adv. G.H.Q. " I " repeated to Army and Corps H.Q. aaa The officer will be detained at Div. H.Q. pending instructions from G.H.Q. aaa Guards and 62nd Divisions to ACKNOWLEDGE aaa.

From VI Corps.

Time 11.20.

This message naturally caused great excitement among all ranks. The idea of German envoys crossing our lines to ask for a truce seemed almost too good to be true. One had so often wondered and talked of how peace would come, and sometimes asked South African veterans about it, and now it really seemed near at hand.

However, rather to our disappointment, no peace envoys appeared, and between 6 and 7 p.m. a message was received that they were not to be expected on the British front, but would pass through the French lines.

Meanwhile, there was still work to be done. During the day another message from the Corps had stated—

" that the enemy appeared to be withdrawing along the whole length of the Third Army front, and that, if the infantry had lost touch with the German rearguards, the cavalry must regain it." [1]

On the 8th November the advance continued all along the Corps front. " A " Squadron moved to Le Cambran Farm. Patrols sent out from Second-Lieutenant Wise's troop from La Longueville towards Maubeuge were held up 1,000 yards east of Les Mottes. [2]

At 5.40 a.m. on the 9th, Second-Lieutenant Wise's troop pushed patrols from Les Mottes to Faubourg St. Guislain and Faubourg St. Quentin ; finding these unoccupied, the whole troop pushed straight into Maubeuge, which it entered at 6.45 a.m., " being the first British troops to enter the town proper." [3] The troop then pushed on to Assevent and Boussois, and tried to get to Marpent, but was held up by machine-gun fire from Fort de Boussois, and also by

[1] Headlam, *The Guards Division in the Great War*, vol. ii, p. 229.
[2] The Scots Guards captured La Longueville early that morning.
[3] Regimental Diary.

the destruction of the bridge over the river. A German officer and nine other ranks were captured during the day. The Guards and 62nd Divisions both claim to have been the first British troops to enter Maubeuge. It seems clear, however, that although one if not both of these divisions had small patrols in the outskirts shortly after 2 a.m., they had not penetrated into the centre of the town at the time Lieutenant Wise passed through.)

At 10.15 a.m. Lieutenant Smetham's troop moved off from Neuf Mesnil and pushed on to Ostergnies, where it met with some opposition, and subsequently to Marpent, where it was held up.

Meanwhile, the reports of a general enemy withdrawal had been confirmed, and the demand of the VI Corps that the cavalry must regain touch with the German rearguards where lost by our infantry had been met. It was considered that the time had now come for the employment of cavalry on a larger scale than in small detached patrols, and some at least of the mounted units were accordingly re-grouped in their brigades. The following order was issued to all units of the 4th Cavalry Brigade.

Secret. Copy No. 2.

4th CAVALRY BRIGADE ORDER No. 40

Ref. Valenciennes 1/100,000 9th Novr. 1918.

1. The enemy is retiring rapidly on the whole Army front. Maubeuge has been taken.

2. The VI Corps is to assume the rôle of Advance Guard to the Third Army.

The 4th Cavalry Brigade has been placed at the disposal of the VI Corps to cover the advance guard and keep in touch with the enemy.

All regiments of the 4th Cavalry Brigade will come under the control of G.O.C. 4th Cavalry Brigade as soon as practicable.

  •   •   •   •   •   •

(Sgd.) C. A. HEYDEMAN,
Captain,
Brigade Major 4th Cavalry Brigade.

Issued at 15.15 hrs.

At 8 a.m. on the 10th November the Regiment left Frasnoy and went into billets at Les Petites Mottes, " C " Squadron rejoining from the V Corps ; " A " Squadron sent patrols to Fort de Boussois and Bois de Jeumont, both of which were found to be still strongly held by machine guns.

On the morning of the 10th we heard that the Kaiser had abdicated and fled to Holland. That night the Regiment was ordered to advance next day to the Beaumont–Givry road, about 7 miles beyond the existing outpost line.

The 11th November dawned bright and sunny, a glorious morning with a sharp frost. At 7.15 a.m. the Regiment moved from Les Petites Mottes to Assevent. It was not then known that the armistice had been signed in Marshal Foch's train at 5 a.m. that morning, although a premature announcement of the news had been made in some high quarters the night before. The actual signature did not in fact take place till 5 a.m. on the 11th, and the news was officially received at VI Corps Headquarters about 7 a.m.

Meanwhile, at 7.30, a patrol of " A " Squadron, under Lieutenant Soame, pushed on to Fort de Boussois, to find the enemy gone.

At 8 a.m. the following message was received :

" An armistice has been declared and begins at 11.00 hours to-day. Units will, as laid down in Brigade Order No. 42, gain the line of the Beaumont–Givry road and then halt.

"Any Germans coming towards our lines must be taken prisoner, although the armistice will be in force.

" C. A. HEYDEMAN,

Brigade Major 4th Cav. Bde."

11.11.18.

At 9.30 " A " Squadron left Assevent, pushing patrols to Elesmes, Grand Reng, and Vieux Reng, which were found to be unoccupied, and the squadron subsequently took up an outpost line on the Givry–Beaumont road, just inside the Belgian frontier.

At 9.30 " D " Squadron also left Assevent and sent patrols to Erquelinnes (on the Belgian frontier, now the customs

examination station for the Paris–Berlin express), which was
found to be lightly held by machine guns. Having cleared
the village of enemy by 10.55, an outpost line was taken up
on the Givry–Beaumont road, with patrols over the road,
and at 2 p.m. the Regiment went into billets at Erquelinnes,
Vieux Reng, and Grand Reng.

The calm windless weather made the silence of the guns
yet more impressive. So much has been written about men's
thoughts and feelings that day that little need be said here.
Everybody knows how those at home, especially in the great
cities, went wild with excitement and " painted the town red,"
and how those at the front kept their emotions to themselves
and went about their work, silently rejoicing. So at least
we have read. But, in truth, our impressions were very
vague. Officers and men were very tired, and little inclined
either for wild excitement or deep reflection. They felt
pride in victory, perhaps, when they thought about it ; but
yet more they felt relief and relaxation after great strain,
quietly thankful that it was all over.

Captain Wellesley gives the following account of " D "
Squadron's advance to Erquelinnes :

" I sent Lieutenant Tompkins out on the left of my front,
and went myself with Lieutenant List and No. 1 Troop on
the right, leaving Lieutenant Allfrey in charge of the
remainder of the Squadron. Both the advance troops had
patrols well out in front, and—beyond a certain amount of
desultory rifle fire—little opposition was met with. About
10.30 we came with the advance troop on the right under
long-range machine-gun fire, and withdrew into some dead
ground.

" A patrol under Corporal Stockford pushed on round the
edge of Erquelinnes—immediately beyond which was our
final objective, the main road. I followed the patrol, and
on reaching the outskirts of the town was met by a cheering
mass of inhabitants, some of whom sang, others wept, and
others begged me to be careful as German machine guns
were in position round the corner. (To these civilians, of
course, it was complete news that an armistice was at hand.)

" So great was the crush that, having sent back for the squadron to come on, it was with the greatest difficulty that I got down to the market-place on foot, only to find that the last of the enemy had just gone.

" On returning to my pony, I found her bestraddled by a huge fat Belgian who was addressing the crowd from her back.

" Having kicked him off, I went on to investigate, charged through mobs of wildly excited inhabitants, and finally got through the town and out on to the main road beyond. Here I met the patrol, who had come round the outskirts, and we established a Hotchkiss post on the road and sent back for the squadron.

" Meanwhile, Stockford and I tried to round up some escaping Boches, who finally jumped into the river Sambre !

" Tompkins's troop arrived almost simultaneously on the road half a mile to our left, and reported having obtained touch with ' A ' Squadron, who had also reached the objective.   I sent a patrol down the road on my right to Solre only 600 yards away, but found the village full of Germans.

" On the arrival of the squadron, posts were put out along the road, and we began to take stock of the situation.

" At 11.15 it was found necessary to end the days of a Hun machine gunner on our front who would keep on shooting.   The armistice was already in force, but there was no alternative.   Perhaps his watch was wrong, but he was probably the last German killed in the war—a most unlucky individual !

" Considerable difficulty was experienced by the men, owing to the pressing attentions of the civilians, who besieged all our posts with presents and souvenirs of every kind, while they were trying to keep their eyes skinned for the enemy.

" I remember, too, noting the enormous extent to which a comparatively small body of troops—advancing over any considerable distance of ground—is inevitably depleted by the necessity for sending back despatch riders (often in duplicate) at the end of each bound.   Regimental H.Q. was 7 miles back at Assevent, and when the two leading troops reached the final objective only some 60 per cent. of their strength was available to take up the line of outposts.

" At about 12.15 things had settled down, and I had just started to drink some much-needed coffee in a cottage,

23

when a galloper arrived post-haste to ask that I would come to the right of the line, where there was a nasty-looking party of Germans with a white flag in front of one of our Hotchkiss gun posts.

" I found that the party contained three officers and two orderlies all mounted, and a cyclist, the senior officer carrying a dirty white flag on a stick. He explained that he commanded the troops in Merbes-le-Château (a village 1,000 yards away on our front)—that he had received orders concerning a cessation of hostilities—and that he wished to make sure that we had similar orders and would not attack him.

" Having received the necessary assurance, he thanked me and prepared to withdraw, but this, as it seemed to me, could not be permitted. Previous experience during the war had taught me nothing as to the correct manner of handling white-flagged parties, but I had a dim idea that the correct etiquette for the enemy to have observed would have been to come unarmed and blindfold into our lines, if they wished to be treated as ' parlementaires.' As it was, they were all armed to the teeth, and had had full opportunity to observe the disposition of our line. I there-fore informed them that they must consider themselves my prisoners, disarmed them, and sent them off *on foot* under escort to Regimental H.Q.

" The party protested most vehemently that this was a violation of all military laws, emphasizing, I remember, the fact that no Englishman would have been treated so dis-courteously at the hands of the Germans !

" It is interesting to note here that the higher authorities seem to have been equally in doubt as to what should be done. From Regimental H.Q. the party was passed in turn to Brigade, Division, Corps, and finally to Army H.Q. at Le Cateau—a nice little walk for the ' parlementaires ' !

" At Army H.Q. they remained for some days until a special order was received from G.H.Q. directing that they be passed back through our line. The order further stated that all horses, bicycles, arms, etc., which had been taken from them were to be returned by us. Now it so happened that the senior officer of the party had come in on a very serviceable black mare. Strange to relate, a most unfortu-nate accident (?) occurred to this mare on the very morning that the party returned and she trotted out dead lame !

We therefore most unselfishly offered the party another horse in exchange. No. 1 troop provided an aged 'hairy' which they had been trying unsuccessfully to cast for the past twelve months—the Germans rode off satisfied, and the mare remained with us. We named her 'Peace,' and when I left the squadron I handed her over to Sergeant Harper—on whose farm at home she may be seen to this day."

CHAPTER XI

CONCLUSION

AFTER the armistice the Regiment, in common with the rest of the Army, remained halted in billets for six days.

On the 12th November small parties of all sorts began to approach our line from the German side. Many of them were German soldiers who had deserted from their units during the general break-up that was taking place. Others were batches of English prisoners, released or escaped during the German rout. There were also quite a number of English soldiers who had been in hiding since August 1914, when they had been cut off during the German advance past Mons. One of these had for over four years been concealed in a wood-stack by day and taken out only at night by the Belgian family who befriended him throughout this period.

Captain Wellesley gave a ball in Erquelinnes town-hall on the 15th November. Over 800 people came and as many more could not get in and went away disappointed. The hall was beautifully decorated, and in the middle hung the old " D " Squadron sign, battered and bruised, but crowned with a wealth of laurels. A full orchestra was in attendance, but the crush was too great to dance, and people just hopped up and down. Soon after midnight the party broke up, amid much singing of national anthems.

When " D" Squadron took Erquelinnes, they captured amongst other prisoners a German pioneer. Captain Wellesley put him on parole and made him undo all the mines in the village, telling him that if anything went up he would be shot. If none went off, he would be kept with the squadron and treated well. This worked admirably. He undid 54 mines and none went up in the village. He was subsequently dressed as a civilian, nicknamed " Alphonse," and taken on towards Germany with the squadron transport, his duties being to make himself generally useful in the officers' mess. Two months later he was pushed over the German frontier in the dead of night.

At 9 a.m. on the 17th November, a bitterly cold morning, with a black frost, we began our march to the Rhine.

At Erquelinnes the Mayor and deputies, wearing top-hats and accompanied by the town band, were in attendance in the Square, where they presented an address to the Colonel. The Mayor read a special poem, and presented the illuminated manuscript to Captain Wellesley, commanding " D " Squadron, while printed copies were distributed by ladies to all the men.

The Regiment stopped the first night at Castillon and Boussu-lez-Walcourt, going on next day to Oret and the neighbouring farms. Here they stayed three nights, and on the 21st continued their march to Yvoir, Anhée, and Houx, on the banks of the Meuse. Next day they marched to Emptinne and Hamois, and on the 23rd came to Melreux, Fronville, and Deulin, on the river Ourthe. Here orders were received that the Second Army only would proceed to Germany, and the Regiment remained in these billets till the 29th, when they marched to new billets at Dochamps (Headquarters and " C " Squadron), Samrée (" A " Squadron), and Bérismenil (" D " Squadron), all near Laroche, in the heart of the Ardennes.

The retreating Germans were about three or four days' march ahead of us. We formed the advanced guard to the infantry, and moved with patrols out in front just as in war conditions. Throughout the march the population turned out to cheer us. Most of the villages were decked with triumphal arches formed of fir trees and garlanded with festoons and Chinese lanterns, and in some places the band turned out and played " God save the King," specially learnt for the purpose. Occasionally the Mayor produced a bottle of champagne, but this was a rare honour, for billeting parties only.

The news that we were not going to Germany caused much

disappointment. But this soon wore off, and we probably spent a pleasanter, if possibly less interesting, winter in Belgium.

The gravest feature of this time was the so-called " Spanish 'flu." It had begun in the early summer, but there were comparatively few cases in the Regiment till about the time of the armistice. From then onwards it raged for two or three months, and really became a miniature plague. Several died of it, often, sadly enough, men who had come through the whole war with a splendid record.

The Regimental Diary ends on the 29th November with the remark : " Rations very irregular and short owing to breakdown in train service. Mails also very irregular." This had been the case ever since the armistice and was of course due to the destruction of roads and railways farther back.

Letters to or from England were taking six days on the journey. Officers who went on leave to Paris had to go round by Brussels and Dunkirk, and took four days to get there.

Colonel Dugdale left us while we were at Dochamps and went home to England, having commanded the Regiment continuously since the war began. He had been with it in every important action in which it had taken part, and had practically never been absent, except for the ordinary periods of leave. He was succeeded by Major Nicholl, who was gazetted Lieutenant-Colonel on the 21st January 1919.

Early in December the Regiment moved with the rest of the Brigade to permanent winter billets in the country east of Liége. Regimental Headquarters and " C " Squadron were at Trooz, on the main line from Liége to Verviers and Cologne. " A " Squadron had a château near by ; and " D " Squadron occupied the village of Olne, a few miles north of Trooz.

Here they were all very comfortable, and probably for most of us the next two months were the best holiday of our life. The war was over ; the worries of peace had not

COLONEL DUGDALE AND MAJOR NICHOLL.
(1915.)

OXFORDSHIRE HUSSARS PLAYING POLO (1915).
Lt. E. H. Chinnery, Major V. Fleming, Lt. A. J. Muirhead, Lt. F. Weatherby, Major R. E. U.
Hermon-Hodge, ——————, Major J. W. Scott, Capt. H. A. Fane.

begun ; there was almost nothing to do but enjoy ourselves, and we did it. The surrounding country was delightful, the people exceedingly friendly. The one shadow on the scene was the gradual process of demobilization. But only a small proportion of the Regiment left before Christmas, and there was still a substantial nucleus to enjoy the numerous festivities arranged. Chief among these was a great dramatic performance by " D " Squadron, in which a series of short plays was given, one by the officers, another by the sergeants, a third by the men, and the last, on a bigger scale, by all ranks combined. The show only ran one night, but was an immense success, receiving tremendous applause from the very large audience, drawn from all squadrons of the Regiment, and containing also representatives of the 3rd Hussars and other units in the Brigade.

We also held two very successful race meetings, besides numerous dinners and other parties.

Of work there was very little beyond grooming and exercising horses. Voluntary educational classes were started in subjects such as the writing of English, book-keeping, etc., and were rather popular, but did not come to much, owing to continual demobilization.

It was a very hard winter with much frost and snow. By the end of January demobilization was in full swing. About the end of February Colonel Nicholl went home and handed over the command of the remnant to Major Villiers.

Lieutenants Soame, Williams, and Hodgson, S.S.M. Elliott, and a number of men volunteered for a year's service with the Army of the Rhine, and were attached to the 3rd Hussars, where they were very kindly received, and are reported to have served with credit to their Regiment of origin.

Captain Keith-Falconer was appointed D.A.Q.M.G. on the British Armistice Commission at Spa (30th March 1919).

Major Villiers stayed on to the end and brought the Regiment back to England in May 1919. On their last journey out of Belgium they narrowly escaped a nasty accident : the coach containing the officers and several of the men ran off the rails and overturned, but no one was hurt. They eventually arrived at Catterick Camp and dispersed to civil life.

During the spring of 1920 the Government decided to convert all but ten of the fifty-five yeomanry regiments into artillery batteries or machine-gun squadrons. The ten selected for retention as cavalry were those appearing as senior in the official table of precedence, which were not necessarily those with the longest continuous history. As shown in the introduction, the Q.O.O.H. have an earlier origin than that by which their place in the seniority list was determined. Moreover, they alone of the yeomanry regiments which fought in France retained their horses and served in a cavalry division from 1914 to 1919. However, as in 1827, it was decided that they must be among the units to be sacrificed, and in February 1920 a private meeting of officers was held to consider the question and to find out how many were likely to convert. It seemed clear that very few would be able to give up the time necessary to become even amateur artillery officers. None knew much of the technical working of a battery, beyond at best such knowledge as every cavalry officer should have.

However, the issue was postponed by a decision of the Government in March to reconstitute all the pre-war yeomanry regiments as cavalry for a provisional period of two years, during which time it was hoped that a sufficient number of the old officers and men would get together again to reawaken the now rather flickering interest, collect new recruits of the right sort and generally revive *esprit de corps*. They would then be asked to convert into the new units required by the War Office.

Major H. W. Hamilton, 5th Dragoon Guards, our former Staff Captain, and later D.A.A. and Q.M.G. on our Divisional Staff, was appointed Adjutant, and worked hard to make the regiment a success, aided by Captain Goldie the Quartermaster.

His Majesty the King was graciously pleased to approve of the appointment of Her Majesty the Queen as Colonel-

in-Chief of the Regiment on 25th March 1919, and on 11th
March 1921, on the occasion of Her Majesty's visit to Oxford
to receive the degree of D.C.L., the Regiment provided an
escort to and from the railway-station, under the command
of Captain Hutchinson.

Almost the last occasion on which any considerable body
of the Regiment was assembled officially was on the 17th
September 1921, when the musketry finals were shot off
at Gravenhill Butts, near Bicester.

On 31st March 1922 the Regiment was finally disbanded,
and ceased to exist as a military unit.

Some time afterwards it was awarded the battle honours
shown at the beginning of this book—more in number than
those of any other yeomanry regiment.

Two batteries of field artillery were raised by slow degrees
and united with two Worcestershire batteries to form the
100th (Worcestershire and Oxfordshire Yeomanry) Brigade,
R.F.A.   Major Muirhead was appointed to command one
of the two Oxfordshire batteries, both of which take their
name and badge from the old Regiment.   But the batteries
are recruited mainly from the towns, and must of necessity
develop a new spirit and a new tradition, very different
from that of the old yeomanry cavalry.

NOTE TO APPENDICES

THE first five appendices (A to E) have been compiled from the lists kept during the war and attached to the Regimental Diary, and have been largely supplemented and revised, in the case of A by the official publications *Officers Died in the Great War* and *Soldiers Died in the Great War*, and in the case of D by the *London Gazette*. Unfortunately no such revision has been possible in the case of Appendices B and C, for which the only source of information available is the list attached to the Regimental Diary. This is probably fairly complete except for a strange gap between July 1917 and March 1918, during which no casualties of any sort are recorded, although it is tolerably certain that some occurred.

Regimental numbers, rank, initials, spelling of names, and dates, are given, in Appendix A as in *Officers Died in the Great War* and *Soldiers Died in the Great War*; in Appendices B and C as in the regimental lists; and in Appendix D as in the *London Gazette*. To avoid misunderstanding, it may be explained that letters indicating honours, such as D.S.O., M.C., etc., are appended to names only when the recipient had actually received the award before the date at which his name occurs.

The following abbreviations have been used: K., killed in action; D.W., died of wounds; D., died from illness or other cause, not in action. Such an entry as " D.W. Potijze," or " D. Roquetoire," does not mean that the man in question actually died at that place, but that he died of wounds received at Potijze or of illness contracted at Roquetoire.

Although the utmost care has been taken to make these lists as complete and accurate as possible, it is too much to hope that some errors and omissions have not crept in. To any who may find their name omitted or their particulars incorrectly given, the compiler offers his sincere apology and regret.

Finally, it should be added that, while in Appendices A and D the net has been spread as widely as possible, so as to include all those who ever wore the regimental badge, whether serving with the " first line " or not, and also all officers and men of other units attached to the Regiment in France, the names in Appendices B and C have of necessity been restricted to those actually serving with the Regiment at the date of being wounded or captured.

APPENDIX A

OFFICERS, NON-COMMISSIONED OFFICERS, AND MEN KILLED IN ACTION, DIED OF WOUNDS, OR OTHERWISE DIED ON SERVICE IN THE GREAT WAR, 1914–1918

Rank and Name.	Date of Death.	Remarks.
Captain B. C. B. Molloy	1/11/14	K. near Messines
Captain G. Bonham-Carter, 19th Hussars, Adjutant Q.O.O.H.	15/5/15	D.W. near Potijze
2nd Lieut. W. H. L. Vernon	7/10/16	K. on the Somme. Attd. Oxford & Bucks Lt. Inf.
Major (Temp. Lt.-Col.) J. W. Scott, D.S.O.	23/4/17	K. near Arras, Comdg. 8th Bn. Somerset Lt. Inf.
Major V. Fleming, D.S.O., M.P.	20/5/17	K. Gillemont Farm
2nd Lieut. F. S. J. Silvertop .	20/5/17	K. Gillemont Farm
2nd Lieut. J. A. P. Whinney .	22/6/17	K. Gillemont Farm
2nd Lieut. A. J. L. O'Beirne .	28/7/17	D.W. Attd. R.F.C.
2nd Lieut. H. E. Biederman .	10/8/17	K. Attd. R.F.C.
2nd Lieut. L. Dove, Bedfordshire Yeomanry, attd. Q.O.O.H.	1/4/18	D.W. near Amiens. With "Carey's Force"
2nd Lieut. J. P. Higgs . .	14/4/18	D.W. Attd. 4th Machinegun Squadron
Captain H. A Fane, M.C. .	11/8/18	D.W. Battle of Amiens

No.	Rank and Name.	Date of Death.	Remarks.
2039	Private N. Sheasby	1/11/14	D.W. Messines
1700	Private H. F. Archer	3/11/14	K. Wulverghem
1865	Private A. E. Horne.	16/11/14	K. Wulverghem
1718	Private F. B. Dallow	22/11/14	K. Kemmel
1995	Private F. Nixey .	21/1/15	D. Roquetoire
2061	Private R. Dickins .	22/2/15	K. Zillebeke
2440	Private J.T. Tompkins	18/3/15	D. England
2016	Private A. Woodcock	30/3/15	D. Pradelles
1502	Private H. Wood .	21/4/15	D. France
1436	Sergeant C. Hyde .	27/4/15	K. Vlamertinghe
1883	Private J. E. Batchelor	28/4/15	D.W. Vlamertinghe
2078	Private R. J. Paice .	28/4/15	D.W. Potijze
1897	Private R. C. Quinion	17/5/15	K. Potijze
1932	Private A. E. Bennett	23/5/15	D.W. Potijze
1577	Corporal L. F. Gale .	26/5/15	K. Zouave Wood
1607	Private W. R. North	26/5/15	D.W. Potijze
1625	Private G. W. Jones	27/5/15	D.W. Potijze

No.	Rank and Name.	Date of Death.	Remarks.
1498	Sergeant W.E.Roberts	28/5/15	K. Zouave Wood
2043	Private R. Gibbs .	5/6/15	D. Wallon Cappel
1979	Private H. Stevens .	14/6/15	D. England
1884	Private A. Kitchener, R.A.M.C., attd. Q.O.O.H. . . .	27/6/15	D. France
2375	Private F. J. Wilson	16/7/15	D. France
2103	Private F. G. French	13/9/15	D. England
2305	Private A. G. Bowden	14/1/16	D.W. Vermelles
1489	Corporal G. Wassell .	14/1/16	D. England
1853	Corporal R. O. Bolingbroke . . .	27/1/16	D.W. Vermelles
2330	Private T. W. S. Jones	31/1/16	K. Vermelles
3089	Private R. C. Claridge	3/2/16	D. England
1849	Private T. P. Stone .	8/2/16	K. Vermelles
2241	L. Corporal A. Tutty	24/6/16	D.W. France
1784	L. Corporal T. Hartley	27/12/16	D. Caumont
286200	Private A. E. Burton	28/3/17	D. England
2468	L. Corporal S. A. Hopcroft . .	29/3/17	K. Arras
2951	Private J. Markham	30/3/17	D.W. Arras
2193	Sergeant E. H. Price	10/4/17	K. Arras
285508	Private E. Roads .	18/5/17	K. Gillemont Farm
285484	Private G. N. Buswell	20/5/17	K. Gillemont Farm
285727	Private L. G. Gillett	20/5/17	D.W. Gillemont Farm
285091	Private J. Lovejoy .	20/5/17	K. Gillemont Farm
285483	Private C. White .	20/5/17	K. Gillemont Farm
285034	Sergeant V. Gare, M.M.	24/5/17	K. Gillemont Farm
285803	Private A. G. Milligan	27/5/17	K. Gillemont Farm
3513	R.S.M. A. Collier, M.C., D.C.M. .	1/6/17	D. England
286046	Private C. T. Cunnington . .	13/6/17	D. England
285510	L. Corporal H. H. Jennings . .	22/6/17	K. Gillemont Farm
285883	Private T. H. Ayris .	22/6/17	K. Gillemont Farm
285491	Private W. J. Berry	22/6/17	K. Gillemont Farm
285406	Private W. Butler .	22/6/17	K. Gillemont Farm
285852	Private H. Castle .	22/6/17	K. Gillemont Farm
285579	Private S. F. Cator .	22/6/17	K. Gillemont Farm
285862	Private T. R. Deane	22/6/17	D.W. Gillemont Farm
280739	Private A. Farnsworth	22/6/17	K. Gillemont Farm
285745	Private J. Flux .	22/6/17	K. Gillemont Farm
40272	Private H. Goddard	22/6/17	K. Gillemont Farm
285480	Private M.F. Saunders	22/6/17	K. Gillemont Farm
285429	Private A. Shayler .	22/6/17	K. Gillemont Farm
285604	Private T. G. Stevens	22/6/17	K. Gillemont Farm
285894	Private W. Watson .	22/6/17	K. Gillemont Farm
285033	L.Corporal W. Blelock	1/7/17	K. Templeux Quarries
285826	Private F. Cox .	1/7/17	K. Templeux Quarries
285934	Private F. W. J. Macey, M.M. .	1/7/17	K. Templeux Quarries
285319	Private C. H. Thompson . . .	1/7/17	K. Templeux Quarries
285121	Sergeant W. A. S. Bayliss . .	5/7/17	K. Gillemont Farm

No.	Rank and Name.	Date of Death.	Remarks.
285891	Private G. L. Buckle	5/7/17	K. Gillemont Farm
281123	Private J. Hamilton.	5/7/17	D.W. Gillemont Farm
285763	Private A. Old. .	5/7/17	K. Gillemont Farm
285462	Private A. J. Podbery, M.M. . . .	5/7/17	K. Gillemont Farm
285932	Private C. A. Hitchman . . .	28/10/17	K. France
29821	Private G. Tustin .	28/10/17	D.W. France
285754	Private H. Lindsay.	29/10/17	D.W. France
285716	Private F. Woodley .	29/10/17	D.W. France
285783	Private R. Buggins .	2/11/17	D.W. France
285403	Private C. E. Beckingham . . .	27/11/17	K. France
285542	Private A.R. Smewing	27/11/17	K. France
285379	L.Corporal E. Lovell	2/12/17	D.W. France
285680	Private C. F. Canning	11/12/17	D.W. France
285122	Private G. A Drewett	1/1/18	D.W. France
285138	Sergeant H. V. Drake	21/3/18	K. Battle of St. Quentin
285708	Private F. E. Bayliss	21/3/18	K. Battle of St. Quentin
285681	Private E. Claridge .	21/3/18	K. Battle of St. Quentin
285837	Private G. W. Coles .	21/3/18	K. Battle of St. Quentin
29470	Private A. G. Darcy	21/3/18	K. Battle of St. Quentin
285237	Private E. Freeman .	21/3/18	K. Battle of St. Quentin
285037	Sergeant E. E. Hall	23/3/18	K. Battle of St. Quentin
285209	Corporal R. Lines .	23/3/18	K. Battle of St. Quentin
285404	Private A. H. Boyles	23/3/18	K. Battle of St. Quentin
285251	Private J. Castle .	23/3/18	K. Battle of St. Quentin
230498	Private U. J. Clarke	23/3/18	K. Battle of St. Quentin
285498	Private C. J. Dale .	23/3/18	K. Battle of St. Quentin
285339	Private J. Foster .	23/3/18	K. Battle of St. Quentin
280545	Private W. Beevers .	25/3/18	K. near Noyon
285796	Private W. J. Lewington . . .	25/3/18	K. near Noyon
285074	L.Corporal L. W. Saunders . .	26/3/18	K. near Noyon
285396	Private G. Freeman	27/3/18	D.W. near Noyon
29428	Private J. H. Hersey	29/3/18	D. England
285069	Sergeant H. Kidman	30/3/18	D.W. Battle of St. Quentin. (Missing, 23/3/18)
285505	L.Corporal D.C. Carter	1/4/18	K. Rifle Wood
45705	Private J. Anthony .	1/4/18	K. Rifle Wood
285879	Private B. Atkins .	1/4/18	K. Rifle Wood
285409	Private E. W. Didcott	1/4/18	K. Rifle Wood
285515	Private W. J. Dunn	1/4/18	K. Rifle Wood
285445	Private E. Ford .	1/4/18	K. Rifle Wood
285306	Private H. A. French	1/4/18	K. Rifle Wood
285725	Private F. G. Hunnisett . . .	1/4/18	K. Rifle Wood
285700	Private C. W. C. Maasz . . .	1/4/18	K. Rifle Wood
288946	Private A. P. Miles .	1/4/18	K. Rifle Wood
285381	Private W. J. Mortimer . . .	1/4/18	K. Rifle Wood
285524	Private H. N. Parker	1/4/18	K. Rifle Wood
285049	Saddler G. Avery .	1/4/18	K. Rifle Wood
285006	Sergeant A. Hawtin .	2/4/18	D.W. Rifle Wood

No.	Rank and Name.	Date of Death.	Remarks.
285474	L.Corporal F. J. Rouse	2/4/18	D.W. Rifle Wood
285173	Private R. G. Farn-brough . .	2/4/18	D.W. Rifle Wood
285265	Private G. H. Hicks	10/4/18	D.W. Rifle Wood
285422	Sergeant J. Johnston, M.M. . . .	15/4/18	D.W. Rifle Wood
285450	A./Corporal J. Clift .	18/4/18	D. England
288829	Private G. H. Vince	24/5/18	D. England
285021	S.S.M. R. T. Shrimpton	9/8/18	K. Battle of Amiens
231149	Private A. J. Jarman	10/8/18	K. Battle of Amiens
285295	Private T. C. E. Newell . .	10/8/18	D.W. Battle of Amiens
288935	Private W. C. Timms	10/8/18	K. Battle of Amiens
80704	Private E. Tompkins, Essex Yeomanry, attd. Q.O.O.H. .	10/8/18	K. Battle of Amiens
285834	Private E. Edmunds	12/8/18	D.W. Battle of Amiens
40283	Private R. J. Howkins	22/8/18	D.W. Battle of St. Quentin. (Missing, 23/3/18)
39681	Private D. Swift, MM.	6/9/18	D.W. Battle of the Dro-court–Quéant line
285610	Private O. W. Buck-ingham . .	30/9/18	K. Battle of the Canal du Nord
285482	L.Corporal W. A. H. McIntosh, M.M. .	30/9/18	K. Battle of the Canal du Nord
285790	Private S. A. Sheppard	20/10/18	D. France
285698	Private C. B. Fowler	24/10/18	K. Battle of the Selle
286038	Private W. Youens .	27/10/18	D. England
285426	A./L. Sergeant J. Coleshill . .	1/11/18	D. England
255235	Private W. Scott .	3/11/18	D. France
285062	Sergeant E. J. Butler, M.M. .	5/11/18	D. England
285440	Private J. B. Cross .	5/11/18	K. Battle of the Sambre
275404	Private J. A. Guy .	8/11/18	D. France
281841	Private A. E. Jones .	11/11/18	D. France
285391	Corporal G. J. Tomp-kins, M.M. .	19/11/18	D. France
285194	L.CorporalG.W.Smith	22/11/18	D. France
285180	Sergeant L. North .	24/11/18	D. France

APPENDIX B

OFFICERS, NON-COMMISSIONED OFFICERS, AND MEN WOUNDED

Rank and Name.	Date of Wound.	Remarks.
Major F. G. Proudfoot, R.A.M.C., attd. Q.O.O.H.	27/4/15	Vlamertinghe
2nd Lieut. J. Kingscote .	30/4/15	Wieltje
2nd Lieut. G. V. Wellesley .	1/5/15	Wieltje
2nd Lieut. F. Weatherby .	3/10/15	Loos
2nd Lieut. R. L. Worsley .	26/5/17	Gillemont Farm
Major R. E. U. Hermon-Hodge	29/5/17	Gillemont Farm
2nd Lieut. W. B. Riddell .	1/7/17	Templeux Quarries (Shell-shock)
2nd Lieut. A. C. Rawlinson .	4/7/17	Gillemont Farm
Capt. H. A. Fane . . .	23/3/18	Battle of St. Quentin
Capt. W. Pepper . . .	23/3/18	Battle of St. Quentin
Capt. G. H. Palmer .	23/3/18	Battle of St. Quentin
2nd Lieut. W. J. Mason .	23/3/18	Battle of St. Quentin
Major Hon. A. G. C. Villiers, D.S.O.	1/4/18	Rifle Wood
Lieut. R. L. Worsley . .	1/4/18	Rifle Wood
Lieut. A. E. MacColl . .	1/4/18	Rifle Wood
Lieut. B. H. Matthews . .	8/8/18	Battle of Amiens
2nd Lieut. E. W. Hunt . .	3/9/18	Battle of Amiens, the Drocourt–Quéant line

No.	Rank and Name.	Date of Wound.	Remarks.
2184	Sergeant W. Kingston	31/10/14	Messines
1375	Corporal J. Beesley	31/10/14	Messines
1782	Private M. Batting .	31/10/14	Messines
1944	Private B. Smith .	31/10/14	Messines
1805	Private B. Bury .	1/11/14	Messines
2162	Private C. H. Daniels	3/11/14	Wulverghem
1266	Sergeant M. Rice .	3/11/14	Wulverghem
1811	Corporal A. Coppock	6/11/14	Wulverghem
2010	Private F. Jones .	6/11/14	Wulverghem
1047	Sergeant W. Perrin .	16/11/14	Wulverghem
1493	L.Corporal R. Holmes	20/11/14	Kemmel
1784	Private N. Harcourt .	20/11/14	Kemmel
1954	Saddler S. Harris .	20/11/14	Kemmel
1632	Private T. Bosbury .	22/2/15	Zillebeke
1977	Private R. G. Gale .	22/2/15	Zillebeke
2158	Private A. E. Coles .	27/4/15	Vlamertinghe
1885	Private W. F. Burton	27/4/15	Vlamertinghe
2145	Private E. S. Street .	27/4/15	Vlamertinghe
2315	Private W. J. Paice .	28/4/15	Potijze

No.	Rank and Name.	Date of Wound.	Remarks.
1947	Private R. Lines .	28/4/15	Potijze
2382	Private E. Roads .	28/4/15	Potijze
2097	Private T. P. Palmer	28/4/15	Potijze
2129	Private G. R. Jeffreys	28/4/15	Potijze
1566	L.Corporal W. C. Humphries . .	28/4/15	Potijze
1839	Private A. Stanley .	28/4/15	Potijze
2022	Private F. V. Gee .	1/5/15	Wieltje
1946	Private A. Wilkins .	15/5/15	Potijze
1740	L.Corporal J. Steele .	15/5/15	Potijze
1873	Private C. Brown .	15/5/15	Potijze
2489	Private F. Bryant .	15/5/15	Potijze
2114	Private B. B. Cole .	16/5/15	Potijze
2350	Private W. G. Paice	19/5/15	Potijze
2172	Private R. F. Hawes	23/5/15	Potijze
2207	L.CorporalC.Hounslow	25/5/15	Zouave Wood
1619	L.Corporal M. Bryan	25/5/15	Zouave Wood
1535	Private W. Blelock .	26/5/15	Zouave Wood
2270	Private D. K. Leed .	27/5/15	Zouave Wood
2283	Private J. Sanders .	27/5/15	Zouave Wood
2163	Private W. Darter .	28/5/15	Zouave Wood
971	S.S.M. J. C. Warren, D.C.M. . .	29/5/15	Zouave Wood
1275	Sergeant A. Thompson	29/5/15	Zouave Wood
2160	Private R. Collett .	29/5/15	Zouave Wood
1707	L.Corporal R. Hall .	4/7/15	La Clytte
1174	Sergeant G. H. Elliott	30/7/15	La Clytte
2371	Private C. Nickolls .	30/7/15	La Clytte
2001	L.Corporal A. Castle	30/7/15	La Clytte
1994	Private Machin .	3/10/15	Loos
2363	Private A. Rice .	3/10/15	Loos
2470	Private H. F. Thomas	3/10/15	Loos
1982	Private T. Turvey .	4/10/15	Loos
1719	L.Corporal F. Break- spear . . .	13/1/16	Vermelles
2307	Private B. W. Franklin	13/1/16	Vermelles
2331	Private G. Taylor .	14/1/16	Vermelles
2344	Private G. White .	22/1/16	Vermelles
1815	Private R. Graham .	14/1/16	Vermelles
2138	Private J. Foster .	22/1/16	Vermelles
2036	L.Corporal L. Kinch.	8/2/16	Vermelles
1774	Private H. Martyr .	8/2/16	Vermelles
1706	Private G. Pengilley	8/2/16	Vermelles
2947	Private A. Creed .	18/7/16	Kemmel
1938	Private F. C. Little .	11/9/16	Somme Area
2956	Private W. J. Clack .	15/9/16	Somme Area
2992	Private J. Pickering	8/10/16	Somme Area
2751	Private S. C. Eldridge	6/4/17	Arras
2841	Private F. Green . .	6/4/17	Arras
2452	Private E. Coles .	9/4/17	Arras
2065	Private T. A. Franklin	10/4/17	Arras
1774	Private H. Hedges .	10/4/17	Arras
285807	Private G. Howkins .	20/5/17	Gillemont Farm
285726	Private A. C. Kitchener . .	20/5/17	Gillemont Farm
285148	Private C. Aldridge .	20/5/17	Gillemont Farm

24

No.	Rank and Name.	Date of Wound.	Remarks.
285264	Private J. Hancock .	20/5/17	Gillemont Farm
285481	Private G. W. Surman	21/5/17	Gillemont Farm (Gas)
285503	Sergeant H. Quarter-man . . .	26/5/17	Gillemont Farm
285774	Private B. East	26/5/17	Gillemont Farm
285573	Private E. Sirett .	26/5/17	Gillemont Farm
285801	Private J. H. P. Sanders . .	27/3/17	Gillemont Farm
285050	Sergeant T. Orpwood	29/5/17	Gillemont Farm
285147	Corporal H. Fifield .	30/5/17	Gillemont Farm
285357	Private R. J. Collett.	30/5/17	Gillemont Farm
285382	Private A. Nichols .	22/6/17	Gillemont Farm
285833	Private A. Bailey .	22/6/17	Gillemont Farm
285159	Private C. Brown .	22/6/17	Gillemont Farm
285297	Private G. Ray .	22/6/17	Gillemont Farm
285329	Private W. Tustian .	22/6/17	Gillemont Farm
285568	Private F. Bryant .	22/6/17	Gillemont Farm
285957	Private J. A. Homer	22/6/17	Gillemont Farm
285804	Private S. Oldacre .	22/6/17	Gillemont Farm
285478	Private C. J. Partridge	22/6/17	Gillemont Farm
285226	Private C. W. Thorpe	22/6/17	Gillemont Farm
285151	Private J. R. Jones .	22/6/17	Gillemont Farm
285723	Private B. Chennels	1/7/17	Templeux Quarries (Shell-shock)
285328	Private C. Simons .	1/7/17	Templeux Quarries (Shell-shock)
285558	Private E. E. Martin	1/7/17	Templeux Quarries (Shell-shock)
285992	Corporal W. C. Hum-phries . .	4/7/17	Gillemont Farm
285569	Private A. N. Bird .	4/7/17	Gillemont Farm
285853	Private P. C. Newell	4/7/17	Gillemont Farm
285559	Private N. F. Thomas	4/7/17	Gillemont Farm
285243	L.Corporal R. W. Hawken . .	5/7/17	Gillemont Farm
285134	Private W. Putt .	5/7/17	Gillemont Farm
285755	Private F. Stainton .	5/7/17	Gillemont Farm
285990	Private H. J. Read .	5/7/17	Gillemont Farm
285869	Private W. G. White	6/7/17	Gillemont Farm
288944	L.Corporal E. L. Reed	21/3/18	Battle of St. Quentin
285737	Private H. C. Draper	21/3/18	Battle of St. Quentin
285168	Private P. Gaydon .	21/3/18	Battle of St. Quentin
285766	Private A. J. Kimble	21/3/18	Battle of St. Quentin
285797	Private R. B. Payne	21/3/18	Battle of St. Quentin
285538	Private J. Surman .	21/3/18	Battle of St. Quentin
285751	Private J. Willets .	21/3/18	Battle of St. Quentin
285022	Sergeant H. Stroud .	23/3/18	Battle of St. Quentin
230489	Corporal J. Clarke .	23/3/18	Battle of St. Quentin
285174	L.Corporal T. L. Easby	23/3/18	Battle of St. Quentin
285382	L.Corporal A. Nichols, M.M. . .	23/3/18	Battle of St. Quentin
13007	Private W. Allardyce	23/3/18	Battle of St. Quentin
285689	Private W. B. Ayers	23/3/18	Battle of St. Quentin
285347	Private R. S. Ashford	23/3/18	Battle of St. Quentin
285695	Private F. Baggott .	23/3/18	Battle of St. Quentin
40703	Private H. J. Bint .	23/3/18	Battle of St. Quentin

No.	Rank and Name.	Date of Wound.	Remarks.
285653	Private A. S. Briars	23/3/18	Battle of St. Quentin
285038	Private H. Brain .	23/3/18	Battle of St. Quentin
285794	Private F. Carpenter	23/3/18	Battle of St. Quentin
285721	Private P. O. Dunklin	23/3/18	Battle of St. Quentin
285831	Private B. Fowler .	23/3/18	Battle of St. Quentin
288945	Private W. Gubbins	23/3/18	Battle of St. Quentin
285202	Private J. Hale .	23/3/18	Battle of St. Quentin
285752	Private H. Hall .	23/3/18	Battle of St. Quentin
285264	Private J. Hancock .	23/3/18	Battle of St. Quentin
285274	Private A. H. Hicks	23/3/18	Battle of St. Quentin
285987	Private H. Hicks .	23/3/18	Battle of St. Quentin
285398	Private H. Hulbert.	23/3/18	Battle of St. Quentin
285090	Private S. V. Hunt .	23/3/18	Battle of St. Quentin
285472	Private N. Jerrams .	23/3/18	Battle of St. Quentin
21708	Private W. King .	23/3/18	Battle of St. Quentin
285476	Private W. Lovejoy	23/3/18	Battle of St. Quentin
285035	Private H. G. Maunder	23/3/18	Battle of St. Quentin
285727	Private A. C. Mead .	23/3/18	Battle of St. Quentin
285287	Private J. Pimm .	23/3/18	Battle of St. Quentin
285686	Private W. Rawlins .	23/3/18	Battle of St. Quentin
16119	Private W. Seben .	23/3/18	Battle of St. Quentin
14104	Private R. Staite .	23/3/18	Battle of St. Quentin
285481	Private G. W. Surman	23/3/18	Battle of St. Quentin
285750	Private T. E. Swann	23/3/18	Battle of St. Quentin
285949	Private F. J. Thomas	23/3/18	Battle of St. Quentin
285715	Private H. Underwood	23/3/18	Battle of St. Quentin
285782	Private E. Vaughan	23/3/18	Battle of St. Quentin
285857	Private F. Wells .	23/3/18	Battle of St. Quentin
285687	Private H. West .	23/3/18	Battle of St. Quentin
43251	Private S. G. Young.	23/3/18	Battle of St. Quentin
285223	Sergeant R. Hoddinott	25/3/18	Near Noyon
285773	L.Corporal S. F. Bennett . .	23/3/18	Near Noyon
285885	Private A. B. Foster	23/3/18	Near Noyon
285830	Private E. Wayt .	25/3/18	Near Noyon
285178	Corporal J. Griffen .	1/4/18	Rifle Wood
285718	Private F. Adams .	1/4/18	Rifle Wood
285781	Private J. Scarrott .	1/4/18	Rifle Wood
285329	Private W. W. Tustian	1/4/18	Rifle Wood
285797	Private R. B. Payne	1/4/18	Rifle Wood
285470	Saddler N. Hill .	1/4/18	Rifle Wood
285605	Private G. A. Higgs .	1/4/18	Rifle Wood
285334	Private S. H. Weeks	1/4/18	Rifle Wood
285705	Private S. B. Clarke	1/4/18	Rifle Wood
285501	Private T. Freeman .	1/4/18	Rifle Wood
285044	Private W. Taylor .	1/4/18	Rifle Wood
285712	Private F. J. Harris .	1/4/18	Rifle Wood
285817	Private L. Fisk .	1/4/18	Rifle Wood
285551	Corporal R. N. Webb	1/4/18	Rifle Wood
285423	L.Corporal H. Mullard	1/4/18	Rifle Wood
285753	Private F. Bultitude	1/4/18	Rifle Wood
285843	Private C. H. Claydon	1/4/18	Rifle Wood
285460	Private A. R. Evans	1/4/18	Rifle Wood
285699	Private J. W. Hitchman . . .	1/4/18	Rifle Wood
285955	Private F. Hudson .	1/4/18	Rifle Wood

No.	Rank and Name.	Date of Wound.	Remarks.
285151	Private J. Jones .	1/4/18	Rifle Wood
285478	Private C. J. Partridge	1/4/18	Rifle Wood
11804	Private B. Wright .	1/4/18	Rifle Wood
285059	Sergeant H. W. Lovell	1/4/18	Rifle Wood
285224	Sergeant A. Bull, M.M.	1/4/18	Rifle Wood
285248	L.Corporal R. Stonor	1/4/18	Rifle Wood
285154	Private L. F. V. J. Lamb . . .	1/4/18	Rifle Wood
285155	Trumpeter S. E. Hickman . .	1/4/18	Rifle Wood
285747	Private A. W. Bond	1/4/18	Rifle Wood
285709	Private A. J. Brunsdon	1/4/18	Rifle Wood
285710	Private W. J. Butler	1/4/18	Rifle Wood
40224	Private Heley .	1/4/18	Rifle Wood
214441	Private H. Monk .	1/4/18	Rifle Wood
285384	Private T. Peverill .	1/4/18	Rifle Wood
285583	Private W. H. Saw .	1/4/18	Rifle Wood
231183	Private W. Wicks .	1/4/18	Rifle Wood
285545	Private W. C. Allington . . .	1/4/18	Rifle Wood
288885	Private A. O'Neill ..	1/4/18	Rifle Wood
285265	Private H. G. Hicks	1/4/18	Rifle Wood
23705	Private H. G. Pearce	1/4/18	Rifle Wood
251373	Private J. Anderton	1/4/18	Rifle Wood
285661	Private Lane . .	1/4/18	Rifle Wood
40721	Private W. J. Howe .	1/4/18	Rifle Wood
285201	S.Q.M.S. E. Chaundy	9/8/18	Battle of Amiens
285340	L.Corporal W. Hackling . .	9/8/18	Battle of Amiens
285269	Private F. Attwell .	9/8/18	Battle of Amiens
288884	Private G. H. Reeves	9/8/18	Battle of Amiens
285866	Private E. J. Smith	10/8/18	Battle of Amiens
45706	Private W. J. Ashton	10/8/18	Battle of Amiens
81137	Private A. Whitten .	10/8/18	Battle of Amiens
285420	Corporal C. A. Webster	3/9/18	Battle of the Drocourt– Quéant line
4690	L.Corporal C. Hobell	30/9/18	Battle of the Canal du Nord
285957	Private J. A. Homer	30/9/18	Battle of the Canal du Nord
40224	Private Heley . .	30/9/18	Battle of the Canal du Nord
285140	Private D. Bayliss .	30/9/18	Battle of the Canal du Nord
300753	Private W. Darby .	10/10/18	Pursuit to the Selle
295362	Private E. J. Durnford	10/10/18	Pursuit to the Selle
285177	Private A. Smith .	10/10/18	Pursuit to the Selle
285507	Sergeant A. Peaker .	10/10/18	Pursuit to the Selle
33295	Private S. Slater .	20/10/18	Battle of the Selle (Gas)
285695	Private C. W. Batts .	20/10/18	Battle of the Selle (Gas)
285786	Private W. A. Fenemore . .	23/10/18	Battle of the Selle
285340	Private F. C. Smart .	23/10/18	Battle of the Selle
285132	L.Corporal W. A. Clack . .	23/10/18	Battle of the Selle
231076	Private H. Elsom .	23/10/18	Battle of the Selle
285096	Sergeant C. Jacobs .	23/10/18	Battle of the Selle
285227	L.Corporal E. O'Neill	23/10/18	Battle of the Selle
285293	Corporal L. Clayton	24/10/18	Battle of the Selle
285788	Private F. Beldom .	24/10/18	Battle of the Selle

No.	Rank and Name.	Date of Wound.	Remarks.
285921	Private A. Jacques .	24/10/18	Battle of the Selle
285491	Private R. Webb .	24/10/18	Battle of the Selle
285353	Corporal H. Bustin .	25/10/18	Battle of the Selle
285643	Private J. Nicholls .	25/10/18	Battle of the Selle
285691	Private S. C. Eldridge	25/10/18	Battle of the Selle
285366	Corporal R. Hawes, M.M. . . .	26/10/18	Battle of the Selle (Gas)
381971	Private A. Cross .	26/10/18	Battle of the Selle (Gas)
285793	Private A. Thompson	26/10/18	Battle of the Selle (Gas)
285569	Corporal A. N. Bird	4/11/18	Battle of the Sambre
285989	L.Corporal J. Hicks, M.M. . . .	4/11/18	Battle of the Sambre
35043	Private N. Frances .	4/11/18	Battle of the Sambre
230605	Private F. G. Short .	4/11/18	Battle of the Sambre
285881	Private A. J. Hickman	4/11/18	Battle of the Sambre
285083	Private D. Alden .	5/11/18	Battle of the Sambre
285340	L.CorporalW.Hackling	10/11/18	Battle of the Sambre
285691	Private S. C. Eldridge	10/11/18	Battle of the Sambre

APPENDIX C
PRISONERS OF WAR

No.	Rank and Name.	Date of Capture.	Place.
285111	Sergeant A. E. Hepworth, M.M. .	22/6/17	Gillemont Farm
285249	Private G. Bulford .	22/6/17	Gillemont Farm
285684	Private R. Lewis .	22/6/17	Gillemont Farm
285738	Private J. F. Richardson . . .	22/6/17	Gillemont Farm
285439	Private W. Summersford . . .	22/6/17	Gillemont Farm
285798	Private H. Thornton	22/6/17	Gillemont Farm
285525	L.Corporal H. C. West . . .	23/3/18	Battle of St. Quentin
281891	Private G. Carter .	23/3/18	Battle of St. Quentin
40283	Private R. J. Howkins	23/3/18	Battle of St. Quentin (Died, 22/8/18)

APPENDIX D

HONOURS AND AWARDS.

Rank and Name.	Date of Award.	Remarks.

COMPANION OF THE ORDER OF ST. MICHAEL AND ST. GEORGE (C.M.G.)

Lieutenant-Colonel A. Dugdale	3/6/15	Regimental Headquarters

DISTINGUISHED SERVICE ORDER (D.S.O.)

Major (Temp. Lt.-Col.) J. W. Scott	1/1/17	Comdg. 8th Bn. Somerset Light Infantry
Major V. Fleming, M.P. .	4/6/17	"C" Squadron
Major Hon. A. G. C. Villiers .	18/7/17	"D" Squadron
Major J. S. S. Churchill .	3/6/18	Staff
Lieut.-Colonel A. Dugdale, C.M.G.	1/1/19	Regimental Headquarters
Major Hon. R. E. U. Hermon-Hodge	3/6/19	"A" Squadron

BAR TO THE DISTINGUISHED SERVICE ORDER

Major Hon. A. G. C. Villiers, D.S.O.	26/7/18	"D" Squadron

MILITARY CROSS (M.C.)

2nd Lieut. (T. Lieut.) G. V. Wellesley . . .	3/6/16	"D" Squadron
Lieut. (Temp. Capt.) G. T. Hutchinson . .	1/1/17	Staff
3513. S.S.M. (A./R.S.M.) A. Collier, D.C.M. . .	17/4/17	"C" Squadron
2nd Lieut. (Temp. Lieut.) A. J. Muirhead . . .	4/6/17	Staff
2nd Lieut. (Temp. Lieut.) H. M. Worsley . .	17/9/17	"C" Squadron
Temp. Capt. F. A. Grange, R.A.M.C., attd. Q.O.O.H. .	4/2/18	Regimental Headquarters
Lieut. (A./Capt.) G. E. Schuster	3/6/18	Staff
Capt. H. A. Fane . . .	26/7/18	"A" Squadron
Capt. W. Pepper . . .	26/7/18	"A" Squadron
Lieut. (Temp. Capt.) J. A. Moncreiffe, D.C.M. .	26/7/18	4th Machine-gun Squadron
Lieut. (A./Capt.) F. Weatherby	26/7/18	Regimental Headquarters

BAR TO THE MILITARY CROSS

Capt. A. J. Muirhead, M.C. .	1/2/19	Staff

Rank and Name.	Date of Award.	Remarks.

DISTINGUISHED CONDUCT MEDAL (D.C.M.)

Rank and Name.	Date of Award.	Remarks.
971. S.S.M. J. C. Warren .	3/6/15	" D " Squadron
2516. Private P. Muller .	15/3/16	" D " Squadron
285169. Private T. N. A'Bear, M.M.	25/8/17	" C " Squadron

MILITARY MEDAL (M.M.)

Rank and Name.	Date of Award.	Remarks.
1814. Sergeant H. F. Wise .	11/10/16	" A " Squadron
1811. Sergeant A. Coppock .	11/10/16	" A " Squadron
1549. Sergeant V. Gare . .	11/10/16	" D " Squadron
1798. Sergeant A. E. Hepworth . . .	11/10/16	" D " Squadron
1705. Sergeant S. Waine .	11/10/16	" A " Squadron
2884. Corporal A. J. Champion	11/10/16	" C " Squadron
285811. Private H. J. Collett .	26/5/17	" A " Squadron
285575. Private G. C. Tame .	18/6/17	" C " Squadron
285422. Sergeant J. Johnston .	18/7/17	" C " Squadron
285169. Private T. N. A'Bear.	18/7/17	" C " Squadron
285934. Private F. W. J. Macey	18/7/17	" C " Squadron
285462. Private A. J. Podbery	18/7/17	" C " Squadron
285224. Sergeant A. Bull .	21/8/17	" C " Squadron
285062. Sergeant E. J. Butler .	21/8/17	" C " Squadron
285243. L.Corporal R. W. Hawken . . .	21/8/17	" C " Squadron
285382. Private A. Nichols .	21/8/17	" D " Squadron
285092. Corporal J. L. Saunders . . .	19/3/18	" C " Squadron
285989. Private J. Hicks .	19/3/18	" C " Squadron
285223. Sergeant R. Hoddinott	27/6/18	" C " Squadron
285174. L.Corporal T. L. Easby	27/6/18	" C " Squadron
285366. L.Corporal R. F. Hawes	27/6/18	" D " Squadron
285482. L.Corporal W. A. H. McIntosh . . .	27/6/18	" A " Squadron
285717. Trumpeter A. H. Wells . . .	27/6/18	" C " Squadron
22076. Private F. Brown .	27/6/18	4th Machine-gun Squadron
285264. Private J. Hancock .	11/2/19	" D " Squadron
39681. Private D. Swift .	11/2/19	" C " Squadron
285372. Sergeant N. F. Jones.	14/5/19	" D " Squadron
285171. Corporal F. Coles .	14/5/19	" D " Squadron
285199. Sergeant S. G. Bennett	17/6/19	" A " Squadron
285435. Corporal W. H. Huckerby . . .	17/6/19	" D " Squadron
285167. Corporal P. A. Stockford . . .	17/6/19	" D " Squadron
285391. Corporal G. J. Tompkins . . .	17/6/19	" D " Squadron
285285. Pte (L.Corporal) H. Hunt	17/6/19	" D " Squadron

MERITORIOUS SERVICE MEDAL (M.S.M.)

Rank and Name.	Date of Award.	Remarks.
14101. S.Q.M.S. B. J. S. McFie . . .	1/1/17	" A " Squadron
285036. Sergeant L. H. Gale .	17/6/18	" A " Squadron
285970. Private H. M. Young.	6/9/18	Detached

Rank and Name.	Date of Award.	Remarks.

CHEVALIER OF THE LEGION OF HONOUR (FRANCE)
Major J. S. S. Churchill . . | 30/3/16 | Staff

CROIX DE GUERRE (FRANCE)

Major J. S. S. Churchill, D.S.O.	–/–/18	Staff
Major Hon. A. G. C. Villiers, D.S.O.	10/10/18	" D " Squadron
1555. Sergeant C. H. Hunt .	5/11/16	" C " Squadron

MÉDAILLE MILITAIRE (FRANCE)
285341. Corporal F. W. Quartly| 29/1/19 | " C " Squadron

CROIX DE GUERRE (BELGIUM)

285015. R.Q.M.S. A. G. Thompson.	15/4/18	Regimental Headquarters
285019. Sergeant G. F. C. Sansom	15/4/18	" D " Squadron

MILITARY ORDER OF AVIS OF PORTUGAL
Major J. S. S. Churchill, D.S.O. | –/–/19 | Staff

BREVET MAJOR
Captain A. J. Muirhead, M.C. | 1/1/19 | Staff

MENTIONED IN DESPATCHES

2nd Lieut. (Temp. Capt.) F. A. Gill	17/2/15	" D " Squadron
Lieut.-Colonel A. Dugdale .	22/6/15	Regimental Headquarters
Major V. Fleming, M.P. . .	26/6/15	" C " Squadron
Capt. G. Bonham-Carter, 19th Hussars, Adjutant Q.O.O.H.	22/6/15	Regimental Headquarters
Major (Temp. Lt.-Col.) C. R. I. Nicholl	1/1/16	Regimental Headquarters
2nd Lieut. A. J. Muirhead .	1/1/16	" C " Squadron
Major (Temp. Lt.-Col.) J. W. Scott . . .	15/6/16	Comdg. 8th Bn. Somerset Light Infantry
Major (Temp. Lt.-Col.) J. W. Scott . . .	4/1/17	Comdg. 8th Bn. Somerset Light Infantry
2nd Lieut. (Temp. Capt.) G. E. Schuster	4/1/17	Staff
Major J. S. S. Churchill . .	15/5/17	Staff
Major (Temp. Lt.-Col.) J. W. Scott, D.S.O.	15/5/17	Comdg. 8th Bn. Somerset Light Infantry
Major V. Fleming, M.P. .	15/5/17	" C " Squadron
2nd Lieut. (Temp. Capt.) G. E. Schuster	15/5/17	Staff
Major Hon. A. G. C. Villiers, D.S.O.	11/12/17	" D " Squadron
Major J. S. S. Churchill . .	20/5/18	Staff
Capt. G. H. Palmer . .	20/5/18	" C " Squadron
2nd Lieut. H. B. O. Tompkins	20/5/18	" D " Squadron

Rank and Name.	Date of Award.	Remarks.
MENTIONED IN DESPATCHES—*continued.*		
Qrmr. & Hon. Capt. J. L. Goldie	20/5/18	Regimental Headquarters
Lieut. (Temp. Capt.) A. J. Muirhead, M.C.	30/5/18	Staff
Lieut.-Colonel A. Dugdale, C.M.G.	20/12/18	Regimental Headquarters
Major R. E. U. Hermon-Hodge	20/12/18	" A " Squadron
Major Hon. A. G. C. Villiers, D.S.O.	20/12/18	" D " Squadron
Capt. A. J. Muirhead, M.C.	20/12/18	Staff
Lieut. E. G. Howarth	20/12/18	" D " Squadron
1275. Sergeant A. G. Thompson	22/6/15	Machine Gun Section
1490. Farrier-Sgt. F. T. Cleverly	22/6/15	" A " Squadron
1812. L.Corporal W. A. S. Bayliss	22/6/15	" C " Squadron
1871. Private J. Checkley	22/6/15	" D " Squadron
1718. Private F. B. Dallow	22/6/15	" D " Squadron
2201. Private W. J. E. Napper	22/6/15	" A " Squadron
1555. L.Sergeant C. H. Hunt	1/1/16	" C " Squadron
3360. Sergeant H. G. List	15/6/16	" D " Squadron
1853. Signalling-Corporal R. O. Bolingbroke	15/6/16	" A " Squadron
2185. Sergeant J. J. List	4/1/17	" D " Squadron
285258. O. R. Sergeant W. Turrill	11/12/17	Regimental Headquarters
285340. Pte. (A./L.Corporal) W. Hackling	20/12/18	" C " Squadron

EXTRACTS FROM THE LONDON GAZETTE

(*Note.*—Eight of the awards to officers were accompanied by special notices in the *London Gazette,* not reprinted here.)

No. 971, Squadron Sergeant-Major J. C. Warren. Awarded the Distinguished Conduct Medal. For conspicuous gallantry on the 3rd November, 1914, at Wulverghem, when he took a prominent part with two troops in crawling up a field to fill a gap in the line of trenches, under very heavy shell fire. Has been noted for voluntarily undertaking dangerous and difficult work.

No. 2516, Private P. Muller. Awarded the Distinguished Conduct Medal. For conspicuous good work in night reconnaissances. On one occasion he entered the enemy's sap, which was unseen from our trench, picked up a rifle and fixed it so that the line could be seen by daylight.

No. 3513, Squadron Sergeant-Major (Acting Regimental Sergeant-Major) A. Collier, D.C.M. Awarded the Military Cross. For conspicuous gallantry and devotion. He brought in six wounded men from the front of the trenches under a heavy fire, the men having been left out from the previous day's engagement. He has invariably shown great bravery and coolness under fire, and set a fine example to all ranks.

No. 285169, Private T. N. A'Bear, M.M. Awarded the Distinguished Conduct Medal. Conspicuous gallantry and devotion to duty when at a listening post in advance of our line. During a fierce enemy attack he came under heavy shell fire, but in spite of being isolated he remained unmoved, bombing the advancing enemy and causing them to retire. His splendid determination and courage contributed largely to the failure of the enemy's assault.

(*Note.*—Several of the awards of the Military Medal were also accompanied by a notice of the specific act of gallantry for which they were made, but these have not been preserved in the *London Gazette* and cannot now be traced.

APPENDIX E

ROLL OF OFFICERS WHO SERVED WITH THE REGIMENT IN FRANCE, 1914–1918

SAILED WITH THE REGIMENT, 20TH SEPTEMBER, 1914

Lieutenant-Colonel A. Dugdale.
Major Hon. E. E. Twisleton-Wykeham-Fiennes, M.P.
Major J. S. S. Churchill.
Major C. R. I. Nicholl.
Captain J. W. Scott.
Captain B. C. B. Molloy.
Captain V. Fleming, M.P.
Lieutenant R. E. U. Hermon-Hodge.
Lieutenant Hon. A. G. C. Villiers.
Lieutenant P. Fleming.
Lieutenant G. T. Hutchinson.
Second-Lieutenant H. A. Fane.
Second-Lieutenant W. Pepper.
Second-Lieutenant G. H. Palmer.
Second-Lieutenant J. J. Pearce.
Second-Lieutenant A. W. Keith-Falconer.
Second-Lieutenant F. A. Gill.
Second-Lieutenant A. J. Muirhead.
Second-Lieutenant R. H. E. Hall.
Second-Lieutenant E. H. Chinnery.
Captain G. Bonham-Carter, 19th Hussars, Adjutant.
Quartermaster & Hon. Major B. W. Lidington.
Surgeon-Captain A. H. Hogarth.
Captain W. S. Carless, A.V.C.

REINFORCEMENTS, 1914

Quartermaster & Hon. Lieutenant J. L. Goldie.[1]
Second-Lieutenant J. A. Moncreiffe, D.C.M.
Second-Lieutenant J. Kingscote.
Second-Lieutenant L. Winterbottom.[2]

[1] Sailed with the Regiment as Regimental Sergeant-Major.
[2] Sailed with the Regiment as Private.

REINFORCEMENTS, 1915

Second-Lieutenant E. W. H. Allfrey.
Second-Lieutenant H. G. Page-Turner.
Second-Lieutenant J. L. Shand.
Second-Lieutenant F. S. J. Silvertop.
Second-Lieutenant R. L. Worsley.[2]
Second-Lieutenant G. V. Wellesley.
Second-Lieutenant F. Weatherby.
Captain H. C. Jagger, A.V.C.
Major F. G. Proudfoot, R.A.M.C.
Second-Lieutenant H. E. Evetts.
Second-Lieutenant G. E. Schuster.
Second-Lieutenant T. W. M. Francis.[2]
Second-Lieutenant H. D. Savory.
Second-Lieutenant J. P. Higgs.
Second-Lieutenant H. M. Worsley.

REINFORCEMENTS, 1916

Second-Lieutenant A. C. Rawlinson.
Second-Lieutenant R. C. Byass.
Second-Lieutenant H. J. Soame.
Captain S. E. Whitnall, R.A.M.C.
Second-Lieutenant H. H. Smetham.
Second-Lieutenant A. E. MacColl.
Second-Lieutenant J. A. P. Whinney.
Second-Lieutenant F. Holford.
Second-Lieutenant R. Lakin.
Second-Lieutenant C. T. Hardy.
Second-Lieutenant E. G. Howarth.

REINFORCEMENTS, 1917

Captain F. A. Grange, R.A.M.C.
Second-Lieutenant C. H. Bottomley.
Second-Lieutenant B. H. Matthews.
Second-Lieutenant W. B. Riddell.
Second-Lieutenant D. H. Williams.
Second-Lieutenant S. B. Wood.
Second-Lieutenant G. H. S. Boas.
Second-Lieutenant C. B. Fish.
Lieutenant H. Hodgson, Bedfordshire Yeomanry.

[2] Sailed with the Regiment as Private.

Second-Lieutenant V. H. Bicker-Caarten, Bedfordshire Yeomanry.

Second-Lieutenant L. Dove, Bedfordshire Yeomanry.

Second-Lieutenant A. S. Ingram.

Second-Lieutenant T. A. Mason.

Second-Lieutenant W. J. Mason.

Second-Lieutenant H. C. Reed.

REINFORCEMENTS, 1918

Second-Lieutenant C. R. Jennings.

Second-Lieutenant H. B. O. Tompkins.[3]

Second-Lieutenant H. F. Wise.[3]

Second-Lieutenant J. J. List.[3]

Second-Lieutenant A. D. Pollock, 1st County of London Yeomanry.

Second-Lieutenant A. M. V. Surtees, 1st County of London Yeomanry.

Second-Lieutenant C. Pates.[4]

Second-Lieutenant J. Dixon, 1st County of London Yeomanry.

Lieutenant B. S. Harvey, North Irish Horse.

Second-Lieutenant H. A. R. Lambert, 1st County of London Yeomanry.

Second-Lieutenant F. G. Fairburn, 1st County of London Yeomanry.

Second-Lieutenant M. G. Jemmett, 1st County of London Yeomanry.

Second-Lieutenant H. Bailey, 5th Cavalry Reserve Regiment.

Lieutenant C. E. Venning, Royal 1st Devon Yeomanry.

Lieutenant E. S. Downes.

[3] Sailed with the Regiment as Sergeant.
[4] Sailed with the Regiment as Corporal.

APPENDIX F

1

OPERATION ORDER NO. 54

By MAJOR-GENERAL H. DE B. DE LISLE, C.B., D.S.O.,
COMMANDING 1ST CAVALRY DIVISION

30th October, 1914.

1. (*a*) The enemy have made strong attacks against our line and these have been beaten back, except on the left of the 2nd Cavalry Division, whose line now runs through the INN east of WYTSCHAETE via INN at sixth kilo stone on ST. ELOI–OOST-TAVERNE road to the canal due north of the "H" of HOLLE-BEKE, and thence to bend in canal north of the same village.

(*b*) The 2nd Cavalry Brigade, less 9th Lancers, has been detached to the 2nd Cavalry Division.

2. The 1st Cavalry Division will continue to hold the MESSINES position.

3. (*a*) The 1st Cavalry Brigade, 9th Lancers, 1st Field Squadron, and two Companies 57th Rifles, forming a temporary group under the command of the G.O.C. 1st Cavalry Brigade, will continue to hold MESSINES.

(*b*) The two guns, 6-inch Siege Battery, will remain in their present position, and for the night come under the orders of the G.O.C. 1st Cavalry Brigade.

(*c*) Ammunition Column and Field Ambulances will remain in their present billets.

4. Headquarters, 1st Cavalry Division, will be at NEUVE EGLISE to-night, and will move to the INN half-mile east of WULVERGHEM at 7.30 a.m. to-morrow.

A. F. HOME, *Lieut.-Colonel, General Staff.*

Issued at 8 p.m.

2

OPERATION ORDER NO. 55

By MAJOR-GENERAL H. DE B. DE LISLE, C.B., D.S.O.,
COMMANDING 1ST CAVALRY DIVISION

31st October, 1914.

1. Our counter-attack on MESSINES has driven the enemy towards the eastern edge of the town.

2. The 1st Cav. Div. will continue to hold to the MESSINES position from the WINDMILL on WYTSCHAETE Road to the DOUVE River.

3. The 2nd Cavalry Bde. will to-night take over the defence of the positions gained to-day from the WYTSCHAETE Road WINDMILL to the DOUVE River, linking on the Right with the XI Infy. Bde. and on the left with the 2 Cav. Div.

(b) King's Own Yorkshire Light Infy. and the K.O. Scottish Borderers will come under the orders of the 2nd Cav. Bde.

(c) The Oxfordshire Hussars will come under the orders of the G.O.C. 2nd Cy. Bde.

(d) The Field Squadron will move into [illegible : Div. Tps. area ?] at WULVERGHEM.

(e) WULVERGHEM is placed at the disposal of G.O.C. 2nd Cy. Bde. for billeting purposes.

4. The 1st Cy. Bde. when the positions gained have been handed over will billet in NEUVE EGLISE.

5. Cy. Div. H.Q. DRANOUTRE to-night, move to WULVERGHEM at 6-30 a.m. to-morrow morning.

PERCY HAMBRO, *Maj.*

Issued at 5.15 p.m.

3

Confidential.   To 1st Cavalry Bde.
2nd Cavalry Bde.
Oxfordshire Hussars
31st

SPECIAL ORDER

BY MAJOR-GENERAL H. DE B. DE LISLE, C.B., D.S.O., COMMANDING 1ST CAVALRY DIVISION

The G.O.C. 1st Cavalry Division has been highly complimented both by the Commander of the Corps and by the Field-Marshal, Commanding in Chief, on the gallant manner in which the 1st Cavalry Division defended Messines to-day.   AAA The G.O.C. Corps wishes this conveyed to the troops to-night if possible.

From 1st Cav. Div.

P. HAMBRO, *Major*, G.S.

Time 7.40.

APPENDIX G

Extract translated from a German History of the War describing the fight for Messines, 31st October–1st November, 1914.

MESSINES, 31st OCTOBER–1st NOVEMBER, 1914

To the south, between Ypres and Armentières, it was more a question of fights for hills. The successful assaults on *Wytschaete* and *Messines* were the most important triumphs of German arms here.

Beyond the river Lys the English were occupying a strongly entrenched position Ypres–Messines–Armentières. The key of this position was *Messines*, a fortress-like village, situated on a small hill in otherwise flat country, and which, as an intercepted English order ran, was to be defended to the last.

As regards the capture of Messines (on 1st November), a member of the Württemberg Army Corps, which has gathered fresh laurels there, reported to the *Stuttgarter Neues Tageblatt* :

" After we had thrown back the English west of Lille, we were ordered here, into the neighbourhood of Ypres, where dismounted cavalry of ours were lying in the trenches, and only with difficulty holding out against the English. We relieved them during the night in pouring rain. At first we remained lying quietly in the trenches—the right wing was still too far back—but afterwards, towards evening, we proceeded to attack, the task set to our regiment being to take Messines. The night fell while we were still advancing slowly. The English were firing as hard as they could, with the result that we had to fall back some distance. Further advance, in the night, was impossible against this hellish fire ; we dug ourselves in, but had to be keenly on the alert, so as not to be surprised by counter-thrust of the English. At daybreak we continued our attack, and, with the aid of the artillery, we succeeded, after a hard fight, in driving the English out of their trenches into the village. Of course, we pressed after them, and occupied the eastern outskirts of Messines. Here a terrible struggle ensued, in which the English fought in a way to compel our highest respect, at least as regards their soldierly qualities. In the village itself they had occupied every house, the streets were barred by barricades metres in thickness, the windows of the houses stuffed up with sandbags, the doors barricaded with furniture and stones ; through the walls they had drilled loopholes, scarcely visible ; each house was a small fortress, scattering death and destruction. In the midst of the firing we made a breach in the first barricade and penetrated with fixed bayonets into the empty village street. Right and left of us a thousand bullets were whistling ominously ; here and there one of our men fell. With our hatchet-picks we knocked holes into the walls of houses, through which we entered to clear the next. Thus we succeeded in penetrating to a depth of about 50 metres into the village, until we were brought to a stop by the next barricade. All at once machine-gun fire was opened upon us from immediately behind on the left. There is no help for it—all take refuge in the houses, in the road-ditches, and behind the barricade. What was to be done ? We indeed took some more houses by again breaking through the walls, but afterwards even this was no longer feasible ; anyone showing himself in the road was shot down. Meanwhile it had become night. House to house by the side of the enemy we spent the night ; of course, sleep was again out of the question. Under the cover of darkness a gun was then brought into the street in order to demolish the houses by fire at close quarters. When day broke the first morning greeting, in the shape of a shrapnel shell, crashed into the first house, which collapsed with a crash and rumble, mercifully drowning the terrible cries of the Englishmen buried beneath its ruins."

We are indebted to private letters for the description of the following episode from the fight around Messines, which immediately followed the events just described :

" On the evening of 31st October, 1914, the 6th Battery of the 65th Württemberg Field Artillery Regiment received orders to advance with one section into Messines, where the strongly entrenched enemy was defending himself so stubbornly that the attacking Württemberg Infantry could not overcome his resistance without assistance. As, however, one gun had already arrived there during the night to support the infantry, it was not until early in the morning that, in order to relieve the first gun, two more guns with four ammunition wagons were pushed forward from the direction of Gapaard, first to the outskirts of Messines, and then up to the first barricade. While one of the guns thereupon about 9 a.m. advanced, under most violent infantry, machine-gun, and artillery fire, as far as the second barricade, the second gun first of all brought down the church steeple of Messines, from which the hostile machine guns were firing into the flank of our infantry fighting at the second barricade. After the 13th Pioneers had made a breach in the second barricade a destructive fire was opened upon the rows of houses on the right and left of the street, and when we had succeeded in breaking there as well the resistance of the enemy, men and officers hauled the first gun forward, escorted by infantry advancing on both sides of the road, some distance beyond the second barricade, and continued firing from the position at ranges between 60 and 100 metres. The commanding officer of the battery, Captain Heuss, armed with an infantry rifle, took part in the fierce fight, and when all his gunners had been killed or wounded he himself acted as gun-layer, loaded and fired until the crew of the second gun arrived. Again they advanced, first to a crossing of two streets, the houses of which, still held by English infantry, soon collapsed under the fire of the howitzers. Thereupon the gun was hauled forward at a run another 300 metres up to the last hostile barricade near the market-place of Messines. In most murderous street fighting one house after the other in the immediate neighbourhood was here also brought down by gun fire in the first place, and thereupon the hostile infantry, retreating laterally to the left, was taken under fire. Then a shell from a heavy English naval gun hit the firing howitzer, instantly killing the brave Captain and three of his gunners; brave Lieutenant-Colonel Gundert also was so severely wounded by the same shell that he died shortly after. All gunners, except two who were immediately behind the gun shield, had been killed or wounded. At 11.20 Messines was finally in German hands.

" Captain Heuss had served the gun under a most heavy rain of shells up to his last breath; he fell, an example of manly heroism and devotion to duty. We are indebted for the conquest of Messines, which the English and French had tried to hold with the most pertinacious efforts, first and foremost to the heroic advances of these Württemberg artillery men. All who were witnesses of the fighting affirmed subsequently that they never witnessed, in any of the preceding heavy fights, such boldness and contempt of death."

The letter published in the *Stuttgarter Neues Tageblatt* further relates :

" The village was in our hands. But now it was a question of holding it. The English artillery fired shell upon shell of the heaviest calibre into the village ; if a house was properly struck by a dead hit it collapsed. Behind every wall which could at all afford shelter we crouched, crowded together ; incessantly the ground was trembling beneath our feet, the shells were bursting with deafening crashes, scarcely leaving one stone upon the other throughout the village. At last—at last !—night came, and with it quiet, at least as far as artillery fire was concerned. We dug trenches in front of the outskirts of the village, took from the deserted cellars some bottles of faultless wine, a jar of butter, and another filled with eggs, which we brought with us into the trenches, and made ourselves comfortable. However, first of all we did not care a fig about eating, or about the English or the artillery, but slept—slept at last for the first time after four days, and so soundly that if the English had had sufficient spirit left to attack, they might have carried us from our trenches into their own without our being aware of it. We then finished off the butter and eggs, in spite of all artillery fire. At last, night brought us the longed-for relief."

APPENDIX H

SIR JOHN FRENCH'S SPEECH TO THE 4TH CAVALRY BRIGADE, 12TH JUNE, 1915

" GENERAL PITMAN, AND 4TH CAVALRY BRIGADE,

" I think you all know the very great pleasure it always is to me to come amongst the troops of the branch of the service with which I have been associated practically all my life.

" Once more in the course of this campaign I have come to tell you how deeply I appreciate your good work.

" Now, I do not think you realize what you did in the recent gas attacks. The 47th French Division were holding the line when suddenly there was burst upon them one of the most violent and most deadly gas attacks, causing them to fall back. It was quite unexpected, and the first intimation was when men were found half suffocated in the trenches, and I firmly believe that the finest troops in the world could not have stood it. Nearly 4 miles of ground and 40 guns were lost. If the Germans had followed up that break, it would have broken up our line hopelessly, but they did not do it simply because they are not what they ought to be and we were able to throw the Canadians into the gap and consolidate our line in a new position. I have nothing but praise for the manner in which the troops withstood the heavy artillery fire with little or no trench protection, thus enabling us to adjust the line.

" No doubt you will be wondering why we should hold on so tenaciously to a place like Ypres which is nothing but a heap of ruins, but I can assure you it is of the utmost strategic and moral value.

" I have nothing further to say except again to thank you for your splendid work, which I highly appreciate."

APPENDIX I

LETTER FROM LIEUTENANT-GENERAL SIR C. T. McM. KAVANAGH (COMMANDING CAVALRY CORPS, B.E.F.) TO THE DUKE OF MARLBOROUGH (LORD LIEUTENANT OF OXFORDSHIRE), AND THE DUKE'S REPLY. FROM *THE TIMES*, 1st APRIL, 1919

THE Duke of Marlborough (Lord-Lieutenant of Oxfordshire) has received the following letter from Lieutenant-General Sir C. T. M. Kavanagh (Commanding Cavalry Corps, B.E.F.) :

H.Q. CAVALRY CORPS, B.E.F., *3rd March.*

DEAR SIR,—Now that the time has come for the remaining officers and men of the Oxford Yeomanry to leave the Cavalry Corps on demobilization, I feel perhaps that you would like to hear how well the Regiment and all its members have done during the war.

The Regiment, the first Yeomanry regiment to come out to France in 1914, under Lieutenant-Colonel Dugdale, very soon reached a high state of efficiency, which compared very favourably with the Regular cavalry regiments alongside of whom they were serving. They maintained this high standard of efficiency throughout the hard fighting of the past two years, and all ranks have continually displayed a splendid spirit.

It has been a great honour and pleasure to me to have had them under my command, and I hope and believe that after a short period at home, a large number of men will rejoin, and that before long the Regiment will be re-formed, up to strength, and again ready to take their part in the defence of the Empire, if called upon.

C. M. KAVANAGH,
Lieutenant-General, Commanding Cavalry Corps.

The Duke of Marlborough has sent the following reply, dated 25th March :

MY DEAR GENERAL,—Your generous praise of the Oxfordshire Yeomanry will give pride and pleasure to all connected with the Regiment.

It is indeed agreeable to know on the authority of the G.O.C.

Cavalry Corps that the test of war has amply revealed the merits of the training given to the regiment in the days of peace. During my own long connection with it I fully appreciated the zeal of its principal officers—Lord Valentia, Sir Robert Hermon-Hodge, and others, some of whom bear names known outside the Regiment.

May I say how fully I share your hope that the Regiment will not wish to rest on its laurels, but will again seek to equip itself to play its part in the defence of our land in time of crisis ? There is no need nowadays to emphasize the value of the Yeomanry, least of all in a letter to you, who have commanded them. But there was a time when the reputation of this arm was not so high as now. In looking back on those difficult years I am conscious of the Regiment's debt to its late Colonel-in-Chief, King Edward VII, to whose unfailing sympathy and encouragement the whole Yeomanry force owes so much.

Believe me, yours sincerely,

MARLBOROUGH.

APPENDIX J

SPECIAL ORDER TO ALL RANKS OF THE 2ND CAVALRY DIVISION, BY MAJOR-GENERAL T. T. PITMAN, 11TH MARCH, 1919.

Now that the Division is about to be broken up after a period of four and a half years since its formation, I wish to offer each one of you my heartfelt thanks for your services both individually and collectively. I do so not only in my own name, but in the names of the Divisional Commanders who preceded me.

While some of you enter into civil life, others remain at the helm ; but wherever you may go, I would like you to keep with you a remembrance of the great part which has been played by your Division in the greatest of all wars. The Division has come through four and a half years of war without a stain on its character or a single regrettable incident, and as you will see by the account of its doings overleaf, it has come to the rescue of the Army at many a critical moment.

I hope that each one of you will always remember the good feeling which has kept us together during these years and carry the same into home life in England. Let us do this in memory of those we have unfortunately been compelled to leave behind. May their names never be forgotten !

THOMAS T. PITMAN,

Major-General, Commanding 2nd Cavalry Division.

11*th March*, 1919.

1914

The 2nd Cavalry Division was formed on 16th September, 1914 on the Aisne. It originally consisted of the 3rd and 5th Cavalry Brigades under command of Major-General H. de la P. Gough, C.B. The 4th Brigade joined the Division shortly after the capture of the Mont des Cats. This brilliant operation by the combined action of the 3rd and 5th Brigades first brought the Division to a prominent position as a fighting unit.

The units in the Division have remained the same throughout the war with the exception of the Composite Household Cavalry Regiment in the 4th Cavalry Brigade, who were replaced by the Queen's Own Oxfordshire Hussars on the 19th November, 1914.

The Division distinguished themselves in a contest against overwhelming numbers on the Wytschaete–Messines line from 20th October to the 1st November, and later in the vicinity of Wulverghem until the end of the first battle of Ypres.

1915

In January and February 1915 the Division had their first experience of regular trench warfare in the Ypres salient, the first big mine of the war exploding under one of the trenches held by them.

In March they were in support at the battle of Neuve Chapelle, the 5th Cavalry Brigade making the first attempt of Cavalry to break through the enemy's trench system.

Shortly after returning to billets the Division was again hurried up to the Salient to take part in the Second Battle of Ypres, where the enemy launched poisoned gases against us.

On the 15th April Major-General C. T. McM. Kavanagh, C.V.O., D.S.O., took over command.

Throughout the summer of 1915 large working parties were found for constructing defences in the vicinity of Kemmel.

On the 15th July, Major-General Sir P. W. Chetwode, Bart., C.M.G., D.S.O., took over command.

In September and October the Division was in support at the battle of Loos.

1916

The Division spent the first two months of the year in the trenches at VERMELLES, when mining and countermining were of almost nightly occurrence.

From June to September they were in support of the Second Army, which had been considerably weakened to find troops for the battle of the Somme.

In September the Division moved south to the Somme, where they remained in vicinity of Dernancourt until the beginning of November.

On the 16th November Major-General W. H. Greenly, C.M.G., D.S.O., took over command of the Division.

1917

Early in the year the Division furnished strong working parties for railway construction, and in the beginning of April took part in the battle of Arras under very trying conditions for the horses.

From there they went into the trenches in front of Ronssoy. A most successful raid was carried out at Gillemont Farm, and a few days later a stubborn defence was put up when the Germans counter-raided the same position.

On the 16th November, after a short spell in billets, the Division moved east to take part in the battle of Cambrai. The mounted scheme having failed to materialize, a dismounted brigade was formed which had very heavy fighting in the defence of Bourlon Wood.

On the 30th November, when the Germans made their big counter-attack, the 2nd Cavalry Division assisted the Guards in restoring the situation.

They ended up the year by going once again into the trenches near Hargicourt.

1918

There they remained until the end of January and afterwards moved into the area round Athies.

In March, in order to meet the threatened German attack, the Division moved to vicinity of Grandru, in support of the III Corps.

When the attack came on the 21st March, the Division was immediately sent up in motor lorries to try to restore the situation. All units of the Division were engaged in very heavy fighting, especially on the Jussy Canal, suffering heavy casualties.

On the 25th March the mounted Division was again re-formed, under command of Brigadier-General Pitman.

On the 26th they made a combined mounted and dismounted attack on the Bois des Essarts. This attack succeeded in holding up the Germans until the arrival of large French reinforcements.

From there the Division, to which was attached the Canadian Cavalry Brigade, made a forced march to Montdidier to support a reported break in the French line, and thence by another forced march to vicinity of Amiens, where the situation of the Fifth Army was critical.

On the 30th March, the British line having broken, the Canadian Cavalry Brigade and 3rd Cavalry Brigade made a mounted attack at Moreuil Wood and restored the situation.

On the 1st April the line having again broken, the whole Division carried out a brilliant dismounted attack on Rifle Wood under cover of their own artillery and machine-gun barrage. The objectives were gained and the line restored, heavy casualties being inflicted on the enemy.

The losses of the Division from 21st March to 1st April were 70 officers and 2,000 other ranks.

The appointment of Brigadier-General T. T. Pitman, C.B., C.M.G., to command the Division with the temporary rank of Major-General was confirmed (dated 29th March).

From Amiens the Division was moved north to vicinity of Blaringhem and Flêtre to support the Second Army.

On the 9th and 10th August the 2nd Cavalry Division took part in the successful operations in front of Amiens which started the final battle of the war.

As soon as the war of movement commenced, there was a general outcry for cavalry, and the Division was split up on a front of three Armies. Playing a prominent part throughout the final operations, they had the satisfaction of knowing that nearly every squadron of the Division was well in front when the " cease fire " sounded on the 11th November ; one regiment taking part in the final attack on Mons, entered the town at the head of the Canadian Corps.

During the advance through Belgium after the armistice was signed, the 2nd Cavalry Division acted as Advanced Guard to the Fourth Army.

APPENDIX K

SPECIAL ORDER OF THE DAY TO THE OFFICER COMMANDING, THE QUEEN'S OWN OXFORD-SHIRE HUSSARS, BY BRIGADIER-GENERAL C. RANKIN, 17TH MARCH, 1919

To the Officer Commanding, the Queen's Own Oxfordshire Hussars

Before the final disappearance of the 4th Cavalry Brigade, I should like to express to you my deep and sincere appreciation of the services of your Regiment. Of Yeomanry and Territorial regiments yours was the first to come out, and I imagine about the last to go back. You have served in the midst of the most highly trained and efficient Regular Cavalry force which there has ever been, and yet there has never been any question of your efficiency being of a lower standard than theirs. In the field your courage and endurance has been equal to the best, in billets your discipline, orderliness, horse management, and good comradeship have been an example to many.

The way in which the Regiment has conducted itself throughout the war, whether in trenches, open warfare, or in billets, the spirit of the Regiment, and the excellent feeling of good-fellowship which exists between all ranks are matters, I consider, for very just pride to one and all of you.

Your services to the country are worthy of tribute from someone who is worthy to give it, and this you will doubtless receive in course of time ; for the moment I beg you to accept from one who has been your Brigadier for eleven months his most sincere thanks for the services of your Regiment and his appreciation of your continuous support.

It would be impossible to conclude without a reference to that gallant officer, your predecessor, who brought the Regiment out, and who remained at his post until the war was over, in spite of having exceeded his period of command by nearly a year ; to him I offer my thanks as well as to yourself, and to all ranks of your Regiment.

(*Sd.*) CHARLES RANKIN,
Brigadier-General, Commanding 4th Cavalry Brigade.

MÉRY (BELGIUM), 17*th March*, 1919.

APPENDIX L

NOTE ON THE 2ND AND 3RD LINES

IT is regretted that no full account of the second and third lines of the Regiment can be given here. The following brief notes have been collected from such sources as were available.

Second-line regiments began to be formed in September 1914, the 2nd/1st Q.O.O.H. being raised under the command of Lieutenant-Colonel A. N. Hall, with Major A. H. Fell as second-in-command. They were at first stationed at Oxford, and used to supply reinforcements to the first line, but in April 1915 all second-line yeomanry regiments were made independent units for service overseas, the 2nd/1st Q.O.O.H. being transferred to King's Lynn. The duty of supplying reinforcements was then taken over by the third line.

In June 1915 Major C. R. I. Nicholl, from the first line, succeeded Lieutenant-Colonel Hall in command of the second line, which now formed part of the 11th (2nd/2nd South Midland) Mounted Brigade, 3rd Mounted Division, Eastern Command. During the winter 1915–16 they remained at King's Lynn, training, and acting as a home defence force. (There were at this time four mounted divisions, six mounted brigades not formed into divisions, and six regiments not brigaded, all, except one brigade, composed of second-line yeomanry, and all apparently in England or Scotland—though of this I am not sure.)

About March 1916 two regiments per brigade were turned into cyclists, and mixed brigades formed of one cavalry and two cyclist regiments.

In July 1916 these brigades were broken up; the mounted regiments formed two fresh divisions, and the cyclists remained separate.

The 2nd/1st Q.O.O.H. were among those turned into cyclists, and moved to Canterbury in June 1916. They were now in the 5th Cyclist Brigade with the 2nd/1st South Notts and the 2nd/1st Derbyshire Yeomanry.

During the Somme offensive in 1916, when reinforcements were urgently required for infantry in France, 5 officers and

383

200 men were taken from each of the second-line yeomanry cyclist regiments and drafted to infantry, in most cases to a battalion of their county line regiment. The draft from the 2nd/1st Q.O.O.H. was sent to the 6th Battalion, Oxford and Bucks Light Infantry, in time for the later stages of the battle of the Somme, and greatly distinguished itself in its first engagement.

In October 1916 the second-line yeomanry regiments at home were filled up with C3 men and made home service units, being amalgamated with other similar units in January 1917 to bring them up to battalion strength. A certain number of the 2nd/1st Q.O.O.H. were allowed to be drafted to the third line for use as reinforcements to the first line in France; the remainder were amalgamated with the 2nd/1st Berkshire Yeomanry to form the 11th Cyclist Regiment, 4th Cyclist Brigade. Lieutenant-Colonel Nicholl gave up the command and rejoined the first line early in February 1917.

By this time only some thirteen or fifteen regiments of second-line yeomanry remained mounted ; the rest were all cyclists.

These amalgamated cyclist regiments were split up again later on, each yeomanry unit forming a separate regiment, so that the brigade had six single regiments instead of three double regiments. Many of them, including the 2nd/1st Q.O.O.H., were sent to Ireland early in 1918, on account of the troubles there.

Even scantier is the information available about the third line. It was first formed at Oxford in the summer of 1915, then moved to Tidworth, and later, in July 1916, to the Curragh, where it remained till the end of the war.

Throughout its existence it was used as a reinforcement depot and training centre for the first line, and supplied nearly all officers and men sent out to the first line after 1915.

INDEX

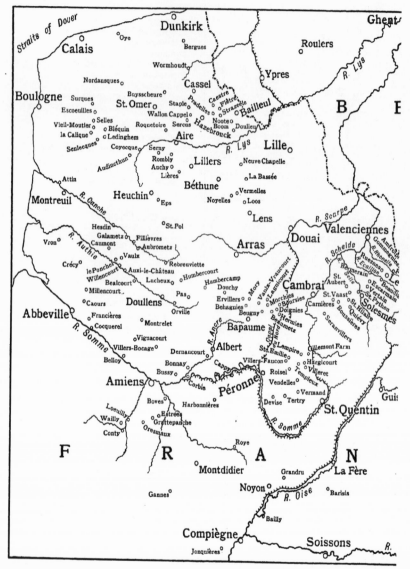

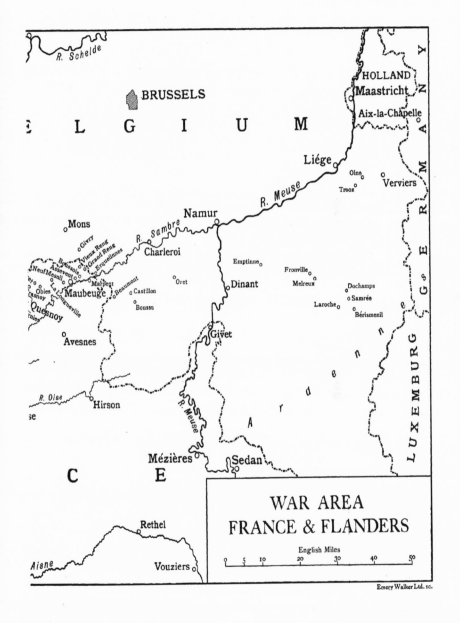

WAR AREA
FRANCE & FLANDERS

English Miles

0   5   10   20   30   40   50

Emery Walker Ltd. sc.

ANTWERP, 1914.
OPERATIONS,
3rd.—8th. OCT.

Map compiled by
Historical Section (Military Branch).

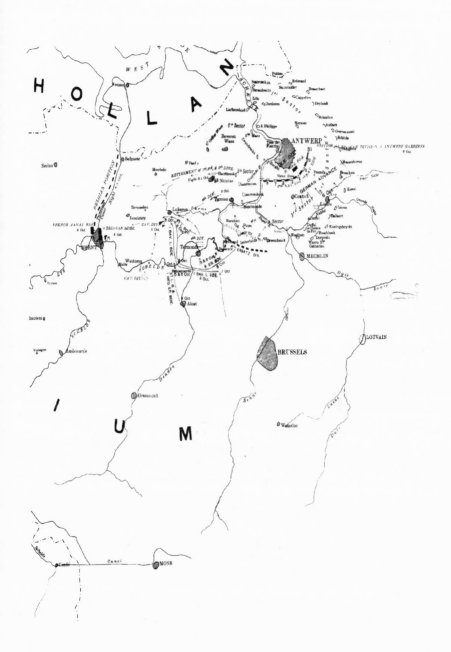